BIBLICAL STUDIES
AND WISDOM FOR LIVING

Biblical Studies and Wisdom for Living

Sundry writings and occasional lectures

Calvin G. Seerveld

Edited by
John H. Kok

Dordt College Press

Cover design by Willem Hart
Layout by Carla Goslinga

Copyright © 2014 Calvin G. Seerveld

Fragmentary portions of this book may be freely used by those who are interested in sharing the author's insights and observations, so long as the material is not pirated for monetary gain and so long as proper credit is visibly given to the publisher and the author. Others, and those who wish to use larger sections of text, must seek written permission from the publisher.

Dordt College Press
498 Fourth Avenue NE
Sioux Center, Iowa, 51250
United States of America

www.dordt.edu/dordt_press

ISBN: 978-1-940567-06-8

Printed in the United States of America

The Library of Congress Cataloguing-in-Publication Data is on file with the Library of Congress, Washington D.C.

Library of Congress Control Number: 2014934733

Cover: The Holy Spirit-given biblical writings bespeak God's everlasting care and wisdom for us corporeal mortals. Just as Susanna Oppliger's ceramic angel shelters the exhausted, scared Elijah (1998), waking him up to carry on the LORD's appointed tasks, just so, following Jesus Christ through this wonder-filled, troubled lifetime bodes strength and hope for the morrow.

Table of Contents

Introductions
    God's Word in God's World
    by Craig Bartholomew... i
    Living as a "Grown Up Child"
    by Peter S. Smith vii

Part One

1. Hearing God's Narrative about "the Way" of shalom.................... 1
2. Reading and Hearing the Psalms: The Gut of the Bible............. 25
3. Psalms are to be Heard Everywhere... 49
4. Five Psalms: For the American Guild of Organists
   a. Psalm 19: Celebrating the good news of God's creational ordinances and creatural glossolalia 75
   b. David Psalm 30: A song written for a consecration service of the house of God... 81
   c. Psalm 96: A song that never gets old is new........................ 86
   d. Isaiah 61:1–4, 8–9, 11: The most human of these is hope ... 89
   e. Revelation 18:21–19:8: Hip-hop millennial culture and Hallelujah! 92
5. Pain Is a Four-Letter Word: A congregational lament................. 97
6. Proverbs 10:1–22: From Poetic Paragraphs to Preaching 101
7. Celebrate the Resourceful Woman (Proverbs 31) 125
8. Herder's Revolutionary Hermeneutic and Aesthetic Theory: The Import of Herder's Hermeneutics for Text Performance of *The Greatest Song* 133
9. Needed: Biblical Recovery of Human Corporeality and Historical Institutionality in God's World 149
10. The Gift and Distraction of Pleasure 185
11. The Smell of your School: A letter of reference? 191

12. A Christian School Song for Parents and Teachers 197

13. Ways-of-life and becoming elderly wise..................................... 203

14. Import of Biblical Wisdom Literature for a Conception of Artistic Truth 215

15. A Modest Proposal for Reforming the Christian Reformed Church in North America 233

16. A Snake and Dove Policy for Redeemer Graduates.................. 263

17. Graduating to Glocal Martyrdom 271

18. Reformed Institutions in Transformation 279

Part Two

19. Book Review: *Reading Ecclesiastes: Old Testament Exegesis and Hermeneutical Theory* 291

20. Carlos Martínez Mime Actor 295

21. A Worship Service Where Two People Walked Out.................. 297

22. Say "Amen!" Somebody: On gospel singing and joyful worship.. 303

23. Longing to Lament: A conversation between Michael Card and Calvin Seerveld... 319

24. The Rule of God... 327

25. Long-range mercy for Africa: The CRC in Sierra Leone 343

26. We are Not Pilgrims: We are called to build tent cities in God's world 373

27. Bastards or Sons of God? 381

28. Operation Fish and Bread for the Ontario Government........... 387

29. The Tender, Tough Mystery of (Married) Love........................ 393

30. "The Rare Gift of a Friend".. 396

31. A Morning Weather Hymn.. 399

32. Reading the Bible like a Grown-Up Child 403

33. Epilogue: A personal testimony... 409

List of illustrations 413

Index 417

List of translated Bible passages printed in these books 420

List of psalms, hymns, and spiritual songs printed in these books ... 421

List of selected Bible translations by Calvin Seerveld published elsewhere 422

Abbreviations used throughout this volume:

NA   Calvin G. Seerveld, *Normative Aesthetics: Sundry writings and occasional lectures*, edited by John H. Kok. Sioux Center, IA: Dordt College Press, 2014.

RA   Calvin G. Seerveld, *Redemptive Art in Society: Sundry writings and occasional lectures*, edited by John H. Kok. Sioux Center, IA: Dordt College Press, 2014.

CP   Calvin G. Seerveld, *Cultural Problems in Western Society: Sundry writings and occasional lectures*, edited by John H. Kok. Sioux Center, IA: Dordt College Press, 2014.

AH   Calvin G. Seerveld, *Art History Revisited: Sundry writings and occasional lectures*, edited by John H. Kok. Sioux Center, IA: Dordt College Press, 2014.

CE   Calvin G. Seerveld, *Cultural Education and History Writing: Sundry writings and occasional lectures*, edited by John H. Kok. Sioux Center, IA: Dordt College Press, 2014.

Introduction to Part One

God's Word in God's World

Craig G. Bartholomew

I count it a privilege to introduce Part One of this volume, which includes more than thirty of Seerveld's talks and writings that fit well under the title *Biblical Studies and Wisdom for Living*. Many readers will have had the moving experience of hearing Seerveld speak and of his invariably weaving Scripture in and out of his address. He is also well known for his dramatic versions of Song of Songs[1] and, more recently, Ecclesiastes. Indeed his dramatic script for Song of Songs has been performed in a wide variety of venues across North America and internationally and receives mention in a major commentary on the Song.[2]

Seerveld is first and foremost a philosopher and aesthetician, to which the other volumes in this series bear eloquent testimony. He is not by training and practice a professional biblical scholar, as he would be the first to admit. However, two points in this respect should be noted. Firstly, Seerveld *has* undergone rigorous training in biblical studies. While a Fulbright scholar in Europe Seerveld studied under Karl Barth and Oscar Cullman and experienced something of an Epiphany while wrestling for days with a translation of the Greek text of Romans. He is thus well equipped to handle the Bible academically, and works easily with the original languages. A browse of the footnotes in this volume indicate a keen interest in and awareness of contemporary biblical scholarship. Secondly, it is by no means necessarily a disadvantage having a Christian philosopher attend closely to the Bible. Contemporary biblical studies is unhealthy in many ways and regularly the best and freshest work has come from outside the guild and not least from literary scholars. The works of the Jewish literary scholars Erich Auerbach,[3] Robert Alter,[4] and

---

1 Seerveld, *The Greatest Song: In Critique of Solomon* (Toronto: Tuppence Press, 1967/1988).
2 Marvin H. Pope, *Song of Songs* (New Haven and London: Yale UP, 1995), 37.
3 *Mimesis: The Representation of Reality in Western Literature* (Princeton and Oxford: Princeton UP, 1953/2003).
4 Amidst Alter's many publications representative examples are *The Art of Biblical Po-*

Meir Sternberg[5] come immediately to mind as well as the magisterial commentary on Genesis by Jewish philosopher Leon Kass.[6] Outsiders to the guild are often able to cut through the debilitating baggage of contemporary biblical studies and enable us to hear Scripture speak in fresh and illuminating ways. This is certainly true of Seerveld's work as the feast in this volume demonstrates.

It must be noted therefore that in this volume we have *a philosopher* attending closely to Scripture. This remains remarkable and is still far too rare a phenomenon. Over the last thirty years or so we have witnessed a veritable renaissance of Christian philosophy in North America. Amidst this marvellous development it remains rare to find Christian philosophers engaging actively with Scripture *in their work*. We are seeing signs of the tide starting to turn,[7] but deep engagement with Scripture has characterized Seerveld's work throughout his career. In this his work is reminiscent of philosophers like Hamann and Kierkegaard. Recent works on Hamann are exceptional not least in requiring a biblical index, a phenomenon that few philosophers could lay claim to.[8] Seerveld would certainly be one of them.

I learnt from John Calvin that a good theology will enable one to be a better reader of the Bible. Indeed, Calvin wrote his *Institutes* to help pastors and ordinary Christians read the Bible whereas it is common today for the move to be seen as from the Bible, to theology, and then beyond without ever returning to Scripture. A test of a theology and a theological framework is that as it takes hold it should lead us ever deeper back into Scripture. Although there are areas in which I would disagree with him, Karl Barth's *Church Dogmatics* is exemplary and unique in

---

etry (Edinburgh: T&T Clark, 1985); *The World of Biblical Literature* (London: SPCK, 1992); *The Book of Psalms: A Translation with Commentary* (NY: Norton, 2007); *The Wisdom Books, Job, Proverbs, Ecclesiastes: A Translation with Commentary* (NY: Norton, 2010); Alter and Frank Kermode, eds., *The Literary Guide to the Bible* (Cambridge, MA.: Harvard UP, 1999).

5   *The Poetics of Biblical Narrative: Ideological literature and the drama of reading* (Bloomington, IN: Indiana UP, 1985).

6   *The Beginning of Wisdom: Reading Genesis* (Chicago and London: University of Chicago Press, 2003).

7   See, for example, Nicholas Wolterstorff, *Justice: Rights and Wrongs* (Princeton: Princeton UP, 2010); Eleonore Stump, *Wandering in Darkness: Narrative and the problem of suffering* (NY and Oxford: OUP, 2010), etc.

8   See Johan Georg Hamann, *Writings on Philosophy and Language* (Cambridge: CUP, 2007); Oswald Bayer, *A Contemporary in Dissent: Johann Georg Hamann as a Radical Enlightener* (Grand Rapids: Eerdmans, 2012); John R. Betz, *After Enlightenment: The post-secular vision of J.G. Hamann* (Chichester: Wiley-Blackwell, 2012).

modern times in this respect. His *Dogmatics* is chock full of theological exegesis, with some 130 pages of careful exegesis of Gen 1-2, for example. A more contemporary example is that of the ethicist Oliver O'Donovan particularly in his political theology, *Desire of the Nations*.

The same, or so it seems to me, ought to be true of a Christian philosophy. Its focus is, of course, different from theology, but it ought to be normed by Scripture, a matter that Seerveld has written about, and it ought to return again and again to Scripture. A danger of Reformational philosophy as it has developed in North America during the last thirty years is, in my opinion, a loosening of the relationship between Scripture and philosophy, with worrying results. It is clear from this volume that this is not the case with Seerveld's work. He brings the insights of his Reformational philosophy to bear on Scripture and he allows Scripture to illuminate his philosophy. This mutual relationship, without placing philosophy on par with Scripture, is an essential ingredient in the ecology of his scholarship, and so it ought to be.

Contra Barth, and rightly so, Seerveld is passionately committed to the possibility and importance of Christian philosophy. It was he, after all, who coined the term "Reformational," to refer to the continental style of Christian philosophy in the tradition of Bavinck, Kuyper, Dooyeweerd, Vollenhoven, etc., the tradition in which he works. That one of the six volumes in this series is devoted to biblical studies should cause theologians, biblical scholars, *and* philosophers cause for reflection. Theologians and biblical scholars will need to reflect on the inevitable role of philosophy in their disciplines and the enormous potential of a Christian philosophical contribution to such work. Advocates of Christian philosophy will need to wrestle with how one's philosophy can be genuinely Christian if Scripture plays virtually no part in it.

In biblical studies *the literary dimension* of the Bible was rediscovered in the 1970s onwards, mainly through the work of Jewish scholars such as Alter and Sternberg. This turn has been remarkably fruitful in biblical interpretation but, alas, before it could be fully appropriated biblical studies was awash with the wild pluralism of postmodernism. In recent years the best hermeneutic approaches to the Bible have recognized the importance of attending to the literary, historical, *and* kerygmatic or theological dimensions of the text, and their interrelationship. Amidst the contemporary pluralism of biblical studies a healthy focus on the literary dimension of the Bible has receded but it remains extremely important. And clearly in this area biblical studies has to draw on aesthetic insight in one way or another.

Enter Seerveld! As an aesthetician Seerveld is particularly well equipped to attend to this area and, as many of the essays in this volume indicate, he has done so with aplomb and nuance. His work speaks for itself and I confine myself to several comments in this respect. Firstly, Seerveld not only attends to the literary aspect of parts of the Bible but to the Bible *as a whole*. Much modern biblical studies has given up on the unity of Scripture but not Seerveld, and he rightly and creatively attends to Scripture as the grand, sprawling, capacious story that it is, the true story of the world.

Secondly, Seerveld has attended in this volume to poetic texts in particular. In this respect it should be noted that far more of the Bible is poetry than is often recognized, especially in the Old Testament. Most of the prophets, wisdom, and psalms, for example, is poetry. We live in an age in which poetry is confined to a shelf or two in bookstores and poets are not held in high regard. For much of Western history and especially for Israel this was not the case, and we need the sort of help Seerveld gives us in hearing again the poetic texts of the Bible.

Thirdly, a rich spinoff of the literary turn has been the discovery that books like the Psalms, Proverbs, and Ecclesiastes, all heavily poetic, are unities and not just random lists. This has revolutionized study of these books and especially in relation to the Psalter[9] and Proverbs you will find in this volume Seerveld's contribution to that development. Fourthly, a fertile development in current biblical studies is *intertextuality* and once again you will find resonances of this in Seerveld's biblical interpretation. He rightly, for example, encourages us to look for resonances of the Psalms throughout the Bible. Fifthly, Seerveld's work exemplifies something I learnt from him several years ago, namely that if your discipline is in an unhealthy state, learn to know its history well and find healthy nodes in its history, nodes that you can translate into the present in order to redirect your discipline. Seerveld's work on Herder is exemplary in this respect.

Sixthly, and somewhat more controversially, Seerveld sees *translation* of a specific sort as central to his hermeneutic.[10] One of Seerveld's great pleasures in life is working away at the biblical text in its original languages, yielding fresh translations that form the basis of readings, homilies, songs, and a variety of performances. A strength of this volume is that

---

9 See, for example, J. Clinton McCann Jr., "Hearing the Psalter," in *Hearing the Old Testament: Listening for God's address*, Craig G. Bartholomew and David J.H. Beldman, eds. (Grand Rapids: Eerdmans, 2012), 277-301.

10 Cf. footnote 4 above for Robert Alter's similar practice of taking translation seriously as an indispensable part of interpretation.

you not only get to sample his translations but, especially in his chapter on Herder, you will find an articulation of his theory of interpretation. In recent decades a great deal of attention has been paid to translation, as evidenced by the great number and variety of translations of the Bible available today. Seerveld is concerned to translate the Bible such that he is faithful to the original while allowing the text to speak with power to us today. Seerveld's evocative translations have been compared, for example, to Eugene Peterson's *The Message*, but they are, I think, quite different, as they are to the *Good News* Bible or the recent *Common Bible*, in which I was marginally involved as a translator. The difference lies, I think, in the literary, almost poetic quality of the translations. This makes the interpretive element in them strong and will not, of course, satisfy those who prefer more literal translations such as the *English Standard Version* or the *NRSV*.

Seventhly, Seerveld is sensitive to the *performative* nature of many biblical texts. Biblical texts may be performative in several ways.[11] In my own work on Old Testament wisdom literature it has struck me that Job and Ecclesiastes in particular perform their own message in the way their texts develop and are structured.[12] Ecclesiastes, for example, enacts the enigma of life in a text that is notoriously difficult to encompass, and doubtless Qohelet would have found it ironic that modern interpreters are divided between those who read the books as primarily depressed and negative and those who read it as primarily positive. Job is dreadfully long but then so is suffering, seeming to go on, and on, and on. The sort of literary sensibility that Seerveld brings to the biblical text alerts him to this aspect of performativity but also to the fact that a central way of hearing many biblical texts is through their performance. Hence the variety of translated texts for particular occasions that you will find in this volume.

In the last decade biblical studies has experienced a renaissance of what is called theological interpretation. Part of this has brought with it a renewed emphasis on *the ecclesia* as the primary context for the reception of the Bible.[13] Seerveld's biblical exegesis certainly fits with this. He rightly sees Scripture as God's Word given to us through what

---

11 See the stimulating work by Shimon Levy, *The Bible as Theatre* (Brighton: Sussex Academic Press, 2000).

12 See Craig G. Bartholomew, "Hearing the Old Testament Wisdom Literature: The wit of many and the wisdom of one," in *Hearing the Old Testament: Listening for God's address*, 302-331.

13 A wonderful expression of this view is found in Mariano Magrassi, *Praying the Bible: An introduction to Lectio Divina* (Collegeville: Liturgical Press, 1998).

I would describe as the deposit, like the silt at the bottom of a river, of God's immersion in the life of Israel and culminating in Jesus. Through Scripture we hear God's address and Seerveld works with the Bible in the service of facilitating such an encounter. He is also an accomplished hymn writer and musician and the songs accompanying translations and talks in this volume bear eloquent witness to his commitment to the primacy of the liturgical context for the reception of Scripture.

However, Seerveld is equally aware that the life of God's people extends into all areas of the creation and that the Jesus we find like the pearl of great price hid in the field of Scripture is the "author of life" so that the address of God is never restricted to ecclesial life in the institutional sense. A rich aspect of this volume is the opening of Scripture in a variety of life contexts in which God's people find themselves, as the footnotes accompanying the essays indicate. Scripture facilitates an encounter with God that is transformative and equips us with wisdom for living in all areas of life.

November 2012.

Craig G. Bartholomew
H. Evan Runner Professor of Philosophy
and Professor of Religion and Theology,
Redeemer University College
Principal, The Paideia Centre for Public Theology

Introduction to Part Two

Living as a "Grown Up Child"

by Peter S. Smith

I first read Dr. Calvin Seerveld's work in 1968 while I was a student at Birmingham School of Art and Design, finally meeting him in the early 1980's. Since that first reading, and later meeting, I have had an ever increasing respect for his work and his kind, perceptive support. His redemptive aesthetic theory, and in particular his ongoing exploration of the notion of allusivity, continue to profoundly affect my work as a visual artist.

He will understand when I say that the framework he provides also leads me to leave his theoretical aesthetic writing at the "studio door." Self-conscious illustrations of a philosophical theory are the last thing that Seerveld would expect from a visual artist. Using a visual language to make something tangible is to have a mindset that thinks in terms of physical making rather than verbal constructs. Only thoughts and ideas that become part of the embodied self, including Seerveld's ideas, manage to make it into the studio.

In his review of Craig G. Bartholomew's book, *Reading Ecclesiastes: Old Testament and hermeneutical theory*, Seerveld commends Bartholomew because, "A pastoral concern always permeates the scholarship." These words also perfectly describe Seerveld's own scholarship. That same pastoral concern shines through this collection of his book reviews, articles, and essays. We also see how wide-ranging Seerveld's interests are: from preaching and biblical studies to issues of academic freedom; from missionary travels in Africa to next door neighborly pastoral support near to home; from childlike pleasures in simple playful experiences to meditations on the nature of lament; from the music of Thomas A. Dorsey to hymns about the weather.

While reading these pieces I realized that I have embodied more than just his work in aesthetics. Seerveld's attitude to his calling to scholarship and his wide ranging interests flow from his winsome way of being a Christian. While his aesthetic theorizing helps with analysis and reflection, his encompassing Christian worldview is one of the seedbeds for my attitudes to what and how I make. His example and exhortations concerning what it means to live redemptively find their way not just into the studio but into my life.

"Reading the Bible like a Grown-up Child" is such a good way to describe Seerveld's understanding of the Bible. He twice records a significant and life transforming moment when he was a graduate student in Basel in 1956. During a period of intense preparation for an examination, in which he was expected to translate Paul's Letter to the Romans from Greek into German and exegete on the spot, he reached the end of chapter eight: ". . . . suddenly I had a sense that the New Testament Greek text I was holding in my hand was veritably GOD before me." His immediate response was to put the text carefully down on the stool and get down on his knees to pray. But Seerveld's earthy Christian self-awareness was also present at this significant time. He knows that he has been studying hard over a two-week vacation period in self-imposed solitary confinement. "Maybe it was the crazy intensity of the whole business," he muses. Nevertheless the conclusion stands. "The sense that the Bible is God talking to me live has never left me."

This understanding of the Bible, as "God talking to me live," runs throughout all Seerveld's life and scholarship. Don't imagine that this view of the Bible leads to the triumphant attitude found in some Christians, whose boast is that the only book they need or read is the Bible. This is not what Seerveld means. In fact reading his Bible is the incentive that leads to reading many more books and to a life devoted to study.

As a Christian who was unwittingly steeped in a tradition that used the Bible almost always as a personal self-help book and a theological argument-winning textbook, Seerveld's critique of that sole use of the Bible was a much needed challenge to me. "Don't get me wrong. You can base doctrines and lifestyle on Bible study. But to read the Bible like a prosecuting attorney, marshaling evidence and scoring points, is to squeeze the juice of compelling mystery out of God's living word. It is to leave it behind like a dried-out shell, as exhibit A or exhibit B. Whenever do-it-yourself theology or even an official partisan theology calls on the biblical texts as evidence to set somebody else straight, someone has lost the key to Bible reading. And that can lovelessly bind burdens on other people's backs."

In this way Seerveld's study of the Bible and his work in translation and exegesis has brought the Bible, and especially the Older Testament, alive again for me. "The Bible is not a pacifier, and it is not an inspired almanac of God's solutions for what ails you. It is not the mother of all self-help books. And it is not written, I believe, to make us feel good. The Bible is, instead, a true account of what God has done in history and the way the Lord does things and wants things done on earth."

To read the Bible like a grown-up child is perhaps to also live like a "grown-up child." I had wondered why there was a sense in which I feel "at home" in the world when all I seemed to be hearing was that I should think of myself as estranged from the world. Better to think of myself as a kind of pilgrim in a foreign land who is just passing through an alien landscape in which I have no place. Seerveld's understanding of the Bible, working within his Reformational heritage, points us in another direction. "Sin and godless culture may make us feel sometimes like aliens and exiles. But humans are not cosmic strangers in God's world. . . . we humans are defined by the task to tend obediently to the earth with the gifts the Lord who is a-coming gave us." This transforms one's daily tasks and presses home the fact that this present reality is the place where God is at work. It is this place that is redeemed in Christ. It is this place that has a future. As Seerveld says, "I believe that this world belongs to God. . . . So as a human creature I am at home in God's world of marvels, from the eclipse of the sun to the birth of a baby."

In the world but not of it takes on a new dimension. Cultivation and to engage in culture are fundamental to what it means to be a person in God's world. Exodus is there, but not as an incentive to world flight. "The fact that Genesis is first and establishes that the human generations are here to cultivate the Lord's garden (even before sin laid us waste, Genesis 1:26-31), takes away any obsession for us to have to go somewhere else than the world where God purposely placed us, as man and woman." He counters our desires to identify some special, more spiritual place or experience and set it apart from our daily experiences of life, as though daily experiences are spiritually inferior. "So, to bypass daily creational activities provided us personally by God as if you have to get somewhere else for a special blessing or an oracle—to Delphi, Mecca, Lourdes, to 'do' Jerusalem as a tourist, or even ascend to heaven—is to be ungrateful to our saving Creator Lord." Being like a grown-up child is to "Be joyfully thankful for creational gifts. It is the amazing grace of God that elicits wonder from children who at a seaside discover the laughing pleasure of having mud ooze between your toes. . . ."

We would do well to remember though that being like a grown-up child is as much about being grown-up in our trust in God's grace as it is about being "childlike." Seerveld can encourage us not to be ". . . blind to that soft incandescent sunlight after a supper hour when green foliage turns golden and shimmers like a bewitching hour" and then remind us of something else that frames our present circumstances. We must be joyfully thankful for creational gifts at the same time as grasping our broken situation. After that encouragement to see God's world with eyes wide open, he talks of ". . . the ability to weep quietly after someone you love has been inexplicably, deeply hurt. . . ."

In my own work I seem to be drawn to the bitter sweetness and sweet bitterness of our experiences here and now. What joy there is seems to be inevitably tinged with a deep sadness. There was a time when I imagined this to be some kind of failure in my faith because the world I was representing was not all sweetness and light. In my Christian thinking I had little place for lament and no real way to articulate it. When it forced its way into my visual language it became an anxious presence. Seerveld shows how lament has a rightful, vital, and biblical place in our Christian experience.

"I have learned" he writes, speaking as a church elder, "congregation members were not really so happy-go-lucky as they appeared in Sunday-morning services. I think that inside and outside church buildings we need popular songs that give vent to the genuine sorrows of our lives and the world—songs that still allow the grit of patient faith in our Lord to come through."

For Seerveld the place of lament in the Christian life is not optional. "The Bible warns that we can fulfill the law of Christ only if we bear one another's burdens through passionate laments (Galatians 6:2)." His concern is that the neglect of lament in our individual experience and in the corporate life of the church is less than the full counsel of God. Is this why maybe as Christians we don't respond ". . . to these Scriptural appeals to groan and weep in our songs because we don't hear nonhuman creatures groaning or our human neighbors weeping." Lament, however heartfelt and urgent, is not just us letting off steam and shouting at God. It embodies the admission of our own sin and is "uttered in faith when we are *helpless* before evil." It is also not something we only engage in alone because lamenting is "wrestling with God in communion on behalf of others, not a freelance protest business."

We can see something of all these strands in Seerveld's being a Christian in his long, detailed, and passionate account of the time he and his wife spent in Sierra Leone with missionaries from the Christian

— Introduction to part two —

Reformed Church. He gives us an engaging description of the landscape, animals, daily life, and culture of the Kuranko peoples of West Africa. In these descriptions there is an empathy and admiration for much of Kuranko culture because he believes, "Christian mission work without humble cultural knowledge and patient nurturing is irresponsible." It is these qualities he finds and admires in the mission workers he meets. There is the same empathy and thankfulness not only for the work they do but for the way they do it. "We learned much more from the mission workers than we could ever have taught them." We learn that what they don't need are Western management methods and target setting imposed from thousands of miles away from the reality of their circumstances. The task of bringing the Gospel into someone else's culture involves generations rather than years if you are to witness a genuine transformation of all that is good in Kuranko culture: ". . . forming a Christian way of life is not a short-term project. It's never like making a cup of instant coffee, where you boil the water, pour in the powder, mix and serve. Nurturing a Christian vision and way of life could certainly not be a short-term project when it comes to helping a first-generation of African Christians find their own Christian style of life." This is one of the keys to his heartwarming account of this Gospel work in Africa. It wouldn't be Seerveld if there was not some honest analysis about what might be unhelpful and sinful in current Kuranko culture, but this is set in the context of ways that culture could flourish rather than be destroyed. "The Kuranko love of children, their gift of storytelling, their praise-singing and rhythmic body movements, the keenness for riddles, and sturdy directness . . . needs to be treasured and reformed."

All this comes together as he explores "The Rule of God." Seerveld suggests that, "We have a hard time getting a heartfelt grasp of the Rule of God on earth because we tend to believe, 'you only get what you pay for,' and we are normally intent on hanging on to something for ourselves. . . . The *liberating Rule of God is free*. And the Rule of God is something you don't hoard for yourself: you *give it away to your enemies*."

His pastoral concern prevents him from ever being a passive commentator or ivory tower theoretician. He always presents us with a challenge not only to our thinking but to who we are and what we actually do. "The Rule of God is hampered when God's children act as though they are God—raising up and putting down disobedient people, inflicting guilt, judging hearts, and meting out rewards. Scripture tells us, instead, to give away our special gifts of the Holy Spirit to one another, to our neighbor, and to do good things even for our enemies."

In his "Epilogue: A Personal Testimony" Seerveld provides a final insight into what it means to be a scholar. "'You spend too much time in your study,' some people say. 'What about life?' That's the one thing I have learned from the Lord: study is life too. Ideas can kill people, or make them alive. Simple words can be seductive, brutal, or give direction and bring healing. The whole world of cultured history with all its sin, vanity, lust, and waste pass before me in my study. I sometimes have felt like St. Anthony in those paintings, tempted all alone by incredible visions of grandeur that are threatening monsters, appearing like genii out of the rubbed bottles of my books. Does anyone these days pray for scholars living and dying in their studies?"

I know that I am one of many who are prayerfully thankful for Seerveld's hours of lonely scholarship. You will find that the words you are about to read are the kind that make you alive, give you direction, and provide healing.

Peter S. Smith
Richmond upon Thames, England

HEARING GOD'S NARRATIVE ABOUT "THE WAY" OF SHALOM

Jewish Persian Queen Esther's husband General Xerxes invaded ancient Greece in 480 BC with his world dominant army and navy, and was soundly defeated. In the aftermath, the polis Athens developed a brilliant imperial culture of Parthenon architecture, the tragedies of Sophocles and Euripides, statesman Pericles, historian Herodotus— This is about the time when a remnant of Jews were rebuilding devastated Jerusalem under Ezra and Nehemiah (c. 460–420 BC), and Malachi was a prophet of Yahweh. Confucius had recently died in China (c. 551–479 BC). Over in Sicily lived a Greek medical thinker named Empedocles (c. 484–424 BC) who developed an important philosophy out of the belief that **everything in the world comes down to four basic matters: earth, water, air, and fire**. Plants, animals, humans, and you can even think of gods like fiery thunderbolt Zeus and his watery goddess wife Hera who promotes marriage and bearing offspring: everything! said Empedocles, becomes and begoes as a loving bonding or struggling-to-separate-out mixture of these four original elements.

Now it is not my intention to give you a lecture on how Empedocles' fourfold primal matters played into a Materialist worldview held by Asia Minor philosopher Democritus (c. 460–370 BC) and the Roman poet Lucretius (c. 96–55 BC), and has been variously embraced throughout world history by Ludwig Feuerbach (1804–72)—*Man ist was er ißt* (You are what you eat)—and leaders like Joseph Stalin (1878–1953) and Mao Tse-Tung (1893–1976). I am not even focused on how Empedocles' nomination of earth, water, air, and fire, as the fundamental building blocks stirred by Love and Hate, constitute at bottom the Nature of the world: how that perspective supported Hippocrates' (c. 460–c. 377 BC) analysis of health and sickness. You get sick, said Hippocrates, if you have a disproportionate amount of fiery warmth (fever) or watery moistness

---

Address for The Arts Gathering, Montemayor, Cordoba, Spain, in May 2008.

(dripping nose) or cold air (chills) or dry earth (constipation). So you use leeches to get rid of the excess blood, and go sit in the sun to dry up the excess moisture, and get your four bodily juices back into a blended harmony—blood, phlegm, yellow and black bile.

You probably know, Empedocles and Hippocrates form the background to the rough-and-ready, popular psychology typing of persons and characters in the writings of Chaucer (c. 1340–1400) and contemporaries Cervantes (1517–1616) and Shakespeare (1564–1616)—sanguinary blood-thirsty fellows, watery phlegmatic people, dried-up frigid women, darkly morose men. Carl Jung's (1875–1961) complex theory of extrovert and introvert personalities picks up traces of these ideas and says people are especially susceptible to psychical disturbances today because they have mostly lost any sense of the mysterious, numinous character of our natural physical phenomena like Empedocles' earth, water, air, and fire.

And that is precisely where I want to make my first point: it would help human sanity and also the well-being of society if we treated earth, water, air, and fire with the respect they deserve as creatures of God. It is hard for us self-serving Humanists to realize that soil, rain, air to breathe, and warmth are telling us about God! Such inanimate creatures God created are not just givens to be taken for granted, "stuff" for our whimsical disposal. The sun, a fireball of energy [#1], as this x-ray photo shows, with its regular run across the skies (as we see it), warming the earth but not sustaining vegetation on our moon, and the Swiss alps, Canadian Rockies and Spanish range of Pyrénées mountains, though getting older and their earthen rock being worn down, have been around much longer than us human inhabitants, telling us—if you are not hard of hearing—their long-lasting staying power and amazing reliability outshine anything we men and women

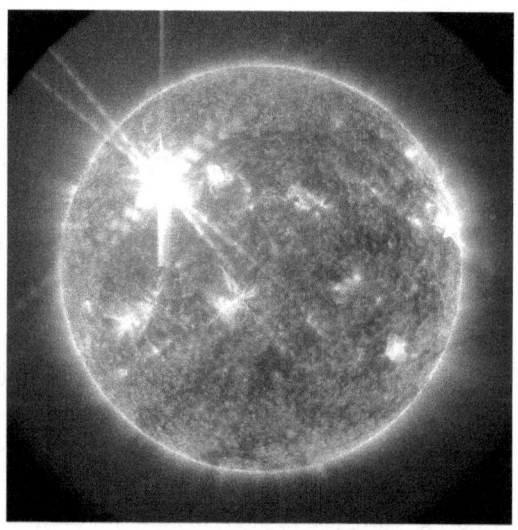

[#1] A Fireball of Energy

[#2] Castle Geyser's Steam in Yellowstone National Park

can do. The amazing properties of water—a liquid that can vaporize into steam at 100 degrees Celsius [#2] or turn into ice a heavy person can walk on (and give evidence you have poor roof insulation [#3])—water

[#3] Wonderful icicles testifying of poor house insulation

is not magical—but such versatility of an inanimate creature presents the reality of a cosmic order that invites incredible variety. And the see-through air all around us—more essential for life even than water—has weight but is as invisible as are most angels: you can marvel at what air makes possible, childhood play, blowing bubbles [*NA* #24], and terrible destruction [#4].

I happen to know that **air, water, fire, and hard earth, like rock and minerals, are messengers of God.** You may think I'm joking, but I know this because the Bible tells me so. Psalm 19 says:

> The heavens are telling the glory of God;
> the very shape of starry space makes news of God's handiwork.

One day is brimming over with talk for the next day, and
each night passes on intimate knowledge to the next night
—there is no speaking, no words at all, you can't hear their voice—
   (but)
their *glossolalia* travels throughout the whole earth!
their uttered noises carry to the end of inhabited land! (vv. 1–4)

Psalm 148 and the apostle Paul's letter to the Romans reports that **these strange, inaudible, non-human sounds of night and day declare the provident care of the Creator God of the universe: everything *tells* of the LORD God's setting limits for creatures**, like gravity, temperature, osmosis (Psalm 148:5–6, Romans 1:18–23). If you do not realize the so-

[#4] Oklahoma Tornado

[#5] Curious tree in Bath, England

[#6] Fan-shaped fern, Indonesia [#7] Huge aloe plant in South African *veld*

[#8] Glorious cover of dandelions, suburb of Toronto

lidity of the earth and the permeability of air [#5] and the metamorphosis of water and combustion of a forest fire begun by lightning are God's loving ordinances to give trees, for example, a place, an environs in which to grow, then you miss understanding what's going on in the world.

Plants like an Indonesian fern [#6], a wild African aloe stalk [#7], trumpet vine flowers and climatis blossoms kissing one another's shadows, a garden herbal jack-in-the-pulpit, even a lovely lawn of pesky [#8] dandelions: shrubs and flowers are living creatures photosynthetically revealing their immobile dependence upon God's sending them sun and rain, nutrient earth and unpolluted air to stay alive. Maybe you, unlike Shakespeare's Duke in the forest of Arden in *As You Like It* cannot say you find

> ... tongues in trees, books in the running brooks,
> Sermons in stones, and good in every thing. (II, i)

And I do not mean you, like a logical magician, can pull incontrovertible "proofs for God's existence" out of a tall black hat of weeds and bumblebees.[1] It is just that the outlandish shape [#9], look, and colors of an Australian peacock, the intimidating threat to strike back of a cornered Asian rat snake (*elaphe radiata*), and the impossible, lugubrious visage of a Canadian walrus [#10]—not to mention the ubiquitous bugs and [#11] insects: fantastic animals bespeak for me the imaginativity of the LORD God who uses a rainbow as well as ivory tusks to give us an oblique word of promising forgiveness (Genesis 8:20–22, 9:8–17) and an incitement to bewonder [*NA* #52] and praise God's majestic humor.
...

If you have ever been out alone quietly paddling a canoe in a large Northern lake just before a thunderstorm, and in the eerie silence that falls

[#9] Peacock at close range, Australia

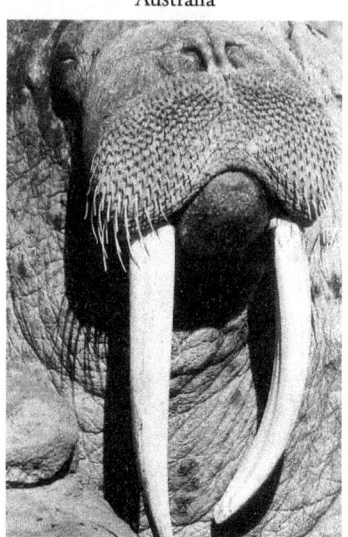

[#10] Canadian walrus

---

1   In *Christianisme et philosophie* (Paris: Librairie philosophique J. Vrin, 1949) Etienne Gilson questions why, in the overwhelming presence of creational revelation of God, John Calvin's admission that the structural bent of humans is to reach disquietedly for a resting place (à la Augustine, *inquietum est cor nostrum, donec requiescat in te,* in *Confessiones,* I,1) cannot be credited as valid "natural knowledge of the true God" (58–64). Calvin's answer is: *Omnis recta Dei cognitio ab obedientia nascitur* (all true knowledge of God is born out of obedience), *Institutio Christianae religionis,* I,6,2. Corporeal recognition and response to God's creational ordinances needs to be focused in thanksgiving sanctified by a heartfelt submission to the Rule of God revealed in Jesus Christ's Way before it counts as "a right knowledge" of God.

portending the danger of lightning soon to be criss-crossing the empty sky you hear the melancholic cry of a loon, you are blessed if you remember Psalm 104 celebrating God's animals (vv. 10–30), and how God self says in the biblical book of *Job* how much God really enjoyed mountain goats, crocodiles, ostriches, and

[#11] Praying Mantis

"Leviathan" before any humans were around (chapters 38–41). That is, stones, plants, and animals communicate God's marvelous loving care and goodness, which we Humanist humans have tended in history to mess up (Romans 8:18–23).

Many people misread "the most elegant book of the universe,"[2] and do not hear the silences of the stars, clouds, snow, the sprint of a tarantula towards its prey, the rustle of a bird's feathers, the hiss, bark, and grunt of animals, as a thanking God for life and sustenance that invites us humans to join in their praise of the LORD God. That's why I call the speaking silences and sounds of non-human creatures *glossolalia*, God's mysterious lala-tongue-talk, which needs the language of the Bible to interpret aright.

The "narrative" of God's non-human creatures has an oracle character: sunshine is God speaking in "heavenly" tongues; seedtime and harvest is God backhandedly telling you of God's faithful presence. **God's *glossolalia* has epigrammatic character: the story line is intriguing but fragmentary, unfinished, without its superintending focus up front. If you do not have ears to hear God's *glossolalia* as a call to prayer and praise, then either you think it is merely interesting, unintelligible noise like thunder** (cf. John 12:27–36) **or you come to overvalue the "talk" of rubies, the West wind, candlelight, and the surf.** Because Empedocles missed hearing the prophet Malachi speak of God's grace, human sin, and a coming Messiah, Empedocles unfortunately missed the true message of earth, water, air, and fire, and made the elements themselves the ontological key to saving knowledge.[3]

---

2 Cf. article 2 of Guido de Brès' Reformation testimony called the *Belgic Confession* (1561).

3 Cf. the good poem by Francis Thompson, "The Hound of Heaven" (c. 1906); also,

We humans who have the gift to communicate in Spanish, English, French, German, Persian, Hausa, or Chinese languages also have the human specialty of books. Certain writings like I Ching, Bhagavad-Gita, the Scriptures sacred to Jews, which Christians call the Older Testament and hold together with a Newer Testament to constitute the Biblical canon, and the Qur'an, are written texts purporting to be, or at least are esteemed to be by many intelligent people, more than ordinary, run-of-the-mill human disquisitions. These legendary or God-originated texts are authoritative for giving direction and contours for living to Daoists, Buddhists, orthodox Jews, Christians, and Muslims. Other people put their faith in writings like the *Communist Manifesto*, the *Financial Times* newspaper, or consult horoscopes for revelation on why, how, and what to live for. Humans who have no final reading source are apt to be wandering, drifting to wherever the prevailing trade winds are blowing.

I should like to describe succinctly for you the Older and Newer Testament Biblical writings and "the Way" to which they focus the *glossolalia* of animal, plant, and mineral creatures, and open up human activity to make art for the imaginatively handicapped, or to do proximate justice in society for the poor-off, and for instituting long-range well-being that will draw a smile to God's face.

The Older Testament Biblical writings tell the story of the LORD God's creating the universe filled with all kinds of creatures, and how humans foolishly tried to displace the Almighty God to call the shots by themselves. After all, the LORD had given the earthling (*adam*) the task of freely naming and caring for all the other creatures (Genesis 1:26, 2:19–20). Then the LORD God of *chesed* (חסד– that rich Hebrew word meaning "an everlasting, intimate bonding quality of providing merciful justice") watched the human race debauch themselves and despoil the earth. So the LORD God, according to the story, chose Noah and family to start over, and later, selected Abraham and his progeny to become the people of Israel: **the LORD God entrusted the mission of making daily life holy with shalom,**[4] **and of giving away God's grace to the nations of the world to this ragtag people of obstreperous Jews.**[5] And if you know the story of Egyptian university-trained Moses' leading God's bitching people in the wilderness for 40 years (Exodus 16–17, 32–34), and later

---

Luke 11:52.
4 Exodus 20, Leviticus 19, Deuteronomy 5.
5 Genesis 12:1–3, 22:15–18, 26:1–5, 28:10–17; Isaiah 42:5–8, 49:5–7, 60:1–18. Cf. Galatians 3:6–9.

how shepherd boy David became top general King and pop song writer (1 Samuel 16–18, 2 Samuel 23:1), and how God's chosen people with their anointed leaders defaulted again and again on their assigned task to which a series of prophets kept reminding them, then you have a rough idea of how the Older Testament is a record of God's disappointments, and of the Lord's continually seeking out remnants of God's adopted people nevertheless to carry on, with the promise of a Messiah still coming who shall fulfill God's will (Psalms 2 and 110).

This Older Testament Biblical tale is told in a narrative meant to be taken as a literary historical account of what actually happened in front of the living God's scrutiny. Miriam's song and dance in Exodus 15 celebrating God's destruction of ancient Pharaoh's war machine took place once upon a time, unlike Aeschylus' depiction of how the departure of Agamemnon's army for Troy was held up until his daughter Iphigenia would be sacrificed to appease the goddess Artemis—a dramatic incident full of meaning in the ancient Greek world vision of multiple Olympian gods, male heroics, and one's fated life, but that event at Aulis did not really happen.

The very nature of the Biblical Hebrew language supports what I just said. Biblical Hebrew is heavy on verbs, not adjectives and detail as one finds in Homer. There is not one adjective in Psalm 23. And there are only two verb tenses in Biblical Hebrew, along with participles, which denote ongoing action: the imperfect tense used for uncompleted action, and the perfect tense, which signifies completed action. What beguiles translators or drives them to distraction is that this history-telling imperfect tense in the Bible is omnitemporal—past, present, and/or future!—and the perfect tense is a preterit referral to what did happen, could happen, and is sure to be happened.

Biblical narrative keeps both past and future in the crucible of reporting what is incompletedly happening . . . because the everlasting God superintends all creatural historical action. Biblical narrative holds connected the pasted (Heidegger would say) responsibilities and futural possibilities, for example, of Nazarite judge Samson's vivid immoral and faith-filled present accomplishments, because the Lord God of enduring *chesed* is One who in the clutch faithfully forgives any repentant wayward prodigals (Judges 13–16). **So, particular and peculiar about the true story-telling of the Older Testament Bible is its disinterest in establishing cause-and-effect sequences so dear to modern Positivist historians, yet its terse presentations of actual events are**

mysteriously contexted as playing a role in a God-intended new restoration of shalom acoming for all peoples.

I'll give just one example that characterizes such everlasting God-drenched Biblical narrative. When God personally called Moses at the burning bush to help extricate God's people who were enslaved by Egyptian culture, and Moses demurred, the LORD God said, אֶהְיֶה עִמָּךְ, "I will be with you" (Exodus 3:12). The imperfect tense connotes, "I was, I am, I will be with you." When Moses persisted in getting five-star credentials and said, "The people fathered by Abraham, Isaac, and Jacob will ask, 'What is the name of the God who sent you.' What shall I tell them?" Then God says, אֶהְיֶה אֲשֶׁר אֶהְיֶה (Exodus 3:14), **not** "I AM WHO I AM," as if it were an obfuscating Parmenidean ontological conundrum, **but** simply a repeating, reassuring, "I am the One who will be (with you"—understood). That is, this firsthand dialogue between God and Moses recalls the LORD's conversation with Eve and Adam, Cain, Noah, Abraham, and pinpoints the reality as the Bible exposits it: God is intimately, permanently involved with our history because this is God's world, headed eventually for the unobstructed, liberating Rule of *chesed*. That is the reality the Biblical Older Testament reveals: caterpillars [#12] that become moths [#13], and rock that becomes [#14] a grand canyon, and polar bears [#15] going extinct like dinosaurs, and well-fed humans starving [#16] other enslaved humans, **happens under the focus of what the prophet Isaiah later formulated as "Immanuel" (God-with-us)!**[6]

The true stories told in the Older Testament Biblical writings and the non-narrative poetry strewn throughout the varied books have an oral, God-voicing nature that confronts you for an answer. If you intently read Dostoevsky's *Crime and Punishment* (1866), James Joyce's *Ulysses* (1914–22), William Faulkner's *Absalom, Absalom!* (1936), Gabriel Marquez' *Cien años de soledad* (1967), or Ursula LeGuin's *The Left Hand of Darkness* (1969), such fascinating literature can stretch and modify your personal picture of the world and your place in it. But you can take it or leave it, no sweat. Special about Biblical literature, however, is that its invitation to those who give it time to be **heard** is not just to add some ideas and possibly norms to what you already hold, if you wish, but **the Biblical writing requests that you trust its thrust enough to fit the heart and contours of your life into *its* God-speaking eschatonic story line, because this text is God talking/calling to you and your neighbors for a life-committed response.**

---

6   Isaiah 7:14; cf. Matthew 1:18–23.

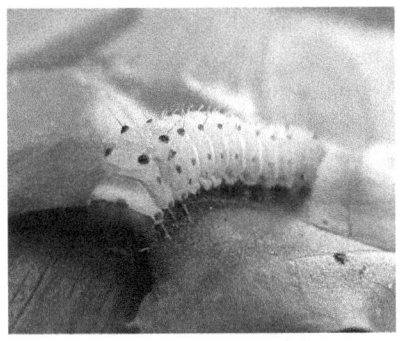
[#12] A larval Luna Moth

[#13] Luna Moth

[#14] Marble Canyon, Arizona

[#15] Polar bear

[#16] Refugees in South Sudan

The wordless talk without syntax of animal, plant, and mountain *glossolalia* praise of the Creator God may sound like stammering to many people, but the original Hebrew, Aramaic, and Greek languages of the Biblical texts are in human tongues, decipherable, able to be translated and clearly understood. The Older Testament documents are not only the scroll and codex records of speech remembered and passed on for generations, but they have themselves a speaking, proclaiming, vocative-imperative character. The Older Testament stories are God asking, "Do you love me? Do you respect your neighbor and yourself?" (Deuteronomy 6:4–7, Leviticus 19:17–18) And if one's response is, "Who are you?" then the biblical text says, "If you will take my hand, and listen, I'll tell you a true story that can make you wise. I am the One who will always be with you through thick and thin—"

It is so important to catch the tone of God's voice in the Biblical writings. The famous Ten "Thou shalt not" Words of Exodus 20 are not to be heard as damning prohibitions backed up by a raised club, but rather as the LORD God's beseeching [#17] fragile mortals not to disregard God's protective hedges lest you get off track and badly hurt. The wild story of Elijah's out-performing 450 prophets of the Canaanite Baal god on Mount Carmel and then marathon running for his life from murderous Queen Jezebel until exhausted, suicidal . . . upon falling asleep, an angel of the LORD touched him [#18] awake, gave him food and water, did it twice, so that Elijah could continue his journey to a forsaken place where the LORD God self gently "in a still small voice" told the depressed but cheeky Elijah to hang in there with the other failures; and God gave Elijah strength for a new assignment (1 Kings 18–19): angels are real epiphanies of God's provident care today too,

[#17] Ernst Barlach, *Schwebender Gottvater*, 1922

[#18] Susanna Oppliger, *Der Engel mit Elia*, 1998

and may guard a person from evil unawares, and could be some hospitable stranger not wearing wings.[7] And the love songs written to God called Psalms, both trusting and lamenting God's silence and at time slowness to act, reveal how incredibly receptive God is to human cries uttered in faith: I know, You keep [*RA* #104] all my tears in your bottle! (56:8) Yes, you give us elderly codgers like palm trees fresh sap so we can bear juicy fruit in our old age! (92:12–15) But how long, good LORD, do we have to wait for you to stop the excruciating pain our friend is suffering? (13:1–2) Yet I trust You, my Lord, "My life time, my times, the timings for me, are in your hand" (31:15).

The Older Testament Biblical writings, which ask to be **read aloud** so you realize the worded text is intrinsically oral—**God speaking in human voices!**—reveal the LORD God's abiding angry mercy toward us humans, and authorize those who take God at God's word to vent their frustrations honestly at evil (in which we humans are complicit), to plead for forgiveness ourselves, and to thank God for the breath of life, food and drink, difficult neighbors to love, and variegated tasks to cultivate the earth we inhabit. The Older Testament Bible is a ferment of intertextual allusions, a rich resonance of echoing symbols, a complex unity of narrative and poetry that, above all, is **not** dictated declarations and regulations like the Qur'an, but is **a Holy Spirited true story inviting anybody**—not prejudging—**to listen, to wrestle [#19] with the LORD God self offering merciful justice as "the Way" to find fulfillment of our human nature.**

[#19] Jacob Epstein, *Jacob wrestling with the Angel*, 1940

And if a person is unwilling to get an ear full? afraid of limping for life after wrestling with the angel of God (Genesis 32)? too grown-up and self-assured to ask for direction? to want to become like a little child up for adoption by God (cf. Matthew 18:1–4)?

The Newer Testament Biblical writings up the ante, because they pres-

---

7   Cf. Hebrews 13:2, as happened to Abraham and Lot (Genesis 18–19) and to Jacob (Genesis 32:22–32).

ent Jesus Christ as the Messiah whom God's people of the first Older Testament Covenant expected (Hebrews 8:6–13, Jeremiah 31:31). Most people do not doubt the historical existence of rabbi Jesus crucified under orders of Pontius Pilate outside Jerusalem around 30 AD. But the main question is: was Jesus Christ a human teacher of good morals, a pretentious fake who thought he was a god, or was the Jesus Christ to whom Saul of Tarsus, medical doctor Luke, and other "gospel" writers witness really God-in-your-face, the preposterous God-man born from the womb of a virgin named Mary, the Messiah who lived, died, was resurrected! and returned to where God oversees world affairs? Ancient Greek philosophers mocked such a monstrosity (Acts 17:16–32), sadly the Muslim *Qur'an* damns those who believe such an enormity as if Jesus be God to hell,[8] and many disbelievers in our post-Christian culture treat the whole matter of a Jesus Christ, if they think about it, as fiction.

Whatever stand you take with respect to Jesus, it is evident, according to these Scriptures held to be holy by Christians, that Jesus came onto the scene not to supersede but to fulfill, that is, to intensify and give invigorating body to the Older Testament story, message, and promises (Matthew 5:17–20). The apostle Paul picks up this knotty problem of continuity and updating the LORD God's old covenant with the specific people called Israel in God's letter to the new Christians in Galatia: don't treat God's earlier Word in a legalistic, rule-book fashion, as if the **alphabet letters** of the *torah* need to be obeyed. Christ's resurrection, which overcame death, and Christ's offering the Holy Spirit also to non-Jew believers (Acts 10), frees Christians from the inordinate pagan dependence on "the rudimentary particles holding the world together" (τὰ στοιχεῖα τοῦ κόσμου)—earth, water, air, fire—**and** saves Christians from reducing God's Older Testament speaking direction and comfort to its elemental letters, the basic particles (στοιχεῖα) of language—a letter-bound, literalistic reading—myopically missing the narrative flow of the story about who the LORD God is and God's will to bring shalom to the nations of the world (Galatians 4:6–11, Colossians 2:8–23).

---

8   *Al-Qur'an*: "They are surely infidels who say: 'God is the Christ, son of Mary.' Whoever associates a compeer with God, will have Paradise denied to him by God, and his abode shall be Hell . . ." (5:72); ". . . the Christians say: 'Christ is the son of God.' That is what they say with their tongues following assertions made by unbelievers before them. May they be damned by God: how perverse are they!" (9:30); "It does not behoove God to have a son. Too immaculate is He! When He decrees a thing He has only to say, 'Be,' and it is" (19:35). Translation by Ahmed Ali (Princeton: Princeton University Press, 1993).

The Newer Testament epistles of Paul, Peter, James, and John bring explicitly to the fore, with one voice, the central Older story theme but with a new emphasis: **the LORD God now fully revealed in Jesus Christ is God of all creatures, παντοράτωρ [#20], and God of all nations.**[9] The Kingdom of God, the Rule of "Heaven," the Holy Spirited "ordering" Jesus Christ bespeaks was sounded by the prophet Micah long ago— **"What is required of you, O people, but to act justly, love to show mercy, and walk humbly with your God"** (Micah 6:8). The Newer, updated formulation reaching out forcefully to neighbors and strangers is: "Bear one another's burdens, and you will be carrying out the *torah* of Christ!" (Galatians 6:2; cf. Romans 13:8–10).

[#20] *Christus Pantokrator*, apse of Monreale cathedral, Sicily, c. 1180–1194

I'd like to slip in here a brief tragic note before I characterize the narrative of the Newer Testament writings. The apostle Paul's masterful, rhetorically shaped letter to the Jewish and Gentile Christian believers at Rome tells the tale of Israel's forfeiting its favored nation status if it persists in not recognizing Jesus Christ as the Messiah and Son of God. Yet thank the LORD! writes Paul, because this failing has occasioned an historical opening to bring the good news of God-given shalom **directly** to non-Jewish ethnic peoples (Romans 9–11; cf. Matthew 21:33–46, vv. 42–43).

The deep Jewish thinker Martin Buber (1878–1965), from his Jewish perspective, held that what has distinguished the people of Israel from all other nations is the fact that they were betrothed to God at Mount Sinai,[10] and given the mission to show to other nations **as a people** the shalom Way of the LORD as God's Rule for **all** peoples. Tragically, says Buber, Israel reduced the LORD God of the universe to be their national God; so Israel can no longer as a people represent God's Holy Spirit leading the nations of the world to the LORD God of the universe. Israel has

---

9 Matthew 12:15–21, 25:31–33; cf. Revelation 1:7, 15:1–4, 21:22–27.
10 Cf. Genesis 17:1–8, 2 Samuel 7:22–24, Amos 3:1–2.

become nationalistic like all the other non-elect nations who struggle to subdue their neighbors by military power. The Christian faith, continues Buber, absorbed "the people of God" task, but atomized peoplehood into a collection of saved individuals, and then in short-sighted, power-hungry fashion set up "Christendom," a kind of sacred empire, Churchianity, with an infallible pope demanding nation-status; so Christians too lost the non-partisan authority to invite the nations of the world to become members in "the kingdom of *God*."[11]

But Jesus Christ spent the 40 days on earth after his resurrection, says the Bible, speaking not about doing evangelism or forming an organized church: Jesus spent 40 days straight **speaking of the kingdom, the Rule of God** (Acts 1:1–3)! Christ's disciples still had a very poor grasp of how **unlike** "kingdoms" and authoritarian, power-trip "Rulers" was the "kingdom" and "Ruling" for which Jesus Christ was speaking.[12] **The "Way of the LORD"** the prophet Isaiah and later Baptizer John had announced their hearers should prepare (Isaiah 40:3–5, Matthew 3:1–3)—the very "Way" Jesus Christ walked on earth—was and is: **to be building a community of thankful healed persons busy in redeeming ordinary activities with joy,**[13] **sharing gifts and goods to fill communal needs** (cf. Acts 4:32–35), **quietly exorcizing the spirit of vanity, violence, greed, and pride infecting leaders like a deadly virus.**[14] This "Way" Jesus walked (John 14, v4) is precisely what the Newer Testament biblical writings mean by "seeking the kingdom of God and God's mercifully just doing **first**" in *this* **world now**, not some future world (Matthew 6:24–33).

And Jesus spoke the healing he practiced in parables. The Newer Testament gospels report in spare, laconic language how Jesus told stories in the vernacular to learned and uneducated people often in a rural idiom, "A sower went out sowing seed . . ." to face his audience with the metaphorical point, "Are you hearing God as hard ground, rocky soil, a thin skin of dirt, thorny matter, or as rich receptive earth?" (Mark 4:1–20, Matthew 13:1–23, Luke 8:4–18). People were captivated but often puzzled by the parables, even though parables come out of the Older Testament

---

11 Martin Buber, "The Gods of the Nations and God," in *Israel and the World: Essays in a time of crisis* (New York: Shocken Books, 1948), 199–202, 212–213.
12 Mark 10:35–45//Matthew 20:20–28//Luke 22:24–27; Mark 9:33–37; John 13:3–17. Jesus' "triumphal entry" into Jerusalem on an ass (Luke 19:28–44) is an ironic corrective to the Roman imperial chariot and horses (Zechariah 9:9–10).
13 Matthew 11:2–6, Luke 11:14–23, v20, Philippians 4:4–6.
14 Matthew 23:1–12, 26:47–54; Luke 16:1–15, 18:9–14.

rabbi teaching praxis of speaking proverbs, because the Jewish people of Jesus' day had grown accustomed to being commanded without a blink what to think by their Pharisee and Sadducee leaders.[15] Nicodemus with his Th.D. did not get it. "What do you mean, 'A person must be born again?'" (John 3:1–15). But the non-Jewish Syro-Phonecian woman with a demoniac daughter who responded in metaphorical kind to Jesus' bluntly telling her, "It's not good to take the children's bread and throw it to the house dogs," "Yes, Lord, but even the house dogs eat from the crumbs that fall from the master's table." And Jesus said, "Great is your faith, O woman. Your daughter is healed" (Mark 15:21–28//Matthew 7:24–30).

Jesus' ministry was oral, face-to-face; and that the Newer Testament narrative highlights this tale-telling parable format of Jesus' expositing this upside down "kingdom of God" is important. **The parable narrative embodies the truth that "the Rule of God" is not first of all a doctrine-to-be-instructed but is a life-to-be-lived, a Way-to-walk, a tale your history is to embody and tell.** The very oblique, literary character of a parable gives the listener room to respond at varied levels of hearing and willing. **The intrinsic ambiguity and ellipticality is good, hinting that the kingdom of God's grace, which the story articulates, is not logically cut-and-dried but is unfinished! open to surprises! an invitation to catch on to what is really going on in the world, which takes visionary faith and hope rather than proven sight.**[16] **The parabolic revelation of the Way-of-the-Lord expects your walk to embody imaginatively, with quirks, let's say, the merciful just-doing that pleases God.**

[#21] Masaccio, *Adam and Eve Expelled from Paradise*, 1424–1425

I'll tell you just one of Jesus' parables in today's language, using a series of five photographic artworks entitled "The Return of the Prodigal Son" (1982) [*CP* ##32–36]. I'll tell it the way I think the Newer Testament writings wanted the tale to be **heard**: Like a mirror [#21] image of Masaccio's Adam and Eve expelled

---

15 Cf. how the overbearing leaders treated the ordinary people as being stupid, John 7:45–52.
16 Luke 17:20–21, Romans 8:22–25, Hebrews 11:1.

from paradise, the naked son enters from the right into a room where the Father is leisurely scanning *The New York Times*. The startled older man looks at the youth bowed in shame. The father loosens his shirt to protect the other's nakedness, and then thoughtfully removes all his clothes to give them to the younger one. Finally the naked old man gingerly gives the returned son a hug offering reconciliation.

Jesus' parable is about **the prodigal God!** who in overflowing love did for us human sinners and the polluted world of earth, water, air, and fire, what will restore us to normality. God went naked in sacrificing God's only begotten son for both us prodigal younger sons and daughters **and** us older brothers and sisters, who have wasted our inheritance from God too, our gifts, by keeping them locked up selfishly at home without joyful giving them away thankfully to neighbors. Duane Michals' pictorial retelling of the story also describes the Way Jesus Christ acted as the good shepherd who lays down his life for the sheep. Jesus Christ, says the Newer Testament, laid down his life, went naked on the cross, to give those who respond to the happening gratefully, to give those persons redemptive openings to be clothed in deeds of becoming a ready hand and a sure foot, a perceptive eye and listening ear, or a wise mouth for our fellow handicapped, poor sheep (John 10:1–18, 1 Corinthians 12).

The fact that the Lord God's direction and wisdom is offered in tales told not with sound and fury signifying nothing, but in a roundabout, offhand gentle way, facing listeners indeed person-to-person with a decision for genuine life or for prolonged dying, but offering the fateful choice in a kindly, child-friendly fashion, is indicative of how the Newer Testament biblical writings are to be taken. One would do well to hear the Scriptural injunction to "destroy arguments and every proud obstacle raised up against the knowledge of God," which the apostle Paul pronounces (2 Corinthians 10:3–6), as a suggestion **not** to try to figure out a more sophisticated, logically tight way to dispute with disbelievers, but to humble the theologians and still the noise of argument simply by telling parable stories that make the convincing truth of God's Word available to people who have ears to hear.

I began by suggesting God speaks through the unmediated *glossolalia* of creatures at large, telling us in tintinnabulating sounds of God's *chesed*. Then I spoke about how God revealed God self more fully in Jesus Christ whose pivotal place in the history of the universe is told by the Older and Newer Testament Holy Spirited writings, which voice clearly **"the Way"**

of the Rule of God: practicing merciful justice that brings the fruit of shalom. I should like to conclude now by showing with oral comment just a few graphic artworks that in my judgment bear the spirit of wisdom that testifies to the cosmic, glocal Rule of Jesus Christ, which is acoming historically, and therefore is **artistry echoing God's voice with an obedient imaginative response**. Artistic images can be a kind of underpainting layer that a worded glaze elucidates.

[#22] Matthias Grünewald, *The Small Crucifixion*, c. 1505–1519

Singular about the LORD God that Christians confess is the ugly death [#22] of Jesus Christ who quoting the Older Testament Psalm 22 cried, "My God, my God! Why have you forsaken me!" The Messiah Jesus, as the story goes, made good for our human wrongs by dying in weakness, practicing a justifying mercy (צְדָקָה, *tzedaqah*), the Way of grace with which God rules God's creatures (2 Corinthians 13:4, Isaiah 53:4–6). A contemporary installation [*RA* #17] with a burning arc of live electricity where the head would be gives "crucifixion" the proper note of torture used in prisons today too. The Canadian Yukon Indian believer Stanley Peters' *Totem Cross* (1976) [*CP* #31] replicates the lament of the Newer Testament Romans 8 about the non-human creatures groaning for the redemption of human bodily activity by raising up a mythic Thunderbird on a cross like a bronze serpent,[17] to remind us, "God did not send the Son into the world to condemn the world, but in order to save the whole cosmos" (John 3:17)—tundra, snow, Arctic air, Northern lights, and animals, not just humans!

Two hundred years ago to this very day an atrocity happened in

---

17 Cf. Numbers 21:4–9, John 3:14–15.

Madrid (3 May 1808), which Goya unerringly depicted in its stark, coldblooded terror. *J'accuse!* such senseless evil, paints the artist. But we humans continue to murder one another . . . in Iraq, Palestine, Darfur, Tibet, megalopolis ghettoes, can be anywhere. . . . The New York Jew Abraham Rattner's World War II crucifixion! painting entitled *There was a Darkness over All of the Land* (1942) [#23] coalesces, it seems, Golgotha and Auschwitz. The faces of soldiers bloody in the light of their torches form a barricade between viewers and the paschal lamb sent to take away

[#23] Abraham Rattner, *There was a Darkness over All of the Land*, 1942

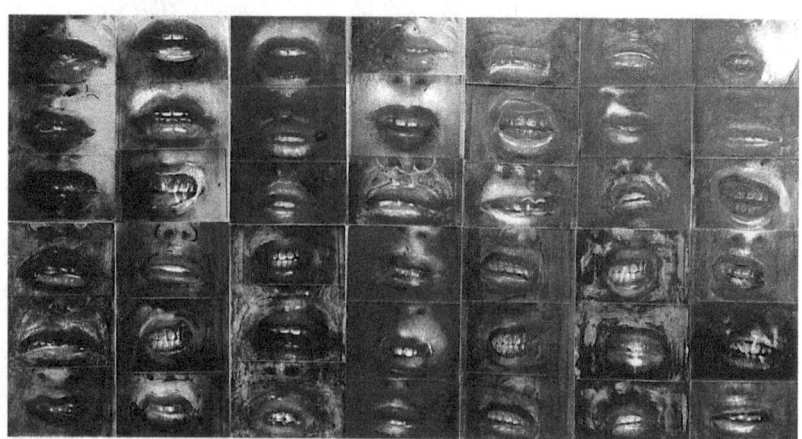

[#24] Warren Breninger, *Gates of Prayer* [detail], 1993–2008

the sin of the world, because men militarized into soldiers not only kill the landlord's son (if you know the parable in Luke 20:9–19) but also militate against letting anybody get near to the Peace of the world. Australian artist Warren Breninger has produced a series of 44 mouths called *Gates of Prayer* (1996) [#24]. Each 50x75 cm. painting can be put in different arrangements to fit whatever a given prayer communion of Job-saints needs. These are mouths pleading for help, uttering clenched teeth curses against the evil powers we cannot seem to match—not specific people—but the principalities of Greed, Rage, Hate, which drive humans to become cruel, ruthless, implacably violent. Like the imprecatory laments of the Older Testament psalms—two of which Christ quoted on the cross—these mouths, while confessing *mea culpa*, wrestle with God for a blessing: do not leave us and our neighbors as prey for evil-minded predators, but come back quick! Lord Jesus (Revelation 22:20). And in the meantime give us communally the visionary wisdom and stamina to do proximate justice—right the wrongs nearby us in our own societal environs—so that the discouraged may take heart and the weak be restored to able-bodied, self-respecting service.

The Way of shalom the Bible directs us humans to live in God's world is not namby-pamby but faces evil in society. Yet God promises to humans who listen to God's voice in creatures, in the Scriptures testifying of the God-man Jesus Christ, and in the witness of humans faithful to the call to follow Jesus Christ: **God promises the courage to repent and to be thankful for creatural normality**. Emile Nolde's vibrant colors in *Christus und die Kinder* (1910) [CP #22] celebrate Christ's inviting children into the communion of saints, while the thick-lipped disciples hem and haw in disapproval behind Christ's back. Enigmatic Hundertwasser grapples [CP #25] with human habitation and city life: *On the Sunny Side of the Street* (1953) places a warm yellow rectangle next to red shadows, while all the primary colors swim around pleasantly, as if clothes are waving on clotheslines outside. His [CP #26] *Rainbowhouse* (1976–77) is wonderfully messy, lived in, crisscrossed by a rainbow of grace. Gerald Folkerts incorporates a derelict street-person named *Ralph* (2005) into our human company [NA #79], as Christ gave special attention to outcasts, and practically grants the sad-eyed fellow an "assumption" in the rising steam of a hot coffee in paper cup resting on the lowly pavement next to his worn out shoes.

Catalan Joan Cots (1927–2004) baptizes the wonderful plasticity of clay with a happy mysterious quality. Cots' steles [#25] remind one of faces that are both intimate and strong, each with an uncanny personality, [#26] weather-beaten, firmly aristocratic. There is a glow of warm desert sands to some of these "signposts," which look both severe and delicate to my eye. When you see a whole family [#27] together, you think of a reunion of very different, polyethnic persons who somehow still belong to one another: they have idiosyncrasies, this communion of creatures, whether human or not does not matter. It is the sturdy, forthright, friendly character of Cots' artwork that breathes, it seems to me, a holy spirit. And Rouault's *Sarah* (1956) [*NA* #87] for me anticipates and symbolifies the joyful laughter of the bodily resurrection that those who become God's adopted children may expect. Rouault's cheerful *Sarah* artwork helps one realize again that the biblical narrative of God speaking is "**good news**," not bad news demanding self-help work-righteousness. **The Newer Testament beatitudes are not hortatory but congratulatory!** The Bible story is **not**: "Try to become meek, so you will inherit the earth." No! Those who meekly, childlikely accept the biblical story as true come to know in your bones—and you can see it in *Sarah*—that despite the trouble and patient endurance the coming of God's merciful just-doing kingdom entails (Revelation 1:9, cf. 1 John 3:11–17), **God's children are free to giveaway together to the neighbors whatever gifts the LORD God has created us with—***that is the Way of the Lord!* (Galatians 5:22–6:2). And God says then, "You shall be blessed with laughter through the tears" if in your art, in your speech, in your political governing, in your buying and selling, you give

[#25] Joan Cots, ceramic stele in his studio, Torrelles de Llobregat, Province of Barcolona

[#26] Joan Cots, ceramic stele

[#27] Joan Cots, ceramic stele

your fellow humans the daily bread of merciful justice instead of a beautiful but weather-beaten, unresponsive stone (Matthew 7:7–12).

"Offering of bread rather than a stone"
Photo by Ines and Calvin Seerveld

Selected sources consulted
Alter, Robert. *Canon and Creativity: Modern writing and the authority of Scripture* (New Haven: Yale University Press, 2000).
———. *On Biblical Narrative* (Eugene: University of Oregon Humanities Center, 2000).
———. *The Art of Biblical Poetry* (New York: Basic Book, 1985).
Alter, Robert and Frank Kermode, eds. *The Literary Guide to the Bible* (Cambridge: Belkap Press, 1987).
Auerbach, Erich, "Odysseus' Scar" (1946) in *Mimesis: The representation of reality in Western literature*, translated by Willard Trask (Garden City: Doubleday Anchor, 1953), 1–20.
Balkenende, Jan Peter and Roel Kuiper, Leen La Rivière, eds. *The Art of Living: The cultural challenge of the 21ˢᵗ century* (Rotterdam: International Association of Christian Artists/CNV-Kunstenbond, 2001).
Benjamin, Walter. "The Storyteller: Reflections on the works of Nikolai Leskov," in *Illuminations*, ed. Hannah Arendt, translated by Harry Zohn (New York: Shocken Books, 1969).
Buber, Martin. *Israel and the World: Essays in a time of crisis* (New York: Shocken Books, 1948).
Delling, Gerhard. στοιχέω in *Theologisches Wörterbuch zum Neuen Testament* (*TWNT*), ed. Gerhard Friedrich (Stuttgart: W. Kohlhammer Verlag, 1964),

7:666–687.

Eagleton, Terry. "Introduction" to *Jesus Christ, the Gospels* (London: Verso, 2007).

Fuchs, Ernst. "Die Sprache im Neuen Testament," in *Das Problem der Sprache in Theologie und Kirche.* Ed. Wilhelm Schneemelcher (Berlin: Verlag Alfred Töpelmann, 1959), 21–35.

Liebenberg, Jacobus. *The Language of the Kingdom and Jesus: Parable, aphorism, and metaphor in the sayings material common to the synoptic tradition and the Gospel of Thomas* (Berlin: Walter de Gruyter, 2001).

Löwith, Karl. "Die Sprache als Vermittler von Mensch und Welt," in *Das Problem der Sprache in Theologie und Kirche*, 36–54.

Michaelis, Wilhelm. ὁδός in *TWNT*, 5:42–101.

Michaels, J. Ramsey. *Servant and Son: Jesus in parable and gospel* (Atlanta: John Knox Press, 1981).

Price, Reynolds. *A Palpable God: Thirty stories translated from the Bible with an essay on the origins and life of narrative* (New York: Atheneum, 1978).

Schelhaas, David. *The God of Material Things: Poems* (Sioux Center: Dordt College Press, 2007).

Schilder, Klaas. *De Openbaring van Johannes en het sociale leven* (Delft: Meinema, 1924/1951).

Wilder, Amos N. *The Language of the Gospel: Early christian rhetoric* (New York: Harper & Row, 1964).

Wink, Walter. *Unmasking the Powers: The invisible forces that determine human existence* (Philadelphia: Fortress, 1986).

Zimmerli, Walther. "Die Weisung des Alten Testamentes zum Geschäft der Sprache," in *Das Problem der Sprache in Theologie und Kirche*, 1–20.

With James C. Schaap at Dordt College, before "The Meaning of our Nakedness" (1969) lecture in November 2013

Reading and Hearing the Psalms: The Gut of the Bible

Since this conference encourages us to be living in Scripture, we should start by doing it, by standing and reading out loud together Psalm 115.

The text is antiphonal, back-and-forth between liturgist and people, a call and response primed to help you realize you are not alone but in a communion of *tsadiqim, chasidim,* saints. And together by reading Scripture in faith we invoke God's presence, testify to whatever hope be in us, make our urgent requests known to God, and then wait to hear the Lord's blessing.

Psalm 115 [*for communal responsive reading aloud*]

leader:	Not for us, Lord, not for us,	1
	but do something glorious for Your name!	
	Make something solid and shining to show your covenanting grace and utterly dependable faithfulness!	
	Why should the peoples all around say, "	
	And where now is their God?"	2
people:	Our God is in heaven!	3
	Everything that pleases God, God completes!	
leader:	Their "gods" are solid gold and silver,	
	[but] made by a human hand.	4
	Their fake gods have a mouth, but cannot speak;	5
	they have eyes, but cannot see!	
	Ears they have, but cannot hear;	6
	a nose is there, but they cannot smell—	
	their hands cannot touch things.	7

First presented at a "Living the Scriptures" conference at Dordt College and published that spring in *Pro Rege* 27:4 (1999):20–32.

	Their feet cannot go for a walk. No sound passes through their throat…	
people:	Like them become those who made them! Like them become all those who feel secure with them.	8
leader:	Israel! get to feel secure with the LORD God:	9
people:	a relief and protection is the LORD for such people.	
leader:	[Priestly] house of Aaron! bind yourselves only to the LORD God:	10
people:	a relief and protection is the LORD for such people.	
leader:	You [newcomers] who fear Yahweh! trust— trust the LORD God:	11
people:	a relief and protection is God for such people.	
leader:	The LORD God has kept us in mind: God shall bless—	12
people:	Bless the house of Israel! Bless the [priestly] house of Aaron! Bless those who fear the LORD God!	13
leader:	—the unimportant ones together with the very important ones…	
	May the Lord God prosper you, you and your children. May you all be blessed by the LORD God, who made heaven and earth.	14 15
	Heaven [you know] belongs specially to the LORD: The earth is what God gave for the sons and daughters of man [to tend].	16
	Dead men and women do not praise the LORD, not one of those who have gone down to where it is deathly still. But we people here, let us praise the Lord! from now on and for ever more:	17 18
people:	thank God—hallelujah!	

(translation 1969)

Scripture is a live wire. You need to take hold of it and be charged by its power. The script has to become oral; you have to hear the voice of God speaking for reading the Bible to be right.

Naturally, it is important to pick up subliminally on imaginative features of a psalm text. For example, that a repeated line is not a copyist's error. Repetition in poetry—whether it be Robert Frost's "And miles to go before I sleep, and miles to go before I sleep," or Bertolt Brecht's refrain in "Das Lied des Freudenmädchens," or God's word of Psalm 115, ". . . a relief and a protection is the Lord for such people"—repetition brings amplification, intensification, a purposeful supply of extra meaning that counts in between the literal lines.

It's also good to catch a sense of setting, if possible. The initial two verses of Psalm 115 sound as if God's chosen people are in difficult straits and want the Lord's *chesed* (Covenantal grace) and *'emet* (dependable Faithfulness) to kick into gear, because the surrounding nations' jibe is, "Isn't your almighty God going to show up?" Psalm 115 fits well if you lived at the time of Nehemiah, surrounded by enemies, rebuilding the blasted wall of Jerusalem, crying together as a people because the second temple being put up looks like an outhouse compared to the one Solomon had built: "Not for us, Lord, not for us, but do something glorious for Your name!" Psalm 115 contends with God precisely the way Moses did in Exodus 32, and argues for what Ezekiel 36:22–32 reports God-self says God shall do: restore Israel to their home in order to vindicate God's holy name. So Psalm 115 has the tenor of being written perhaps after the Jews returned from exile in the 500s BC.

A good time for the Church to have read Psalm 115 would have been when the Romans were putting the squeeze on Christians calling only Jesus Christ *kurios,* Lord, and demanding that they call Emperor Augustus *kurios,* Caesar, lord, or the congregation would be martyred.

Are Dordt's rising graduates under siege? Beset by idols? Are a group of you seniors coming back from spiritual exile? Then it would be appropriate to declaim Psalm 115—this communal, responsive, shouting piece of God's Word written—allow it to come into its own. And you do justice to God's Word written if you merely read it silently in a private "quiet time" before you fall asleep?

My presuppositions

Before we go any further, I should be open about my presuppositions and where we are headed here. Even if you don't share my perspective, I'd like to make a couple of psalms meaningful to you, God willing, and freshen our language for talking with God.

Credo (I believe) this holy scripture in its canonic form is God-speaking literature given us historically, booked in the human language of Egyptian-educated Moses (Acts 7:20–22), philosopher-poet Isaiah, medical doctor Luke (Colossians 4:14, Luke 1:1–4), converted to Pharisee bachelor Paul (2 Thessalonians 3:17), and many other gifted, colorful anonymous men and women over a millennium of years for our learning by faith the one true story of *magnalia Dei* (God's great deeds) and the Lord's Rule acoming in this world, which belongs to God revealed in Jesus Christ. *Credo* the Bible is mysteriously kerygmatic: the very text understood pulsates with God's voice existentially, and compels one to respond with, "Amen! Lord, speak to me more, I'm listening," or "God loves sinners into repentance?—preposterous!"

That is, God's Word written, in front of us, in its full-orbed counsel, is meant to be heard (said Buber), accepted as it is. Studied, sure, to catch the deep resonances of subtle meaning embedded in the text from Genesis to Revelation, but the Bible must be studied on your knees, so to speak, so you don't start pretending to hover over the text and try to master it, pick out its fleas, flaws, or even proof texts to argue for this or that special partisan point you want to make. You are not supposed to get the Bible's message in your theologistic grip: the Bible is supposed to get you, change you, turn you around, discipline-disciple you, give you direction on pivotal matters like life or death, truth or the lie, and face you with the Way of shalom or vanity, wisdom or foolishness.

If you meet the living God in reading holy Scripture, then other good things can happen too, like a Holy Spirited way of life, fashioning a biblically Christian worldview, sound churchly doctrine, responsible societal reformation, and missionary endeavor. The key thing is to submit your reading, in the communion of saints living and dead, to the given writings as a trustworthy, imaginative, historical record of God-speaking-to-us awaiting our discovery.

So, from the standpoint of this Calvinian Reformational reflective faith tradition, I should like to explore with you how we humans are to go about reading the biblical psalms with supple maturity (sensitivity, intelligence, imaginativity, competence). We need to hear God's Word sound through the marvelous crisscrossing cathedral variety of 150 pieces that cohere as a single, edited book of the whole Bible—aware that both Older and Newer Testaments assume the Psalter to be integral to the whole Bible and quote it cross-referentially in profusion.

The psalms as an edited book

For me, the psalms in the biblical canon are not loose bits and pieces, free-form devotional lyrics, or approved mantras for TM. The psalms as we have them are songs ascribed variously to pop-song writer David, to King David's poet-laureate Asaph and the composers-singers who bore that family name (Psalms 50, 73–83). Certain psalms were written down, the text says, by the temple guild of liturgical leaders named Qorah (Psalms 42–49, 84–85, 87–88), and many are available to us through the God-breathed writing (cf. 2 Timothy 3:16–17) of nameless, skilled wise men and women artists.

A fact that has not received enough attention until of late is that God's Spirit had certain persons—nobody knows who, exactly when, or why—edit at different times (?) all those 150 songs into five books (see *Table A*). The last verse of the first four books (41:13, 72:18–19, 89:52, 106: 48) quotes in abbreviated form a doxology found in 1 Chronicles 16:34–36—which is the chapter that reports on the time when David organized the first musicians' union to write songs and become professional composers and musicians for the worship services among God's people:

> Blessed be the Lord, the God of Israel.
> From everlasting on for ever and evermore.
> Amen and amen!

Book V ends with a flurry of five hallelujah! songs (Psalms 146–150). It seems that a jubilant doxology is a good way to end any size collection of songs intended specifically to address the Lord God.

Psalm 72:20 adds onto its doxology: "Here end the intercessory prayers of David, son of Jesse," as if books I and II had formed an earlier completed psalter (because other psalms scattered through books III, IV, and V are credited by somebody to David's pedigree too[1]). And one can find that Psalms 120–134 all have the same title, "A song for the goings-up," and thus comprise, following Psalm 119, a small collection of 15 psalms inside book V, apparently tailored for singing on pilgrimages up to Jerusalem, if not used on the actual return from Babylonian and disparate exiles.[2]

There are other editorial notes beside the attribution of composers; for example, what sort of piece the psalm is (*Table B*): Is it text for a song-chant (*shir*)? Should it be accompanied by instruments (*mizmor*)? Is it an intercessory prayer (*tefillah*), a meditative poem (*maskil*), or an

---

1 Viz., "with David's signature": 86, 101, 103, 108–110, 122, 124, 133, 138–145.
2 Cf. Psalms 121, 126, and nearby Psalms 136, 137.

exultant celebrative shout (*hallelujah!*)? All those notes provide clues to the psalms. There are also occasionally fascinating historiographic glosses: Psalm 3, "when David was fleeing from his son Absalom" (cf. 2 Samuel 15–17); Psalm 34, "when David made-believe he was crazy in front of [Philistine king] Achish-Abimelech in order to make his getaway" (cf. 1 Samuel 21:10–15).

Did you realize there are duplicate psalms? Psalm 14 and Psalm 53 are exactly the same, except Psalm 14 has the "Yahweh" name and Psalm 53 has only "Elohim" to name God. Psalm 40:13–17 is Psalm 70 precisely, again only with the "Yahweh" and "Elohim" name difference. If you live in Scripture, start to spend quality time there, become familiar with the book of psalms as a definite book of the Bible, you start to notice things.

Instead of becoming skeptical about "What in the world is going on here?" one needs to remember that serious Jewish authorities and ancient Church councils were somehow prayerfully led by God's Spirit to receive as "sacred" what we know as the canon. The edited Psalter we have, along with these credits, superscriptions, and musical designations, was set and accepted already earlier than the Septuagint translation of the Hebrew text in the Greek language, c. 270 BC, because some of the musical terms were so old the Alexandrian Greek translators didn't know what the Hebrew meant: "David's tune of Psalm 8, the choir director is told, should be played according to Giffith." Who knows what that means? (It's probably like saying a certain blues tune, before the oral tradition became literate, should be played in the Memphis style, not in the Chicago blues way.)

The incredible diversity of the psalm writings, which came out of historically specific, artistically honed, lived faith experiences, are still all of one piece because God's Holy Spirit permeates the texts. 2 Peter 1:20–21 puts the nature of the Psalter right:

> First of all you (should) know this: no declaration of Scripture comes to be from a private interpretation; no (scripted) utterance was ever brought about by the will of man or a woman; but humans led by the Holy Spirit spoke from God.

So the Psalms first of all have God talking . . . in David's troubled cries (Psalm 22) or Asaph's meditative history (Psalm 78). The broken-hearted as well as joyful psalms tell me about God, about who God is, how the LORD does things with God's creatures, what God says to us humans. Faithful readers of the psalms will distill from the human wrestlings with God found in the psalms what God's nuanced will is for our lives today, since basically the psalms are God talking. That's why, as the Belgic Confession of my communion puts it (article 5): ". . . we believe without a doubt all things contained in [the canonical psalms]."

If we take seriously now the editing of the 150 psalms into one book, then it makes good sense to expect the first two untitled psalms,[3] not even called songs, to have been set there like a preface or foreword to give you a prospectus of what follows in the book. What happens if one takes that tack? Psalm 1 centers around *torah*, and Psalm 2 introduces Messiah. Those are the orienting horizons, I think, to the books of the psalms: God's will, which when followed, satisfies, and the Lord's anointed one is here and coming.

Orienting the first psalm: the Lord's *torah*
Let me read the quieting, matter-of-faith first psalm of the book:

Psalm 1

That man or woman is a happy one	1
who does not practice the clever thought	
habits of godless people	
who does not go stand around the way sinners do,	
or sit down with mocking, scoffing company.	
[That man or woman is a happy one]	2
whose pastime rather is the *torah* of the Lord.	
who ruminates on the *torah* of the Lord day and night.	
That person is like a tree transplanted near running waters,	3
a tree which bears its fruit on time	
and whose leaf does not wither—	
all that man or woman does is prospered!	
It is not so with godless people.	4
They are like the chaff which wind blows to bits.	
That is why godless people	5
—the sinners within the covenantal congregation too—	
that is why they cannot and shall not withstand Judgment:	
[they are like chaff which the wind blows to bits.]	
The Lord God keeps close watch on the	6
way-of-life the tried-and-true faithful lead:	
the way the wicked walk, however, shall end in	
permanent destruction.	

(translation 1966–1999)

---

3   The first two psalms are the only ones in the Septuagint with no superscriptions.

The first psalm begins with a beatitude: Happy/blessed is the person who loves to spend time with the LORD's *torah*, who simply enjoys sitting down with God and marveling, pondering, rechewing the cud of the LORD God's magnificent ordering of the heavens and earth, the intricate ordinances the LORD has put in place for fulfilling human lives, for ruling nations of people and sorting out the complexities of myriad societal relationships. *Torah* for Israel included also the special treatment the Lord had given them in forging the covenant with Abraham and Sarah, the great deeds of deliverance from Egyptian captivity, the ten Words Godself had even written in stone for Moses on Mount Sinai: remembering all that *torah* (the LORD's worldwide guidance), a person engrossed with God's *torah*, says the first psalm, is like a tree transplanted near running waters; so you never dry up, but bear fruit on time.

Unfortunately god-less people—the smart operators who have no truck with boundaries, who are blind to the fact that God's *torah* covenanting is a protective embrace creatures can rest within; intelligent, godless hot-shots—are not rooted, they have no source of living water, they're just blowin' in the wind, blowing bits in fact. But the LORD God takes intimate loving care of the *tsadiqim,* the tried-and-true faithful ones who walk the way of *torah*-life, bearing good and mature fruit.

Torah has this cosmic, historical-redemptive scope, I dare say, because Psalm 19 backs up Psalm 1 as to the life-giving nature of *torah* (Psalm 19:7)[4] and keeps the cosmic ordinances that govern the bridegroom sun's daily rising and setting (vv. 1–6) unified together with the testimonies, statutes, commands, and tasks the LORD prompts us humans to follow if we would produce what is good (vv. 7–11). God's "law" (*torah*) is a many splendored reality.

The long 22-stanza alphabetic acrostic Psalm 119 also emphasizes the variegated richness of the LORD's *torah* by using 8 to 10 different near synonyms of *torah* (see *Table C*) in each line of every eight line stanza. It's as if the psalmist is serenading the wonders of the LORD's *torah* on an 8–10 stringed lyre, playing variations on the Word of God, the speaking/willing/doing of the Covenantal LORD God toward all creatures, especially toward Israel as God's own special folk.

Psalm 78:1 begins, "Open your ears, my people, to my *torah!*" and then Psalm 78 recounts the story of God's patient, punishing, forgiving, directing, leading of God's pigheaded people circuitously wandering through the wilderness toward the Promised Land and David's royal

---

4 Cf. my *Rainbows for the Fallen World* (Toronto: Tuppence Press, 1980/2005), 10–18, for a translation and exposition of Psalm 19.

rule—that's *torah* in action!

Buber carefully translates *torah* as *Weisung* (guidance), like *Wegweisung* (leading, directing the way to go) [related to *Unterweisung* (teaching)]. The crux of what we need to hear about *torah* from Psalms 1, 19, 119, 78, and many others is that *torah* is the actual guiding hand of the living God Almighty, as close as the snow and change of seasons (Psalm 148:3–10) and as revealing of the Lord God's everlasting compassion as God's constantly providing time for both wicked and sinful godly people to be afoot in this marvelous world.

Torah as God's intimate love letter
It is so important to catch the tone of intimacy in the first psalm about *torah* in order to understand the book of psalms as the very gut of the Bible. *Torah* is the Lord God's graciously extended hand to steady us on our feet like a child learning to walk. *Torah* holds the congealed passion and jealous love of God for the life of us creatures: God doesn't want us dead! So the Lord spoke, speaks, in the orderly *glossolalia* of mountains, trees, and animals; in the birth of a child and the face of a neighbor, in leading God's folk through ages of persecuted weakness; and in the trustworthy scripted Word we know as the Bible, which gives focus to our vision and hearing on which way to walk—that all is *torah*. And the first psalm presents this beginning simple good news: if you would truly stay alive, bear good fruit, on time, get close to *torah,* the Word of God, and discover the way the Lord expects things to be, and you will be blessed with shalom. Wicked, perverse humans miss the boat.

And this direction is proffered by the first psalm with the same gentle, inviting firmness God shows in covenanting with Moses, as reported in Deuteronomy 30:11–20:

> Do you see, I have set right in front of you today genuine life and what's good, or death and what's perverse . . . choose life so that you and your children's children may live, loving the Lord your God, responding to God's voice, cleaving to the Lord. . . . (cf. Genesis 2:24!)

Psalm 1 faces us readers with the same decision Proverbs 9 pictures with the two attractive women asking a young, inexperienced boy to come in and dine. One says,

> "Come, eat the meal with me; drink the wine I have all mixed.
> Let your one-track simplemindedness go so that you may live and walk the way of insight."

And the other woman says,

"Stolen waters are sweet.
And a meal of secretly hidden (delicacies) tastes so delicious. . . ."

But the poor fellow doesn't know, comments the text, that the last house for dinner is full of dead men.

Jesus, too, includes in his "Beatitudes" this counsel: "You cannot serve both God and Mammon. . . so first of all search out the rule of God, God's way of doing right and then [the cornucopia of blessings] will be given you in addition" (Matthew 6:24, 33).

Don't ever let anybody mislead you into thinking God's *torah* is God's big stick to knock you back into line, or a legislated set of rules to make your hell-bent yen for the open road miserable. That misconception of "law" is exactly what infiltrated the intertestamentary writings on wisdom (which is not imported into the canon[5]), and became the program of crowd control used by the scribal leadership of God's people: the "law of God" as a repressive measure that you have to obey and do what's right to the letter, if you want to be saved. But that's a frame-up! God is not an autocratic, mean-spirited parent with inflexible rules, and is not interested in punitive damages (cf. John 3:17).

Jesus said it clearly: "Don't you people suppose I came to abolish the law and the prophets. I didn't come to overthrow but to carry out (God's *torah*)! . . . However, if your 'right-doing' does not top the correct

---

5 In my judgment, despite good insights Walter Brueggemann misreads Psalm 1 here as a "simplistic" tract that claims that all is right in God's world, moral obedience fends off trouble, and the wicked perish (cf. in "Bounded by Obedience and Praise: The Psalms as canon," *JSOT* 50 [1991], especially 66–79). Brueggemann's exposition misses the stereo tone of Psalm 1 (with Psalm 2) of God's troubled beckoning hearers to become blessed as embattled anointed ones rather than to stand around as scoffing sinners pressed by judgment.

As best as I can determine, Brueggemann works self-consciously out of a dialectical scheme (orientation, disorientations, new orientation) that, despite *caveats*, he forces upon the psalm book so that the "trustful naiveté of Psalm 1," which "is not adequate to lived experience," has to be "overcome, transcended, and superseded" via psalms like pivotal 73 before one reaches the uncluttered praise of Psalm 150.

Because of his dialectical philosophical frame (and concern to upset a mindless conformist piety in the church), Brueggemann introduces and prioritizes, it seems to me, notes of "subversive" protest and "countercultural activity" (cf. *Praying the Psalms* [Winona: Saint Mary's Press, 1982], 15–25; *The Message of the Psalms: A theological commentary* [Minneapolis: Augsburg Publishing House, 1984], 9–23; "Response to James L. Mays, 'The Question of Context,'" in *The Shape and Shaping of the Psalter*, ed. J. Clinton McCann [*JSOT Supplement* 1 59, 1993], 40–41; also with Brueggemann's questioning whether "'book as context' is desirable," p. 30). This "subversive" project is foreign, I think, to the thetical affirmation of trusting the LORD to come through in our pained but certain Melchizedek service.

deeds of the scribes and Pharisees, you all shall never walk into the Rule of heaven" (Matthew 5:17, 20). And Paul struggled years with the Jewish work-righteous legalists in Corinth, Rome, and Galatia, who had twisted the Lord's "child-leading" *torah* (cf. *paidagogus,* Galatians 3:23–4:7) into a pseudo-mediator detached from the speaking mouth of God: Paul argued that the dilemma of either "keep the law intact" or "enjoy an antinomian freedom of the spirit" is false. God's grace (*chesed*) was given us in Christ for us to grow up, to mature into disciplined, winsome members of the Holy Spirited body of the Christ (Ephesians 4:7, 12–16).

Psalm 1 talks about the Judgment (*mishpat*) coming, but introduced an amazing thought—so characteristic of the psalms that follow—did you catch it in v. 5b (which I translated as a clause between dashes)? God does not require "the righteous" (*tsadiqim,* the covenantal congregation) to be sinless! We know that's true, personally, as well because David was a major biblical psalm writer. But remember that truth as introduction to the psalm book: God does not blink at there being sinners among "the righteous"; God simply wants to transplant them near the Lord's *torah* so they won't fail to withstand what's coming for the wicked.

Psalm 1 says the world we inhabit is like a burning bush where God is speaking; so take off your shoes, you grownups, and walk barefoot like an exploring child through God's world. Psalm 1 also shows that the psalms are God's love letter to you (Jeremiah 17:5–10 replays Psalm 1). A person thrives on reading a love letter someone has written to him or her.

Orienting second psalm: the Lord's anointed one(s)

The other introductory piece to this edited book, Psalm 2, in tandem with the meditative Psalm 1, has quite a different vigor and immediately gets down to historical brass tacks of political struggle and the Lord's provision for anointing public leaders to rule in God's name. Envision a chorus of voices: a wise person; a priest (whom God used to anoint leaders in Israel); and then a king, royalty, an "anointed one" whom God addresses as "my son."

Psalm 2 (*for choral reading in a worship service*)

> *The wise cantor*
> Why do peoples of the world rage about [like madmen]?   1
> Why in the world do the different nations
>   keep on thinking up stupid schemes?
> Earth kings get together "for a consultation"—   2
> important rulers hold conferences all together

against the LORD God and against God's anointed one (*mashiach*).
[These earthly rulers say:]
"Let us smash the chains of this god that holds us down!   3
Let us throw off the reins of God's 'anointed one'!"

Another liturgete, perhaps a priest
The One who sits enthroned in heaven begins to laugh,   4
my Lord mimics their foolish bluster,
and then God turns to them in (holy) anger,   5
stops the upstarts short with God's fierce outrage:
"It was I! it is I who have set up my anointed king on Zion,
    my set apart mountain."   6

Princely ruler taking official part in the liturgy
Yes, I will recite the decisive appointment by the LORD God.   7
God said to me:
"You are my son. Today is the day I have borne you.
Ask it of me and I will give you peoples of the world
    for your heritage;   8
the most distant nations of the earth will be yours to tend.
You may have to break them with a rod of iron.   9
You may have to smash them for remolding
    as a sculpting potter reshapes her clay dish—"

Wise cantor again
So now, you (small-time little) rulers, you had better wise up!   10
You who (only) judge on the earth,
hadn't you better get the point?
Serve the LORD God with an attentive awe—   11
Take joy (in your task only) with trembling—
Give homage to this (adopted) son (of God too)—   12
lest he also get worked up, and you obliterate any way
    [for you to walk],
for God's anger can flash up like lightning. . . .

Congregated chorus
Blessed are all those who have run to take shelter
    with the anointed one.

                             (translation, 1980/1999)

While Psalm 1 situates us in the cosmic theatre of God's *torah*, Psalm 2 pulls us into the thick of public life where earthly rulers challenge gods and mock those whom the LORD has consecrated, installed as holy men and women (v. 6) to bring about a rule of God's compassionate justice. Even when you are called upon to smash an evil setup (v. 9), you break it in pieces like a potter who wants to reclaim the clay to build a new, good vessel. The antagonism (the "antithesis") comes only from those who dream up schemes to oppose God's redemptive way in the world (v. 3).

In reading the second psalm, it is critical that we hear it as describing the real world: *Meshiah* (the Messiah, anointed one) is not something esoteric, mythical, or foreign to our usual experience. In Israel they ceremoniously poured sweet-smelling oil over Aaron's head, letting it drip off his robes, to consecrate him ritually as high priest of the nation, signing and sealing him off from impurity, as it were, so he could mediate the people's sins by overseeing their atoning sacrifices (Leviticus 8–9, Psalm 133).

Saul, David, and Solomon were anointed with oil by prophet-priests to be kings in Israel (1 Samuel 10:1–8, 1 Samuel 16:1–13, 1 Kings 1). That was God's way of showing what Nathan told David God said verbally about Solomon, "I will be to him as father, and he will be to me as son" (2 Samuel 7:1–17). I adopt you, says God to the anointed one, and shall protect you from the power-grabbers in the world, and teach you to lay down your life so that the weak, like widows and orphaned children, shall receive reliable relief from your royal administration for their distressing needs (cf. Psalm 82:1–4), because God's "anointed ones" are sustained by their receiving wisdom from the indwelling of the Holy Spirit (cf. 1 Samuel 10:9–13, 16:13, 1 Kings 3:28).

Psalm 2:7 gets quoted at the baptism of Jesus Christ in the Jordan river (Mark 1:9–11): "A voice from heaven said: 'You are my son, the one I love, in whom I am well pleased.'" That event was God commissioning Jesus with the second psalm, says the apostle Paul in his Antioch sermon (Acts 13, especially vv. 16–41), to be the incorruptible successor of David's mortal line, whose resurrection from the grave brings us the good news of forgiveness for sinners, not more prescriptions one needs to fill. So the second psalm reaches out, according to the Newer Testament, to our baptism. When you are baptized into the name of the Father, Son, and Holy Spirit, you become an adopted child of God, an "anointed one" whom the Lord expects to mature into ordering things and ruling with a holy wisdom. God gives you diplomatic immunity for that task, says Paul: "God speaks comfort through us who are ambassadors for Christ" (2 Corinthians 5:20).

On this very matter I cherish the Heidelberg Catechism question/answer 32:

Why are you called a Christian?

Because by faith I am a member of Christ
and so I share in his anointing.
I am anointed
to confess his name,
to present myself to him as a living sacrifice of thanks,
to strive with a good conscience against the sin and the devil in this life,
and afterward to reign with Christ over all creation for eternity.

The psalms hold for us today

With the second psalm as introduction, one may expect following psalms to deal with the rough and tumble of ordinary life: governing, fights, enemies, smashed dreams, tension, perseverance. Do you know how the earliest Christian believers were living in Scripture? Breathing in and out with Psalm 2, for example? Let me read you the straightforward passage of Acts 4:23–31:

> When Peter and John [who had been arrested, held overnight incommunicado, then interrogated and threatened by the Jewish clerical authorities] were allowed to leave, they went to their own kind of people and reported everything the higher-up priests and the elders had said to them. When those who were close to Peter and John heard it all, they raised their voices all together to God [in prayer]:
>
> Oh Sovereign LORD, You who made the sky, the earth, the sea, and every creature in them—you LORD, who through the mouth of David our father, your child, moved by the Holy Spirit, said [quoting Psalm 2],
>
> "So why to the non-Jewish nations foam at the mouth?
>
> And why do people think up stupidities?
>
> The kings of the earth step up to show themselves, and the rulers are assembled together against the LORD and against the LORD's anointed one."
>
> —that's true [continues their prayer]: there were assembled in this very city against your holy child Jesus whom you anointed, Herod and Pontius Pilate, with both the non-Jewish nations and the peoples of Israel—they were assembled . . . to do whatever your hand and your deliberate counsel ordained would

> happen.
>
> And now, Lord, look over their threats, and make it possible for your servants to speak your Word with all kinds of boldness, while You stretch out the hand for healing, and let signs and wonders be done through the name of your holy child Jesus.
>
> When they had finished praying, the place in which they were gathered shook violently; and all of them were filled with the Holy Spirit, and they took to speaking the Word of God with boldness.

Luke recounts how followers of "the Way" (Acts 19:9, 23 and 24:22) heard Psalm 2 speak directly to their current affairs and persecuted life before the LORD. Living in Scripture they prayed an updated version of Psalm 2: "Kings of the earth like the traitor Herod, and rulers like what-is-truth Pilate, and leaders of Israel, in this very holy city, trumped up charges and executed the son of God! But you were laughing at them, LORD! Because Jesus Christ is raised from the dead as You ordained. So now, please, LORD of the nations—we are your anointed ones too—amid the threats to get us, make us able to speak your Word with all kinds of boldness, while You bring healing into the world."

Acts 4 legitimates, I take it, as *bona fide* for us Newer Testament Christians to take Psalms 1, 2, and the whole book of psalm-prayers on our lips this way, provided we are pure-in-heart (as Psalm 15 asks), are not self-righteously judgmental (as Jesus puts it, Matthew 7:1–5), and if we can discern surely what battle God wants waged. It is not the USA vs. Saddam Hussein; it is not "concerned conservatives" vs. "progressive liberals"; that is, the battle that counts is never "us" against "them" ("Not for us, LORD, not for us"—remember Psalm 115). The basic battle is between the LORD's name and Rule in world history under attack by godless, idolatrous, falsely good, deceptive forces within us as well as outside us undermining the faith of the anointed body of Christ. That fight is as close as our personal greed and as real as mass-advertised Materialism, sophisticated academic Skepticism, and the weaseling principality of Secularism. The second psalm brings a believer today the gut courage to wield "the 'sword' of the Spirit," as Paul's rhetoric has it (Ephesians 6:10–20) in challenging God's enemies:

> You earth judges and rulers, don't plot against God's people, but follow their lead!

If you are living in the psalms, you will receive "much grace" (cf. Acts

4:33) to speak with such humble boldness, running to take shelter with God's Anointed One.

Illustration: reading and hearing Psalm 23 with this orientation
One more matter here: let me illustrate what I've been proposing on the edited nature of the Psalm book, where the first and second psalms sketch horizons of the cosmic panorama of the LORD God's *torah* as a backdrop for an embattled public war theater where God's presence takes on Herod, Pontius Pilate, bad leaders of God's folk, and anybody in the headlines (or by-lines) of 1999 AD. How does recognition of the Psalm 1–2 literary focus make a difference in reading psalms? I'd also like to show how those last chorus lines of Psalm 2 have earthly grit and are not just a pious wish in the sky. Let me read PSALM 23 in your hearing:

PSALM 23 (*A song for musical accompaniment, by David*)

The LORD GOD is my shepherd (too).   1
    I lack nothing.
In quiet spots of soft green grass   2
    the LORD lets me settle down in peace.
(My shepherd) leads me out to flowing waters giving rest.
The LORD brings me back to myself.   3
The LORD leads me in the tracks of doing what's right
for the sake of God's (holy) name!

Even if I have to walk through the
    Valley of the shadows of Death,   4
I will fear no evil because You are with me.
Your shepherd crook and your strong club reassure me.
You set a table for me with a meal   5
    right in front of my enemies!
You anoint my head copiously with oil.
My drinking cup is overflowing!—

It's true! (Your) covenantal mercy (*chesed*) and   6
    what's creaturely good shall follow me up
all the days of my life,
and (someday) I shall dwell in the house of
the LORD God for as long as there are days. . . .

                                                               (translation 1997)

Many people use this favorite Psalm 23 for personal devotional comfort—good. One must be careful, however, not to restrict God's written

Word to servicing one's own pressing peculiar problems. The first and second psalms prepare us to read and hear the book of psalms as public, communal tête-à-tête sessions with the living God. Not every psalm is oriented liturgically for a public worship service, but the very fabric and outreach of these deeply personal, poetic prayer-songs is not individualistic, but the expression of a communion of faith.

The Bible is clear: the Lord is a shepherd of a people, a flock of sheep, if you will. The psalms use the image again and again: we are the people, the sheep of God's pasture (Psalm 79:13, 95:7, 100:3). Important for anybody who reads Psalm 23 is to remember you are one of the flock. You are not alone, even if you feel that way, or want to be alone. That's why I slipped into the translation what is understood, "The Lord God is my shepherd (**too**)." We've got to overcome our individualism without adopting a "herd mentality." There are black sheep among us, stubborn sheep, a few who bleat a lot, some have blemishes, others limp, several are on rocky, slippery slopes, and some desperately need a rest—this is the Psalm 1–2 picture frame around Psalm 23. So when I read Psalm 23, my confession is: I am not the only sheep in the fold; the Lord God is my shepherd **too**. And I look around gratefully.

Psalm 23 is edited between Psalms 22 and 24—if you want to live in the psalms, then you always look at the psalm's neighbors in the book to pick up overtones. Psalm 22 is the sober song Christ knew by heart and quoted on the cross, "My God, O my God! Why have you left me in the lurch!" (vv. 1–11). Like ravenous wild dogs the enemies are circling in on me for the kill (vv. 12–21).

Enemies, according to the Bible, include death, cancer, depression, and any sinful violence that breaks down God's good creation and brings tears to our eyes or disfigures our face. So Psalm 23 is not a Victorian pastoral idyll of private sweetness and light; instead it grapples with death and my enemies, which have societal dimensions. If a follower of the Christ (Messiah) has no enemies—God-enemies which are wicked—you probably have poor faith-eyesight, weak biblical antennae. And then you would miss out on the promised prospect of Psalm 23 that God prepares a festive meal for you right in the thick of what's evil—Alzheimer's disease, antichrist hypocritical abuse, wretched poverty—I am an "anointed one" (v. 5), so I'll still be safe! Psalm 23 practices exactly what Psalm 22:22–24 promises: thank the Lord in the midst of the congregation for the Lord's coming through when it counted.

And Psalm 24 seems to celebrate what the last verse of Psalm 23 hopes for: entering the dedicated house of God to cheer the glorious

LORD God of the mighty angels! Psalm 24 revels in the relaxing safety of being at home among God's people away from the enemies. "To dwell in the house of the LORD God" (Psalm 23:6) does not mean you stay cooped up in a church building for eternity. Since Jesus was born, "the house of God" is "the body of Christ." One may revel in the liturgical celebration of word and sacrament for centering ourselves as a cohering body with interlocking ligaments, but we are to exercise the communion of saints in daily life amid neighbors and enemies—Dordt College is to be "a house of God"—and the "shelter" provided us anointed ones is "the Word of the Lord," the leading of "the good shepherd" (John 10:1–30) who was able to feast thousands on five loaves of bread and a couple fish (Mark 6:30–44, 8:1–10) and stands nearby . . . outfitted with a club.

I cannot explicate now, as I should like, penitential psalms and the paeans of *halelu yah* in the psalter, nor the psalms that lament and the psalms with curses, because I must say something about the most important psalm in the book, and want to end with a couple of suggestions about living in the psalms.

Reading and hearing the gut of the Bible

What is so exciting for me is that I'm just discovering the psalms book as a whole edited book, and that if you give attention to the canonic literary shape of the Psalter and tease out hints of historical setting, you can become a more acute listening object! of the speaking text in its full-orbed revelation of God, God's will for human lives.

I still have to check out *Table D* in more detail how Psalm 1 to 145 plus the final doxology of Psalms 146–150 orient the book to the LORD God's *torah* and its affording wisdom to those who heed God's call, and how Psalm 2 to 144 cohere roughly with Psalm 72 and 89 as bookends around the revelation of God's redemptive working in history through the LORD's "anointed one" David and show that the covenant with Israel under the promise of Messiah holds open, if you will, the prospects of God's rule mediated through the priesthood of Jesus Christ.

It seems sound to me at this stage of my development to read books I, II, and III as Spirit-led collections of psalms conceived during Israel's monarchy and experience of temple worship (although not all these psalms were originally liturgical);[6] and books IV and V, introduced by the premonarchic figure Moses' Psalm 90 and the *hodu leyahweh* ("Give thanks to the Lord") Psalm 107 (cf. also Psalms 118, 136) are post-exilic,

---

6 For example, verses 18–19 were added to Psalm 51 by God-breathed editors for use in the worship service of Israel.

Sprit-led collections of psalms that emphatically confess the sin of God's folk Israel—there are no more kings in David's historic line!—and look forward to the victory of the LORD God and God's Messiah over the enemies of God's people on earth, proclaiming the LORD God's royal rule over all nations.

Psalm 110 is maybe the most important psalm in the book, intensifying the message of Psalm 2 in a book V way, because it is the most quoted Older Testament psalm in the Newer Testament. It follows the severe, screaming imprecatory Psalm 109: "Damn the merciless enemy, LORD (vv. 6–19); your *chesed* (vv. 12, 16, 21, 26, 31) demands you rescue the helpless being scornfully martyred—your name and Rule is at stake," especially since, as Paul states in Acts 13, this Jesus was the expected Messiah that Psalm 2 foretold (cf. Acts 13:32–43).

PSALM 110

> This is what the LORD God says to my Lord: 1
> **"Sit at my right hand**
>   **until I have put down your enemies**
>   **as a footstool for your feet."**
> The LORD will give you free reign to the
>   official scepter of your power, (David).   2
> Go ahead, rule from Zion in the thick of your enemies!
> On D-Day your folk will be willingness itself,   3
> wrapped in the splendors of consecration.
> Just as dew (springs) from the womb of a sunrise,
> so shall your youthful strength surprise you.
> (I repeat,) this is what the LORD has sworn,   4
> and God will not have second thoughts (about it):
>   **"Henceforth you are a priest forever**
>   **in the order of Melchizedek."**
>
> [to the people]
>
> My Lord is at your right hand!   5
> My Lord shall break kings to pieces in the day of his anger.
> My Lord shall set things straight in the
>   nations filled with corpses!   6
> My Lord shall shatter (those who are) head
>   over most of the earth—
> (God's anointed one) shall be able to drink water
>   from the running stream   7

nearby the way (of judgment):
that is why God's anointed one shall be able to
hold the head up high!

Let me read Psalm 110 as a commentator. Where are the breaks in poetic structure? Who is being addressed? The Revised Standard Version correctly, I think, takes v. 4 with vv. 1–3, a matter important for interpretation. The psalm begins as if the poet is reporting a scene of how Nathan might have spoken to David: "My lord, last night the LORD God said...."

The first paragraph (Psalm 110:1–4) says: David, when you go out to fight the Philistines, the heathen Syrians, Ammonites (2 Samuel 7, 10), and everybody under the sun, remember, (1) In your kingly office as an anointed one of the LORD, you have the power of sitting on God's right hand (110:1), and (2) You are a priest-king, not a warlord; you are a priest-king like old Melchizedek ("Melchizedek" means "king-doing-deeds-that-prove-true") of Salem, Jerusalem, in the days of Abraham (Genesis 14); you are called upon to fight and rule with deeds of setting-things-right as a priest, one who mediates between God and human creatures, who brings the paltry sacrifices of the people to the LORD and the rich blessings of God back to the people (110:4).

The poet next (Psalm 110:5–7) addresses the people about David, "my Lord" (v. 1). What followers refers to David as anointed ruler, vice-regent for the LORD in Zion. These verses also refer to Jesus Christ, as Newer Testament quotations make clear (Matthew 22:43–45, Acts 2:34–36).

"God's anointed one" refers to sinful saint David, Jesus Christ on the cross, and those who confess Heidelberg Catechism answer number 32. As a follower of Jesus Christ I am "a priest forever in the order of Melchizedek"!—if that drills through your mind into your heart, you become a new creature (2 Corinthians 5:17–19)!

If you are not just dipping into the psalms for spiritual kicks, like checking God's yellow pages in the divine phonebook for something you want for the weekend, but are seriously reading to hear the gut of God, what it cost God to save us piddling sinners and set straight the mess we have made of God's world and human society, then your Christian reading of the Older Testament psalms needs to ponder their enduring, multiple fulfillment overlay: the psalms' good news (1) in the original BC time-setting when they were spoken and scripted; (2) in the Newer Testament AD period when God's people received the psalms as sacred scripture revealing God's promises at hand; and (3) in our "last days" (cf. 1 Timothy 4:1–4, 2 Timothy 3:1–9, 2 Peter 3:1–7), the era after Jesus

Christ's resurrection until the Lord comes again. Catch how Psalm 110 holds out the sterling mandate to be an "anointed" priest-king-or-queen for the LORD in the order of Melchizedek (1 Peter 2:9–10).

Jewish zealots read Psalm 110 enthusiastically, except verse 4. That's why the Newer Testament book "to the Hebrews" makes so much of Melchizedek (Hebrews 4:14–8:13): not by Aaron/Abraham blood, but by an anointing in faith from the Holy Spirit do you become a true child of Abraham, adopted by the LORD God; and the Rule of the LORD is not a put-down, but is a caring, leading rescue operation effecting reconciliation even among enemies, though it cost you your life (cf. 1 John 2:18–29).

The biblical psalms are God's love letters written to you, me, anybody able and willing to read the script and listen to God speak from God's gut. The psalms are oral poetry; so we should read them out loud (the way people used to read), sing them in public together.

If you want to live in the psalms, I have three suggestions: (1) **Dwell in the book**. Become immersed in the text; read and reread the whole, the five parts, clusters of neighboring psalms. Yield to what the psalm text says, let it come over you. Memorize the psalms, or write tunes for them. Just you and God for a while, possibly with a reliable written companion (see bibliography) before you share reading God's love poems aloud with others.

(2) **Study the psalter in wonderment**. If at all possible, read the psalms also in a language that is not your mother tongue, because then you have to read more slowly, look up words in a dictionary, puzzle over meanings. Accept what at first seems strange: God is blamed for eating away what is dear to me like a moth! (Psalm 39:11); God finally got up like a ranting drunk (says Psalm 78:65)—is this a way to talk about God? Well, take it in, don't read the psalms first of all like a theologician, as if the text be a repository of themes or proofs for and against certain dogmas. This is God-breathed poetry where you are meant to meet the Holy Spirit, and the Holy Spirit is not a systematic theology or a worldview but a real person who powerfully inhabits a human and gentles you out of your sinful wits into becoming a wise child able to love one's unlovable neighbor, fulfilling the Lord's *torah*! (cf. Romans 13:8–10, Galatians 5:25–6:2).

(3) **Discover echoes of the psalms throughout Scripture**. If the book of psalms becomes familiar to you, its details will not be loose trivia but will start to resonate everywhere in the Older and Newer Testaments.

The pained reality the psalms confess in faith reveals the "suffering servant" side of God, too, and gives an Older Testament memory, grit, and color to the Newer Testament message about the Way of thankful salvation incarnated in Jesus Christ.

Table A

Edited books of the Psalter

41	I	anonymous	1–2, 3–41:13	(mostly "…of David")
31	II	Qorah	42/43-72:18–19,20	(mostly "…of David")
17	III	Asaph	73–89:58	(mostly Asaph & Qorah)
17	IV	Moses	90–106:48	(mostly anonymous)
44	V	anonymous	107–145/146–150	(mostly anonymous)
150				

Table B

Titled sorts of psalm (approximations)

30	*shir*	song to sing, chant
57	*mizmor*	melody for music, tune
1	*shigaywon*	dirge
6	*miktam*	script
5	*teffilah*	intercessory prayer
13	*maskil*	meditative poem
1	*tehilah*	praise song
16	*halelu yah*	exultant shout of celebration

(21 without any specification)

Table C
Near synonyms for (1) *torah* (*Weisung*, guidance, leading)

(2)	*'edut*	testimonies, *testimonia, magnolia Dei*
(3)	*piqqud*	command, 10 word covenant, *mandata*
(4)	*choq*	cosmic ordinance, providence, *statuta*
(5)	*mitswah*	task, *praecepta*
(6)	*mishpat*	ordering judgment, *jura*
(7)	*dabar*	authoritativer, saving, working word, *verbum*
(8)	*'imrah*	authoritative speech (poetic)
(9)	*derek*	way
(10)	*'orah*	path (poetic)

Table D
Editorial framework for psalm book

1	2	3		72	73		89	90		107		144	145
						Royal Covenant Frame (spans 3–144)							
	Final Wisdom Frame (spans 2–145)												

Gerald H. Wilson, "Shaping the Psalter: a consideration of editorial linkage in the book of psalms" in *The Shape and Shaping of the Psalter*, ed. J. Clinton McCann. Sheffield Academic Press, 1993, p. 81.

Bibliography

Aalders, G. Ch. *Oud-Testamentische Kanoniek* (Kampen: J.H. Kok, 1952).

Alter, Robert. *The World of Biblical Literature* (San Francisco: Basic Books, 1991).

Calvin, John. *Commentarii in librum Psalmorum* (Amsterdam: J.J. Schipper, 1997); translated James Anderson, *Commentary on the Book of Psalms* (Grand Rapids: Eerdmans, 1949), 4 vols.

Childs, Brevard S. *Introduction to the Old Testament as Scripture* (Philadelphia: Fortress Press, 1979).

Diessler, Alfons. *Die Psalmen* (Düsseldorf: Patmos, 1964).

McCann, J. Clinton. *A Theological Introduction to the Book of Psalms* (Nashville: Abingdon Press, 1993).

Peterson, Eugene H. *Answering God: The Psalms as tools for prayer* (San Fransisco: Harper, 1991).

Ridderbos, J. *De Psalmen, 1–106*, 2 vols. (Kampen: J.H. Kok, 1955/1958): 1–106.

Smith, Mark S. "The Theology of Redaction of the Psalter: Some observations," in *Zeitschrift für die Alttestamentliche Wissenschaft* 104 (1992): 406–412.

Van Niejenhuis, Herman. Sermon on Psalms 1–2, Evening service, 6 October 1996.

Wilson, Gerald H. "Evidence of Editorial Divisions in the Hebrew Psalter," *Vetus Testamentum* 24:3 (1984): 337–352.

Brad and Helen Breems,
Blue Island–Chicago, Illinois, 2010

Psalms are to be Heard Everywhere

To begin our session on "Psalms are to be Heard Everywhere" we shall listen to the important Psalm 1, focusing attention upon the *torah*, the Law, the Guidance (*Weisung*—Buber, cf. Psalm 119:105) of the Lord God, which it is wise to meditate upon day and night! Since the Older Testament *torah* is not restricted to the Ten Words spoken at Mount Sinai but includes the order, the ordinances God set "in the beginning" for all God's creatures and their doings (cf. Psalm 148), after we hear Psalm 1, please stand to sing in unison Genevan Psalm 8 extoling the amazing *torah* Word of the Lord.

Psalm 1

> That man or woman is a happy one 1
> who does not practice the clever thought habits of godless people
> who does not go stand around the way sinners do,
> or sit down with mocking, scoffing company.
> [That man or woman is a happy one] 2
> whose pastime rather is the *torah* of the Lord.
> who ruminates on the *torah* of the Lord day and night.
> That person is like a tree transplanted near running waters, 3
> a tree which bears its fruit on time
> and whose leaf does not wither—
> all that man or woman does is prospered!
>
> It is not so with godless people. 4
> They are like the chaff which wind blows to bits.
> That is why godless people 5
> —the sinners within the covenantal congregation too—
> that is why they cannot and shall not withstand Judgment:
> [they are like chaff which the wind blows to bits.]

Plenary address for the Calvin Institute of Christian Worship Symposium, Grand Rapids, Michigan, January 2005, with organist Dr. Chris Teeuwsen. A CD of this address is available from the Calvin Institute for Christian Worship.

The LORD God keeps close watch on the
way-of-life the tried-and-true faithful lead:
the way the wicked walk, however,
    shall end in permanent destruction.

(translation 1966–1999)

Psalm 8

LORD God, how great your won-der-ful cre-a-tion!
A-mazed at night I scan the sky and ling-er
LORD, you have made us hu-mans tru-ly lord-ly,
LORD God, how great your won-der-ful cre-a-tion!

Your Name re-sounds through earth each gen-er-a-tion.
to see the moon and stars made by your fing-er.
crowned us with cul-ti-va-ting might and glo-ry.
Your Name is heard at large by ev-ery na-tion.

Weak ba-by cries still cel-e-brate your laws.
What good are mor-tal hu-mans on the earth?
Mar-vel-lous crea-tures— birds and fish and beast—
Grant us the grace and wise hu-mil-i-ty

Your stun-ning deeds make e-ven scof-fers pause.
Why do you gent-ly care for us from birth?
You have sub-jec-ted un-der-neath our feet.
to claim and serve your rul-ing ma-jes-ty.

Text: Psalm 8, vers. Calvin Seerveld, 1986 ©   11 11 10 10
Tune: Louis Bourgeois, 1551   Genevan 8

In workshops on "Voicing God's Psalms" I shall try to make convincing the need to reinstate singing psalms in congregational worship services, but here I should like to resurrect the old Reformation idea that psalms could be voiced, sung, and heard anywhere, everywhere.

Psalm 8 would be great for the opening assembly of a school year, or, if everybody knew it, you could lustily sing Psalm 8 at the start of a group vacation, waiting at the airport together or as the Greyhound Bus drivers are having the baggage loaded....

In 1543 John Calvin's expanded introduction to the developing French Psalter said: "...singing at home and even in the fields should be an incentive for us to praise God, to elevate our hearts to God, to console ourselves by ruminating on God's power, goodness, wisdom, and justice..."[1]

Court poet of Francis I, Clement Marot, whom Calvin used to versify the biblical psalms for singing, had written a poem "To the Women of France" about the good times coming when ploughman at the plow, artisan in his or her boutique "would lighten their labor by singing a psalm or song . . . exalting the holy Name of their Creator!"[2]

That ordinary people affected by the Reformation actually sang psalms in the streets is attested to by Michel de Montaigne in his essay "On Prayers," where he sanctimoniously groused: "It is certainly not rational to see the holy book of the sacred mysteries of our faith meddled

---

1 "Combien que l'usage de la chantrerie s'estende plus loin: c'est que mesme par les maisons et par les champs ce nous soit une incitation et comme un organe à louer Dieu, et eslever nos cœurs à lui. Pour nous consoler en méditant sa vertu, bonté, sagesse et justice: ce qui est plus nécessaire qu'on ne sauroit dire." John Calvin, Introductory letter to the reader of the revised Psalter, 1543, in *Le Psautier Huguenot du XVIe Siècle, Mélodies et documents,* ed. Pierre Pidoux (Basel: Édition Baerenreiter, 1962), 2:20.

2   O bienheureux qui veoir pourra
    Fleurir le temps, que l'on orra
    Le laboureur à sa charrue,
    Le charretier parmy la rue,
    Et l'artisan en sa boutique,
    Avecques un pseaume ou cantique
    En son labeur se soulager !
    Heureux qui orra le berger
    Et la bergere 'au boys estans,
    Faire que rochers et estangs
    Après eulx chantent la hauteur
    Du sainct nom de leur Createur.
Clement Marot, "Aux Dames de France touchant lesdicts pseasumes," in *Œuvres complètes* (Paris: Garnier Frères, 1829), 2: 284–5.

with by uncouth fellows and kitchen help."³

Whether you be couth or not, consider it far-fetched? I invite you to let your imagination go as we chorally read Psalm 115, Martin Buber's favorite psalm. What would it be like for elected representatives to read Psalm 115 aloud at the opening of a legislative session in your state capital? Maybe pipeline construction workers of the Christian Labour Association of Canada are tensed to take a strike vote because of unsafe labor conditions, or Seventh Day Adventist leaders have just had their permission to open a medical hospital in a foreign country rescinded by a newly elected government wanting money under the table.

It is the right time to pray Psalm 115 out loud, where the key point is: people become like the gods/the idols they worship. If you worship Military Prowess, you become a Militarist, as single-minded as a bullet. If your God is Money, you become a Materialist, and everything you touch turns to golden metal. Protect us, Lord God! Bless us to serve only You!

> When "the people" repeat the response, please do not hesitate to come in on the rhythm of a chant ("a relief and protection is the Lord for such people"). Where the three lines are "Bless the house of Israel" (=God's people as a whole who are pure in heart); bless the priestly house of Aaron (=confessional leaders, ordained clergy, charismatic leaders—and we could include today's Levites—music directors and worship leaders); bless the newcomers who fear the Lord (= "seekers" who may still find God fearsome);

> those lines should get louder and stronger each time, the chant becomes an invocative cheer! . . . in the legislature, before the tribunal, in the courtroom, reaching out to God with the brusque gumption peculiar to God's psalms.

PSALM 115 [*for communal responsive reading aloud*]

leader:	Not for us, Lord, not for us,	1
	but do something glorious for Your name!	
	Make something solid and shining to show your covenanting grace and utterly dependable faithfulness!	
	Why should the peoples all around say,	
	"And where now is their God?"	2
people:	Our God is in heaven!	3

---

3 "Ce n'est pas raison qu'on permette qu'un garçon de boutique, parmy ses vains et frivoles pansements, s'en entretienne et s'en joue ; ny n'est certes raison de voir tracasser, par une sale et par une cuisine, le sainct livre des sacrez mystères de nostre créance" (Montaigne, "Des Prieres," *Essais* [Paris: Ernest Flammarion, 1908], 1:372.

	Everything that pleases God, God completes!	
leader:	Their "gods" are solid gold and silver,	
	[but] made by a human hand.	4
	Their fake gods have a mouth, but cannot speak;	5
	they have eyes, but cannot see!	
	Ears they have, but cannot hear;	6
	a nose is there, but they cannot smell—	
	their hands cannot touch things.	7
	Their feet cannot go for a walk.	
	No sound passes through their throat…	
people:	Like them become those who made them!	8
	Like them become all those who feel secure with them.	
leader:	Israel! get to feel secure with the LORD God:	9
people:	a relief and protection is the LORD for such people.	
leader:	[Priestly] house of Aaron!	
	bind yourselves only to the LORD God:	10
people:	a relief and protection is the LORD for such people.	
leader:	You [newcomers] who fear Yahweh! trust—	
	trust the LORD God:	11
people:	a relief and protection is God for such people.	
leader:	The LORD God has kept us in mind: God shall bless—	12
people:	Bless the house of Israel!	
	Bless the [priestly] house of Aaron!	
	Bless those who fear the LORD God!	13
leader:	—the unimportant ones together with	
	the very important ones…	
	May the Lord God prosper you, you and your children.	14
	May you all be blessed by the LORD God,	
	who made heaven and earth.	15
	Heaven [you know] belongs specially to the LORD:	16
	The earth is what God gave for the sons and	
	daughters of man [to tend].	

Dead men and women do not praise the LORD,	17
not one of those who have gone down to	
where it is deathly still.	
But we people here, let us praise the Lord!	
from now on and for ever more:	18

people: thank God—hallelujah!

(translation 1969)

In parachurch settings like a long-term nursing home, a shipside military funeral, hospital wards, chaplains often find that the familiar psalm gives the most comfort to the sick, the dying, and the bereaved. The simple tetrameter/trimester ballad measure of the Scottish psalter tradition also can provide a gentle, steady beat in which to cradle one's anxieties. The *Kilmarnock* tune, like the lovely well-known *Crimond*, has a reassuring lilt to its line with just enough stretch and color to carry the dark side of Psalm 23, following up Psalm 22, which Christ cried out on the cross, and to anticipate the celebration of the Lord's presence Psalm 24 extols.

    I have wrinkled the Common Meter to 8786 and made "the Shepherd" who leads us in paths of just-doing peace explicit for today as "the Christ," but it stays a psalm text.

The Shepherd Psalm Today

1. The LORD my shepherd satisfies our ev'ry anxious request by leading us to verdant grass where flowing streams give rest.
2. The LORD restores me to myself, brings us resolve for God's sake to follow Christ in making peace, and find just paths to take.
3. When death's dark shadows fall my lot, I still will fear no evil, for You, my Lord, hold us so close, ward off what would do ill.
4. The enemies can only stare while You prepare our banquets with overflowing cups of wine, anoint with joy our heads!
5. Your covenantal mercy, Lord, and promised Presence extend rich blessing to our coming lives: shalom will never end.

Text: The Shepherd Psalm Today, Calvin Seerveld © 2004   8786
Tune: Neil Dougall, 1831   KILMARNOCK

There are two song traditions I know that seem to be especially built structurally to handle the astonishing mixture of yelling at God in hurt faith and in the same or second breath concluding with a chastened "Oh my Lord, thank you for holding on to me": the modal Genevan melodies of the 1500s and the pentatonic Afro-American spiritual tunes and early Blues.

I hear an aesthetic kinship in both these redemptive melodic patterns. They pulse with an irregular rhythm and natural tonal intervals that can catch both the desperate sorrowful quandaries of the human heart and a quieted trusting expectance, a reluctant but also hopeful acceptance of what the Lord metes out to God's often stymied, woebegone creation.

The hypo-Phrygian *la-mi* central frame to Genevan 51 (*mi sol sol la mi sol sol re fa mi*) gets to the core of the fervent grief embodied in the biblical psalm laments, and provides the tonality in which to hear the curses in God's psalms. Imprecatory psalms (like 35, 58, 69, 83, 109, 137) are not vindictive diatribes by small-time losers (Christ's cursing anathemas in Matthew 23 have even more edge), but are agonized pleas by God's defenseless faithful interceding for the victims of systemic violence: "Stop the wicked in their tracks, Lord, because we can't do it! Lighten the burdens of your people, *Adonai!*"

Just as Käthe Kollwitz's (1867–1945) charcoal-ink drawings (*Sleeping Child*, 1903) present the vulnerability of a sleeping child [#28], the

[#28] Käthe Kollwitz, *Sleeping Child and Child's Head*, 1903

helpless sadness (1924) of a poverty-stricken pair, etches in a taut solitary clump of naked flesh the enormity of a mother's anguish over the fruit of her womb (*Woman with dead child*, 1903 [*NA* #41]) untimely robbed of life by the last enemy, Death: just as Kollwitz quietly depicts—good art is never sensational—the listless waste of endless time (*Prisoners, Peasants War* #7, 1908 [*RA* #124]) prisoners of war undergo waiting, the brutal rape ravaged particularly on women in the hideous aftermath of the political failure we call "war" (*Raped, Peasants War* #2, 1907 [*RA* #125]), so "A Congregational Lament" quietly remembers and cries "Why?!" to the Lord about personal tragedy, calamity in a congregation, public disaster, in the psalmodic embrace of the inimitably sad Genevan 51.

As Chris Teeuwsen plays the lament, please choose to read stanza 2 if you know a lonely person stifled in a prison, stanza 3 if you have a loved one wracked by the evil of cancer, stanza 4 if there be the wreckage/salvage of lives dear to you in the grip of divorce proceedings; choose to follow stanza 5 if someone in your family or whom you know well has died by accident, and read stanza 6 if you have a special concern for certain troubled persons who do not make the TV news. After that stanza of silent reading/hearing, let all who are able stand to sing stanza 1, as if at a vigil held by Amnesty International in South America or while remembering the fourteen women students massacred in Montreal (1989), and the countless killed civilians in Palestine, Iraq, Darfur, and especially fellow followers of Jesus Christ around the world whose blood cries out, documents Paul Marshall (*Their Blood Cries Out* [Dallas: Word, 1997]), for the LORD to show that the God of the Angels is at hand mercifully, justly to punish violators in the grip of Shameless Evil principalities (Philippians 4:4–7). May our intercessory psalm lament epitome be like a godly Mother hen (*Saatfrüchte sollen nicht vermahlen werden*, 1941–42) trying to protect her children from conquistador predators, and be a prayer for the undefended weak as Kollwitz' terracotta piece for a tombstone says, "Resting in the peace of his hands" [*RA* #127].

5 Why, Lord, did you abruptly take him home?
　Could you not wait to summon him before you?
　Why must we feel the sting of death's old cruelty?
　Come quickly, Lord, do not leave us alone.
　We plead: Repair the brokenness we share.
　Chastise no more lest it destroy your creatures.
　Hear this lament as intercessory prayer,
　　and speak your powerful word to make us hopeful.

6 Why, Lord, must any child of yours be hurt?
　Does all our pain and sorrow somehow please you?
　You are a God so jealous for our praises—
　　hear this lament as prayer that fills the earth.
　We plead: Repair the brokenness we share.
　Chastise no more lest it destroy your creatures.
　Hear this lament as intercessory prayer,
　　and speak your powerful word to make us hopeful.

Early Afro-American melodies also bespeak hope from the ash heap, exactly in tune with the biblical psalms (cf. 1 Samuel 2:1–10, Luke 1:46–55), because the Lord of Holy Scripture is not a fix-it god, but is the faithful Almighty One, the Precious Lord, who takes your hand and hugs you through the dark hours before the morning breaks and there are the "broken cries" of joys, as Psalm 30:4–5 puts it.

I am not a habitué of North American bars, but I have watched and listened to recovering alcoholics standing on overturned milk crates preaching as street corner evangelists near Times Square, New York City; and once around midnight in an offbeat Grecian nightclub, Thessaloniki, I heard a second generation gypsy Christian rend our hearts with his powerful song pleading for his Roma people to be given not constant ruthless suppression but acts of *agapé*.

Psalm 56 reveals God keeps my tears in a bottle; they are so precious to the Lord! It probably was a wineskin pouch and not a beer bottle. But I am wondering, if the prophetic group *U2* can rock in strange places, why could God's psalms not find their way into clubs full of bottles, where desperate people "in their cups" often find sharing pain, shame, intractable troubles, easier than in a happy-happy church congregation.

Imagine that the lights have dimmed and your wine cups have been overflowing in Psalm 23 fashion, and Jacqueline (Bessie) Rhodes takes stage-center under a spotlight and begins to sing, "There's people out to hurt me bad," and you pick up the call-and-response song habit of the Afro-American tradition—precisely what Older Testament psalms do—and come in with your congregational line after stanzas 2, 3, and then the resolutionary thanks at the end of stanza 6 in the upbeat last half of the psalm.

— Psalms are to be Heard Everywhere —

God Keeps My Tears in a Bottle
Psalm 56:8

Text: Calvin Seerveld, © January, 2001   87 87 with Refrain
Tune: Calvin Seerveld, © 2001   GIOIA IN GOD'S BOTTLE BLUES
harmonization, Jean-Pierre Rudolph

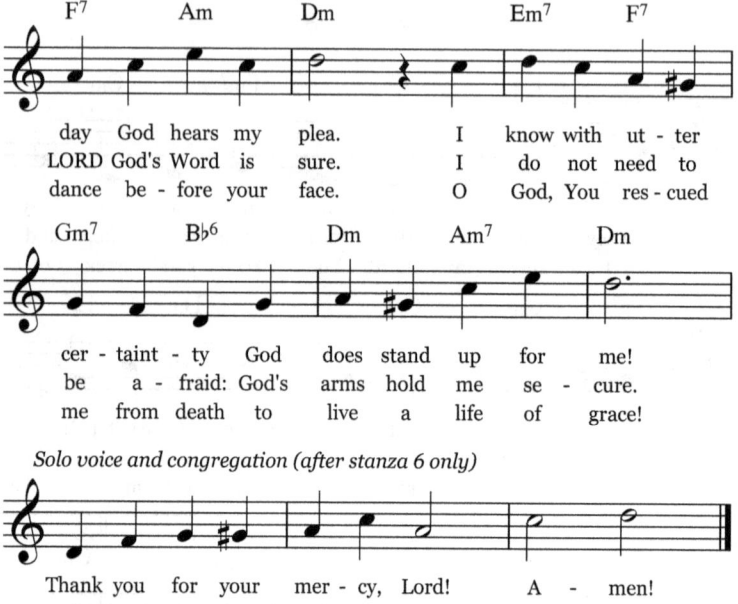

I am wondering, if the prophetic group *U2* can rock in strange places, could *Blues 92* come through in a jazz club where there are hot guitars, drums, and sax doing gigs? where those on expense accounts "know the ropes so well," have been "double-crossed . . . on the rocks," and maybe realize over a whiskey they're "getting old," hair thinning, "bones drying up," and would be interested in hearing God's promise to be made "strong as a wild ox!"?

Following again the Afro-American song habit of call-and-response, please answer the first phrase Jacqueline (Bessie) Rhodes sings by repeating it, and also sing the final musical phrase of each stanza, like "but my LORD the Rock ain't crooked!"

After *Blues 92*, sing out stanzas 1 and 4 of *Genevan 92*, to catch the playful syncopated rhythmic similarity with the Blues and how such a long 13 (6+7) syllabic line can be speaking both light-hearted fun and happiness but also a more serious message that God can keep older people fruitful, succulent, full of juicy sap.

Blues 92

The LORD en-joys a hot gui-tar, with drums and sax to cook it. God moves some-times it seems so slow, but my LORD the Rock ain't crook-ed.

I watch the wick-ed get a-head; they know the ropes so well. "Yeah, those poor en-e-mies," says God, "they're find-ing the road to hell!"

I had it bad not long a-go, double-crossed, was on the rocks. But you know? the LORD was e-ven there: made me strong as a wild ox!

I'm get-ting old, bones dry-ing up, not grow-ing like a tree. "Oh, don't you wor-ry," says the LORD, "You'll get good fresh sap from me!"

The LORD en-joys a hot guit-ar, with drums and sax to cook it. God moves some-times it seems so slow, but my LORD the Rock ain't crook-ed.

Text and Tune: Calvin Seerveld, © 1999 BLUES 92

Genevan Psalm 92

Sing praise to God, be play-ful, God's cove-nant love is sure:
Why wick-ed seem to flour-ish can not be un-der-stood
LORD God, how strong You made me, stout as a strong wild ox!
Just per-sons thrive like palm trees, like ce-dars which ma-ture;

sun-rise and night en-dure to glad-den, make us grate-ful.
un-til their bril-liant good is seen to slip and per-ish.
Your hand a-noints my walk with heal-ing oil of safe-ty.
plant-ed near God, se-cure they al-ways blos-som with ease.

My hap-pi-ness, O LORD, needs skill-ful mus-ic and voice
Fools stup-id-ly a-void your glor-y, prac-tise de-ceit,
Now those who stalked my steps, placed traps to am-bush, trick me,
Those who do right stay fruit-ful e-ven when they grow old.

to help me laugh, re-joice, and cel-e-brate your great deeds.
but You plan their de-feat—God's en-e-mies are des-troyed.
I clear-ly hear and see, shall, yes, them-selves be laid waste.
Their ag-ed fer-tile hold shows God, my Rock, is truth-ful.

Text: Psalm 92, vers. Calvin Seerveld, © 1999   13 13 13 13
Tune: Genevan Psalter, 1562   Genevan 92

Now comes the hard one that will stretch your faith as well as your imagination, the psalm most quoted in the Newer Testament, which lies neglected in most christian Bibles today, unpreached, not even a verse of it mentioned in *The Revised Common Lectionary* (three year cycle, 1992) used by many, many churches: Psalm 110.

I don't have time here and now to explicate the seven compacted verses of Psalm 110, the confusing change of voices, the different persons addressed, why verse 4 was not in the Pharisee Bible, how "Lord" all in capital letters refers to God and "Lord" not all in caps refers first to Ruler David, gradually dissolves to focus on the Messiah, and finally takes on the overlay of referring to anybody as "lord" who is anointed by the fire of the Holy Spirit—a bona fide "Christian," a Christ-follower who leads in the Way of the Lord (all capitals).

But the early post-resurrection Church had no trouble understanding Psalm 110 and its direct link to the commanding orientation of Psalm 1 and especially Psalm 2 about God's "anointed ones" coming to rule the nations of the world! Newer Testament Christians claimed outright the promise of God in verse 1: the Lord will subject the enemies of God's anointed ones like a footstool! beneath your feet. And those naïve followers of the ascended Jesus Christ gladly accepted investiture "in the order of Melchizedek," verse 4—a key focus of the whole Newer Testament book *To the Hebrews* (4:14–10:39). That is, Christians who took God at God's Word in Psalm 110 knew they were in a life-and-death historic struggle as the Lord's delegated priest-kings called to act with merciful justice and to abhor whatever feast-killed, wasted the meek as prey.

Psalm 110 (like Psalm 2) is "political" all right, but not a song for the Evangelical Far Right anymore than it is a text for the Liberal Left Gospeliers. Psalm 110 authorizes the easy-fitting yoke of Melchizedek Rule over the shoulders of God's fighting adopted children, which means: you lay down your life in the struggle against principalities, powers, and dominions like insatiable Greed for MORE, missile Violence, consuming Vanity, the Big Lie of Technocratic Progress world without end. Even as you unhandily contest and mediate justice for the weak, the destitute, the sick, handicapped, the self-satisfied, the ignored lonely ones, the societal bullies, and you yourself, like Baptizer John in Jesus' day, question what's up (cf. Luke 7:18–23) and bewail your own impotence, you still sing Psalm 110?

As Muslim, Zionist, Christian, Hindu, Shinto, Secularist FUNDAMENTALISMS come to the fore, I hope we who have heard tell of ye olde persecuted Huguenots marching through the streets lurching against their chains, singing Genevan psalms striking fear in their captors: we may need to learn anew how to sing Genevan 110, even if it upset ecclesiastic decorum. God's psalms are rough and tough, and Genevan psalms need a rugged, unconcertized voicing. Genevan 110 must not be Schubertianized; it is not Robert Shaw Chorale material. We need to learn to sing Genevan psalms like lusty *boeren*, long-haul truck drivers, butchers, bakers, and candlestick makers, judo street-fighting singers protesting as it were, pro-theses! because psalms wrestle tenaciously with the LORD and God's promises as if at the Jabbok ford. Genevan psalms are not pretty, but gritty.

Would to God Genevan 110 could become a common song of God's people, the way the "We Shall Overcome" makeover of C. Albert Tindley's hymn became the theme of '60s Protest Marchers. Genevan 110 is less premillennial perhaps, more self-critical, not in automatic melodic gear, but is just as eschatonically sure on "overcoming."

Shall we rise to sing Genevan 110 in unison as an exercise in preparation for when we too in North America will be joining Christ's followers around the world who even now in distant lands are being expropriated, maligned, made refugees, killed—without having been taught to sing a psalm in God's world.

Psalm 110

Text: Psalm 110, vers. Calvin Seerveld, © 1980
Tune: Louis Bourgeois, 1551; harm. Dale Grotenhuis, 1988

11 10 11 10
Genevan 110

"Let your forbearance be known," God had Paul write to the churches, since it is the LORD God who wreaks vengeance, not Melchizedek priestly rulers (Romans 12:14–21). "The Lord shall smash all military forces that proudly feast-kill, waste the meek as prey." Suppose Psalm 110 were sung soundly before the regular prayer breakfasts held in Washington, D.C., and Ottawa, led by our godly rulers. Would Genevan 110 alter their coffee conversation?

Would your faith be offended if you hear me think out loud that a defense policy of pre-emptive strike (*The National Security Strategy of the United States of America,* September 2002, section 5, p. 15) is in stark antithesis to the Melchizedek Rule Psalm 110 enjoins? At least this is certain: just as the huddled believers in Acts 4 prayed Psalm 2 out loud as referring to Pilate, Herod, and the Sanhedrin (Acts 4:23–31)! God's psalms are directly relevant today! To our personal, communal and national life. God's psalms are dynamite! And God's people deserve to be led in singing dynamite psalms both outside and inside congregated church walls.

Before we sing a last Genevan psalm tune to go on our way rejoicing, let us accept the blessing of Psalm 126 into our lives tendered by an exquisite German Reformation tune that blends in one song the tentative musing sadness of exiles returning to a devastated homeland and a childlike joy skipping with laughter, confident in the LORD's intimate concern to make things new and right in our lives. To introduce our singing this gentle psalm so appropriate for many of God's people, since as "recovering Christians" we are often coming back it seems from exile somewhere foreign to the Lord's Rule, not knowing exactly whether or how we will be received by God and God's people, let me show you an unusual reading of the Luke 15 parable Jesus told about the prodigal God who in Melchizedek style celebrates returning sons (and daughters).

In Duane Michals' *The Return of the Prodigal Son* [CP #32–36], the naked son, like a mirror image of Masaccio's Adam expelled from paradise enters from the right into a room where the father is leisurely scanning *The New York Times.* The startled older man looks at the youth bowed in shame. The father loosens his shirt to protect the other's nakedness, and then thoughtfully removes all his clothes to give them to the younger one. Finally, the naked old man gingerly gives the returned son a hug offering reconciliation.

Jesus' story in Luke 15 ends with the Father offering the same gracious forgiving fresh start to the older son who "wasted" his inheritance by hoarding it joylessly, without thanksgiving. Both Luke 15 and Psalm

126 reveal the everlasting redemptive sacrificial giveaway nature of the Covenanting God revealed in Jesus Christ, "the true Melchizedek," who promises to all the repentant wastrels and discouraged faithful who may be present: "who sows with tears, but perseveres, comes back again with sheaves of grain, surprised by God's salvation."

When God Brought Zion's Remnant Band

Text: Psalm 126; vers. Calvin Seerveld, 1985, ©
Tune: J. Klug's Geistliche Lieder, 1535; harm. Dale Grotenhuis, 1985.

847 847 887
MAG ICH UNGLÜCK

There is no time to include the psalm-song of Jonah versified for the vigorous, tossing Welsh melody *Eifionydd*, bound to captivate christian grade school students. So we shall conclude with "a praise song" good for this conference occasion, for a three-generation Fiftieth Wedding Anniversary, or for a centennial celebration of your christian group whatever it be.

But first, a plea to all pastors, preachers, music directors, congregational song leaders, church musicians, and liturgetes who ostensibly spend night and day, as Psalm 134 says, "in the house of the LORD," married as it were to the Scriptures: sometimes married people come to take the familiar for granted, relax on "dating protocols"—you don't dress up, you slough off on imaginative surprises, go cheap on flowers rather than lovingly expensive—if your profession has eased your "marriage" to Scripture toward the humdrum through overwork, routine, overfamiliarity, how about "dating" the psalms again?

If the song leaders of God's people do not "fall in love" passionately with God's psalms, no amount of exhortation will get the psalms active in believers' lives and voices. And if the current North American generation remains ignorant of Reformation psalm songs, including the skillful, apt sinewy Genevan melodies, then we leaders will have failed, defaulting on a very rich treasury of the Church. We can find other ways too to bring whole psalms back into circulation, like the British *Psalm Praise* of the '70s (which is now a generation old), find new vigorous language for the Scottish reservoir, and tap into the Afro-American spirituals connection; but consider the wonderful repristination our believing Japanese brothers and sisters have produced: an up-to-date CD of Genevan psalmody sung with consummate musical devotion and scintillating verve[4]—check it out if you are willing to give the Genevan Psalter a fair trial for reinvigorating psalm-singing.

In the pop-song composing course I have taken at York University in Toronto, the basic commandment for writing text and tune was: "Keep it simple, stupid!"

Well, God's psalms are not simple, and need tunes that are strong, wiry, deep, robust, resolute. Doing justice to singing the psalms in church worship or anywhere is the birthright of God's people, and must not be sold off for a mess of delicious potage. God's psalms need to be spoken

---

4 *Psalms from the Genevan Psalter in Japanese*. Bach Collegium Japan, Masaaki Suzuki, conductor (30MCD-1026) 1996. Cf. also a lecture-recital CD by Calvin Seerveld and the Pax Christi Chorale under the direction of Stephanie Martin, *The Gift of Genevan Psalmody: Sprung from its historical context*, 2011.

and sung until they are stamped, stored up indelibly in our communal memory as prayers—I learned the expression from my wife—"for when the hard times come."

Let us conclude this session in anticipation of being saints singing the psalms in chapter 19 of Revelation, remembering Grünewald's (c. 1460–1528) triumphant "Resurrection" scene and Georges Rouault's *Sarah* (1956), a contemporary Ravenna-like symbol of the laughing resurrection that awaits the tried-and-true faithful followers of Jesus Christ, as we sing in unison stanzas 1 and 6 of "A Congregational Paean" to Genevan psalm tune 89.

A Congregational Paean

1. How shall we thank you, Lord, for joy and this sur - prise?
2. How good it is to see Your heal - ing touch of health
3. How good it is to have all toil-some ten - sion past.
4. How good it is to know Your grace fills out one's life
5. How good it is to see our *bro - ther face to face,

You have come through a - gain to re - cre - ate our lives.
re - store (**'s) blood and breath to nor - mal life's prime wealth.
You have sup - plied a fruit - ful fin - ish now at last.
from sol - i - tar - y walk to wed - ded hus - band - wife.
brought back from ex - ile sound, kept safe by Your em - brace.

We stand a - mazed: Your prov - i - den - tial hand looks af - ter
Gone is the pain, the doubts, *his feel - ing un - pro - tect - ed:
Strug - gles and set - backs plagued the ar - duous un - der - tak - ing,
In - ti - ma - cy and pas - sion joined by love are gift - ed
Cap - tiv - i - ty is cruel and breaks the best com - mun - ion:

**insert the name of the one who is intended for commemoration
* use his/her/their or brother/sister/member as appropriate

Text: A Congregational Paean, Calvin Seerveld, © 1992   12 12 13 13 13 13
Tune: *Genevan Psalter*, 1562; harm. Jacobus J. Kloppers, 1985, alt.   Genevan 89

— Psalms are to be Heard Everywhere —

6. How good it is to taste exultant jubilee!
   You feed us from the honeycomb, and make us free.
   Your generosity provides more than requested:
   teach us to dance and sing, Your children glad and festive—
   praised be Your name, O Lord, You have redeemed our story!
   We cheer your mystery and celebrate Your glory.

Stanza 1 usually is sung first. Then the congregation sings the stanza appropriate for the occasion.
Stanza 2   For unexpected healing
Stanza 3   For completion of a difficult task
Stanza 4   For second, late, or remarriage in the Lord
Stanza 5   For release of captive of hostage
Stanza 6   For other special festive events, or use as final stanza

— Biblical Studies and Wisdom for Living —

Singing Genevan Psalms under the guise of Christmas Caroling, in the popular Tim Hortons coffee shop at Bathurst & Finch, Toronto, Canada, December 2009. Left to right: Seerveld, Charles Im, John Declou, John Meiboom. Photo by star reporter Ian Jameson.

FIVE PSALMS: FOR THE AMERICAN GUILD OF ORGANISTS

PSALM 19: CELEBRATING THE GOOD NEWS OF GOD'S CREATIONAL ORDINANCES AND CREATURAL GLOSSOLALIA

The sun does not stumble sleepily tired out of bed in the morning, but rises like a man or a woman having been refreshed by a night of deep sleep after the nuptial excitement of satisfying sexual intercourse, says Psalm 19:4b–6. Just as human passion basks in memories of past trysts where intimacy was bathed in trust, so the sun relishes its daily task, utterly faithful, full of news—every day is new!—not at all worn down by an office routine. As the sun circles in view overhead, all creatures come to know the sun is uncontrollable. We clever humans can box ourselves in by hiding from its heat in cooled chambers. We Americans can even walk on the moon, desecrate its forbidding space with left-behind debris made-in-USA. But who can stop the sun?! No wonder ancient civilizations worshiped this mighty creature of God.

The constellations of stars at night too, like diaphanous sunlight during the day, are telling—the Hebrew calls it "sky-writing"—proclaim the weighty majesty of God. "There is no lightness-of-being in God," broadcasts one day to the next day. And every clear night or stormy one passes on the inside knowledge to the next night, says Psalm 19:1–2, about the glory of God: the amazing, merciful care the eternal Creator God shows for each of the myriad complex creatures and cosmic arrangements at large (cf. Psalm 104:24–30, Isaiah 40:12–31). God's divine power houses the sun, orders summer and winter, seedtime and harvest, so long as the inhabited earth shall remain (cf. Genesis 8:20–22).

And fascinating about this hum of communication going on night and day by sky and sun is that there are no words! no intelligible speech. Humans cannot even hear what is voiced, says Psalm 19:3–4a, although the sounds carry throughout the whole earth! It's like the high-pitched

---

Homilies for the American Guild of Organists, New York Region II convention in July 1999, Long Island, New York.

whistle noise a dog can hear but their masters cannot. And not only all things bright and beautiful like frost and wind, dolphins and butterfly wings, but also creatures lugubrious like mud and snakes, whirlpools and dragons (Psalm 148:7–10), are constantly busy in this massive, unintelligible babble of praise, affirming the marvelous wisdom of their Creator. All things made by God thankfully confess God is LORD, says Psalm 145:10. The spacious heavens and subterranean currents deep in the oceans attest, says Psalm 97:6, that God is the tried-and-true One who always comes through with right-doing (*tsedeq*); God always acts in a reliable way creatures can count on.

That's a clue to why Psalm 19 follows up the opening description of this worldwide chorus of *glossolalia* with a tribute to the *torah* of the LORD (Psalm 19:7–10). The ordinances that the Creator God set up for sun and moon, planet and star to follow—"which they do not overstep" (Psalm 148:3–6)—are of a piece with the commands the LORD God gave men and women through Moses at Mount Sinai once upon a time, in writing (cf. Exodus 31:18, 32:15–16). When a human creature does not murder, abuse a fellow creature sexually, steal, lie, or covet possessions, that person is as free for a life that promises gladness and laughter, says Psalm 19:8a, as a bird is to fly in a world structured by gravity, because the Creator God's order [*piqqud*] for human shalom is to give birth rather than to kill, to experience mutual erotic fulfillment rather than stymied sexuality, to giveaway your goods with generosity rather than be a miser, and to bear true witness to what happens.

The LORD God's *torah* is not repressive, reveals Psalm 19:7a, but is truly liberating. The LORD God's *torah* (which Buber translates as *Weisung*, guidance) can lead humans deadened into robotic zombies by their mesmerizing idols of greed, orgasm, or corrupting power, back to life again by restoring their actions to be within human creatural limits, in the way that gravel, stubble, and decaying matter obey the laws of petrification and properly become solid, wonderful mountains. Once creatures know the LORD God's task [*mitswah*] set out for them in their kind (cf. 1 Corinthians 15:39–41), those creatures flourish (Psalm 19:8b).

Also, the magnificent deeds of the LORD (cf. H. Bavinck, *Magnalia Dei*) celebrated throughout the Older Testament, from the creation of the universe (Genesis 1–2) and the exodus of God's people from Egypt (Exodus 3–15), to the raising up of David's lineage for the Messiah (2 Samuel 6–7, Psalm 110), and bringing back the LORD's folk from Babylonian exile (Ezra, Nehemiah): all these acts of God [*'edut*] fill out historically the cosmic redemptive scope of the LORD God's *torah*, which, says Psalm 19:7b, upon being experienced, makes a generation wise.

Whether God said in the beginning, "**Let there be** creeping crawly creatures squirming in the grass" (Genesis 1:24–25), or later said, "**Thou shalt keep a day free** in the week so families, servants, even your domesticated animals, can rest a bit on the strenuous journey" (Deuteronomy 5:12–15): God's ordering judgments [*mishpat*] are good for creatures, as good as gold, no, better than gold, sweeter than honey manufactured by bees and desired by bears and humans alike (Psalm 19:9b). The covenanting LORD God's creative and providing will is firmly **pro** creatures. That's true even after sin came in to spoil God's good creation, as the Later Testament makes explicit in John 3:17: "That's right, God did not send the Son into the world in order to condemn the world, but so that **the world might be saved through him**."

Finally Psalm 19 gets very personal. Given the hallelujah chorus of responses by all God's non-human creatures in this worldwide theatre of God's good creation, and given the special loving attention the passionately jealous Yahweh spends on humans, putting ordinances for society down in writing we can read and grasp, it makes sense for us men and women to recognize the many-splendored order God wants in the world as God's rich embrace of us historical creatures together.

To stand in awe of the LORD God's covenanting with us this way, which will bring out what is good in our various natures if we men and women obediently follow the LORD's guidelines the way the sun, seaweed, and tortoises do: such respectful compliance before the face of God [*jir'at jhvh*] would be cleansing, says Psalm 19:9a. You get the idea that facing up to God's creational will would be like standing under a refreshing, pulsing stream of clear water that showers you clean, so you don't stay sitting in a hot tub of your own dirty bathwater.

"But," says the psalmist who is not uptight or defensive; "I can't do it! I know firsthand your creational fiats, your ordinantial Word, is a searchlight for my feet, bright illumination for the path I need to walk (Psalm 119:105), but I stumble around, I am inherently deceptive—so good-looking on the outside but crooked, twisted in knots deep inside— I'm a bluff! I pretend, I never say quietly in public, 'Lord, be merciful to **me, a sinner**' (cf. Luke 18:9–14). I can't see straight, I can't talk straight; even the inarticulate groanings of my heart—*abba!*—are impure. I want to be your servant, LORD [the psalmist says it twice in the closing verses], like the sun and the rain, the trees and wild animals (cf. Isaiah 55:8–13), which You love so much, O Lord, enjoying their praise; but I'm a loser! Could You not somehow take me out of hock, and make what comes out of my mouth acceptable to You!? O LORD God, my stalwart Rock, my *go'el* [=redeemer]!" (Psalm 19:11–14).

Many psalms begin *de profundis*, switch gears, and conclude with thanksgiving. Psalm 19, however, starts with this panoramic service of praise and ends almost the way the Pharisee-trained christian Jew Paul finishes a paragraph in Romans 7:24, "Wretched human creature that I am! Who shall be a *go'el* for me, who will rescue me out of this deadly corporeality?!"

But there are three matters here in Psalm 19 that can help us get our bearings straight in God's world, also as organists and church musicians:

(1) Creatures at large are a sounding board for Creator God's voice, the golden echo that "give(s) beauty back, beauty, beauty, beauty, back to God, beauty's self and beauty's giver" (to quote Gerard Manley Hopkins). The praise of non-human creatures Psalm 19 reports reveal God's almighty power and divine glory. So creation structured by the LORD's "Let-there-be" Word is good news, "gospel" you could almost say, as to how creatures are to respond to their Maker—enact the LORD's will! make the Creator LORD God known abroad and respond with adoration!

But humans do not naturally understand creatural *glossolalia*. Romans 1:18–25 backs up Psalm 19 on this very point, to say no human has an excuse for being ignorant of the Hound of Heaven (cf. Francis Thompson's poem), since creation from the beginning has made the Creator God audible, visible; but humans apparently perversely don't get it! Instead of joining the hallelujah chorus of creation, humans tend to worship the fabulous teeming earth, water, air, and fire, or their own human prowess, and sing their own praises rather than worship the Creator.

In proclaiming the good news of creation Psalm 19 gives an orientation that undercuts all Humanism as well as every variety of Naturalistic idolatry. The true living God **is** being praised, says Psalm 19. Do you men and women want to be part of it, or not? Yes, humans are special in God's world, as Psalm 8 puts it, "almost like a god, crowned with a lordliness to administer the handiwork of the Creator." But creatural praise is SATB. No prima donnas, please. Humans may often take the melody, but the basso continuo of trees clapping their hands (Isaiah 55:12), mountains dancing like deer (Psalm 29:16), and lions growling as they chew the bones of their food provided by the LORD's hand (Psalm 104:20–23), is the kind of concert that pleases God.

Can we women and men Humanists—an **ism** always wrongly exaggerates the importance of something—hear Psalm 19? If we humans play God or abuse our fellow non-human creatures' *glossolalia*, pollute their praise, then we humans are culpable for the false notes and shall suffer judgment, like the huge submerged mass of rotting flesh and garbage floating in the Atlantic Ocean adrift not so far off Long Island.

(2) Creation is a fundamental tenet of **faith**—*credo in unum Deum, patrem omnipotentem, factorem caeli et terrae*. Attempts to prove in some supposed neutral fashion that this world is a creation of Almighty God has always struck me as misguided. If you have to check rock strata and measure light years or get your premises in line with their terms distributed logically before you can read and believe Psalm 19, you are unfortunately a person to be pitied, it seems to me. The genuine faith-based insight that this world reality where the miracle of birth happens, and the grace of warmth can be experienced, and the blessing of a smile takes place, is a creation God made good and ordained for us humans, animals, plants, and minerals to inhabit: when one **knows in faith** reality is God's creation, that certainty holds an assurance of things hoped for and a conviction of glories still to come (cf. Hebrews 11:1) that provides a sure foundation and sanity sorely needed in our technocratically driven culture.

Also, if the Church neglects to confess vigorously and recognize as primary that this is God's world, and we guests for 70 or, by reason of strength, 80 years are at home here as the Lord's grateful creatures: if the Church misses the primordial, key importance of the doctrine of creation, then the faithful tend to lose focus on our creatural task to tend the garden, and people go off on tangents—competing narrowing fundamentalisms, commercialized world-flight evangelism, or a mania that the millennial sky is falling—instead of being centered by the sweet, enduring gospel of Psalm 19.

And (3) let me close with a note on the import of Psalm 19 for church musicians congregated to worship the Lord.

The testimony of Psalm 19 to the creational ordinances God has provided for humans to honor as they interpret the *glossolalia* all around us and compound its joyful clamor with human praise does not promote esoteric moralisms about being devoted to "the mystical music of the spheres," but is very down to earth. How sounds become tones, thanks to the pressure of air in a pipe cut to certain length, which can be assembled and forged with other tones into an harmonic ensemble, interests God, since the Creator God instituted the setup for making music possible. The

Psalm 19 revelation about *torah* has God touching down into the dirt of a diatonic scale, the genial or harsh dissonance of chromatic notes, the tenor of a Dorian or Phrygian modal melody, the different temper of an open fifth or a minor third—God is in the details of creational order, also the order for music-making. So making music at any time—outside the special place of congregational worship too, in the home, at campouts, in the concert hall—rests in the Creator God's creatural framework provided for us.

We humans are responsible for the music we make in God's world, whether it be choral, instrumental, or rhythmic drum music and dance. Psalms 19 supports all kinds of edifying musical traditions—"And God heard a ninth chord in the blues scale, and behold! it was very good"—and expects only that the music we make have an imaginative quality and be skillfully performed (cf. Psalm 33:1–5). Within the Creator's gift of vocal, tonal, body-movement creatural terms available, we compose and present a permutation of what thanks the Lord for our creaturehood, which God's covenantal grace sustains, in whatever setting it be.

Church musicians, as I understand it, are called almost like priests of old, like levitical ministers of music around the ark, to embody in music the faith confessed by the gathered saints and sinners, celebrating the fact that the Lord revealed in Jesus Christ is God of the historical universe, and that the bodily resurrection is sure—thank God!

And that's where it gets very personal, and the concluding paragraph of Psalm 19 fits well. I as a theorist and you as organists, church musicians, persons of any endeavor or calling, have the mandate from Colossians to "let the word of Christ dwell in you richly, teaching and focusing the consciousness of one another in all wisdom, and with gratitude in your hearts be busy singing psalms and hymns, holy spirited songs, to the Lord" (Colossians 3:16). And hold us back—your avocational musical servants, Lord—from overweening presumption; help us to be living **offerings** of patient and excited love (cf. Romans 12:1–2).

Now may the singing of our mouths, the playing of our hands and feet, and the inarticulate groanings of our hearts for the wretched of the earth be something acceptable in front of your face, O Lord God, our Rock! the Faithful One who always comes through as Redeemer to set us free from the bondage of our isolated vanity.

Hallelujah!

David Psalm 30:
A song written for a consecration service of the house of God

> I am celebrating You, Lord God, because You pulled me back up;
>> You did not let my enemies enjoy themselves at my expense.
> Lord, my God, I cried out to You, and You have made me whole again—
> Lord, you have raised me up and away from the grave!
> You have let me breathe again! after being so close to those who have gone down into the opened earth.
>
> O you faithful folk of God—all of you—sing out and play music to the covenantal Lord God!
> Let there be thanksgiving in remembering God's holy presence:
> if sudden ill wrinkles for a little while from God's grievous anger,
> our having life and being alive issues from the Lord's gracious favor.
> If some evening you have to spend a night weeping,
> there shall be—count on it!—broken cries of joy when it is morning.
>
> I said to myself, I did, when I was disarmed, at ease,
> "I shall never be shaken up."
> Lord God, by your gracious good will You had set me up sturdy, a mountain of solidified strength;
> but when You turned your face aside, I was shaken, completely bewildered.
> I called out to You, Lord God!—I begged my Lord for mercy—
> "What good is my blood to You? in my going down into the bottomless pit?
> Can dust praise You? Can broken clods of earth announce your steadfast faithfulness?
> Hear me, O Lord God, be gracious to me!
> O Lord God, be my helpmate…
>
> Tja! You have turned my weeping about death, You have turned it around for me [Lord] into dancing!
> You have undone my sackcloth of mourning, and girded me with gladness!
> so that my deepest insides may sing and play music for You, and I

not be devastatedly stilled—
O LORD God, my God, I will give You thanks forever and ever and ever!

C. Seerveld, translation 1982.

This psalm came to be used by Older Testament believers, says the subtitle, for a service of rededicating the meeting place for worshiping God as a community. So it is most fitting for Newer Testament believers to hear its forthright comfort and direction at matins in wanting to rededicate our human bodies as temples of the Holy Spirit for this workweek, and for consecrating what we shall playfully do the next few days as a communion of the faithful who normally lead others in communal worship. Psalm 30 covers the gamut of human experience and rolls the false security, sudden disaster, argument with God, and grateful rescue all together into a poignant prayer of reflective thanksgiving to God that we may adopt too, if the shoe fits.

After the trauma I went through, says the psalmist—"You pulled me back up, LORD, like a bucket out of a deep well after the hauling rope had been cut and dropped"!—now that I can breathe again after being so close to the stillness of death down in that hole, I'm going to celebrate You, LORD, the incredible way You do things! (vv. 1–3).

I was sitting pretty, and then it happened: disaster struck. Like prosperous Job before the Satan put him through the wringer, like victorious David before his son Absalom made him a sorry refugee, like good king Hezekiah whom God's angels had just saved from the pillaging Assyrian hordes of Sennacherib, before Hezekiah got cancer: it is so easy to forget God until you're in a jam (vv. 6–7).

But Job steadfastly wrestled in faith with the LORD through his trials (Job 19); David repented seventy times seven times in his pock-marked reign, and clung tenaciously to the love of God (Psalm 51, 32); Hezekiah prayed as if his life depended on it, and the LORD gave him 15 extra years (Isaiah 38). Psalm 30 too does not use God just as an accident insurance policy, but reveals precisely three things about how the faithful children of God are to struggle with the LORD in trouble.

(1) "You can't let me die, God! How could I praise You then?" (vv. 8–10)! And that argument changes God's mind, if your daily life is a continuous song of thanking the Lord, and not just a debater's ploy pulled out for the occasion (James 5:13–18).

(2) When evil comes to someone who belongs to the LORD, you

may count on its being brief (v. 5). The certainty of the rescue and healing and God's coming through does not erase the punishing pain, fear, and often hard-to-take consternation, but the sure prospect of the LORD's coming through—maybe only at the resurrection!—does help a woman or man of faith to hang on to the truth that the LORD's gracious goodness is the bed we sleep in, and the ordeals that burden us are, *credo,* essentially transient (2 Corinthians 4:16–18).

(3) Our sadness and mourning which the LORD converts into gladness and dancing is not the self-pitying complaining Cain tried on God (Genesis 4), but is the heart-rent, repentant weeping pleas of God's adopted children who trust the LORD to bring forth good fruit out of our labor pains (vv. 11–12, Joel 2:12–14).

When my wife and I spent time in Africa in the '80s, 200 miles inland up-country in Sierra Leone with one of my students teaching literacy in Alikalia there, life was wonderfully focused on what counts: was Jesus Christ the Son of God on earth, and can you drink the water? The plastic wrappings of our North American cultural concerns seemed so much glossy waste material, which drowns your life in minutiae.

Psalm 30 is like that African experience. Sin is very simple. That's why it's easy to do—do your own godless thing (cf. Judges 21:25). But the results of sin are terribly complex, distorting different layers of human life differently as you bruise those close to you and even neighbors far away. But Psalm 30 does not ask you to walk around guilt-ridden. Psalm 30 is a confession of God-dependence by someone deeply **forgiven.** So the psalmist talks up the LORD's reliable mercy (*chesed*) with fellow believers, and says, "Let's make music, people, dance and sing our thanks to the LORD!"

Let us do that now so we may own Psalm 30 ourselves, by hearing the music of Matthew van Brink (1999), kinesthetically live into the dancing of Nicole Loizides (1999), and voicing the tune of Norman Warren (1969).

The atonal music bespeaks the imploding tentativity and squirreling contentious vagaries of our sackcloth-clad, contemporary faith-lives in the city, far from the diminished sevenths of sunsets and major C chord resolutions where the turbulent underside to life is denied. But there is a turn in the organ, strings, and percussion into the shuffling joy of dance; not ballroom dance or the rococo pirouettes of classical ballet, but the stomp of Jewish or Slavic folk dance, the happy footwork of persecuted gypsies, the kind of roughhewn bodily exertion the God of the Bible enjoys (cf. Exodus 15:20–33, Psalm 150, Jeremiah 31:10–14), and we two right-footed Christians would do well to learn.

> Tja! You have turned my weeping about death, You have turned it around for me [Lord] into dancing!
> You have undone my sackcloth of mourning, and girded me with gladness!
> so that my deepest insides may sing and play music for You, and I not be devastatedly stilled—
> O Lord God, my God, I will give You thanks forever and ever and ever!

— Five Psalms: For the American Guild of Organists —

I Worship You, O LORD PSALM 30

1 I worship you, O LORD, for you have raised me up;
  I cried to you for help, and you restored my life.
  You brought me back from death and saved me from the grave.

2 Sing praises to the LORD, all those who know his name;
  for while his wrath is brief, his favor knows no end.
  Though tears flow for a night, the morning brings new joy.

3 I said, "I am so strong, I never shall be moved";
  but you, LORD, shook my life— my heart was in distress.
  I cried out for your help and pleaded for your grace:

4 "What good am I when dead,
  while lying in the grave?
  Can dust recount your love,
  the grave proclaim your praise?
  O hear me, gracious LORD,
  in mercy be my aid!"

5 My mourning you have turned
  to dancing and to joy;
  my sadness you dispelled
  as gladness filled my soul.
  And so I'll sing your praise,
  my God, through all my days.

Words: st. 1-3, 5: James E. Seddon © 1973 The Jubilate Group, admin. Hope Publishing Company; st. 4: Calvin Seerveld © 1982 Calvin Seerveld
Music (BISHOP TUCKER 6.6.6.6.6.6): Norman L. Warren © 1990 The Jubilate Group, admin. Hope Publishing Company

All rights reserved. Used by permission.

Psalm 96: A Song That Never Gets Old Is New

You people, sing the Lord God a fresh new song!	1
Let all the earth sing to the Lord!	
Sing to the Lord, praise God's name—	2
proclaim God's liberating rescue day in and day out—	
tell the story of God's glory to the nations abroad,	3
make God's marvelous deeds known	
among the peoples [of the world]!	

Yes, the Lord God is great and greatly to be praised!   4
Among the gods it is the Lord before whom one is to be awed.
That's right, all the "gods" of the
    (various) peoples are no-god idols: 5
it is the Lord God who fashioned the heavens of starry space.
Splendor and majesty accompany God;   6
strength and brightness are found in God's holy presence.

Recognize in the Lord God,
    all you generations of the world's peoples,   7
recognize the Lord God's glory and strength!   8
Recognize the glory of the Lord God's Name!
Bring an offering, and come to the place
    where God is available,
worship the Lord God in the splendor of holiness—   9
let all the earth tremble before God's face!
Say to the-folk-who-do-not-know, "The Lord God rules!   10
—that's right, the inhabited world is firmly set up,
    it's not going to teeter-totter—
[the Lord God] governs the peoples with evenhanded fairness."

Let the heavens cheer up, let the earth be exultant;   11
let the sea make its noises,
    and all the creatures that swim in it;
let the cultivated field
    and all the plants growing in it be happy   12
—a time is coming when the trees of the wood
    shall shout out joyfully before the Lord God,   13
    because God is coming!
The Lord God is coming to get an accounting from the whole

> earth—
> The LORD God will judge the inhabited world
> with genuine justice,
> the peoples of the world with God's sterling truth—

The Bible has little truck with novelty, which soon wears out. God always brings enduring news.

In our secularized media you hear and see mostly the old stuff of sensational violence, wars, and rumors of war—that's not new! It's as old as human sin: Cain killing Abel, Lamech boasting to his wives of his military prowess (Genesis 4), the prophets of Baal making a storm of music in their ritual sacrifice on Mount Carmel at the time of Elijah, King Ahab, and Queen Jezebel (1 Kings 18). No, sing to the Lord a **new** song, says Psalm 96, music and song that stays fresh with the good news of the LORD's marvelous deeds in history of rescuing people from their dead ends!

The makeshift gods of so many nations are made of wood and stone or steel and air waves. But the LORD God of the Scripture created the actual galaxies we are still discovering! So, you people in the know, make the Name of Yahweh, the LORD God whose world we inhabit, make the true God's Name known among the peoples of the world.

Then Psalm 96 turns the injunction to sing God a new song toward the very theme Jesus Christ spent his forty days on earth after the resurrection talking to his disciples about (Acts 1:4): the LORD rules! The splendid, even-handed Rule of the LORD is in force over the peoples and nations of the inhabited earth.

The Psalmist enjoins God's people to enter into the holy presence of God to worship the LORD with offerings: show everybody at large by your song and deeds, the dedication of your treasures—poetry, research, inventions—that you humbly bring to God; show to the people-who-do-not-know that this LORD, revealed in Jesus Christ, is One who blesses what is good, punishes what is evil, and saves what is lost.

Striking about Psalm 96 is its expectant temper. There are no second thoughts about how we are to rhyme evil like sickness, poverty, and death with the good LORD's loving Rule of all creatures. Psalm 96 was probably composed by the Asaph brothers for the most significant event in the history of David's kingship, bringing the wilderness tabernacle up to Jerusalem to turn the capital into "the city of God," Zion, where the LORD's justice would be done (cf. 1 Chronicles 16). Not the mean-spirited justice of, "Give me my pound of flesh," but the LORD God's amazing generous justice, which knows forgiveness.

That is something truly **new** in the world: forgiveness! You forgive somebody's debt, and they get a **new** start. It's like being rescued from drowning: you receive a **new** lease on life. Any redemptive deed is **new,** according to Psalm 96, because redeeming acts open up what was closed, renew what looks like failure. God's acts are always **new**—full of surprises, unexpected until they happen, and then utterly promising, because **God's deeds regenerate what is dying and** then **last forever.**

"You people, sing the LORD God a fresh new song!" That means: songs that never get old, songs that are expectant, insightful, vibrant, rather than frayed or soon worn out.

Puer natur est nobis. That **do-sol** birth announcement, "It's a boy!" introducing the Christmas morning mass is a new song, biblically speaking. Pachelbel's chaste canon, Luther's grace-note-beginning *"Ein feste Burg ist unser Gott,"* Bach's chorus, *"Wir setzen uns mit Tränen nieder... Ruhe sanfte! Sanfte Ruh,"* the Afro-American song, "Go, tell it on the mountain," are all **new songs**, because they are waiting for the Lord to come.

And the Church of Jesus Christ, unlike much of North American culture, realizes that history is not past—we are not post-anything—but like the future to come, what has historically happened is veritably present, percolating under our daily patterned lives. There is "nothing new under the sun" except that which God's Holy Spirit touches with the redemptive mark of everlasting joy and thanksgiving.

Such newness is God's gift and calling for anyone here who would be "redeeming the time," that is, singing, working, playing the organ, being wise for the next generation, permeated by the prospect of **Jesus Christ's coming again!**

"The LORD God **is** coming to get an accounting from the whole earth!" says Psalm 96. That's why the psalm concludes, almost like Romans 8:18–25, where all creatures are waiting for the redemption of us human bodies: "Let the heavens cheer up, let the earth be exultant, let the sea make its glossolaic noises, let the plants in the field be happy, because **a time is coming** when the trees of the wood shall shout out unpollutedly, joyfully with God's people before the LORD God who has come back to retore creation forever new."

Isaiah 61:1–4, 8–9, 11:
The most human of these is hope

The spirit of my Lord, Yahweh the Lord God, is on me   1
because the Lord God personally anointed me and sent me
to proclaim Good News to the poor
    [those who have been meekly humbled],
to bring healing for those whose heart is splintered in pieces.
[I am sent] to unbind those who are bound up, captive,
to holler out, "A year of Jubilee from the Lord God!"   2
    "A Day of Punishing Judgment from our God!"
so that all the people who have been
    weeping shall be comforted.

[The Lord God anointed me and sent me out]
to encourage the sorrowing ones in God's city   3
by replacing the ashes on their heads with colorful scarves,
by removing the mournfulness they have cloaked themselves with,
    [rubbing on] the sweet-smelling oil of celebration,
by changing the spirit of beaten-down despair to one of laughing
    hallelujah,
so that they might be called "sturdy oak trees of tried-and-true
    right-doing,"
    "a veritable planting of the Lord God,"
to let the Lord show God's munificent glory!

Then [the disheartened people of God]
    shall start rebuilding the ancient ruins;   4
they shall raise up again the things that were demolished;
they shall renew the ruined cities, the devastations
    left earlier by generation after generation. . . .

[You see] **I am Yahweh, the Lord God who loves**
    setting things straight,   8
who hates deception, crookedly taking things away from people;
I will most surely give the people what's coming to them faithfully.
I hereby establish with them a covenant that shall never end:
their children and children's children shall be specially known
    among the nations,   9
their descendants [shall have a place] right in the midst of the

> peoples [of the world].
> All who see them will recognize that, Yes!
> these are a line of children who are indeed blessed
> > by Yahweh the Lord God.
> . . . Yes, as surely as the earth lets its rich plant life shoot up
> > [fresh in the spring]   11
> and as a garden lets what is sown in it grow and thrive,
> so surely shall my Lord, the Lord God Yahweh, let what is true
> > right doing
> —what is a laughing hallelujah of praise—
> grow and thrive right in front of all the nations.

The Bible seems more a book for losers than for winners. God's written word brings hope not so much for "the haves" (cf. Matthew 19:13–30) as for "the have-nots." Paul told the unruly city-dwellers of Corinth that the Lord chooses those who are weak in the world to confuse and shame the strong-arm boys (1 Corinthians 1:26–29). And our Isaiah 61 has the prophet claim he was anointed by the Spirit of God to bring good news to those who have been brought low into hard times, and healing for those whose deepest desires have been shattered to bits.

The original circumstances for this passage is probably the return of God's people from Babylonian exile to the unprotected, broken-down ruins of their one-time splendid "holy city of God." Where do you start after two generations of neglect, plunder, and devastation? The overwhelming odds against giving your children a normal life again make you as older generation cry and despair.

But No, says the text, the Spirit of God enables me to comfort you who are hurting, to convert your mournfulness into colorful laughter, and to get you into rebuilding the city God gave you for showing the Lord's compassionate love to set things straight. Believe it or not, it is time for Jubilee! God's Day of Judgment for the godless, who are not expecting it (1 Thessalonians 5:1–11), is paired with the promise of jubilee for the Lord's weather-beaten refugee people—cessation of troubles, a new beginning, certainty of free time to play and sing.

Then the last verse does it again: Isaiah contexts the Lord's covenant for human redemption within the Lord's faithfulness to the earth. The Lord certifies by seedtime and harvest (cf. Genesis 8:21–22) that God's woebegone people shall indeed lift up their voices and sing, "Hallelujah!" before all the nations of the world.

Jesus Christ took this Isaiah 61 text, when he taught in the synagogue of his hometown Nazareth, as the mandate he had the mission to fulfill. Because Jesus intimated to his believing home-town audience that they were too affluent to be poor, too trim and fit to need broken-hearted healing, too sure of themselves to bear this ministry of Spirit-led rebuilding of God's people, and therefore as successful Nazarites were unfit for Isaiah's good news, they ran him out of town and tried to kill him (Luke 4:14–30).

For followers of the Christ who have become **new creatures**, as Paul puts it (2 Corinthians 5:17), who have been anointed by the Holy Spirit of wisdom to lead and comfort others, as the prophet Joel (2:28–29) and the apostle John (John 16:12–15, 1 John 2:20, 27) tell it: **the ministry of hope Isaiah 61 holds out** is a god-send for the grunt-time between when we were born and when Christ comes again. God's people are usually coming back from some Babylonian captivity or other of our own making. Sometimes we are just taken hostage by Fundamentalist infighting over doctrinal minutiae or mores, or are left adrift and depressed by sophisticated indifference in one's hometown congregation. When all is said and done, however, and the three matters that remain as earnest of the **new creation coming** (cf. Galatian 6:12–15) are faith, hope, and love: the most human of these is hope, because hope is the nerve of faith and love.

As we believers wait for the Lord to come back, in glory this time, that is, as we pray while we work (*ora et labore*) at rebuilding what pleases God in our neighborhoods during the week as well as at Sunday worship, anticipating the celebration of Jubilee and a fulfilling Judgment by the Covenantal Lord, we may take heart ourselves in the certainty of biblical hope, marked by the Lord as those who have been blessed to faithful gentleness by the Spirit of God.

You know that apocryphal story about Martin Luther, who was asked what he would do if Christ was coming back tomorrow: he said, "I'd plant a tree today." If Johann Sebastian Bach had been told Jesus Christ was coming tomorrow, I'm certain he would have said, "Choir rehearsal tonight!"

That's the laughing spirit of hope Isaiah 61 asks us to give away to the nations of the world—free organ recitals for the poor!—so that our music-making practice testifies to the truth that the meek who listen to **new song** and whose hearts sing along are already beginning to inherit the earth (Matthew 5:5).

Revelation 18:21–19:8:
Hip-hop millennial culture and Hallelujah!

And one strong angel picked up a rock,
    big as a millstone, and heaved it into the lake, saying: 21
That's the way—boom!—the great city of Babylon
    shall get the heave and never be found again.
The sound of guitarists and folk singers and flautists
    and trumpeters shall nevermore be heard   22
        in your city;
no artist, in any of the arts, shall be found
    any more in your (great) city.
The sound of the mill (stone grinding) shall be heard
    among you no more forever, and
the lamp light shall shine
    no more among you forever,
    and the voice of the bridegroom
    and the bride shall nevermore be heard among you   23
—your businessmen were the big shots of the earth!—
nevermore, because all the people were misled
    by your clever artistry.
They found blood too in that (city), Babylon,
    blood of prophets and saints   24
and all those (believers) who were
    butchered to death on the earth. . . ."

After that I heard something like the mighty sound
    of a huge crowd in heaven singing,   1
"Hallelujah! Shalom and glory and
    power belong to our God!
God's judgments are trustworthy and come through
    doing what is right: 2
God has judged the Master Harlot who polluted the
    earth with habitual immorality;
God has avenged the blood of God's servants
    taken by her hand."
Once more the multiple voices cried, "Hallelujah!
    Babylon's smoke goes up forever and ever!"   3

Then the 24 elders and the four living creatures

> fell down and worshiped God 4
> who was seated on the throne, and they were singing,
> > "Amen! Hallelujah!"
> And from near the throne came a voice chanting, 5
> "Praise our God, all you servants of God,
> you who stand in awe of God
> —the unimportant persons as well as the very important persons."
>
> Then I heard [again, says John,]
> > something like the sounds of a huge crowd, 6
> the rushing sound of many waters and
> > the sound of thunderclaps, speaking [as it were in tongues],
> **"Hallelujah! The Lord, our Almighty [*Pantocrator*] God rules!**
> **Let us rejoice and be exuberant—give glory to God,**
> **For the marriage of the Lamb has come!** 7
> The Lamb's bride has made herself ready—
> it was granted her to be dressed with fine linen,
> > bright and pure." 8
> [by 'linen' is meant the redemptive deeds of the saints]. . . .

Even a fragment from the last book of the Bible gives especially a church musician pause: instrumental music, massed choirs, and congregational song seem almost central to life lived before the throne of God. Also, musical artistry can apparently be lethal as well as life-giving.

The audio-visual aid the apostle John exiled on the island of Patmos was given, about what is coming on the final Day of Judgment and the Wedding Feast of the Lamb, is sobering as well as exhilarating. You can't have the happy consummation of a bright, pure linen-clad jubilee on the new earth without the eradication of evil culture symbolized by Babylon. A final celebration of the fullness of grace and a final extermination of sin go together in the Bible.

"Babylon" in Scripture is bad. Not the town on the south shore of Long Island, but the skyscraper Babel cultural center mentioned in Genesis 11, or the glittering city of Babylon Nebuchadnezzar built to show off his world empire-building power, are what "Babel," "Babylon," mean in the Bible: the ruthless, respectable centralization of artistic, cultural privilege and influence that at core is vanity—that's "Babylon."

A visitor might think there's a good candidate for a contemporary Babylon beginning fifty miles west of here—doesn't the whole world somehow dance to the tune of New York City (and Washington, D.C.)?

or envy the way of the American cinema industry, the level of monied technology, and unparalleled corporate financial authority located here?

But the term "Babylon" is as tricky as sin, because sometimes Scripture judges "Jerusalem"! the supposed city of God, to be the Master Harlot (cf. Isaiah 1:21–31, Malachi 3:1–5) that is misleading the nations by its self-indulgent, corrupt hypocrisy rather than practicing a radical ministry of redemptive, hope-giving culture. It would be as if the Church joined forces with the commercialization of human life: that would be "Babylon" too, where MONEY and entertainment, like an Ebola virus, kills the very faith fabric of consecrated deeds, converts lament and praise before God into a vaudeville sham, and spoils the tithe of charity into becoming simply a tax write-off.

—One must not use the book of Revelation as a Rorschach test to point fingers at your favorite malignancies (or to push your own millennial time-table [cf. Matthew 24:36]). Chapter 18:24 does say, though, that there will be the blood of prophets and saints in the grooves of the records sold in Babylon's marketplace. I understand that to cover both what happens to teenage catechumens enamored by gangsta rap **and** middle-aged adults buying CDs of saccharine hymns and pious "Precious Moment" mementoes. Commercialization of what lies at one's heart is no respecter of age or persons, and can murder in cold blood or drug you with sweetened poison gas.

I've wondered whether you members of the American Guild of Organists feel beleaguered in our hip-hop millennial culture blanketing the globe with its fervent rap theologies, mesmerizing rhythmic beat, and the color of *uhuru!* gone hedonistic, Inc. The apocalyptic temper of early rap, which germinated nearby here in the '70s Bronx, when good neighborhoods there were destroyed by the Cross Bronx Parkway, was a cry for justice! But the success of outcast anger was a cross-over product able to make millions of dollars for everybody, has had its insightful bite co-opted, I'm afraid, and sloughed off into the morass of amusing ourselves to death.

Revelation chapter 19 tells those who are guardians of earlier sounds like "Hallelujah!" and "Amen!" simply to keep on performing and composing music with that focus (as your chartering principles spell out)[1]:

---

1 "For the greater glory of God, and for the good of his Holy Church in this land, we, being severally members of the American Guild of Organists, do declare our mind and intention in the things following:

"We believe that the office of music in Christian Worship is a Sacred Oblation before the Most High."

"**Shalom and glory and power belong to *our God*!**" as the glossolalia of creation's rushing white water sounds and thunderclaps testify (vv. 1–2, 6). It's true, just as the hallelujahs tend to cluster toward the end of the Psalm book in the Bible (nos. 111–113, 117, 146–150) and punctuate the victory of those who have survived the blandishments of Babylon in the book of Revelation, praise must be seasoned with the struggles of the saints, or the "Amen!" rings hollow. And make certain, says our text, that seemingly unimportant persons—like children—as well as VIPs, learn to worship the LORD and the Lamb with songs that will last for generations, to keep the line of God's children connected.

As Church we live in the advent of Jesus Christ's coming again to complete God's covenantal Rule with the historical earth. We know from the book of Revelation that at that time the refined treasures of the rulers of the earth shall also come to be at our disposal (Revelation 21:22–27)— and there are certain to be surprises at the music and song God considers worthy to be saved. But the new earth will not be just one long pipe organ worship service or concert with Western civilization repertoire. Drums and David's acoustic guitar will be on hand to lead the dances of the redeemed too. Diversity need not threaten but can express enriched communion of the saints.

So, we should not let the numerical medallion of 2000 constantly dangled before our faces hypnotize us into buying its passing moment as something important. Instead, following Psalm 96, Isaiah 61, and Revelation 18–19, let us live expectantly for Christ's unexpected! coming by being faithful, thankful, Holy Spirit-filled priestly children of God whose music, voices, and song—tears mixed through the joy—provide hope for the world, and carry the redemptive texture of fine linen so God's people will be clothed for the marriage feast coming.

". . . We believe that at all times and in all places it is meet, right, and our bounden duty to work and to pray for the advancement of Christian Worship in the holy gifts of strength and nobleness; to the end that the Church may be purged of her blemishes, that the minds of men and women may be instructed, that the honor of God's House may be guarded in our time and in the time to come."

"Wherefore we do give ourselves with reverence and humility to these endeavors, offering up our works and our persons, in the Name of him, without whom nothing is strong, nothing is holy. Amen."

(The American Guild of Organists is a professional organization of organists and choirmasters from diverse denominations. It was founded in 1896 largely through the efforts of Gerrit Smith [1859–1912], organist-choirmaster of the South [Dutch Reformed] Church of New York.)

PAIN IS A FOUR-LETTER WORD:
A CONGREGATIONAL LAMENT

Soon after September 11, 2001, I received requests from various congregations throughout the United States for permission to sing from "A Congregational Lament" in worship services (supra pp. 58–59). They needed a song to fit the evil besetting them. They wanted to mourn the terrible loss of life and to cry out to God for the Lord to lessen their pain somehow in what seemed so brutally destructive. As believers they wanted to sing a sad song of faith that did not pretend in Stoic fashion to take on the chin whatever happens.

They wanted a lament that would voice exasperation with what had occurred in God's world on their doorstep, while still trusting that the Lord would come through.

A Lament Born Out of Experience

The text of "A Congregational Lament" was born out of experience. As an elder in our communion who visits members of the congregation regularly in their homes to inquire respectfully about the health of the family faith-life and to encourage a deepening rather than a thinning out of their Christian confession—as an elder I knew that the glad Sunday morning worship service of well-dressed propriety and order can be deceptive.

Were the truth told, the gathering might be more like a meeting in the emergency room of a hospital. But how can we openly express our private pain in a public liturgical setting?

- A member of our local congregation is sent to jail. Can we sing about that together without exonerating or being judgmental (st. 2)?
- One of our congregational youth is struck with MS. How can we

---

First published in *Reformed Worship* 72 (2004): 6–7. Reprinted with permission © Faith Alive Christian Resources.

lift up our dismay to the Lord with psalmodic upsetness (st. 3)?
- A daughter of the church undergoes a divorce. Instead of gossiping or taking sides, we believers must lament the waste (st. 4).
- A young mother is killed in an automobile accident by a drunken driver; she leaves behind three little children and a husband. That should not happen in God's world! So we need to reach deep down into our faith and remonstrate with God about it (st. 5)—that is the nature of a believing Job-like lament.

A Tune Strong Enough to Carry Heavy Lament
The text was conceived in the womb of the Genevan melody for Psalm 51. Its Phrygian modal tone (think of a scale from E to E rather than from C to C) embraces human sorrow in its long lines of regularly mixed 10 11 11 10 10 11 10 11 syllables in a way that common meter (iambic tetrameter and trimeter) cannot match. Claude Goudimel's open fifth harmonics ending the second, third, and fourth phrases evoke the empty-stomach feeling that the text speaks. And the C$^\sharp$ following an open A minor chord stings your ear instead of sounding major. The mournful melody is perfectly honed to the excruciating confession of David in Psalm 51: "O God, blot out all my violent sins! Don't take your Holy Spirit away from me (as you did to Saul)!" The Genevan 51 melody is wedded to crises and to facing inexplicable evil in faith.

Some may object, "But the melody is difficult and unfamiliar. Our praise team wants something more upbeat. And there are no guitar chords. . . ."

My pastoral reply would be, "September 11 was certainly not simple, and it deserves a complex response.

Its horrific terror may become gradually more familiar to us in North America. Maybe the congregation needs a trained 'lament team' too, for when the hard times come. Often the best way to pray to God naked in the ash heap is without instruments. Let your choir or a strong voice lead the congregation in a haunting a cappella unison voicing of this bare lament so your sorrow has the silence to breathe."

How to familiarize your congregation with an infrequently used lament tune takes a little imaginative planning. One way a music director could teach the wonderful sadness of Genevan 51 with its underlying tincture of certain hope, to be ready for crises, is to use the melody occasionally in the weekly service of confession and assurance. Stanzas 1–3 of Stanley Wiersma's fine versification of Psalm 51, "Be Merciful, Be Merciful, O God" (*Psalter Hymnal* 51), are primed for a heartfelt pleading

[#29] Henk (Senggih) Krijger, *"I will not let thee go except thou bless me,"* 1972

repentance asking for forgiveness of the *Agnus Dei*. Once a congregation has a rich melody embedded in its consciousness, it functions like a reference book in one's library: you may pull it out only on occasion, but its rich treasury is familiarly there when you need it.

On September 11, 2001, the world did not change. Instead, America joined the world. If we North American believing congregations want songs to match our faith to the terrible sorrows of our neighbors, we could do worse than learn the laments of the psalms sung to melodies with Genevan grit, and keep them on reserve in our library of congregational song. If our hymns be only uncomplicated and thin, we may lack the seasoned, expectant, and wounded, robust faith it takes to wrestle with God for a blessing in our fearful day (cf. Genesis 32:22–32) [#29].

It is possible a given congregation needs to be weaned from its comfortable tunes and choruses to sing the tough stuff by learning to give voice to "the hard Psalms." One could practice by living into the singing of Psalms 39, 69, 130, and 141 as steps toward learning the grit for singing "A Congregational Lament." It would be good for us to be found faithful also in the range of our repertoire for singing to God when the Lord returns (cf. Luke 18:1-8).

Proverbs 10:1–22: From Poetic Paragraphs to Preaching

As a Christ-believing amateur in scholarship on the book of Proverbs, I have been protected from much wrong-headed professional study in "wisdom literature" because I naively took seriously the canonic shape in which Proverbs has been accepted by the church. As a great-grandchild of the historic Reformation, my Bible reading is one that assumes "the Bible be read as sacred Scripture." This we do in the communion of the saints, living and dead, carefully trusting the text will lead the community of faith enough to find definite direction in "the entire manner of service which God requires of us."[1]

Such a trusting experience is crankled by practically all Proverbs commentators—from the higher critical Crawford H. Toy (1899) to the more recent Protestant evangelical Derek Kidner (1964).[2] They treat the text like a collection of individual sayings, loose from any defined context—a kind of anthology of nuggets of wisdom arranged in apparently random fashion for our benefit and admonition. The assumed contextlessness of the sayings collected in Proverbs 10–29, however, easily makes their interpretation arbitrary, truistic, or opaque (not exactly a fertile source for a twenty-minute Sunday sermon that would bring Bible-exposited Good News).

A brief history of exegesis

The background to this state of affairs is fairly well-known. In 1924,

---

1 *Belgic Confession,* articles 2–7; cf. Brevard S. Childs, *Introduction to the Old Testament as Scripture* (Philadelphia: Fortress, 1979), 27–106.

2 Crawford H. Toy, *A Critical and Exegetical Commentary on the Book of Proverbs* (Edinburgh: T. & T. Clark, 1899); Derek Kidner, *Proverbs* (Downers Grove: InterVarsity, 1964).

First published in *Reading and Hearing the Word from Text to Sermon: Essays in honor of John H. Stek,* ed. Arie C. Leder (Grand Rapids: Calvin Theological Seminary and CRC Publications, 1998), 181–200.

Adolf Erman claimed that Proverbs 22:17–23:11 was derived from the Egyptian instruction of Amenemope. Later, Johannes Fichtner argued that biblical wisdom was derived from the ancient Near Eastern eudemonistic teachings that the Hebrews gradually nationalized with Yahwist references.[3] Subsequently, scholars sought to track these refinements, which they claimed moved from teaching a mundane "folk" wisdom, to the more acceptable, pious "theological wisdom."

The influential result was William McKane's decanonization of proverb sentences into three groups: advice for living a successful life, admonitions against harmful deeds to society, and Yahweh God-talk.[4]

As late as 1979, R.N. Whybray suffered the same geneticistic approach and kept reading Proverbs as an attempt by a Yahwist editor to be "bringing 'secular' wisdom under the umbrella of Yahwism."[5] Claus Westermann still holds to the presence of unresolved opposites of "profane" and "isolated propositions about God" in Proverbs, even though he admits that this has kept biblical wisdom from playing a central role in the proclamation of the church.[6]

Udo Skladny set the record straight, as I see it. He argues that the earliest original calling of biblical proverbial wisdom is for people to respect and follow the Lord's order for everyday life, which is first of all ordering to be trusted ("*eine geglaubte Ordnung*") and obeyed truly as the Lord God's will, full of blessing.[7] Likewise, Zimmerli affirmed that "wis-

---

[3] J. Fichtner, *Die altorientalische Weisheit in ihrer Israelitisch-Jüdische Ausprägung* (Giessen: Töpelmann, 1933).

[4] William McKane, *Proverbs* (Philadelphia: Westminster, 1970), 10–13, 415.

[5] R. N. Whybray, "Yahweh-sayings and Their Contexts in Proverbs 10, 1–22, 16" [1979] in *La sagesse de l'ancient testament,* ed. Maurice Gilbert (Leuven: Leuven University Press, 1990), 162. Later on he writes, "it would seem we have to acknowledge three stages: a) a morally 'neutral' attitude ('old wisdom'); b) a moral attitude which expresses itself in terms of an immanent force making for just reward; c) a recognition that this just reward is not simply immanent but directly due to the personal will of Yahweh" (165). In a later work (*Wealth and Poverty in the Book of Proverbs* [Sheffield: Sheffield Press, 1990], 68, n. 1) Whybray modifies his earlier formulation: "I should no longer use the term 'secular.' . . . The 'Yahweh-proverbs' may be said to represent a theological development in so far that they reflect a tendency to *clarify* Yahweh's involvement in all that happens; but—contrary to a widely held view—there is in my opinion no reason to suppose that the absence of reference to Yahweh in the majority of these proverbs necessarily implies a lack of recognition of that involvement."

[6] Claus Westermann, *Forschungsgeschichte zur Weisheitsliteratur* 1950–1990 (Stuttgart: Calwer Verlag, 1991), 46–47.

[7] Udo Skladny, *Die ältesten Spruchsammlungen in Israel* (Göttingen: Vandenhoeck & Ruprecht, 1962), 89–91.

dom theology is Creation theology."⁸ It is a false start to pit secular proverbs against sacred proverb glosses and to spend time guessing at probable stages of compositional genealogy. Such a split orientation fosters treating Old Testament "wisdom" as a topic foreign to "salvation history."⁹

The purported derivative nature of biblical wisdom sayings, culturally dependent upon comparable Egyptian and Mesopotamian "wisdom," is no longer considered compelling today by various specialists.[10] But McKane's wrenching apart of what is canonically given operates as a smokescreen that leaves exegetes uncertain as to what is actually given for us to read in the booked Proverbs. This is especially true in the contemporary atmosphere of wanting "living proverbs" fit for quick reading in the fast lane.

The effort to center the discussion of the proverb on its presumed oral folk wisdom origins also pushed scholarship in the wrong direction.[11] Through this approach the booked Proverbs (especially those in Proverbs 10–24) came to be considered an anthology of atomistic *logia* treating a miscellany of topics arranged at most by catchwords (Boström's paronomasia) or grouped loosely around similar themes. Perhaps Proverbs 25–29 signals a firm move from oral to "transcribed" proverbs (25:1), that is,

---

8   Walther Zimmerli, "Ort und Grenze der Weisheit im Rahmen der alttestamentlichen Theologie," in *Gottes Offenbarung. Gesammelte Aufsätze zum Alten Testament* (München: Chr. Kaiser Verlag, 1963), 302. This essay is translated as "The Place and Limit of the Wisdom in the Framework of the Old Testament Theology," in *Studies in Ancient Israelite Wisdom*, ed. James L. Crenshaw (New York: KTAV Publishing House, 1976), 314–326.

9   That is, as the biblical story of the exodus to the promised land. Patrick Skehan (*Studies in Israelite Poetry and Wisdom* [Washington: Catholic Biblical Association of America, 1971], 23) argues that "to ascribe a primitively 'secular' character to the origins of any phase of human life in ancient times, in or out of Israel, is to go against all that we know of ancient man. . . . The 'secular' basis for the supposition is altogether gratuitous in afflicting some unidentifiable group of ancient sages with the misfortunes of the modern agnostics." Childs (*Introduction to the Old Testament as Scripture*, 553) writes, "As sacred scripture the book [of Proverbs] was not to be read according to a history of development in the concept of wisdom, rather from a fully developed confessional standpoint."

10 The Egyptologists K. A. Kitchen, "Proverbs and Wisdom Books of the Ancient Near East: The factual history of a literary form," *Tyndale Bulletin* 28 (1977): 69–114; "Egypt and Israel during the First Millennium B.C.," *Vetus Testamentum Supplement* 40 (1986): 107–23; Jutta Krispenz, *Spruchcomposition im Buch Proverbia* (Bern: Peter Lang, 1989); John Ruffle, "The Teaching of Amenemope and its Connection with the Book of Proverbs," *Tyndale Bulletin* 28 (1977): 29–68.

11 See, for example, the work of Otto Eissfeldt, *Der Maschal im Alten Testament* (Giessen: Alfred Töpelmann, 1913).

literary deposits by education court scribes.¹² But the presumption that the book of Proverbs is a largely unedited compilation of now contextless oral one-liners continues to dominate wisdom scholarship.¹³

Recently, however, this atomistic approach has been questioned by a qualified and tentative attempt to find unifying edited contextuality within the Proverbs text, a *Sitz in Text*.¹⁴ Already in 1968, Hermission carefully treated the sayings of Proverbs 10–15 with considerable cohesion, paying particular attention to how their aesthetic quality intimated a connecting order.¹⁵ In 1988, Van Leeuwen argued: "If the text presents us with larger, unified blocks of proverbial material, the exegete possesses a much surer basis for interpretation than if only a random accretion of isolated proverbs exists."¹⁶

That is precisely the thesis of this article, which is dedicated in thanks to John Stek. He has always served Christ's body with his Old Testament scholarship, dedicating an incredible amount of his lifetime to carefully annotated translation (NIV study edition) of the Bible, and giving insightful lectures and valuable syllabi on Old Testament books to theological students at Calvin Seminary, in Toronto, and elsewhere over many years.

I state my thesis as follows:

> Expect poetic paragraphs within the booked Proverbs 10–29, because the artful comparisons (מְשָׁלִים) and oblique riddles (חִידֹת) are rooted historically and professionally in the office of wise leaders recounted in the Bible and have been written down by God-breathed educated literary scribes.

---

12 So R. B. Y. Scott, "Solomon and the Beginnings of Wisdom in Israel," *Festschrift for Harold Henry Rowley. Supplement to Vetus Testamentum III*, eds. M. Noth and D. Winton Thomas (Leiden: Brill, 1960), 272–274.

13 McKane (*Proverbs*, 414) and Westermann (*Forschungsgeschichte*, 46) assert that didactic instruction like Proverbs 1–9, the longer and later artistically worked pieces, has a tradition separate from the original popular aphoristic tradition.

14 Brian Watson Kovacs (*Sociological-structural Constraints upon Wisdom: The spatial and temporal matrix of Proverbs 15:28–22:16* [Dissertation Vanderbilt University, 1978], 308) writes, "the catchword and paronomastic patterns which connect various proverbs simply cannot be adventitious nor accidental. Groupings of sayings must be accounted for, along with disruptions and incursions into the text." See also Raymond C. Van Leeuwen, *Context and Meaning in Proverbs 25–27* (Atlanta: Scholars Press, 1988), 37, and Duane A. Garrett, *Proverbs, Ecclesiastes, Song of Songs. The New American Commentary* (Nashville: The Broadman Press, 1993). In a series of articles in *Vanguard* (1972–1979), I exposited Proverbs 25–29 as an anthology of gnomic poems.

15 Hans-Jürgen Hermission, *Studien zur israelitischen Spruchweisheit* (Neukirchener Verlag, 1968), 180–181.

16 Van Leeuwen, *Context and Meaning in Proverbs 25–27*, 6.

Finding the poetic parameters in Proverbs 10–29 so as to discern the unified paragraphs[17] will open up the book of sayings for good preaching.

Context and Task

Before demonstrating this thesis with Proverbs 10:1–22, I will sketch the historical and literary setting, and then present evidence that "the wise" men and women in Israel had a special task and way of presenting a word from the Lord to God's people. These matters are critical for a proper reading of the booked proverbs.

The Literary Setting

Since the superscriptions of Proverbs 1:1, 10:1, and 25:1 suggest c. 950–700 BC[18] to be the historical parameters for the bulk of the written material, then Proverbs should address not nomads but settled city dwellers who were becoming fairly prosperous and secularized. There was a strong farming community at the time, but the younger generation was leaving the countryside to make its fortune in Jerusalem, where the building of the temple and the royal palace were causing a construction boom. Along with the extremely high inflation rate caused by Solomon's enormous deficit financing (1 Kings 9–10, esp. 9:10–14, 10:27), the labor force's shift from herding sheep to city work upset a traditional lifestyle and the accompanying faith-commitment. Freedom from parental control and moving outside the country confines of cultic worship and rituals of sacrifice also increased the importance of education for the next generation.

These dates for Proverbs also cover Ahab and Jezebel's appropriation of Naboth's familial homestead and Jehu's subsequent rough-and-ready retribution (1 Kings 21, 2 Kings 9). The prophets Elijah, Amos, Isaiah, and Micah proclaimed God's justice during the generations when the wise sayings and admonitions would be particularly relevant. And good kings like Hezekiah needed to train young scribes and princes to carry out godly civil administration in the outlying districts of Judah away from the courtly precincts, where judgments in civic disputes would be given orally.

It took Christa Kayatz's 1966 dissertation[19] under Gerhard von Rad

---

17 It may be useful to think of something like the various Psalms (although in Proverbs the poetic paragraphs are epigrammatic poems for speaking, not songs for singing).

18 This dating is also supported by Kitchen on external historical-literary grounds. Cf. Kitchen, "Proverbs and Wisdom Books," 102, 108–110, and "Egypt and Israel," 119–23.

19 Christa Kayatz, *Studien zu Proverbien 1–9. Eine form- und motivgeschichtliche Untersuchung unter Einbeziehung ägyptischen Vergleichsmaterials* (Neukirchen-Vluyn: Neu-

to overturn earlier authorities' (e.g., Eissfeldt, Kittel, Sellin, Gressmann) post-exilic dating of Proverbs 1–9. She argued that Proverb's 1–9's familiarity with ancient Egyptian wisdom literature undermines the hypothesis that later Hellenistic sources account for biblical motifs present.[20] With Childs,[21] I hold that the Masoretic text version the church has come to live with leads it to read Proverbs 10–29 in the light of Proverbs 1–9. So the artistically nuanced Proverbs 1–9 provides a clue to the poetic compositional character of chapters 10–29, since that is the way "the wise" formulated God's word.

If Proverbs 1–9, like Proverbs 31:10–31, exemplifies the kind of poetic paragraphs booked by "the wise," then Proverbs 1–9 not only provides, as Van Leeuwen writes, "a worldview and hermeneutic introduction to the short sayings and admonitions which follow,"[22] but also suggests the poetic format normal for biblical proverbial literature. The prevalent notion that "each proverb is an independent unit that can stand alone and still have meaning," and that "textual context is not essential for interpretation," is wrong, and invites a myopic reading of Proverbs. Garrett significantly adds, "Context, however, sometimes qualifies or gives a more precise meaning to a given proverb."[23] But even Garrett's attempt to "collect" proverbs into groups needs, I think, to be driven more radically by the realization that what we have here first of all are poetic paragraphs. In poetry the chicken comes before the egg—the paragraph whole determines the sense of the separate lines. One must accept that literary critical point in order to read and exhort from the booked Proverbs in a way that "plows the word of truth rightly" (2 Timothy 2:14–19).

The Historical Setting:
The Place and Task of Wise Counselors in Israel

Leadership in Israel: Priests, Prophets, and Kings
After God covenanted with Israel at Mount Sinai, Moses ordained Aaron and his sons to care for the tabernacle and the ark (Leviticus 8). They were

---

kirchener Verlag, 1966).

20 Roland E. Murphy ("Assumptions and Problems in Old Testament Wisdom Research," *Catholic Biblical Quarterly* 29 [1976]: 413) still maintained, "It is generally agreed that Prv 1–9 is a later addition and introduction to pre-exilic collections of wisdom sayings." Westermann (*Forschungsgeschichte*, 46) also still thinks Proverbs 1–9 is late. These earlier traditions of thinking about Proverbs die hard.

21 Childs, *Introduction to the Old Testament as Scripture*, 552–555.

22 Raymond C. Van Leeuwen, "In Praise of Proverbs," in *Pledges of Jubilee*, eds. Lambert Zuidervaart and Henry Luttikhuizen (Grand Rapids: Eerdmans, 1995), 313, n. 12.

23 Garrett, *Proverbs, Ecclesiastes, Song of Songs*, 46.

in charge of sacrifices for propitiation and for thanksgiving to offset the people's sin, they gave liturgical leadership, and they were set aside for the important protocol of moving the ark (Numbers 10:33–36). Levites were officially consecrated to assist in such priestly tasks in Israel (Numbers 1:47–54; 3:5–13).[24] After Joshua's death, the regularly ordained priests of Aaron and Eleazer's line tended the ark at Bethel (Judges 20:24–28), but do-it-yourself priesthoods during the days of Israel's judges (Judges 17) showed how Israel's priesthood could deteriorate to the nadir of the abusive sons of Eli, and end shamefully with Ichabod (1 Samuel 2:12–17, 22–25; 4:1–22).

The angel of the Lord (מַלְאַךְ יהוה) had brought crucial messages from God since the olden days—to Hagar (Genesis 16:7–16), to Abraham about to sacrifice Isaac (Genesis 22:9–19), to Moses at the burning bush (Exodus 3:1–4:17), to Balaam and his ass (Numbers 22:21–25), to Gideon (Judges 6:7–10), and to Samson's prospective parents (Judges 13). The prophet Samuel was trained by the old priest Eli during a time when the Lord God, says scripture, was not speaking much to Israel, and when revelatory visions were infrequent (1 Samuel 3:1). The Bible tells of an unnamed seer in Gideon's day who already used the typically prophetic phrase "Thus says the Lord" (כה אמר יהוה) (Judges 6:7–10). Such speaking is what prophets were supposed to do, and that's what judge-prophet Samuel did when he anointed Saul to be the first king of Israel, saying, "I'll sound out to you the word of God" (1 Samuel 9:27). By the time of Elijah, Ahab, Elisha, and Jehoshaphat, there were schools for prophets in Bethel and Jericho (2 Kings 2:1–3, 15–18). When Amaziah, high priest of corrupt King Jeroboam II, labeled Amos "a visionary" (חֹזֶה), Amos was glad to tell him that he had not been to any such school, but to "Hear the Word of the Lord!" (שמע דבר־יהוה) anyhow (Amos 7:10–17).

The kings of Israel were anointed to rule and protect God's people, particularly to administer justice (Deuteronomy 17:14–20; 1 Samuel 8). There seems to be a sorting out of leadership tasks among Israel's first kings. King Saul—anointed one of the Lord (מְשִׁיחַ יהוה)—made sacrifices in Gilgal when Samuel was late, and lost his kingship because they were disobedient sacrifices (1 Samuel 13:2–15; 15:22–23). David tended burnt offerings and peace offerings before the Lord when he brought the ark to Jerusalem to centralize his tribal administration in Jerusalem, the city of God. His priestly dancing pleased the Lord, if not Michal (2 Samuel 6). Young King Solomon sacrificed in Gibeon (1 Kings 3:1–15) and

---

24 As artisans, for example, the charismatic Bezaleel from Judah, and Oholiab from Dan had crucial roles in the construction of the Tent of Meeting (Exodus 35:30–39:43).

later offered a long priestly prayer with untold offerings at the dedication of the new temple (1 Kings 8) without punishment for mixing priestly duties with his royal tasks. King Solomon also exemplified the wisdom of God, with an encyclopedic horticultural and animal knowledge and the ability to ferret out the truth needed for making just judgments (1 Kings 3:16–28; 4:29–34).

So leaders among God's people were anointed to be priests, prophets, and kings. These posts of trust were quite differentiated, even though historical overlapping of duties existed on into the early monarchy. What needs attention, however, if we are to understand the booked Proverbs, is the fact that there emerged a loosely differentiated group of "counselors" (יָעַץ) of the Lord, distinct from mediating priests of the Lord in Israel, from oracular prophets of the Lord in Israel, and from the Lord's kings in Israel. They made professional in Israel the kind of guiding, teaching leadership practiced by Moses, the village elders at the gates, and the charismatic tribal judges. These "wise" persons, who served as a core of special advisers to royalty, held a definite office as normal and highly valued in the court of Israel as in the courts of surrounding countries.

Leadership in Israel: The Wise
When Pharaoh's counselors failed to interpret God-sent dreams, the wise-man Joseph because Pharaoh's secretary of state. Scripture reports Pharaoh saying, "This is a man in whom is the Spirit of God; nobody sees through things as you do" (Genesis 41, esp. vv. 7–8, 38–40). Moses was also trained in Egyptian wisdom (Acts 7:17–29; Hebrews 11:23–28; cf. Exodus 2:1–15). That Moses was a highly literate commander-in-chief of God's folk wandering through the desert is evident from the elaborate memorial songs he composed (Exodus 15:1–18, Deuteronomy 32:1–47) and the poetic benedictions recorded in his name (Deuteronomy 33). Balaam, son of Beor at Pethor on the Euphrates, was Balak's highest paid "consultant" or "wise man" (Micah 6:5). King Balak needed advice on dealing with the horde of Israelites camped on his borders. After missing out on the honors Balak had offered him, Balaam proved his credentials as an evil "wise man" (cf. James 3:13–18) by later providing the elders of Midian with an intermarriage policy that would break the Lord's favor upon Israel (Numbers 25; 31:1–20).

Such counselors of royalty—like the princesses (wise women, חֲכָמוֹת) attending General Sisera's mother (Judges 5:29)—held humble positions early among the Lord God's people. To help him rule the unwieldy multitude of Israelites, Moses appointed "wise men, insightful, seasoned persons" selected by the various tribes to head up the civil order and to judge disputes without playing favorites (Deuteronomy 1:9–18; cf. Exodus 18:13–27). The tasks of these "wise ones" was allied with ruling; they did not make laws, but they had important judicial responsibilities.

That there was still a definite place for "the wise" to give counsel in Israel during King Saul's day is clear. It was reported that the Lord was no longer answering King Saul's prayer for direction, either by the Urim (used by the priests for making important decisions—Exodus 28:30, Leviticus 8:5–9, Ezra 2:59–63), or by prophetic seers, or by dreams (the peculiar interpretive task of "the wise," 1 Samuel 28:6). During King David's reign, the established practice of "wise women" in the countryside is matter-of-factly told. Joab requisitioned "a wise women" from Tekoa—Amos's hometown—to act out a kind of morality playlet designed to give the pining David a rationale for recalling his murderer son Absalom (2 Samuel 14:1–24). It was in the office of "wise woman" that a leading woman in the city of Abel debated with General Joab and then convinced her townspeople to throw the head of Benjamite insurrectionist Sheba over the wall to save the town's inhabitants (2 Samuel 20:1–22).

The seer Nathan was King David's confidante. His story of the one little ewe lamb (2 Samuel 11:26–12:15) is a characteristic way for "the wise" to bring fools to their senses, and to give suggestive, persuasive advice to those in power. With considerable eloquence, Nathan got the dying King David to let him and Zadok the priest quickly anoint the boy Solomon to be king to foil Adonijah's bid for the throne (1 Kings 1). This consummate story-telling, roundabout, deferential, yet surprising way to bring God's specific direction to bear on life problems stamps the activity of "the wise." The crucial role Hushai and Ahithophel played at the court of David and at the headquarters of renegade Absalom is comparable to the role of the "wise women" mentioned above. Counsel was highly prized in Israel. "In those days the counsel (עֵצָה) that Ahithophel delivered was as if one consulted the very word of God" (2 Samuel 16:23).

Even King Solomon's prodigious wisdom was backed up by ranks of courtly counselors. They outlived Solomon's apostasy and death and saw their good counsel dismissed by Solomon's son Rehoboam when he formed a new cabinet of more modern "wise men," who led him to speak in a harsh spirit to the people seeking redress (1 Kings 12:1–20). This overturning of good counsel by poisoning advice (עֵצָה), with historic results of a split from David's line, was overseen by the Lord, says Scripture (1 Kings 12:15).

By the time of the God-fearing Hezekiah, the composition of

a courtly council with wise counselors included figures like Shebna, a scribe or secretary, and Joah Asaphson, an historian or record keeper. They knew Aramaic, the international language of diplomacy, and entered into high-level negotiations of royal decisions (2 Kings 18:1–19:7). So "the men of Hezekiah, King of Judah," who were given the precious task of "transcribing" the artful comparisons of Solomon (מִשְׁלֵי שְׁלֹמֹה, Proverbs 25:1), were not underpaid copyists. They were educated, cultured wise men concerned with editing a canon for instructing the inexperienced and for providing "the wise" with disciplined training for setting their consciousness in awe of the Lord.[25]

Even in the run-down court of King Jehoiakim there were polyglot wise men like Daniel, Hananiah, Mishael, and Azariah. When they were taken to the palace of Babylonian Nebuchadnezzar, Daniel and his wise friends proved to be better than any of the Chaldean sorcerers, astrologers, wiseman counselors, and interpreters of dreams, because God's Spirit revealed to Daniel mysteries and made him and his God-fearing friends wise (Daniel 1:1–2:30, esp. 1:4; 2:27–28; 5:10–12).

R. N. Whybray argues for an intellectual tradition in ancient Israel that is "distinct from other traditionalists such as the historical, legal, cultic and prophetic." At the same time he maintains that there is no societal institution carrying this tradition, no school, "no special professional class."[26]

I find the term "intellectual" too disengaged from the determinative faith orientation that was present from the very beginnings of Israel's leadership, even in Abraham's exodus-response to the Lord (Genesis 12:1–9). It is also problematic to over-define terms like "counselor," "teacher," "wise man," and "scribe," as if each excludes the other. Gerhard von Rad, for example, has argued that the biblical words "discipline" (מוּסָר), "discernment" (בִּין), "insightful action" (שֵׂכֶל) "circumspection" (עָרְמָה), and "handiness in knowing what's up" (לֶקַח) are differentiated from the other, but that these differences overlap within the family of "wisdom."[27] Moreover "wisdom" in the Old Testament is not a matter of having a "superior degree of (personal) intelligence,"[28] but of "knowing what God wants done." God can give such "understanding" to the for-

---

25 The word "counsel" (תַּחְבֻּלוֹת) in Proverbs 1:5, reminds one of the phrase "instruction of the Lord" (νουθεσίᾳ κυρίου) in Ephesians 6:4.

26 R. N. Whybray, *The Intellectual Tradition in the Old Testament* (Berlin: Walter de Gruyter, 1974), 70, 49.

27 Gerhard von Rad, *Wisdom in Israel*, trans. James D. Martin (London: SCM Press, 1972), 13.

28 Whybray, *The Intellectual Tradition in the Old Testament*, 9, 117.

eign soothsayer Balaam, just as he can call the unbelieving Persian Cyrus messiah (מָשִׁיחַ) among the nations (Isaiah 44:23–45:8).

I have shown how the calling to be "wise" is at home both in the tribal society Moses organized and in the precincts of Solomon's extravagant royalty. "Wise men" and "wise women" exercised a leadership among God's folk that was variegated, fluid, but constant, with certain features that identified its practice as "counsel" (עֵצָה). Differentiation of "the wise" had become commonplace by the time the prophet Jeremiah's adversaries spoke their oath to do him in, when they said, "Come, let's make plans against Jeremiah, as surely as a priest is never without law-guidance (תּוֹרָה), wise man without counsel (עֵצָה), and prophetic seer without the word (דָּבָר)" (Jeremiah 18:18).

After the exile in the day of Ezra and Nehemiah, when kings had forfeited their office among the people of God, the wise men and scribes came to the fore. Ezra was known to Artaxerxes as "priest, scribal scholar in the worded precepts of Yahweh and the ordinances for Israel" (Ezra 7:11). Indeed, that is what scribes in Israel became—Torah specialists. And it needs to be said that when the charisma of wisdom died because there was no vision among God's people, and when "the wise" began to trust their proverbs more than "standing in awe before the Lord God," when these leaders began to put stock in the Abrahamic blood rather than in obeying Yahweh's will, then we see "wise men" like Job's friends and like the scribes of Jesus' day, whether orthodox Pharisee or heterodox Sadducee.

Qoheleth[29] was one of the "wise" teachers in post-exilic Israel who was trained to lead the people in a back-and-forth, speaker-assembly, communal-probing way to determine the right direction to take. Qoheleth is a counselor and folk leader.[30] He speaks words of wisdom, makes artful comparisons, tells riddles and stories to help keep them on the Way of what is right in the eyes of God.

The Imaginative "Yes, but" Pedagogy of "the Wise," and the Literary Configuration of Proverbs 1–9

If you hear Scripture as a true story, as I do, you are startled and impressed by the way young King Solomon distributed the wisdom of God's justice when he told his courtiers to cut a child in half to determine which harlot

---

29 The title of the book Ecclesiastes/Qoheleth designates the official speaker to the people assembled (קָהָל) for a special occasion.

30 This is why in his day Luther translated the title Ecclesiastes/Qoheleth as *Prediger*, that is, "preacher."

was the mother (1 Kings 3:16–28). If such a dramatic ploy was part and parcel of "wisdom" in that day, the contests Solomon held with Egyptian and Babylonian wise men (remember Moses and Aaron's test before Pharaoh's wise men, Exodus 7:8–13)[31] were imaginative, live-wire contests to show wisdom on an international scale (1 Kings 4:29–34).

In fact, Solomon's quasi-dramatic way of bringing God's Word so vividly to bear on life's problems is the very way "the wise" we have discussed above were trained to lead the people in God's directives. I call this parry-and-thrust, parable-telling, decoy method of making a point, the "Yes, but" way of teaching God's will.

This "Yes, but" methodology permeates the artistic literary configuration in the canonically booked section of Proverbs 1–9. There are cohering "my child/my student" (בְּנִי) paragraphs that spin out variations on the central theme, which resonates everywhere:

> To stand still, listening before the Lord God Yahweh gives you a head start in full-bodied knowledge, in wisdom and corrective discipline—exactly what fools despise. (1:7)

These בְּנִי paragraphs sport vivid quotations of tempters (1:11–14; 7:14–20) and provocative alliterative epigrams (1:17; 6:26–28). In counterpoint to these paragraphs, there are stirring appeals by Wisdom in the first person, appealing to the inexperienced to follow the ordinances of Yahweh (1:20–33; 8:1–21). Hymns about Wisdom also highlight the authority, power, and glory of living as children of Wisdom (3:13–20; 8:22–31). These poetic passages act like antiphonal recitations, heightening the one basic thrust of the whole book: live straightforwardly before the Lord, knowing what counts in all kinds of daily life matters.

And there are specially pregnant, capsule summations of the double-edged message permeating the בְּנִי paragraphs (3:11–12; 8:32–36), which festively recapitulate the theme of 1:7. Chapter 5 balances a warning about "the strange woman" and an encouragement to take joy in your wife's erotic love with an interspersed commentary. The structure of chapter 9 is similar. It climaxes the whole proem of chapters 1–9, spelling out the God-breathed point: to live with (Holy Spirited) Wisdom and to know that what God wills shall bring shalom, but to set up a housekeeping with godlessness and to use good gifts illicitly leads to utter ruin.[32]

---

31 ". . . wise men, hieroglyphic specialists, and mumbling magicians"—the narrative pokes fun of them (Exodus 7:11) but recognizes their important official courtly task as Pharaoh's cabinet of advisors.

32 One could schematize the antiphonal artistic structure of chapters Proverbs 1–9 as follows:

The literary configuration one needs to appreciate in order to understand Proverbs 1–9 and (my proposal) the book as a whole is this: think of paragraphs of variegated gnomic poetry, artistically juxtaposed as point and counterpoint, as example and repeated refrain, as graphic vignette and extended metaphor supplementing one another or in polemic contrast. Proverbs 1–9 is like a chorus of stimulating reflections, voices orchestrated on the principle of "Yes, but." The gambit "Yes, but" is the pedagogical tactic of a wise one leading the less experienced person by saying "It seems so, but have you considered this?"

God's revelation booked here in the "wise man and wise woman" format presents arranged paragraphs that need to be studied like poetry. They give an oblique presentation of reflective truth compressed rather than in a direct indicative plus imperative direction (as is the wont of Paul in the New Testament). This "Yes, but" nuanced complexity ranges in the Bible from the chorus of voices lyrically contesting erotic human love called "The Song of Songs" (7:1–9a bespeaks lust, in my reading),[33]

```
                                    introduction 1:2–6
                                    theme of the whole 1:7
paragraphs on                       WISDOM passages
decisive living & temptation
by what is "strange" to the Lord
1:8–9, 10–19 (with vignette vv. 11–14)   1:20–21; 22–31, 32–33 appeal of Wisdom
2: 1–22
3:1–10, 11–12                       3:13–18, 19–20 hymn to Wisdom
3:21–35
        4:1–9 on Wisdom as a pearl of great price
        4:10–19 godly Way and godless way contrasted
        4:20–27 obedient heart and bodily acts
                    5:1–6, 7–14, 15–23 strophic caesura
        6:1–5 on surety
        6:6–11 on lazy fellow
        6:12–15 on deceiver
        6:16–19 on seven-hated matters
6:20–21, 22–7:27 (with parable of seduction 7:6–23)
                                    8:1–21 appeal of Wisdom
                                    8:22–31 hymn of Wisdom, in beginning
                                    8:32–36 closing appeal of Wisdom
                                    9:1–6, 7–12, 13–18 strophic culmination
```

33 Cf. my *The Greatest Song: In critique of Solomon*, freshly and literally translated from the Hebrew and arranged for oratorio performance [1967] (Toronto: Tuppence Press, 1988). (I cannot help but wish Duane Garrett, who repeats G. Lloyd Carr's severe judgment [InterVarsity Press, 1984], "that the Song, as it now stands, is unactable" [*Song of Songs,* The New American Commentary, {1993}, 359–60] could once attend one of the many performances I have directed in the last thirty years in Canada, the United States, and Europe. Their error is to force the chorus of voices in the Old Tes-

to the book of Job with speeches permeated by laments, to the dialogical monologue wisdom of Ecclesiastes with refrains of thankful joy, to the teachings of rabbi Christ. Although booked wisdom is not in the "Thus says the Lord" manner of the prophet, and is not an atoning sacrifice offered by the priest, the "Yes, but" Scripture of interwoven poetic paragraphs is still an authoritative kerygmatic word of the Lord that gives healing words of direction.

To show the reach of the "Yes, but" way of "the wise" into the New Testament, one need but notice that Jesus renewed the wise man way of revealing God's will to the people after the intertestamentary commentators and scribes of Jesus' day had dried up its blessing (cf. Matthew 7:28–29). And Jesus "dramatized" teaching in other ways than by using parables (e.g., Matthew 13). Christ's teaching on the hillside epitomizes the living wise man tradition of the Qoheleth-rabbi: "You have heard it said, but I say"; "If your hand causes you to sin, cut it off"—cut the living baby in two! (Matthew 5–7).

Also, Luke reports how Jesus carried out the wise man tradition of unrehearsed interchange with disciples, crowd, and Pharisees, right after Christ's spirited exchange with those who said he exorcised by Beelzebub. Christ had just told the story (Luke 11:24–26) of the unclean spirit that is cast out, returns to find its old hideout clean but empty, gets seven other spirits worse than itself, and returns, so that the fellow is permanently worse off—filled with self-righteous demons!

> Now it happened that while Jesus was speaking these words, some woman or other in the crowd raised her voice and hollered to him, "Blessed is the belly that carried you around and the tits that gave you suck!" But Jesus said, "That's fine, [lady,] but the point is, 'Blessed are those who hear the Word of God and are busy doing it!'" (Luke 11:27–28)

Luke 11:27 (like Proverbs 10:15) is not a text for "Mother's Day" ("May your children be like Christ")! Luke records this incident under the Spirit's guiding to show how superficial the response of Jewish approval often was to rabbi Jesus' teaching, and how Jesus here did a wise man "Yes, but" *au point*.

The woman sensed Christ had done a great deed, and defended his ministry of healing at a very fundamental level, but she didn't have a clue that Christ's exorcism act showed that the glorious rule of God was already begun on earth, and she didn't grab the story (which Mark 3:23 calls a parable) of an exorcised evil spirit returning with seven worse ones.

---

tament text into a Greek/Shakespearian concept of "drama" in order to dismiss "the dramatic interpretation.")

So the lady says, "A son like you makes a mother glad."

Christ corrects her immediately in the next verse: thank you very much, ma'am, for the support, *but* (μενοῦν) more to the point, don't put down self-righteous people in their logical contradictions, not even to be freed from dumb-making devils. The point is that you need to be cleansed from sin in order to do what God wants done. Don't congratulate me, woman. Repent and believe, fear the Lord, love your neighbor, be a steward of God's gift to you on earth.

Poetic Paragraph of Proverbs 10:1–22

Aware of the historical setting and literary penchant of the indirect, polemical way "the wise" make God's will known, one can hear how chapter 10:1–22 presents Wisdom (act *coram Deo,* 1:7, hate evil, 8:13) correcting the worldly-wise street "wisdom" of the day. I contend that 10:1–22 is almost as tightly composed a piece as chapter 2, which is one single ode-like sentence holding the dependent "if, then" balanced clauses together in twenty-two verses that snap shut as a poem should.[34]

Translation[35] *and Commentary*

1. A wise son or daughter makes a father or mother's heart merry,

---

34 2:1 My son/daughter if you take hold of what I say. . .
   2:5 *then* you shall catch on to standing still listening before the Lord and truly find a full-bodied knowledge of God. . .
   2:9 *then* you shall get to understand doing what is right, the just thing, and doing things simply the way they are set up to be—what is creationally good. . .
   2:12 snatching you away safe from the way of evil. . .
   2:16 snatching you away safe from the strange woman. . .
   2:20 *so that* you shall be walking on the way of creationally good things. . .

35 The layout of my translation hints at the counterpoint connections that make the whole intelligible. "My son" (בְּנִי) paragraphs are not just referring to teenage boys. בְּנִי has the meaning of "my son, my daughter, my child, my student, my disciple," and can include adults who are humble enough to sit at the feet of "the wise" to receive teaching in God's way. So the translation embraces the fact that בְּנִי is not gender-restrictive. My translation of רְשָׁעִים in verse 3 as "those who like to cut corners" and in verse 6 as "those who don't act straight" may set the teeth of purists on edge. But scriptural words are more than technical terms. The words are not jargon but poetically wrought; so putting the Hebrew into English needs a little play to allow this literary quality of the worded thought to have its force. I always check out my translations with purist Buber who wrenches German into the same refined Hebraicized term every time the word appears, lest one stray beyond aesthetic limits. "Blockhead babbling" in verse 14b is my metaphoric equivalent for פִּי אֱוִיל even though "blockhead babbling" hides the fact that the Hebrew has "mouth of a fool" sounding again the "mouth of the crooked" from verse 11b.

and an insolent, godless child breaks its parent's heart to pieces.

2. Treasures gotten by underhanded dealings are of no use at all: doing what is rightly just, however, saves you from death!

3. The Lord God Yahweh never lets a man or a woman who is actually righteous stay hungry,
but God rams the greedy desire of those who like to cut corners right back [down their throats]!

4. "A negligent empty hand brings on poverty:
the grip of the diligent makes one rich."

5. "A fellow who gathers in at harvest time
knows what he is doing:
a fellow who oversleeps at harvest time is
simply disgraceful!"

6. Genuine blessings halo the head of whoever come through with just deeds,
while the mouth of the people who don't act straight casts up a smokescreen over deeds that violate others.

7. The person who has persevered in doing what is just will be remembered as a gift of shalom, while the good name of those who have been guilty of crookedness shall decompose.

8. A person who is at heart wise simply carries out
[his or her] tasks:
it's the pair of slippery lips that will be smashed to bits.

9. "Who walks in wholesome ways will walk securely
unafraid:
who chooses his paths to be twisty will be discovered
[tied in knots]."

10. An eye that blinks the double-crossing wink
makes bitter trouble;
[I repeat:] it's the pair of slippery lips that will be
smashed to bits!

11. The mouth of folk kept truly just is a bubbling source
of life;
while the mouthing of people who don't act straight
[I repeat] casts up a smoke-screen over deeds that
violate others.

12. Hate rouses bickering, blistering discontent,
while love dresses all kinds of rebellious misdeeds with clothes.

13. You will find wisdom on the lips of an experienced, discerning person,
    but, "You need a stick for the backside of anybody who at heart lacks sense."
14. Judicious men and wise women are thrifty with hard-won knowledge,
    but blockheaded babblings are pregnant with disaster:
15.   "Possessions are a citadel of strength to a man of wealth. It's poverty that ruins the poor—"
16. [No!] the handiwork and wages of a tried-and-true man or woman is full of life,
    but the income of the crooked fellow only increases his or her sin.
17. When one faithfully follows a nurturing discipline, you are on a pathway of life;
    but to pay no attention to corrective judgments will leave you wandering around lost!

18.   Lips of deceit conceal hate,
        and whoever spreads gossip is a godless, insolent fool;
19.   wherever there is too much talk, the upstart misdeed will not fail to materialize—
        whoever is more chary of his or her lip movements has more sense.
20.   The tongue of a tried-and-true woman or man is as valuable as the choicest silver,
        while the heart of the connivers is worth next to nothing.
21.   The lips of a tried-and-true woman or man will nourish many [to new life!]
        Stupidly closed fools, however, because they lack sense at heart, drop dead!
22. It is only the Lord God Yahweh's blessing that makes one rich: all your troubled struggle doesn't add a bit to it.

10:1 gives the usual setting, posing the alternative of "Wisdom or foolishness" in a two-generational context so important to the covenanting Lord. This introductory verse probably doubles as a common subtitle to the paragraphs that follow in chapters 10–15 until 15:33 paraphrases the cornerstone of 1:7 to end the section.

10:2 formulates the theme of the whole paragraph: crooked success is worthless, but right-doing (צְדָקָה) keeps you from a dead end. And 10:3 proclaims the Good News that the Lord provides the one with integrity (צַדִּיק) with sustenance, but frustrates the greedy wicked. It takes a saving faith to believe this thesis (as Psalm 73 and the book of Job affirm), because such truth is not observable to the naked eye.

10:4–5 counter the theme and thesis of 10:2–3 with what "people today say." Imagine verse 4 as the quip of an entrepreneur leading one of Solomon's trade missions to Hiram's court, and verse 5 as the "wisdom" of a city foreman to a work crew building the temple or Solomon's gorgeous palace, that is, as an incentive to country boys displaced in Jerusalem trying to make big money.

But 10:6–7 counters the street-smart sense and half-truth of "industry-makes-rich" (v. 4) and "those who work hard get ahead in the world" (v. 5) with the wisdom that lasting blessings (בְּרָכוֹת) come to the one with integrity (צַדִּיק, vv. 6–7) while the wicked (רְשָׁעִים) are deceitfully violent and short-lived. That is, 10:6–7 reinforces 10:2–3[36] after the false lead of 10:4–5 by positing that "just-doing versus crooked acts," not "riches versus poverty," is the framework for thinking and doing wisely.

10:8–11 is a brief commentary on the point of verses 1–3 and 6–7, to make clear that being wise (חָכָם) consists in following the Lord's ordinances (מִצְווֹת, v. 8) for life. In other words, the voice of a just person, which brings life (v. 11), is precisely the opposite of being foolish (v. 8) and wicked (v.11).

Repeating verse 8b in verse 10b and verse 6b in verse 11b corrects the false courtier's mode of operation and teaches the audience to avoid the conflagration caused by slippery lips in a competitive workforce, and a glib tongue at the office or in the neighborhood (cf. James 3:1–12). Duplicit speech entails actual destruction (vv. 8b, 10b); the death of the deceitful (v.2) is the antithesis of life (v.11a) for the righteous (צַדִּיק).[37]

Between 10:2–11 and 10:13–22 we find the central verse of this poetic paragraph. Proverbs 10:12 exposes the nature of crookedness (רֶשַׁע) and of integrity (צַדִּיק) on which one's life or death hangs. Arousing contention (making this crooked, מְעַקֵּשׁ, v.9b) is hatred in action, while love is action that covers over the nakedness of your neighbor's wrongs and evil (פְּשָׁעִים).

---

36 No wonder the LXX added יהוה after בְּרָכוֹת in v.6. R. B. Y. Scott (*Proverbs*, The Anchor Bible [Garden City, NY: Doubleday, 1965], 83) repeats Toy (*The Book of Proverbs*, 203) to second-guess why v. 11b doubles v. 6b. They represent an earlier generation that read doubling as scribal error rather than as poetic emphasis.

37 The alliteration in verse 9a הוֹלֵךְ בַּתֹּם יֵלֶךְ בֶּטַח hints that it is a known aphorism; so the converse in verse 9b may be minted fresh for this occasion.

In the context of 10:1–22, verse 12 is as resounding a statement as Micah 6:8, which proclaims: "What does the Lord require of you? Nothing but doing what is just, loving to keep your promises, and walking humbly with your God." James quotes Proverbs 10:12 from memory as the punch line that sums up his whole letter (James 5: 19–20). Peter also quotes verse 12 as the crux for life in the end times (1 Peter 4:7–11). He argues that Proverbs 10:12 teaches how the body of Christ should be "economical" (house-holding) and hospitable with its charismata. This is the clue to withstanding great troubles, says Scripture.

Verses 13 and 14 pick up the "wisdom versus foolishness" theme from verses 1 and 8. Verse 15 exemplifies this theme, but not as a plank in a biblical economic policy. Rather, 10:15 is the slogan of God's people on the make in 1 Kings 5–7: "Capital is the stronghold of the wealthy: poverty is the weak sport of the poor." Proverbs 10:15 is the proverbial recapitulation of 10:4–5 run amuck in a policy of Mammon. This policy is immediately corrected by verses 16–17.

10:16–17 pulls the runaway concern for success and trust in money back into the orientation of Wisdom: integrity versus wickedness. These verses explicitly condemn the acquired gain, possessions, and profit of those who are devious as an increase in sin (חַטָּאת, v. 16). They declare that only the word of the righteous (צַדִּיק) brings life, and that only those who follow the discipline (מוּסָר) of Wisdom are walking on the path of life (vv. 16a, 17a). So the creed of security-in-riches (10:15) is indeed the babble of fools (v.14).

10:18–21 provides an almost line-by-line explication of verses 12–17, except for verse 15. Verse 18 links hate (שִׂנְאָה, v.12) to being a fool (cf. vv. 1 and 14). Verse 19 emphasizes what verses 13 and 14 pronounce— too much talk is prone to misdeed (פֶּשַׁע), while the judicious (חֹשֵׂךְ) are chary of their words. Furthermore, verse 20 exposits verse 16 by saying that the tongue of the righteous (צַדִּיק) is most valuable while the conniver's (רָשָׁע) talk is worthless. Finally, verse 21 echoes verse 17's sentiment that disciplined lips will nourish many; it also sounds the note that fools (אֱוִילִים) who at heart lack sense (בַּחֲסַר־לֵב cf. also vv.13's contrast to v. 8) will wander around in circles, only to drop dead (cf. v. 2).

This poetic paragraph concluding verse, by using the name of YHWH to recall the Good News of verse 3, corrects all the "get rich and be safe" homespun palaver and street-smarts of verses 4, 5, and 15; the blessing of the Lord (cf. v. 6), not hard work, brings riches. Contrary to all the public opinion in boomtown Jerusalem, Judah, and Israel c. 950–750 BC, pulling yourself up by your own bootstraps in the economy, in foreign trade, in the turmoil of civil administration, and in royal court intrigue—scrambling—do not add to one's well-being: riches (v. 4b) are not the fruit of industrious labor; they come only from the hand of the Lord God's blessing upon those with integrity (צַדִּיק, v.6).

The Paragraph and Its Message

Once one grasps that Proverbs 10:1–22 is a tightly knit poetic paragraph, its powerful message of comfort and rebuke becomes evident: curb the drive to reach prosperity by cutting corners, by talking crookedly to be impressive and to get ahead. Say "No!" to such a self-centered, selfish program of clever discontent and fermented strife, because that is hatred in action, and the end of hatred is ruin. Instead, believe that doing your ordained task is the way of genuine life. The compassionate Lord God will surely bless the one who comes through trials, withstands temptations, and deals trustworthily with colleagues and neighbors. Yahweh's blessing of shalom (veritable riches) is not something a hard-working man or woman can achieve. To know in your guts (לֵב) this truth of total dependence upon the Lord is to have a disciplined life and to be wise.[38]

So Proverbs 10:1–22 carries on in detail the very formidable choice with which Proverbs 1–9 faces every new generation: will you succumb to the seduction of what is "strange" to the Lord, the deeply foolish delights that lead to your death in hell (5:15–23, 7:21–23, 9:13–18), or will you hear the cry and accept the invitation of Wisdom to receive the Spirit[39] of knowing what is holy (1:22–33, 3:13–18, 8:4–36, 9:1–12)? Proverbs 10 develops Proverbs 1–9 by explicitly asserting that wisdom

---

38 To put the literary structure of this poetic paragraph in a schematic way:
    v. 1 (setting)
    v. 2 theme: crooked success is worthless: right-doings keeps you from a dead-end
    v. 3 good news! the Lord protects the righteous and frustrates the wicked.
       vv. 4–5 People say. . .
          vv.6–7   But the truth is:
          vv. 8–11 commentary on vv. 2–7
    v. 12 response God wants: love your neighbor; never hate.
       vv. 13–14 It isn't so. . .
       v. 15   People say. . .
       vv. 16–17 But the truth is:
       vv. 18–21 commentary on vv. 12–17
    v. 22 good news (deepening the theme): only the Lord's blessing makes you rich.

39 The NIV misses, it seems to me, a crucial place to help the reader see the "spirit" versus "flesh" horizon to the choice Proverbs is proclaiming by mistranslating (רוּחִי) in 1:23 as "thoughts." The Good News paraphrase is worse: "advice"! Peterson's *The Message* at least reads "spirit." Cf. note to RSV on Proverbs 1:23, "Heb spirit," which is dropped in NRSV.

(חָכָם) shows up concretely in trustworthy right-doing (צְדָקָה), and foolishness (אֱוִיל) is embodied in crooked deeds (רֶשַׁע). Heart and mouth are intimately linked: a wise heart (חֲכַם־לֵב) carries out God's ordinantial tasks with words of life (vv. 8, 11, 21); a vapid heart (חֲסַר־לֵב) vv. 13–15, 21) arouses and courts death.

This message, which links wisdom to just-doing, is in the forefront of the concern of prophets Amos, Isaiah, and Micah, who are contemporary with the later range of the Proverbs book. Spiritual wisdom is false unless is goes beyond pious sacrifices and regulated worship services and enters into the very bloodstream of society by giving justice to the downtrodden, the lonely, and the destitute, and ending the oppression of societal outcasts (Isaiah 1:10–20; 29:13–24; 58–59; Amos 5–6; Micah 2–3, 6).

The oppositional juxtaposition in Proverbs 9 of the woman Wisdom and the woman Foolishness reappears in Revelation 12 and 17 where the woman with child is saved from the dragon and from the whore of Babylonic culture.[40] Proverbs 10:1–22 ties this fundamental apocalyptic decision, which God already spelled out to Israel in the wise speech of Moses generations earlier (Deuteronomy 30: Choose the life of doing good or the death of doing evil.). Proverbs 10:1–22 reveals that the choice between life and death is made when one's mouth nourishes the neighbor (10:21), or when one's "slippery lips" (10:8b, 10b, 14b–15) murder the neighbor with vain, conniving putdowns.

In Pauline fashion, Proverbs 10 takes the wisdom/folly horizons, depicted by Woman Wisdom (Proverbs 8:12) and Woman Foolishness (Proverbs 9:13; Proverbs 2:16; cf. Ephesians 6:10–13), of Proverbs 1–9 into the tangible courts of gentle speech that sets things straight: a just deed (10:11a, 19, 20a, 21a) or the concealed hatred of ambitious, boastful, insolent talk (10:1b, 6b, 18). Later in James 3:13–18, the Newer Testament clearly proclaims this very difference between godly wisdom and demonic "wisdom" as the difference between what seeds the conten-

---

40 All the debate about whether "the strange woman" is a real flesh-and-blood woman (the Septuagint treats 2:16–17 as an allegorical personification and translates אִשָּׁה as ὁδός and אַלּוּף as διδασκαλίαν!), and whether capital "W" Wisdom woman is a rhetorical personification or a mythic hypostatization due to Hellenistic Gnostic influence of Sophia, is simply evidence of how learned theologians do not know how to read poetic lines aright. With heavy-lidded eyes they either over-read the poetry into *theologoumena* or they mistake the allusive truth as mere dress-up embellishment. The "strange woman" (like the Babylonian harlot of Revelation) is poetic reference to your corner-store *Playboy* magazine or the Jaguar you covet to have under you, and the "Wisdom woman" is a poetic Older Testament reference, I believe, to the Holy Spirit (Proverbs 2:6, 8:14–18; cf. Isaiah 11:1–3, Micah 3:8, Daniel 5:10–12).

tion of careers and success and what sows the shalom of restorative justice (δικαιοσύνη, cf. Matthew 5:5–6).

AN OPEN CONCLUSION

How does one determine where Proverbs' poetic paragraphs begin and end? As Hermission carefully said a generation ago, we are looking for an ordering principle that is not commonly practiced today.[41] However, if we come to the text aware that the tradition of "the wise" in Israel assumed a creational theology of Yahweh's ordinances as fundamental to an obedient people of God, and if we approach the booked sayings as poetic writings, that is, as intentionally composed "Yes, but" wholes (varied wholes perhaps as diverse as the canonic psalms are), finding the paragraphic beginnings and endings in the Proverbs book will be less mysterious.

But exegetes and pastors will have to disabuse themselves of the traditional idea that Proverbs 10:1–22:16 is a collection of one-liner aphorisms and precepts.[42] Garrett's remark is true: "Identifying the small collections of proverbs is essential for the use of Proverbs in the church."[43] But Garrett still seems to work with the idea of Near Eastern paranomastic "collection" and didactic "random repetition" of formulaic sententiae.[44]

With the working presupposition that what we need to find are the artistically refined paragraphs that juxtapose and contrast epigrammatic sayings, we need to edit Proverbs into a format comparable to the Psalms. Proverbs 10:1–22 commends itself as such a literary paragraph for the following reasons.

The name Yahweh appears in verses 3 and 22, and wherever it graces a poetic line one may expect something weighty to be stated, so that a Yahweh phrase initiates the train of thought like a leading paragraph sentence, or it brings the movement of a poetic whole to a conclusion, a kind of caesura.[45] Twenty-two verses is also a natural Hebraic pattern for closure, even if the whole is not an alphabetic acrostic like Proverbs

---

41 Hans-Jürgen Hermission, *Studien zur israelitischen Spruchweisheit* (Neukirchener Verlag, 1968), 174.

42 Scott, *Proverbs*, 83.

43 Garrett, *Proverbs, Ecclesiastes, Song of Songs*, 47.

44 Krispenz (*Spruchkompositionen im Buch Proverbia*, 161) argues that Egyptian paranomastic use is unlike that in the Old Testament book of Proverbs.

45 I call this the "firefly" indicator, and am using it as one method to discern other paragraphs in Proverbs 10:23–24:34. You catch the trajectory of a firefly in the night by seeing where it lights up. Wherever Yahweh radiates a spot, a hint is given, I think, of where the poetic paragraphic point is headed.

31:10–31 (or Psalm 9–10; cf. Proverbs 2).

Verse 12, given special attention by the New Testament (James and 1 Peter), and the two flanking four-verse groupings I call "commentary" all highlight the importance of couplets verses 6–7 (double blessing) and verses 16–17 (double life) for explicating the theme of verse 2. There is a kind of sustained, ode-like structure to the whole.

The to-be-corrected nature of verses 4–5 and verse 15 is unambiguous when one sees their contextualization by the whole twenty-two-verse paragraph. That one should not accept Proverbs 10:15 as bona fide biblical wisdom is shown by the subparagraph Proverbs 18:10–12, which renders explicit the phantasmagorical delusions that attend those who are vainly rich.[46]

What the apostle Peter said about brother Paul's writings (2 Peter 3:14–16) is also true about the wisdom of Proverbs: too hard to understand. The poetic paragraphs of Proverbs are not popular verse. Every attempt to market them for reading like Benjamin Franklin's "Poor Richard's Almanac"—as quips for punctuating and motivating the sanctified life—misses their sturdy God-breathed point and their lasting proclamation. So long as our versified published Bible translations neglect to conceive Proverbs and to print them in collocated poetic paragraphs, we may be hindering the "simple" readers from hearing God's message.

It will take courage to buck the established tradition of Wisdom literature scholarship, which has served up Proverbs as Egyptian precepts made kosher by a Yahwist editor, and to go against the stream of making the Old Testament gospel simple. But such work has been begun by Stek, Van Leeuwen, and Krispenz. It needs to be carried on so that the book of poetic paragraphs comes to be heard today as giving substance to the living water.

---

46 If one does not have the twenty-two-verse poetic context, one can take verses 4–5 as a straightforward work ethic opposed to laziness, which, of course, will be "complemented" by other admonitions not to trust wealth (11:28, 15:27, 23:4–5, 27:24; cf. Scott 84). Such restraint of Nature by the caution of Grace may scotch the snake of (North American) self-reliance but will not kill it as it biblically deserves.

Celebrate the Resourceful Woman (Proverbs 31)

10 Any possibility of finding a resourceful woman?
    You could never equal her worth in jewels or red coral
11 Because her husband deep down always feels secure with her—
    he knows he will never lack plenty:
12 Completing what is good for him and frustrating evil that threatens
    marks a resourceful woman life long.

13 Dunning wool and flax for linen,
    hands crinkled rough with joy in the work:
14 Every resourceful woman brings home food for the family, from (near or) far away,
    like a gallant clipper ship in full sail.
15 From before dawn she is up to prepare a meal for the household,
    and outline chores for the young who help.
16 Garden land may catch her watchful eye, and at the right time she takes it;
    a resourceful woman gets a vineyard planted, as fruit of her toiling hands.
17 Her hips and thighs are muscled with strength;
    her forearms flash a solid power—
18 Indeed, she experiences bodily how good her job is!
    —her lamp does not ever burn out at night.

19 Lightly her fingers guide the spinning wheel distaff
    and her hands hold tight the spindle.
20 More so, her open hand strains to protect the defenseless
    and her fingers extricate those hopelessly tangled in poverty.
21 Never does a resourceful woman fear the cold of snow for her

---

Appeared in *Christian Courier*, 57:2689 (6 May 2002): 12–13.

> household,
> since one by one they have been clothed doubly warm.
>
> 22 **O**rnamental cushions and tapestries—she sews them herself!
> her special homemade clothes include fine white linen and wool dyed purple.
> 23 **P**ublic respect greets her husband in the gates of the city
> when he goes to sit down with the grey-haired elders who judge in the land.
> 24 **Q**uick to knit underclothes and even sell them,
> a resourceful woman can barter belts (and goods) with any tradesman.
>
> 25 **R**eady strength and rough-hewn beauty cover her snug
> so that she stands facing the coming days full of hearty laughter.
> 26 **S**he opens her mouth with wisdom:
> the law of covenanting love rolls off her tongue!
> 27 **T**he resourceful woman oversees what goes on in her house so insightfully
> that no one ever has to eat the curds of sluggish laziness.
> 28 "**U**niquely blessed is she!" her children shout in chorus;
> and her husband says, "Give her a hallelujah!"
> 29 "**V**ery many young women show gifts of resourcefulness,
> but you are better than all of them put together!"
>
> 30 **W**ell, it is true: graceful charm can prove disappointing and to be good-looking might just be a mirage,
> but a woman who lives her womanhood plumb before the LORD God—she is worth celebrating!
> 31 **Y**ou all, then, celebrate such a resourceful woman! let her enjoy some of the fruit that comes from her hands herself;
> let people shout her a hallelujah and praise her deeds publically in the gateway to the city.
>
> (Translation of Proverbs 31:10–31, 1974, C. Seerveld)

The book of *Proverbs* closes with an ABC alphabet poem in seven stanzas about "the resourceful woman" (31:10–31). If King Lemuel of Massa was an Arab (31:1), then God used an Arabian queen mother to book this Hebrew poetry. That historical setting helps us understand this composite portrait of a God-fearing wise woman. This woman of *Proverbs* 31 is not presented as an ideal everyone should strive to be like, but celebrates the range and glory of womanhood as God understands it. [#30]

[#30] *Egyptian Coptic woman*, c. 1950

Throughout the Bible, from Eve to the virgin Mary, women have been pivotal in history. Deborah, Rahab, Bathsheba, and Esther shine out in the earlier patriarchal world of Israel. Martha, Mary Magdalene, Lydia, and Priscilla are mentioned in the newer testamented Bible to show the normality of women taking roles of leadership, in the event that men might think they are the sole masters of public life (cf. Luke 22:24–26). And now the poem of *Proverbs* 31 celebrates the many unsung women who serve the LORD.

The whole book of *Proverbs* is about becoming wise. Standing in awe of the LORD God is the **beginning** of wisdom, says the Bible (Proverbs 1:7, Psalm 111:10); and responding to the disciplined call of God's Holy Spirit brings about a life-giving **maturity** in wisdom to discern good from evil (Proverbs 8:32–36; cf. Hebrews 5:11–6:8). *Proverbs* 1–9 metaphorically portrays wisdom as a vigorous, provident woman, in contrast to a fascinating, seductive woman who represents a ruinous stupidity (much as the book of *Revelation* contrasts the glorious pregnant woman of God with the whore of commercialized Babylon, Revelation 12,17–18). So, to have *Proverbs* end with a panegyric poem celebrating a genuinely wise woman shows God's subtle humor in a world where men like to dominate the scene.

[#31] Jean Siméon Chardin, *La Pourvoyeuse*, c. 1739

A good woman can give security to a man [#31], especially a husband, says *Proverbs* 31 (vv.11–12,23). (It is noteworthy that Genesis 2:24 says the grown man will "cling" to the woman, and not the other way around, in their union.) A woman who tirelessly cares for her household, and does it with style, is indeed praiseworthy (vv.13–

15). The poem exults in the woman's providing food "like a gallant clipper ship in full sail," in spinning and sewing fine linen and purple-dyed wool for warm clothes (vv. 19, 21–22, 24). The point is not to be frugal, stinting, dutiful, but to have joy! in your mundane labor, and élan in your deeds, whatever they be (vv. 16–18).

[#32] Verse 26 is the key to the resourceful woman: she speaks *chokmah* (wisdom) and the *torah* of *chesed* (God's guidance of covenanting love)! That, in a nutshell, is the gospel of God's Word of *Proverbs*. When a person becomes wise, you become adept at managing things with tactful, proactive insight (v. 27), so matters don't fall apart. And when you can articulate, embody, and bring into action God's law for faithful, provident care in daily life—from gardening, sewing, buying and selling, nurturing children, reaching out to those who are poor-off (v. 20)—you become clothed with a glorious rough-hewn beauty, and are buoyed up by a sure, robust confidence that the LORD God shall indeed come through in the days ahead (v. 25).

[#32] Johannes Vermeer, *The Lacemaker*, 1669–70

The source of a woman or a man's resourcefulness is the blessing of God, chants the family in this poem (vv. 28–29). And then the reflective commentator (as is to be expected in such biblical wisdom literature; cf. epilogue to *The Song of Songs*, 8:5–14, *Job*, 42:10–17, *Ecclesiastes*, 12:9–14) gnomically rephrases the crucial stanza of verses 25–27 to say that good-looks may be a mirage, but life lived plumb before the LORD God shall surely bear good fruit (vv. 30–31). So, celebrate women who quietly evince a sturdy godliness in their daily walk with God and neighbor.

My mother Letitia [#33] had the deep love to take the time to read me stories when I was a child, which gave my imagination wings. My mother-in-law Ruth [#34] had the grit under God's eye to keep her family spiritedly alive in The Hague when there was next to nothing to eat during the war winter of 1944–45. My wife Inès [#35] has the holy stamina to be unperturbed during difficult turns in the road of life, which has

— Celebrate the Resourceful Woman —

[#33] Letitia Van Tielen (1955)

[#34] Ruth Huber (1988)

[#35] Inès Cécile Naudin ten Cate (1981)

> *. . . a woman who lives her womanhood plumb before the* Lord *God—she is worth celebrating!*

given me a great steadiness to do my work, and kept the family on an even keel. Our gifted daughters Anya and Gioia have borne troubles, but continue to find rays of joy in their busy, complicated lives that testify to the fact that our Lord keeps God's comforting hand on the pulse of what they do. My daughter-in-law Jan has the intelligent reserve and dedication to serve ably at home, church, and office that bespeaks a sanctified nobility. My friend Phyl holds a rich fund of perceptive awareness of the wonders of God's world and its literate history that enriches my vision of being human. . . .

None of the women in my life are perfect, anymore than I am a model man. But these women of flesh and blood I know, and the many more I could name, whose resourcefulness I bewonder, deserve to be celebrated! says the Bible of *Proverbs* 31:31.

Resourcefulness is not aggressive, insistent, militant, or flashy. The resourceful woman of *Proverbs* 31 is also not a virtuous Miss American superwoman, or a media-championed successful Business Woman of the year. She is steadfastly normal.

A resourceful woman or man imbued with the wisdom *Proverbs* 31 celebrates is fruitfully embedded in a circle of persons for whom she serves as home base, as a crosswalk of security in the disquieting streets of daily life. Such a woman could be a mother, a single woman teacher, secretary, sheep-herder, chaplain, artist, or an elderly great aunt. The resourceful woman is faithfully industrious, kindly astute and gentle in dealing with people, patiently preparing for what may still come from the Lord's hand—evidencing the fruits of the Holy Spirit (cf. Galatians 5:22–25). The resourceful woman of *Proverbs* 31 breathes the peace of the Lord abroad, is imaginative, resilient, has a gift for hearty laughter, and knows the fortitude to dig in deeper to trust God when evil does come her way, providing real cheer to the anxious nearby.

Any possibility of finding a resourceful woman today?

Thank God, yes.

. . . You all, then, celebrate such a resourceful woman!

HERDER'S REVOLUTIONARY HERMENEUTIC AND AESTHETIC THEORY

THE IMPORT OF HERDER'S HERMENEUTICS FOR TEXT PERFORMANCE OF *THE GREATEST SONG*

The Herder I propose to examine is the writer of aesthetic theory and hermeneutics from about 1772 to 1782. My focus is on this period of his amazing, wide-ranging work, because during this decade, in my judgment, Herder temporarily left behind the Aufklärung rationality he had preferred at Riga (1764–69) and later reassumed in Weimar in a close working relationship with Goethe (around 1783). This ten-year period begins at a time when he was reconciled to Hamann,[1] and also happens to coincide with the beginning and ending of an epistolary friendship Herder had with the Swiss clergyman Johann Kaspar Lavater, author of *Physiognomische Fragmente zur Beförderung der Menscherkenntnis* (1775–78), and who was a friend of Füssli.[2] That Herder was a revolutionary thinker during his Westphalian Bückeburg sojourn (1770–75) and during the early years in Weimar (from 1776), polemically embattled against the dominant culture of his day, finds one written expression in his manifesto against Enlightenment philosophy: "Auch eine Philosophie der Geschichte zur Bildung der Menschheit. Beytrag zu vielen Beyträgen des Jahrhunderts" (1774). Particularly during these years Herder ranged far and wide to collect Persian, Nordic, and early English folksongs; he

---

1 The review of Hamann that sharply criticized Herder's prize "Essay on the Origin of Language," and the ensuing rapprochement can be found in "Zwo Recensionen" (1772), in Johann Georg Hamann, *Sämtliche Werke*. ed. Josef Nadler (Wien: Herder, 1951), 3:13–24, and in Hamann's letter of 14 June 1772 to Herder followed by Herder's long reply of August 1 and 25, in *Hamann's Schriften*, ed. Friedrich Roth (Berlin: Reimer, 1824), 5:6–14.

2 Cf. R. Haym, *Herder nach seinem Leben und seinen Werken* (Berlin: Gärtners Verlagsbuchhandlung, 1885), 1:503 ff., 2: 146–52.

Presentation at the Interdisciplinary Conference, "Herder Today," at Stanford University, California, November 1987.

himself was writing experimental texts set to music and performed by Concertmeister Johann Christoph Friedrich Bach.[3] Buoyed by a happy marriage to Caroline Flachsland in 1773, busy with two translations of the Old Testament Song of Songs and with plans to translate the whole Bible, as Luther had done, because it was *Urpoesie*,[4] Herder epitomized during this stage of his development what came to be called *Sturm und Drang*.

I shall first sketch the mindset of Herder's aesthetic theory and situate his contribution in the development of aesthetics. Then I shall delineate the genial thrust of Herder's hermeneutic theory at that time and distill certain insights I find important for today. My thesis, with historical hindsight, is that the revolutionary Herder of that decade made an important contribution that needs to be heard today on the historicality and defining imaginative character of literature, and that Herder proposed a theory for interpreting poetry and reading the Bible that has relevance for contemporary debates generated by Gadamer, Langer, Jauss, Tracy, Ricoeur, and all those who do criticism in the wilderness.

I.

Herder's style of writing and reflection exemplify his basic view of the world: the world is a battleground of opposing forces constantly generating and terminating other powers. Each individual soul, a microcosm, stands wide-eyed before the universe and procreates then and there what he or she will. Human beings are unsimple, concatenated creatures swimming in an ocean of impressions that constantly joggle our senses. But we are aeolian harps with a difference, says Herder: we have the art to catch and name by words the things that animate our feelings for the nonce. In fact, our whole human life is a kind of poietics. We create images more than that we see them. An inner poetic sense knows how to join the welter of perceptions we entertain and how to compose imaginative configurations sensitive to the most refined nuances, although our understanding normally sloughs over such matters. All the powers of our soul (*die Seelenkräfte*) like understanding, reason, the ability to abstract

---

3 Cf. "Brutus. Ein Drama zur Musik" (1774, 28:52—58), "Die Kindheit Jesu" (1772, 28:28—33), "Die Auferweckung Lazarus. Eine biblische Geschichte zur Musik" (1773, 28:34–44). Herder called these texts a "Kommentar in musikalischen Hieroglyphen" (cf. R. Haym. *Herder.* 1:476).

4 "In früheren Jahren war es einer seiner Lieblingswünsche, die Bibel zu übersetzen, wo nicht alle Bücher, doch die wichtigsten derselben," *Erinnerungen aus dem Leben Joh. Gottfrieds von Herder* von Maria Carolina von Herder, geb. Flachsland. Ed. Johann Georg Miller (Stuttgart: Cotta'schen Buchhandlung, 1830), 3:115.

and signify things, depending upon our sensibility, imagination, and memory: all by virtue of our language help us order the world (15:523, 525–28, 531, 535).[5]

From Herder's viewpoint poetry originates in this human power to mint spirited, thoughtful images (*Gedankenbilder*) out of our deepest configured feelings, and to stamp such vital, evocative, sounding words upon the natural universe. Just as God spoke and things came into being, we human second creators speak and imprint a human, personal meaning upon the becoming, being, and ceasing of whatever is extant. Poetry epitomizes the human condition, and humanity was and is originally busy poeting. It may seem exaggerated to a cold-blooded deist, says Herder, but Genesis 1 and all the earliest mythologies and poetry reveal with vitality and clarity what is truly going on: the ongoing, deadly struggle between loving and hating forces under the aegis of a God who continually provides new life (15:526–29, 532–33, 535–36; 12:6–8, 10–11).

Hebraic poetry as מָשָׁל, the pregnant, gnomic image, a kind of metaphorical oracle, illustrates in a most pure way the nature of poetry in the beginning. The conjuncture of an original figure compressing a visual thought, like the proverbial cherub or winged sphinx as guardian of what is secret, is the kind of concrete, idiographic presentation of natural

---

5   All references in the main text between parentheses are to volume:pages of the Bernhard Suphan edition of *Herders Sämtliche Werke* (Berlin: Weidmannsche Buchhandlung, 1877–1913), 33 volumes.

"Die Natur ward ein Kampfplatz verschiedener, gegenseitiger, sich einander einschränkender oder einander beistehender Kräfte; und ist sie etwas anders?" (15:535). "Unter seinen Sinnen sind Gesicht und Gehör diejenigen, die aus dem Ocean dunkler Empfindungen ihm Gegenstände am nächsten und klarsten vor die Seele bringen; und da er die Kunst besitzt, diese Gegenstände durch Worte festzuhalten und zu bezeichnen. . . ." (15:523). "Unser ganzes Leben ist also gewissermaßen eine Poetik: wir sehen nicht, sondern wir erschaffen uns Bilder" (15:526). ". . . wir immer eine Aeole-Harfe sind, sofern wir von mancherlei Winden und Elementen belebt werden: so beruhet die Lebhaftigkeit der Vorstellung gerade auf der Mannichfaltigkeit dessen, was wir beim Genuss dieses Gegenstandes damals auf Einmal fühlten. Der innere poetische Sinn weiß dieses so wahr und genau zusammen zu knüpfen, dass wir in seiner Kunstwelt abermals seine ganze lebendige Welt fühlen: denn eben die kleinen Umstände, die der kalte Verstand nicht bemerkt hätte, und die der kältere Afterverstand als Überfluss wegstreicht, sind gerade die Wahresten Striche des eigentümlichen Gefühls, also auch eben dieser Wahrheit wegen von der entschiedensten Wirkung" (15:531). These quotations are from "Über Bild, Dichtung und Fabel," *Zerstreute Blätter*. Dritte Sammlung (1787), which systematizes, in my judgment, what Herder practiced in his ruminating, translating, interpreting writing of the period on which my analysis focuses. Herder himself says of this article: "Die Materialien derselben sind gleichfalls ziemlich alt" (15:5); I have thought about "fable" since 1767. Cf. also R. Haym, *Herder*, 2:318–21.

truth (*eine Naturwahrheit*) that is the very foundation of poetry. Poetry is spoken hieroglyphs, which work mysteriously upon the sensibilities of one's neighbor because the natural forces (*Naturkräfte*) captured in the spoken symbols are as elementary and universal as human sensation. The true poet for Herder is only a translating spokesman, better, a messenger of what is true to passionate life. No poet attempts to amplify the sort of traits known and described in the animal kingdom by Linnaeus. Poetry strives to activate and effectuate the deepest hope and fear, joy and sorrow, the most memorable, original deeds of humankind. The vivid speech of poetry, whether it be solely a striking image or a simple fable about animals, stirs alive that layer of primary passions that breaks through unexpectedly in our unruly moments and agitates openly childhood, our dream life, and is the innate genius of the fierce, unsophisticated peoples of the ancient East. Hebraic poetry is the prototype of the most true poetry, which indeed has method in its "rational madness" (*eines vernünftigen Wahnsinnes*), because the speech of Job, Moses, and David bodies forth in utter innocence the aura of a convicting divine Word and human sensibility inextricably bound together. Such powerful speech is the original tongue of poetry (12:8–10, 12, 14, 16–19, 28; 8:334 n.a., 339–42; 15:534, 539).

A second kind (*Gattung*) of poetic art next to the empowering spoken word-image, מָשָׁל, says Herder, is singing, song. Singing is image-rich speech (*Bilderrede*) heightened by musical tones, dance cadences, and rhyming sounds, which round out poetry with verve (*Schwung*) and a pristine intensity that provides a veritable concert of sensuous experience (*ein Saitenspiel der Empfindung*). Whether the singing be a hymn, elegy, love song, chant, anthem, or ode, the nub of a song (*Lied*) is the melodic movement of the measured human voice carrying a tune to be heard. Singing is as natural as the human heartbeat, and song is native to every folk under the sun (12:20–22; 25:332–33).

Im Anfang war das Lied, Herder means to say, and the original song is always *Volkslied*. Whether you count Lamech's strident verse (Genesis 4:23–24) as the first song or go to the Hebraic psalms and genealogies, the charmed lays of Orpheus, the archaic, epic tales of folk poet Homer, which were composed to be sung in the oral tradition of ballad, the choruses of Aeschylus, the rhapsodic lines of Ossian, the lilting songs in Shakespeare or Lithuanian lullabies: it is all ἀοιδή, song, the limpid lyric in the mouth of a folk. "Folk" does not mean street rabble, for Herder. A "folk" is a people of common language whose unlettered tongue simply speaks what moves the human heart directly (15:537–38; 25:313–16,

323). Folksong is aboriginal musical poetry, the likes of which simplicity, compelling passion, and stirring aftereffects no current verse, says Herder, can match (25:7, 12). When poets stopped singing as minstrels, although both poetry and music developed in craft, poetry lost in power to evoke heartfelt response. And when the otherwise good invention of the printing press induced poets to write in order to be read! instead of being heard in living voice, poetry forfeited its existential impact (*"Würkung . . . für den jetztigen Augenblick"*) and slipped toward the pedantry of formulating understandable "classic" work fixed in a papery eternity (8:411–13).

The remark on paper poetry situates Herder critically in his day. Herder could divide poets roughly into those who ordered their thought clearly and distinctly, like Milton, Haller, and Kleist, and those who let their passions come directly to the fore, like Klopstock (5:184–85). And to please Wieland, editor of *Der Teutsche Merkur* in 1774, Herder could evenhandedly reject as one-sided both Wolfian scholastic thought at the universities and the caterpillar of abstract, Frenchified formulaic philosophy, as well as the butterfly of fanatic enthusiasts with their drunken ideas (9:497–50). But Herder himself loved to sound out the sweetly murmuring lines of Klopstock, was translating Percy's *Reliques of Ancient Poetry* and Shakespeare into short, pulsing German meters, and was immersed in Old Testament biblical poetry, partial to Hamann's idiosyncratic dicta—"Poesie ist die Muttersprache des menschlichen Geschlechts" and "Das Hell kommt von den Juden."[6]

Herder faulted his countrymen for lacking the natural passion (8:342) and folk identity exemplified by Moses and Miriam's triumphal choral song and dance of Exodus 15 welling up as praise for Yahweh under an Arabian sky (12:22). We mince around in the French minuet, and the enlightenment culture eats us away like cancer (25:11)! We teach art and poetry by servile imitation (*knechtische Nachahmung*) and learned thievery from our closets of stored, anthologized images and allegorical tales (15:529). The pioneering Bishop Lowth compares Job to Greek drama, which followed Aristotle's categories,[7] and even our great historian Winckelmann misjudged Egyptian sculpture with a myopic squint by using Greek form as the norm (5:491). Why must scholars persist in thinking the Old Testament prophets should follow the pettifogging rules of Batteaux (10:14)? What is needed, said Herder, to get poetry

---

6 From Hamann's "Aesthetica in nuce" (1762), in Johann Georg Hamann, *Sämtliche Werke*. ed. Josef Nadler (Wien: Verlag Herder, 1950), 2:197, 210.

7 Cf. "Briefe, das Studium der Theologie betreffend" (1780), 10:15, where Herder refers to lecture 33 of Robert Lowth, "Non esse justum drama," in *De Sacra Poesi Hebraeorum* (Oxford: Clarendon Press, 1775), 443–44.

alive and working again in the land, rather than being merely an entertaining pastime (8:436), is self-respect for our native German language,[8] and a recognition that every stage of the everlasting struggle for cultural progress has its own epicenter of sanity and criteria in itself (5:512–13).

With one swift stroke Herder moves past Baumgarten's Schulästhetik and also Sulzer's *Allgemeine Theorie der Schönen Kunste* (1771–74), which lacked appreciation for historical change in basic concepts in aesthetics (5:380, 388). Herder's aesthetic theory is revolutionary because it calls into question the established, intellectualistic tradition on poetry, and resolutely breaks down any abiding standard into being a phase of an ongoing, genetic process. The polite skeptical practice of the Encyclopédistes had only scotched veneration for the past, and the "critical" idealist philosophy forming in Kant was really old-fashioned in its cautious, conservative attempt to unite systematically past conceptual discoveries. By contrast Herder's aesthetic theory presents an iconoclastic geneticism that helped forge certain important insights.

(1) Herder highlighted the irreducible difference between poetic and scientific human activities: poetry was the meld of sensible sound and word with spark (*Reiz*), whose incantational fusion afforded the deepest, most sure, felt knowledge there is; while science meant abstract analysis and less pressing truths.

(2) Herder rejected as necessary the encrusted, emblematic layer of poetry, and identified the simple lyric and song as intact, bona fide art. While he took his cue for *Natursprache* from Eastern, Hebraic sources, Herder actually laid the theoretical ground for the German *Lied*.[9]

(3) Although Herder was too sanguine on the folksong's integrative power to foster national identity, his fascinated research into folksong was an exploratory attempt to curb elitism in art and grope toward the truth that poetry can only flourish within a community of hearers bound

---

[8] In competition for the first prize essay set by the Fürstliche Akademie der Alterthümer in Cassel in 1777, as a memorial for Johann Winckelmann, Herder bluntly excused his not writing in the usual French by beginning his essay: "Zuförderst erbitte ich mir die Freiheit, als Deutscher über Winkelmann Deutsch schreiben zu dürfen. Winckelmann was ein Deutscher und blieb selbst in Rom. . . . —Ich schreibe Deutsch. Verdiente meine Schrift, so werde sie übersetzt. . ." (8:439).

[9] Cf. "Älteste Urkunde des Menschengeschlechts" (1774), 6:302–303. In 1779 Herder revised his 1774 collection of Volkslieder, which had included certain dramatic scenes from Shakespeare's Macbeth, Othello, and Lear, because he wanted more discriminating readers to accept the value of such *lyrics* (25:329–30). He excluded *Minnesinger* and *Meistersänger* on the same principle, that their language and manner were not lyrical enough (25:324).

together by a unifying spirit.[10]

So Herder's aesthetic theory is fundamentally a poetics of oracular speech and incantational song where the power resides in the originary language that bespeaks the folk—poets from whose mouths it sounds. Herder's aesthetic theory breaks new ground by calling into question the credit of learned poetry, without settling for the pleasantry of polite literature, *belles lettres*. Herder does not encourage looking back to the Greco-Roman treasury of culture that the West inherited. Instead Herder pushes us to appropriate what is wonderful and strange, foreign and therefore pristine, as an empowering source of the genial disposition requisite for becoming fully human. Such an exuberant, radical spirit in aesthetic theory bodes ill for the poets and artists who later adopt it as a principled policy but lack the fresh genius Herder brought to his ideas. An untamed prodigality is difficult to maintain, difficult to transmit to a next generation, and tends to burn out.

II.

The changes in taste and manner of thinking (*Denkart*) over the ages are so whimsical, says Herder somewhat puckishly (32:29), you almost become skeptical of trusting our own current taste and perception (*Empfindung*). Still more unsettling is the possibility that the moving genius and humanity-cultivating power of Shakespeare's dramatic poetry is slipping beyond the grasp of our generation, that not even the guardian angel, actor Garrick, can save this colossal voice of history and the world's soul (*Weltseele*) from becoming as awesome but enigmatically remote as the pyramids. When contemporary criticasters test Shakespearean drama by the pedestrian space and time of their pocket watch, they will never come to know that the lightning shifts of scene and the ecstatic deeds that beggar being timed in Shakespeare are as true to Nature as the single, parsimonious event of a Sophocles drama, because each creative poet was true to the human and world historical reality they were depicting and resounding (5:219–21, 224–29, 231). What we need today is not to be enamored by interminable glosses on texts and guesses on their hidden significance, but the will to approach the simple root meaning (*Ursinn*) of the poet and to hear it sound in its original historical horizon (*Ge-*

---

10 Introduction to second part of *Volkslieder* (1779): "Es ist wohl nicht zu zweifeln, dass Poesie und insonderheit Lied im Anfang ganz Volksartig d.i. leicht, einfach, aus Gegenständen und in der Sprache der Menge, so wie der reichen und für alle fühlbaren Natur gewesen. Gesang liebt Menge, die Zusammenstimmung vieler: er fodert das Ohr des Hörers und Chorus der Stimmen und Gemüther" (2:313).

schichtskreise) (12:23).

"History" means concrete particularity, says Herder, and without one's having a situated awareness of the peculiar lived locale of any given poetry (what later came to be called "*Sitz im Leben*"), the living human soil out of which it springs, you cannot give the poetry a true hearing (5:217).[11] The biblical Hebraic poetry of Moses and David, for example, should be read not as versified dogma of a church, or as fiction (which would satisfy the spirit of our day better): Genesis asks to be heard as a straightforward, edited tale—wonders and all—just a trustworthy account of what happened historically, as Moses and later David recalled it in their day. The portrayal of the creation (Genesis 1:1–2:3) is a story recorded in archaic language (*Urworte*) of how Adam and Eve first looked at the universe. The simple, confiding style in which the patriarchs' domestic vicissitudes are recounted is really history writing par excellence, once you grant it comes from the keen eye of nomadic Bedouin shepherds, trained in Egyptian learning (cf. Exodus 2:10, Acts 7:20–22), by as great a legislating nation-former as Solon ever was. Poetry is the natural mouthpiece of historical reality (5:218–19), and the specialness of biblical poetry is violated— as in a similar way Homer, Plato, Herodotus, would be misread—if its historical, eye-witness travelogue factuality would be pressed by scientific search parties to track down Solomon's hidden treasures, or would be treated like a mere fable by bantering Parisian wits. I accept Voltaire's taunt, says Herder: I become a Jew to read David's psalms aright, and all the Old Testament biblical books, even—says Herder with the flourish of "touché"?—as Christ did. One must read every book in the spirit in which it is composed (l0:l7, 19, 22–25, 27, 32–38, 140–44, 159, 161–64, 209, 212–13).[12]

---

11 "Shakespeare" (1773): "Es wird allein erste und letzte Frage: 'wie ist der Boden? worauf ist er zubereitet? was ist in ihn gesäet? was sollte er tragen können?'" (5:217). Herder tends to downplay any "allgemeine Sätze." His stance is really an apologetic for his non-systematic (philosophical) reflection; cf. "Über die Wirkung der Dichtkunst auf die Sitten der Völker in alten und neuen Zeiten" (1778): "Wie kann man die Kraft besser kennen lernen, als in Wirkung? . . . Nur aufs Besondre zurückgeführt bekommt das Allgemeine Anschauung und Kraft der Wahrheit. Nach wenig vorhergehenden Sätzen sei also unsre einzige Wegweiserin, Lehrerin, Rathgeberin—die Geschichte" (8:338 n.l).

12 This principle was enunciated already earlier in 1769, "Fragmente zu einer 'Archäologie des Morgenlandes'": "Jede gesunde Critik in der ganzen Welt sagts, dass um ein Stück der Literatur zu verstehen, und auszulegen, man sich in den Geist seines Verfassers, seines Publikums, seiner Nation und wenigstens in den Geist dieses seines Stücks setzen müsse: und die Hermeneutik der Christen sagts ebenfalls?—Dass man

Once one has chosen a specific piece of Shakespeare, Horace, or the Bible, and sought out the original circumstances in which it was singularly generated, says Herder, then you can forget all the painstaking commentaries on such poetry and simply submit wholeheartedly to its language. Let the characteristic spirit of its author work his or her living presence upon you so that you resonate sympathetically with the heartbeat and soul of the human who is speaking to you. Brooding analysis is not what interpretation of poetry needs. If you do not listen to the subtle sound of each movement in the text as that of an approaching friend or lover, but crassly measure, parse, and dissect each element of what is there, you will never hear its voice and be able to intuit and transmit its worth. The best literary critique is not to take David's psalm, squeeze it analytically, and hand it back to a person like a pressed out lemon, but to enjoy, highlight, echo its flourishing life alive on the tree. Let the poetic text itself speak, and do it by respecting the text's nature and kind: breathe alive its speech by your own kindredly spirited speaking it. Do not even read it: sing its song! (10:138, 145–46; 11:19, 166; 12:208–210; 6:169; 15:529).[13]

Herder's palingenetic theory of interpretation, as he called it, of "artificial respiration" or resuscitation, one might say, was a revolutionary slap in the face of the established, academic biblical hermeneutic practice because it undercut the standard court of scholarly appeal and opened exegesis up wide for unpredictable innovation. Old Testament biblical narrative is a blend of strongly working images, is factual history retold poetically: it takes an unusual blend of childlike naiveté and wide-ranging genius, not to say the Spirit of God, says Herder, as Jerome and Eras-

---

ja nicht ein fremdes System, eine voraufgefasste Hypothese hineinbringen müsse, und die Hermeneutik sagts ebenfalls!—dass ein uraltes, Orientalisches, Poetisches, National- und Populärstück, was lebender Gesang der Tradition seyn sollte, nicht wie ein gerichtliches Testament müsse behandelt werden, das—auch das muss jeder gesunde Exeget zugeben . . ." (6:34–35).

13 "Briefe, das Studium der Theologie betreffend" (1780): "Den Geist Horaz, Homers, Sophokles, Plato lasse ich aus ihren Schriften auf mich wirken: sie sprechen zu mir, sie singen, sie lehren mich: ich bin um sie, lese in ihr Herz, in ihre Seele; so allein wird mir ihr Buch verständlich, so allein habe ich auch, mit den Zeugnissen der Geschichte, das beste Siegel, dass diese Schriften von ihnen sind, weil ihr inneres Bild nämlich, ihr mir gegenwärtiger, lebendiger Eindruck auf mich wirket" (10:146). A review of 1773: ". . . so ist solche einem großen Original nachtretende, nachempfindende Kritik die beste" (5:330). When Herder sent Johann Heinrich Merck his translations of some songs in Shakespeare, Herder told him: "Sehen Sie nun, wie ich Sie befriedige. Aber bei Leibe horchen Sie nur auf Ton und nicht auf Worte: Sie müssen nur singen, nicht lesen." Letter of 28 October 1770, in *Briefe an J. H. Merck von Goethe, Herder, Wieland* et altera, Karl Wagner, ed. (Darmstadt: Diehl, 1835), 13.

mus recognized, to be a reliable interpreter of biblical writings (10:11; 11:169–70).

Behind Herder's critical hermeneutical affront was not only his aesthetic theory, but also a theory of language and of history. Following Hamann's lead on language, Herder rejected the traditional view that language is a makeshift system of signs that serves as carrier for concepts. Instead, the whole world is a kind of glossolalia that the human creature naturally formed into the medium of speech, which is the passionate, proleptic, similating key of knowledge in human life (5:51; 8:170–71; 15:536).[14] So Herder was primed to honor the oral tradition of Eastern poetry and ready to reject the conception of poetry as "letters," *écriture*, as a reduction to something stillborn, especially when the material was biblical "literature."

Although Herder assumed the Semitic tongue was historically first, original, and therefore somehow a best clue to human poetic ability, Herder's view of history as an orderly passing of cultures, better and worse, with different spirits, kept him from attempting to go back and recapture a precious lost datum, or to represtenate contemporary human activity by redoing what was better earlier. Instead, the interpreter attempts to enlarge and deepen our own cultural awareness of what is human by making the dated poetic text accessible and "working," thus spurring. . . us Germans on to speak *die Sprache des menschlichen Herzens* Germanly, enriched today. Herder faces the problem of *Horizontverschmelzung* by positing that the desirable, right reading of an older poetic text (*dies lebendige Lesen*) is a reading that comes truly to know, and that means, says Herder, to love (*das wahre Erkennen ist lieben, ist menschlich fühlen*): the right, true reading comes about by extending yourself empathically

---

14 The cast of Hamann's philosophy of language, which shaped Herder's thought, can be found in statements such as the following: "In Bildern besteht der ganze Schatz menschlicher Erkenntnis und Glückseligkeit" (*Sämtliche Werke,* ed. Nadler, 2:197); "Leidenschaft allein giebt Abstractionen sowohl als Hypothesen Hände, Füße, Flügel; —Bildern und Zeichen Geist, Leben und Zunge—" (2:208); ". . . wir haben an der Natur nichts als Turbatverse und *disiecti membra poetae* zu unserm Gebrauch übrig. Diese zu sammeln ist des Gelehrten; sie auszulegen, des Philosophen; sie nachzuahmen—oder noch kühner!—sie in Geschick zu bringen, des Poeten bescheiden Theil" (2:198–99).

"Vom Erkennen und Empfinden des menschlichen Seele" (1778): "Was wir wissen, wissen wir nur aus Analogie, von der Kreatur zu uns und von uns zum Schöpfer" (8:170). "Die stille Ähnlichkeit, die ich im Ganzen meiner Schöpfung, meiner Seele und meines Lebens empfinde und ahnde: der große Geist, der mich anwehet und mir im Kleinen und Großen, in der sichtbaren und unsichtbaren Welt Einen Gang, Einerley Gesetze seiget: der ist mein Siegel der Wahrheit" (8:171). Herder's "analogy" might best be understood as a natural human act close to what Karl Aschenbrenner calls "simulation," in *The Concepts of Criticism* (Boston: Reidel, 1974), 313–19.

to live within (*beleben*), to divine the humanity-invigorating *Bildung* of the original author.¹⁵ Humanity, Herder believed, is the one same reality through all of its changing configurations (8:177–78, 198–200, 208–9, 435–36; 11:19, 167);¹⁶ so Humanity provides the Archimedean point that generates the line that intersects the hermeneutic circle and heads directly for its illuminating, certifying center.

An epistemology that introduces "love" as the decisive circuit-breaker for true historical knowledge was as little fashionable in philosophical circles then as it is now. For us not to misunderstand Herder's humane point and think it jejune, one needs to remember that Herder is talking *Gefühl* in a deep and full sense not to be reduced to an emotive reaction or to the very physio-organic conception of *Einfühlung* developed much later, for example, by Theodor Lipps.¹⁷ Despite its resident subjectivism, Herder's project for bridging the distance between current interpreter and ancient or foreign text is not to solicit a reader's "response" to a text, but to enjoin the reader's *performance* of the text. That is the most important distillate of what forms, in my judgment, a cluster of insights in Herder's hermeneutic theory most relevant for us today.

(1) Herder exposed the ontological inadequacy of words and paraphrase for introducing a poetic text, yet called attention to the sense of conceiving interpretation to be a propaedutic prolegomenon rather than a tiresome, post mortem analysis.¹⁸

---

15 "Vom Erkennen und Empfinden der menschlichen Seele" (1778): "Im Grad der Tiefe unsres Selbstgefühls liegt auch der Grad des Mitgefühls mit andern: denn nur uns selbst können wir in andre gleichsam hinein fühlen" (8:200). "Wo es der Mühe lohnt, ist dies lebendige Lesen, diese Divination in die Seele des Urhebers das einzige Lesen und das tiefste Mittel der Bildung" (8:208).

16 "Vom Besser-schildern ist hier die Rede nicht: denn die Wahrheit war zu allen Zeiten dieselbe; dass jeder wahrnehmende Mensch aber seinen Gegenstand eigen schildern kann, als ob er noch nicht geschildert wäre; darüber, dünkt mich, sollte kein misstrauender Zweifel walten" (15:530).

17 Cf. "Einfühlung, inner Nachahmung, und Organempfindungen," *Archiv für die gesamte Psychologie* 1 (no. 1, 1903): 185–204. Friedrich Meinecke uses the category of "Einfühlung" to catch the genius of Herder's contribution, in his *Die Entstehung des Historismus* (München: Oldenbourg, 1959, 357–58, 378, 402–3); but again, one must not take "empathy" in a reduced, psychologized sense.

18 Herder complains in his piece on Shakespeare (1773): "Hätte ich doch Worte dazu, um die einzelne Hauptempfindung, die also Jedes Stück beherrscht, und wie eine Weltseele durchströmt, zu bemerken" (5:224–25). Herder castigates paraphrase as "ein widriges Ding" in the theological education of his day, since it misled students into thinking they then had the proper knowledge of their texts (1780, 10:249, 251–53). Klopstock, however, Herder calls the Asaph of the German folk, because Klopstock first helped the German people hear "den wahren Ton des Ebräischen Psalms"

(2) Herder broke through the paralyzing antinomy of the hermeneutic circle with respect to literary art by locating the primary, defining feature of interpretation at performance. For poetry, then, interpretation means first of all reading it aloud; and with foreign texts, interpretation means an engaging translation.

(3) Although Herder can be challenged on promoting eisegesis,[19] his defense, which invokes Edward Young's principle on the strangeness of originality (12:235), claimed that if the unique otherness of the poetic text is respected, then its root truth in the necessary historical overview will materialize in a new reading (10:138; 11:22). There is a text in Herder's class, and like a quasi-subject the poetic text mysteriously asks interpreters to become human chameleons, or something like a ventriloquist's living dummy.

III.

Let me introduce my concluding remarks by referring to a significant example of the genial and upsetting import of Herder's theory for hermeneutical praxis: Herder's treatment of the Old Testament Song of Songs, which turned the received tradition of his day upside-down and has largely determined the standard, modern interpretation of the book as an anthology of love lyrics and erotic songs.

Theological research is best served by study of the biblical writings, says Herder, because the Bible is the source book for being human. It is not written as a prissy primer in heaven for angels. The Bible, like Noah's ark, holds both clean and unclean animals. Although it is couched in symbol-rich language (*Symbolsprache*), the Bible has been so over read into a great code of connected, mystifying significations, we would do

---

(1783, 12:227).

19 Thomas Willi's excellent dissertation, *Herders Beitrag zum Verstehen des Alten Testaments* (Tübingen: Mohr–Siebeck, 1971), questions whether Herder's *einfühlende Exegese* does not confuse what the ancient authors said with what we contemporaries want to know (32). Willi thinks Herder's translations of Homer show "...dass es Herder immer mehr um eigene Nachschöpfung als um treue Wiedergabe ging..." (49). René Wellek's masterful overview of *Sturm und Drang* and Herder comments that Herder's "Shakespeare piece is... lyrical rhapsody rather than a piece of criticism" (*A History of Modern Criticism* (Yale University Press, 1955; 1:193), and judges that many of Herder's theses "... were important sayings, salutary in their time for their stress on understanding, but they also contain the germs of much that is bad in criticism since Herder's time: mere impressionism, the idea of 'creative' criticism with its pretensions to duplicating a work of art by another work of art, the critical errors of excessive attention to biography and the intention of the author, mere appreciation, and complete relativism" (1:184).

better, with Luther, to honor and take its straight, vital, gut sense, and let allegory and typological readings go. The point of the whole Bible, says Herder, is the hardly perceptible yet coming, everlasting Rule of Christ, and it is told so ordinarily, like simple history, about natural occurrences, we would do well to understand that supernatural-godly things, according to the biblical writings, are normally natural, like your being born, and being loved by someone, and the unnatural is ungodly. So the Bible is a charter (*Urkunde*) for human nature rather than a proselyting tract (10:7–9, 147–49, 207, 209, 213–14; 11:12–14; 8:554, 591).[20]

The Old Testament book called Solomon's greatest Song (*Hohelied*) reveals the natural, erotic passion of good, young king Solomon, before he went the way of all *flesh*—*Wein, Weibe und Gesang*—in later, corrupted age (cf. 1 Kings 10–11). These songs of love are a God-authorized *Urlied der Liebe* (primal song of impassioned, sexual human love). Their Eastern frankness may offend our fastidious Crebillonian taste accustomed to off-color double-entendre, says Herder, but if you will let the strange, sensuous purity of this biblical testament, with its wild, innocent tenderness, overwhelm your sensibility, then you will grow in humanity—which is the spirit and thrust of the Bible (8:509–10, 523, 543–45, 591, 594, 628–29, 638).[21]

Of the two different translations of the Song of Songs Herder did, the earlier, unpublished version of 1776 gets closest to the unified chorus of voices the text presents. Herder's interpretive translation, which runs on in rapid, short, rhymed, dithyrambic fashion to mime what he believed was naturally intrinsic to rhapsodic bursts of passion, is accompanied by a constant playful, imaginative replay and foreplay of comment on the subtle images, erotic motifs, and exclamations of desire that echo and reecho one another in the book. The original composer or editor has a fine thread of unity in stringing these songs together to cover the whole gamut of human passions, says Herder, from the first bud of a kiss, through threats and pleasures, until the full flower of joyful bodily

---

20 "Lieder der Liebe" (1776): "Der Geist Luthers in Auslegung der Bibel ging vor mir, der mit seinem Feuerblicke immer so gerade in den ersten Sinn, den klaren Wortverstand drang, und diesen Grund der Auslegung seiner Kirche als Wahrheitprobe, als Feld des Erkenntnisses übermachte" (8:591). "Briefe, das Studium der Theologie, betreffend" (1780): ". . . das beste Studium der Gottesgelehrsamkeit ist Studium der Bibel, und das beste Lesen dieses göttlichen Buchs ist menschlich" (10:7).

21 "Lieder der Liebe" (1776): "Nur kommt Alles darauf an, mit was Herzen du in ihm wandelst? ob mit dem Taubenauge der Unschuld, oder mit einem Blick voll Unzucht und Schalkheit?" (8:591). "Geist der Bibel ists, alles Göttliche für uns zu humanisiren, und Geist der Mystik, alle Formen und Gestalten zu verdrängen, alles Menschliche zu vergötten und hinaufzuhimmeln" (8:638).

consummation is exultingly sung, followed by a concluding sigh. But the felt "connections" do not make it into one piece; these gems of short songs are like single pearls on a string, extolling the rich vagaries and happinesses of rapturous manly-womanly love (8:535, 539, 541, 593, 623, 628, 632–35).[22]

Herder virtually performs the poetic text by letting the text speak its own artistry in Herder's voice, which intently maintains a resounding aesthetic quality for its finish. Ricoeur's attempt to bring phenomenology inside hermeneutic theory is much more sophisticated, but Ricoeur's reading of even the early Husserl is based on a method that treats a text as a metaphor. The interpreter is asked to discover a resemblance there where ordinary attention may find none, and then to present the critically experienced, covert, surplus meaning so it may be publically discovered.[23] Herder's approach counts on surprise too, but does not second-guess a reading so much. Ricoeur's suspicious method intends to move beyond dialogue with a dialectical conversation on the "predicates of discourse" in order to detect the meanings and references to something spoken or written.[24] Herder's hermeneutic theory and praxis on literary texts is more elemental, less intellectualistic, and highlights correctly, it seems to me, that the appropriate, foundational interpretation of literature is to be bona fide aesthetic activity, to be rhetorical, if you will, and not "scientific."

Gadamer is a close relative of Herder in Gadamer's trusting that *Sprache* is not a code that needs to be broken, but is the most human, societal reservoir in which all texts and interpreters of all times play. *Sprachlichkeit* is the universal source of all the "unconsummated symbols" found in one's mother tongue, and therefore guarantees the final intelligibility of every human utterance and any text's questions.[25] Herder is

---

22 For my own translation and interpretation of this biblical book, cf. *The Greatest Song: In critique of Solomon* (Toronto Tuppence Press, 1968/1988). Herder almost recognizes the unity of the piece in 1776, something Luther did not find; but the text that Herder voices seems to miss the kerygmatic, saving note Luther did find, probably because Herder's basic, earlier Humanist stance still crowds in upon his reading.

23 Paul Ricoeur, "Phenomenology and Hermeneutics," in *Hermeneutics and the Human Sciences*. edited and translated by John B. Thompson (Cambridge University Press, 1981), 101–28. Also, Ricoeur, *The Rule of Metaphor: Multi-disciplinary studies of the creation of meaning in language*, translated by R. Czerny (University of Toronto Press, 1977), 321–22.

24 Ricoeur, *Interpretation Theory: Discourse and the surplus of meaning* (Fort Worth: Texas Christian University Press, 1976), 10–12, 15–19, 22–23.

25 Hans-Georg Gadamer, "Rhetorik, Hermeneutik und Ideologiekritik," Metakritische Erörterungen zu "Wahrheit und Methode" (1967), in *Kleine Schriften* (Tübingen:

not so conservative as Gadamer, expecting the *Botschaft des Heilen* by following Plato's affirmation of die *Aktualität des Schönen*.[26] Like Gadamer Herder does not require archaeological reconstruction of a past event to validate an interpretation. But Herder wants more than "adequate truth," and Herder does not settle for a permanent dialogical intersubjectivity.[27] When an interpreter performs the text (as I extract the thesis from Herder's account), while one cannot deny the performer's remaining subjectivity, the relatively dated and located subjectivity of the interpreter is absorbed in the human attempt to listen to the other speak, to let one's neighbor be heard. So there is definite historical closure of a (personally) specific literary meaning, but it is met with an ongoing imaginative openness; there is recognition of an enduring subjectivity that, nevertheless, is determined by a common text-embodiment or artwork objective to our possible plural receptions.

Herder's position is too supple to be caught in the battle lines of either settling for an everlasting dialectic or presuming to make a conclusive judgment. Yet as I understand Herder's thesis that translation is the most fruitful paradigm for hermeneutic activity, and Herder's provocative proposal that interpreters perform poetic texts, Herder's position would also avoid the no man's land of quicksand, the space in-between battle lines, that post-Structuralists try to inhabit. If it is a Deconstructivist project to square analytically the literary circle, or to poeticize theory, the fault lies, as seen from Herder's perspective, in a fundamental, systematic misconstruction that cannot help but lead to textual harassment and psychomachia, not to say hara-kiri, for interpretation. If the qualifying coefficient of literature is symbolific, then the analytically unforecloseable nuancefulness of literary meaning is assured. Although one cannot enforce a canonic reading by argument or by fiat, to pretend that exposition must therefore be interminable ends in trivializing the text one means to save.

If truth in interpretation is more a quality of human responsibility acquitting itself in deed than it is in finding the experimentally verifiable correspondence of concept to datum or in fixing a univocal and unmistakable clarity to speech, then Herder's Columbus egg solution to the vicious hermeneutic circles should commend itself to the current debaters: a translating performance is the most basic, appropriate method. The

---

Mohr–Siebeck, 1967), 1:123, 127–30.
26 Gadamer, *Die Aktualität des Schönen Kunst als Spiel Symbol und Fest* (1974) (Stuttgart: Philipp Reclam, 1977), 18–21,41–43,47–49.
27 Gadamer, *Wahrheit und Methode: Grundzüge einer philosophischen Hermeneutik* (1960), (Tübingen: Mohr–Siebeck, 1972), 344–60, 432–52.

otherness of the text, historical circumstantiality, and the current idiom of an informed . . . artist are all respected.

In fact, my reading of Herder in this chapter is an attempt to practice what Herder preached. A normative translation of texts is similar in nature to the invention of a metaphor, and a good metaphor, a good translation like a sound blood transfusion, provides new life—the very rationale of interpretation.

NEEDED: BIBLICAL RECOVERY OF HUMAN CORPOREALITY AND HISTORICAL INSTITUTIONALITY IN GOD'S WORLD

for Gerald Vandezande
with thanks to God for his many years of
proclaiming biblical wisdom in the public square

To speak under the intriguing title "After Evangelicalism" became somewhat daunting when I realized maybe it was meant to be a post mortem on the communion of saints to whom I belong.

The direction of my remarks take their lead from God's Newer Testamented Word booked "To the Hebrews." Let me read into our hearing just a couple of those tough-love-talking paragraphs:

—There is a lot we could say about this [the Christ as Melchizedekian high priest], which is difficult to make intelligible, since you people have become lazy in your listening. Although by this time you people ought to be teachers, you still need someone to teach you again the ABC's of what God has said. In fact, you have become adults who still need milk and can't stomach solid food!

Everyone who lives on milk [like a baby] is not able to handle the matter of talk and thought that does what is right. Such an adult is infantile. Mature people thrive on solid food. Mature people are those who have habitually exercised their sensitivities to discern what is honest-to-God and what is evil-minded.

Therefore, people, let's get past the basic doctrines of the Christ and move on to mature business. Don't keep on laying down the [same old] foundation of "repent from doing dead works" and "believe in God." I mean, don't keep on again and again about "the teaching of baptismal

---

Spoken at Cornerstone University College, Grand Rapids, Michigan, 17 September 2005 AD.

washings" and "ordination," about "resurrection of the dead and everlasting judgment": let's get past all that elementary stuff! And we **will** grow up [into the mature significance of Christ's highpriesthood]—**God** willing— [Hebrews 5:11–6:3]

Hearing the LORD speak so, to put it biblically bluntly, my thesis is: God asks Evangelicals to grow up.

Auch ich bin ein Evangelischer! albeit from a European Reformational Calvinian faith-thought tradition.

As I researched the topic, read authorities like Sandeen and Marsden on the twists and turns in history of the Evangelicalist church, especially in the United States of America, the 57 varieties there came to be, the terrible energy spilled in identifying the splinters in other believers' eyes, the **Neo**-Evangelicalism's self-consciously distancing itself from Fundamentalism in the 1940s, and now in our millennium Stanley Grenz and Robert Webber's excited expectation that a new generation of "younger evangelicals" are renewing the gospel church witness better fitted to our apostate culture, which has lost its center; and as I recalled my own wholesome rural pietist upbringing on the South side of Long Island, New York (without taboos!) in the 1930s–'40s, the years of rich traditional worship experienced in Reformation churches in Switzerland, Germany, the Netherlands, Australia, a year of singing Gregorian chants in Rome's *Anselmo fuori i muri,* **and** hymns with the persecuted Waldensian believers there in Italy, being present at story telling of Jesus in the Alikalia village square, 200 miles inland in Sierra Leone, breaking bread with the beleaguered Protestants in Mexico and the small faithful church following Christ in Muslim-dominated Indonesia, briefly undergoing the Orthodox monastic regimen on Mount Athos: given a lifetime of blessing in a not strait-laced Bunyanesque but in a raucous Chaucerian pilgrimage . . . to Amsterdam rather than Canterbury, let's say, aware of Vatican II, Lausanne 1974, Newbigin, Appiah, Gordon Spykman, Philip Jenkins, Sander Griffioen, Elsa Tamez, and others, is there anything I could contribute to this bouillabaisse of Evangelicalism and its afterlife? Are there particular ingredients that could foster maturity in the life of the Christ-discipled peoplehood of God who are marked by the Holy Spirit?

My offering for your consideration gives attention to four interrelated matters: (1) the **glossolalia** revelation of **God's creation**; (2) the **good corporeality of humans** Jesus Christ died and was resurrected to redeem; (3) the **historical** blessing of **the Lord's institutional holds** on society; and (4) the unhurried Holy Spirited **eschatonic priestly task** of God's adopted children from every nation under the sun.

(1) Glossolaliac revelation of God's creation. Evangelical Christians are known to stake their identity on being **biblically** orthodox, making conversional mission activity primary, and prescribing a rigorous moral code for living (even if we have a comfortable middle-class Way of life).

But you are not home free if you take the Bible seriously as God's very own proclamation of "good news" to sinners. Do you treat the Bible primarily as a book of doctrines needing to be systematized into a coherent theology that shows the indubitable reasonableness of the christian faith? Is the Bible rather your *vade mecum*, a personal companion, which guides your devotional life and fortifies an intimate reliance on God? Does the Bible actually shape your consciousness, give contour to your outlook, and instigate your doing certain projects instead of others, which take life time? Or do you want to check all of the above?

And where does your Bible start? For persons whose Bible seems to start with "Exodus," there develops a theology highlighting "liberation" for the oppressed "way down in Egyptland." If your evangelical Bible begins virtually with the Newer Testament gospel of John, let's say, or the book "Acts of the Apostles," your Bible reading is likely to have a predominantly Christological incarnational focus, a strong soteriological character.

The Bible I read begins with "Genesis," and the one true story God tells from "Genesis" through to the "Apocalypse of Jesus Christ given to John" is anchored in that initial revelation that **this world, which we inhabit, belongs to God, a creatural world the Lord God created good**. In Eve and Adam we human creatures broke the Lord's trusting us to be care-takers of God's marvelous creatures everywhere; so the Bible relates the merciful *magnalia Dei*, the great deeds of the ever faithful, loving covenantal Lord God's gradually working out the gracious restoration of the world through bunglers like Abraham, Moses, faulty charismatic judges, military generals like David who wrote poetry, and fiery idiosyncratic prophets like Ezekiel, until finally the Lord sent God's own Son, Jesus Christ more visibly himself into history to do the job (Matthew 21:33–41), who then provided the Holy Spirit to equip us earthlings (John 14:15–26) to take up again the ministry of reconciling God's creatural world back to Godself, which shalom Christ will someday coming bring to completion (2 Corinthians 5:17–19).

Creation anchors the true biblical story. Creation itself is already basic good news, provides the founding reality to the panoramic vision we humans need for our faith to grow on. If the truth of creation and the dearness of creatures—like rocks and trees, stalks of corn (Psalm 1, 65, Job 23), fish in the seas (Psalm 104), the cows of Nineveh (Jonah 4:11)—if their existence and continual praise of the LORD (Psalm 19) is not up front in one's Bible, one tends to discount history and may humanistically skew our tasks down to fighting sin. If "creation" is not first in your biblical interpretation, I think one's conception of "salvation" can be thinned out to become an escape for human mortality, rather than allow "salvation" to hold the full-orbed biblical promise and deliverance of a new heavens and a new earth filled with the refined treasures of the nations honoring God (Isaiah 60, Revelation 21:22–27), which tribute to the LORD is especially being inaugurated since Christ's ascension in this very day and age.[1]

—There are two important points I should perhaps try to make clear briefly *en passant* at this juncture about Bible reading and creation, which may be moot for some. The first is this: "**the Holy Scriptures [credo] are God-speaking literature given to us historically for our learning by faith the one true story of the LORD's Reign acoming and the contours of our obedient response**."[2] I take that to mean the Bible is the inscripturation of God speaking about certain actualities (indicative), like the birth of Isaac in Gerar in the Negeb (Genesis 21:1–7), Israel's civil war around 734–732 BC (2 Kings 16), the resurrection of Jesus Christ during the rule of Pontius Pilate (John 19), and the spitable lukewarm complacency of a Laodicean congregation once upon a time (Revelation 2:14–22). This history-telling, which God has had literarily booked, enjoins (imperative) listening readers of every tribe and language to trust the reliability of what has been so precisely written (as medical doctor Luke puts it, Luke 1:1–4) so that you become pricked in your heart and be made wise enough to follow God's direction being given.

For me the biblical "Song of Songs," for example, is not a fanciful allegory about Yahweh and Israel or about Christ and his bride the Church, but is the LORD's critique of old lascivious Solomon's leadership (1 Kings 9–11, Song of Songs 8:11–12) offset by God's exuberant bless-

---

1 Cf. Ecclesiastes 3:15; Luke 10:17–20, v.18; John 12:20–33, v.31; Revelation 12:7–12.

2 C. Seerveld, *How to Read the Bible to Hear God Speak* (Sioux Center: Dordt College Press, 2003), xii; cf. 76–86.

ing of the erotic joy to be experienced by woman and man joined in a mutual jealous vow of love (Proverbs 5:15–23). Biblical imprecatory psalms are not an outdated, overblown barbaric embarrassment for New Testament Christians, but are deeply grieved intercessory prayers by helpless believers for **the Lord** of the angels **to stop! the violence** done to the weak (foreshadowing **Christ's cursing!** us hypocrites in Matthew 23 for perfunctorily minding our tithes but letting slide just-doing, showing mercy, and being faithful in our daily tasks with God watching [Matthew 23:23–24]). Nehemiah chapter 7 and the genealogy of Matthew 1 are not just collected evidential factual archival data, but are imaginatively crafted links in the single biblical story of the Lord's everlasting faithfulness to God's adopted people through generations of misery, failures, exile and evil, and a testimony that even Jesus' lineage was not kosher (Tamar, Rahab, Ruth, the wife of Hittite Uriah, Manasseh), so it is not **our** human performance but **God's** grace that makes the world go round.

That is, the God-speaking Bible is an amazing, trustworthy, intratextually unified variegated **literary** account of how the Lord God deals with God's creatures world without end, explicating Jesus Christ as God incarnate in person! who suffered, died, and has triumphed to give all who believe in him as Lord everlasting life—we may live expecting Christ's splendid return—telling us God the Holy Spirit is monitoring and motivating the faithful who are co-operating in having the Lord's will be done on earth now as it is in heaven. The Bible is not an argument. **Holy Scripture is simply a sterling authoritative testimony telling truly what's up** as it is, has been, will be, and should be, **with the power to change floundering humans living at their wits' end into becoming visionary dedicated followers of Jesus Christ as *kurios*, Lord.** "We believe without a doubt all things contained in the Scriptures," says the 1561 *Confessio Belgica* of the communion to which my wife and I belong, "because the Holy Spirit testifies in our hearts that they are from God" (article 5). A person is asked to accept the penetrating truth of Scripture the way a child trustingly accepts as true the Bible story Mother reads to you before you go to sleep nights—"Jesus loves you."

And if the Bible is not an argument, but no less true because God is speaking in the format of literature, maybe this is a more wholesome, mature!? way to take up and read the Bible than to mistake it in Scottish Common Sense Realist fashion turned Positivist as an inerrant documentation of empirical facts that can be logically harnessed to compel others to agree that its propositions you have selected are not nonsense . . . ?

A second pivotal point on Bible and creation I need to mention in passing takes its cue from Psalm 119:105: "Your Word, [LORD,] is a searchlight for my feet, a bright light upon my pathway."

A wise person will not just stare blindedly into the bright light one has in hand, but use the searchlight to discover the lay of the land where one is to walk. In keeping with such a biblical prompt, in my confessional faith-thought tradition of the Reformation, young John Calvin's metaphor carries on Psalm 119's eye-opening insight by affirming: the Scriptures are the "eye-glasses" for reading God's creational revelation aright.[3] And I should like to extend Psalm 119 and John Calvin's proposal, provided one keep Scripture's single true story nature ever in mind, which I have mentioned, and not just dip in and out of the Bible looking for prooftexts to back up dogmatic assertions: if you veritably swim in the Scriptures, somehow come to live in its narrative kerygmatic wisdom as the very normal unpolluted air you breathe, then you will come to realize **the created world is God's tongue-talk, and the Scriptural message provides us the key of knowledge to interpret creation's glossolalia.**

God's psalms like 19, 1, 8, 104, 119, 148, report on the speechless voices and uttered noises of the obedient sun, verdant trees, earthquaked mountains, wind and wild snakes, telling the wonders of God open for us humans to decipher as a chorus of praise to the LORD. The biblical section of "Numbers," "Ecclesiastes," and "Romans" (especially chapters 9–11 and 12) reveal our world to be a cosmic theatre, *theatrum Dei* (to use John Calvin's term),[4] where so much transpires, everything coming and going, flourishing and passing away, an inherently temporal but eschatonic processional reality that invites us human history-keepers, who make our entrances and exits for 70 or 80 brief years, to discern traces of the trails of human footsteps obedient and disobedient to the LORD's mercifully provident will, and tell those tales to edify our grandchildren (Psalms 78:1–8, 128:5–6). The magisterial texts of "Deuteronomy," "Isaiah," and "Job" make vivid the LORD God Almighty is the absolutely final, permanent over-seeing Sovereign Holy One who really holds all things and events in God's merciful just-doing hands. And "Proverbs 1–9," for example, the Newer Testament gospels and apostle Paul's letters, enunciate clearly the crux of genuine wisdom—standing in awe before the LORD God—lies only in timely serving the God-man mediator Jesus Christ: only in Jesus' redemptive reign is there meaning for what creaturely exists and happens; all else is vanity and foolishness.

---

3 *Institutio Christianae religionis* (1559), I, 6.1.
4 Ibid. I, 6, 2.

Since Holy Scripture declares that all creation, all the kinds of creatures extant, operate under the good ordinances of the covenant-keeping Creator God, it behooves us humans whom the Lord designated to be caretakers in God's world (Genesis 1:26–31; cf. Matthew 13) to find out what the various structural limits be to which we creatures are subject. God's will for falling objects in the atmosphere and aerodynamic flight; God's laws for healthy genetic pooling, for bonding or exclusion in a pride of lions, or developing wholesome emotional intimacy among humans, for bartering goods and services that will not run amok; God's limits put on thinking if it would be intelligible, and God's order for imaginative activity to be pregnant with obscurity: God's creational ordinances for viral disease as different from bacterial infection, for birthing and aging, for governing other humans that does not tyrannically preempt willing responses, are all discoverable blessings, but not in the Bible. **God's will is revealed not just in the Bible.** God's will for creatures resides also in the good ordinantial embraces, the multisplendored *huqqim* ordering creatural activities, which we humans are called upon to posit as norms to be followed for shalom, or be neglected or violated at one's peril.

And it is important for followers of Jesus Christ disciplined by the Holy Spirit to warm to and grow into this exciting, dangerous task of interpreting God's will revealed in the glossolalia of creation, since if God is speaking in tongues through the weathering of rocks, the genes that develop *retinitis pigmentosa*, and the boomerang calamities of war self-righteous people inflict on themselves, and the interpreters lack a biblically tuned ear and have no Scripturally focused vision, people might think the raucous is just unintelligible static or an impressive thundering. But the Lord is revealing in the glossolalia of God's creation how we creatures were created to be before human sin perverted and polluted, inflicted groaning upon the universe, which the Lord still upholds (Romans 8:19–25).

In capsule form what I am giving in my first point is the rationale for evangelical Christians to move on from Bible Institutes to Christian Colleges with "university" in their name, since colleges study God's glossolaliac **universe**, and not just the Bible. Bible institutes are good for the narrow training of biblical evangelists and church workers, the way a *madrassa* is good in its way for indoctrinating Muslim youth in tenets of the Qu'ran. Seminaries are crucial for strengthening prospective pastors theologically in the dogmata of their particular confessional tradition as a Lutheran, Reformed, Methodist, Baptist, or some other creedal church emphasis. A christian college, however, is not a church seminary, even though they may be faith partners, one evolved out of the other, and both tap the same resources.

Confusing a christian college and a church seminary becomes particularly troublesome if the christian community involved thinks "salvation" has privileged precedence over "creation" in the biblical story. Then study of creation becomes secondary, tag-along, if not an afterthought or a time-and-money consuming irritant. **But "creation" is not supplemental to "salvation" in the biblical account. Creation is fundamental, foundational, integral to the matter of salvation.**

Granted that those who would explore God's creational revelation and prepare the next generation for the mission of nursing, providing political counsel, correcting market economics, planning cities, must have ground their biblical lenses well and honed their hearing to God's redemptive psalmodic voice, and be able to give a good account of their biblical faith in the lordship of Jesus Christ (1 Peter 3:13–17): but christian college profs, as I understand it, do not have to have a seminary B.D. or have passed their Hebrew, Aramaic, and Greek exams. Yet Esther Meek and Matt Bonzo and their students are philosophical missionaries. Gerald Vandezande and James Skillen and cohorts are politically engaged missionaries. Jan Disselkoen and Gideon Strauss are full-time missionaries in the field of literacy and economic action—**christian missionaries in God's world, but not clergy.**

And this is precisely where the biblical rubber hits the creatural road with the project of a christian philosophical systematics. The biblical underlay I have stippled in while exegeting the glossolalia of creation—the jealous Sovereign LORD God covenanting with us creatures to provide an ordered diversity among kinds of things and genetic ordinances for seedtime and harvest continuing to the eschaton, with Jesus Christ as the Archimedean point who alone determines meaning—moves congenially into the Kuyperian-Vollenhovian-Dooyeweerdian idea of philosophy as a synoptic, encyclopedic, conceptually precise thetical framework consonant with biblical givens, a notch more analytically rigorous than a biblically christian "world-and-life-vision." Such is the genius of this Scripturally directed Reformational christian philosophy that it provides orientational wisdom (rather than technically arguing expertise) and ecumenically invites in all academic disciplines to be philosophically busy in mapping out their specific terrain of responsibility and in communally endeavoring to interrelate their findings across professional boundaries to all those in the communion of scholarly saints. Communal christian philosophical activity is necessary if an evangelical christian college wishes to mature in its educational enterprise and not rest with a quasi-seminary arrangement where a dogmatic theology (legitimately in a seminary!) has the defining word institutionally.

This is a sticky item often, I think, because the term "theology" is used loosely, referring to "systematic dogmatic reflection," or to "simple Bible knowledge," or even mistakenly as a synonym for "christian" (as if there were no Muslim "theology"). And there may be occasional jurisdictional disputes in allocating the co-operative tasks of a christian philosophical endeavor and a christian dogmatic theology—nobody has a monopoly on appealing to the Bible. But it is not a put-down of professional dogmatic theological scholarship or of evangelists to say that **teachers and students investigating God's creational revelation need a christian *philosophical* proleptic grasp of things and events that takes seriously the threesome of God's Word**:

> God's "let-there-be" light and an irreducible diversity of kinds of creatures, God's **ordinantial Word**;
> the "let my only begotten Son Jesus, the **Word incarnate**, enter history to rescue the world from perishing"; and
> let my **scripted Word**, where the Holy Spirit particularly hangs out, lead my people onto the pathway of everlasting life.[5]

College teachers need that kind of enveloping **philosophical habit of consciousness** to promote the integral working of varied disciplinary thinking examinations of things by God's *laos*, laity, leading to a worldwide understanding of reconciling creatures back to God's ordered Way of doing things. If a dogmatic theology or a seminary tries to do what is properly the task of philosophy or a university-college rather than focus on its specific confessional, ecclesial purpose, it may lose its special gift of deepening biblical learning and enlivening liturgical acts it could contribute to our daily lives and institutional church praxis.

—Just a footnote yet to the first main point about the grandeur of God's glossolalia.

It is fashionable today to reject holding any definitely spelled out overview, because the Rationalistic Enlightenment meta-narrative of European Progress has proved to be a lie to many, without a happy ending.

---

5   Many years ago I contended that the "Philosophy of the (Cosmonomic) Idea of Law" should much better be named "A philosophy of God's structuring Word," to highlight its Scripturally informed character. Cf. C. Seerveld, "Dooyeweerd's Legacy for Aesthetics," in *The Legacy of Herman Dooyeweerd*, ed. C.T. McIntire (Lanham: University Press of America, 1985), 62, 76 n.59. {see *NA*: 68–71}.

Short stories, micro-narratives, a *bricolage* of local snippets are all one can trust, we are told. Commenting on the virtual world that has become our reality, I recently heard Jean Baudrillard lament at York University in Toronto, "There is no one left to thank!" Even sharp-sighted Peter Berger sometimes seems to adopt the twice-shy posture of a final "utopian" horizon, because then the leading "ideal" constantly changes as it recedes before advancing actuality.[6]

I myself, though it seem old-fashioned, think it is a mark of faith-filled maturity to hold steadfastly, like a child, to the biblically spired over-arching story of God's creation, our human fall into sin, Jesus Christ's action of redemption leading to the happy/sad consummation of history when the Lord returns. That grand biblical narrative is best held with utter certainty in its mystery rather than spoiled by disputable dispensationalistic time-tables, so that, as Carl F.H. Henry wrote when I was still a teenager, "Evangelicals need to take time seriously."[7] We evangelicals need to plant our trees today and hold our choir rehearsals tonight even if Christ is coming back tomorrow morning. Such a trusting, plodding diaconal life—we adopted children of God do know who to thank!—may not impress the so-called "new Christians" suffering in two-thirds world countries whom Samuel Escobar noted are tempted by a revolutionary premillenarianism that wishes to skip historical turmoil to a post-temporal end;[8] but calm awareness that **this is God's world we inhabit for us to cultivate redemptively** may unnerve our worried neighbors and act like an unusual gospel fish hook of hope in a world culture going violently awry, drifting. . . .

(2) The good corporeality of humans. Now I should like to put to the test a sketch of a christian philosophical notion of human nature that might give more grit and fiber to an evangelical conception of men and women usually thinking of eternal souls with earthly bodies. Although

---

6 Peter L. Berger, *A Rumor of Angels: Modern society and the rediscovery of the supernatural* (Garden City: Doubleday, 1969), 103–107. Cf. also Grace Davie, "Europe: The exception that proves the rule?" in *The Desecularization of the World: Resurgent religion and world politics*, ed. Peter L. Berger (Grand Rapids: Eerdmans, 1999), 80.

7 That is my formulation for what Henry says in *The Uneasy Conscience of Modern Fundamentalism* (Grand Rapids: Eerdmans, 1947): "The problem of Fundamentalism then is basically not one of finding a valid message, but rather of giving the redemptive word a proper temporal focus" (65).

8 Samuel Escobar, "The Return of Christ" in *The New Face of Evangelicalism: An International Symposium on the Lausanne Covenant* (London: Hodder & Stoughton, 1976), 260–261.

this is not the occasion to explicate in detail its theological documentation and implications, I do believe the notion of human corporeality I propose is supported by the biblical givens, and offers our faith in Christ's redemptive work enriched horizons, a more complete (*teléios*) appreciation of us marvelous bodied creatures.

When you as a person are constipated or have a sinus-blocked, phlegm-sniffling cold, you realize **you are a body**. If you have ever almost died in a terrible accident, heart attack, or bout with cancer out of the blue, and existentially faced the prospect of not being there anymore, and asked "Why?" then you know **you are a mortal body with a special feature of questioning why I should live and not die?**

To make a long story shorter, my proposal is for us to realize a person *is* **a body**; you don't just take along a body to the hospital for treatment. You also **are a soul**—if you use that language: you don't **have** a soul somewhere in your body as a detachable piece, located near the pineal gland in your head, figured the God-fearing philosopher Descartes. No, "when the LORD God formed the human Adam from dust of the earth and breathed into his nose breath of life, **the man became a living soul**" (Genesis 2:7). ". . . 3000 souls (KJV) were added" to the followers of Christ after Peter's sermon on that early Pentecost—3000 whole persons! in their special dearness to the Lord.

And it is that wholeness, unicity, being of-a-piece to us bodied human creatures that encourages one to think of our corporeality, grounded in life-breathing flesh-and-blood, to include not only pain but also our speaking, imagining, buying food, being loyal to someone; thinking is **bodily** activity! intrinsically affected by whether you are well fed, hungry, dispirited, proud, own a Mercedes Benz, or work underneath it as the mechanic. **Corporeality is multidimensional me in concrete functioning action.** Bodily I experience multiple relationships in my worlded existence: loneliness, frustration, doubt, humor; rape does not violate just a part of a person, but injures the whole woman, the entire abused child or man. I am my body, and body memory can be subliminal but persists with my identity.

Along with this perduring whole corporeality of mutually irreducible and constantly intra-penetrating zones of activity which I am as human body is the inescapable neighborhoodedness of human nature. Everybody here has been born from a mother; you begin as a twosome. And whether you curse that innate neighborhoodedness à la Sartre—"Hell is other people"—or idolize it à la Rousseau as an ideal realm—*la volonté generale*—the blessed enter, *Mitsein* (together-being) is specially given to humans, because all men and women, whether they acknowledge it or not, stand under God's command to love your fellow human as you respect yourself. Every human body, including the enemy, is a neighbor. Human skin, our largest organ, protects you in one's unrepeatable singularity, guards each person's own reserve sphere of bodied intimacy amid this ineluctable ontic state of inter-individuality. That is why torture, surgery, forced nakedness **gets to you**: inflicts shame to your Levinas face; the cut is deeply invasive (however benevolent); and the hateful wreckage of body obliterates one's neighborhoodness and thus destroys the victim's bodied humanity. **Neighborhoodedness is basic to human nature**, even when it is violated.

Further, structurally peculiar about human creatures is their bent upon occasion to pray, whether it be to the sun and moon, to an unknown fertility goddess, to the unspeakable Yahweh, to Allah, or the God revealed in Jesus Christ. Persons also make obeisance to human Rationality to solve our world's problems, or bow down to Technical Expertise. **Humans have a builtin inclination to worship something, to trust a supernatural Power**—maybe in themselves! The buck stops somewhere for everybody human, even if it be the Everlasting Search for anywhere to lay your wandering head except here. This propensity for bodied humans to give allegiance to something Absolute, to be inclined to rest in something Ultimate, is at the very hearted center of human corporeal consciousness.

I personally understand this unconscious depth dimension constituent of human selfhood, this structural proclivity of humans subterraneanly to focus and simultaneously refer all they do and mean to the true God or a pretended Archè as the feature that comprises what it means for women and men to be created "in the image of God." Only Jesus Christ **is** the spitting image of God (2 Corinthians 4:4–6; Hebrews 1:1–4, v.3; 1 Timothy 6:13–16). Men and women are not to be like God (cf. Genesis 3:1–7, v.5 !), God-like, somehow divine, not even analogically, in my judgment. For us humans to be *in* the triune God's image (Genesis 1:26–27)[9] is for all of us to carry around indelibly a sense of divine Origin (*sensus divinitatis*), **the imprimatur of being God-responsible to lead development** like no other creature. **Humans are dedicational creatures who in extreme circumstances supplicate**. Even when we humans betray this dedicational directing shape of our

---

9 "Let us make man *in* **our** image, *after* **our** likeness, and let them guide the development of. . . ."

whole bodied existence, turn *imago dei* into *simulacrum dei*, such sinful perversion of our human nature—dedicating all we be doing and stand for to certain idols—does not eradicate our being specially stamped structurally as "God-responsible."[10] Humans are called by the LORD God to be conformed to the image of the suffering servant Jesus Christ (Isaiah 43:1–7, Philippians 1:27–29, Hebrews 12:1–11) and to be infused with a Holy Spirited dynamic (Galatians 5:16–6:2), but are not by nature, as I grasp it, with a chip (an "immortal soul," a *vünkelin*) *off the Divine Being (Eckhart's Gottheit, isticheit)*.

Given this peculiar fold of having **religion** structurally define corporeal human nature—that we are built, so to speak, with a heart-centered invisible axis, a thrusted fulcrum, if you will, of God-responsibility for every way we act—it becomes clear what is at stake in human creatural life: **bring yourself, your body, in line with the liberating will of God made known in your hearts by the Holy Spirit as you all together, Scripturally directed, scrutinize creatural glossolalia.**

All the facets of our human corporeality—from praying, resource-use, and speaking to our feelings and diet—are splendid openings to obey God. Biblical text prompts one to adopt this perspective: "Don't you people know that your body is a sanctuary of the Holy Spirit among you?" (1 Corinthians 6:16–20, v.19). "Don't let sin dominate in your mortal body ... but present yourselves before God as if come alive from the dead; offer your (bodily) members"—I hear, 'all your corporeal ways of functioning'— "as weapons for doing what is just in God's eyes" (Romans 6:12–14).

Such is the process called "sanctification." Becoming a holy sinner is more complicated than I can indicate right now because certain bodily modes of activity normally presuppose sound functioning of other ways we operate, but not necessarily.[11] There is also a self-reflexive intentionality to our selfhooded, human consciousness one could call a "preconscious" field of awareness, since there is room in our human setup for originating intentions to be modified or reconsidered before they surface in one's enacted deed.[12] We humans also harbor a functional "subcon-

---

10 I emphasize the **structural** character of the human *sensus deitatis* because to credit human nature with a natural, valid but truncated ***cognitio*** *Dei* would take our anthropological reflection, I believe, in a wrong direction.

11 Cf. C. Seerveld, "The Importance of Imaginativity in Schooling," *Rainbows for the Fallen World: Aesthetic life and artistic task* (Toronto: Tuppence Press, 1980/2005), 140–141. Autistic children usually have a very active precocious intelligence while being socially handicapped.

12 But Christ rejects the Pharisaical ploy that lustful intention alone absolves one from

scious" layer, the sub-sensitive elemental, rather intractable corporeality of physical drives and biotic "instincts." Augustine complains somewhere, "My conscious life has been fairly pure lately, Lord, but could you please clean up my dreams?" And it is so, one could be a health food activist and have a scurrilous vocabulary; one could be deeply pious yet reside like a rich profligate in a Kinkade-style gated community. The patterns our varied kinds of act-responses take over the years become a person's dispositions, relatively lasting traits we call variously one's character, temperament, style, prejudices . . . and most everybody's psycho-somatic history is mottled, if not a little disjointed. Your hearted selfhood may be firmly in the grip of the Holy Spirit, but it takes time for the whole body to wag its tail into line.

Yet the happy gist of my second point is that God's creating us corporeally whole is a good, wonderful gift! an absorbing mystery exciting to explore, primed for all manner of thankfulness. Whether we eat onions and drink water, socialize or think, scratch an itch or sing a song, do crossword puzzles or caress a loved one, do everything bodily to the glory of God (cf. 1 Corinthians 10:23–33, v.31).

It is putting a curse upon God's handiwork when thinkers in Western culture, like Plato, denigrate body as the visible material stuff, an erotically susceptible drag on the mental spiritual soul part of man: σῶμα is the *séma* (tomb) of the *psyché*; death! is the liberation of the soul.[13] The error comes, it seems to me, by the philosopher's abstracting theoretically a person's corporeality (concrete timed action) and "spirituality" (the peculiar structuring *coram Deo* responsibility) of humans and hypothesizing the results into a deiformic immortal soul substance and a disparaged mortal physical body container. Such a pagan dichotomized and later trichotomized (the life breath God gives and takes away from a person was separately discerned and given apart status) anthropology became the overlay for reading Newer Testament Scripture. Later gifted christian thinkers like Thomas Aquinas, working through Aristotle's refined, tightened up conception of man, christianized the misformation, and Protestant Scholastics have to this day continued the thought tradition starkly formulated by the great Irish poet Yeats:

Consume my heart [soul] away; sick with desire
And fastened to a dying animal.[14]

I don't need to rehearse chapter and verse of the many variations

---

actual fornication (Matthew 5:27–32, Mark 7:14–23).
13 Plato, *Gorgias*, 492e7–493a5, *Phaidon*, 64a4–68c4.
14 Yeats, "Sailing to Byzantium" (1927).

to this dualistic philosophical anthropology, which splits a man into a rational moral soul and a physical body (which physique ascetics and Stoics tend and keep lean so as to trouble least one's soul). But I could mention its depressing effect often found in evangelical circles on understanding and valuing artistry, which is palpably **sensible**, material. In fine Platonic form art is considered kosher only if it illustrates good doctrinal ideas, or transports us earthlings "into the heavenlies," mediates us lowly creatures' encounter with a transcendent ineffable Beauty of the *mysterium tremendum*—construals of human artistry I find wrong and foolish but very popular.[15] Feminists also correctly note the slight women have received from the Platonized dualist view of the human, since women are considered mostly body, at best an instrument for uterine care, at worst a constant stimulus to arouse sexual desire so distracting to rational reflection—

But let me conclude this point on the good corporeality of us human creatures by making clear I am not countering the dualistic soul-plus-body idea with the age-old monist reduction of human nature to being a clump of moving atomic particles in space somehow outfitted with life, sensibility, and the ability to get things done. The prevalent Materialist conception of humans today as a bare consuming Body machine, highly sexualized, which can buy happiness, is a travesty of the full-orbed corporeality I have sketched. "Body" in our apostate culture may be all that humans are made out to be, but such voracious pleasure brutes each have their price and are disposable, in war and in the vacationing peace niche-marketing magazines advertise. However, holy Scripture, which indeed recognizes our bodily fragility—we are "clay jars" writes the apostle Paul—makes plain God hallowed corporeality by self becoming human flesh (sarx!) in Jesus Christ (John 1:14): so God cherishes us humans who "always are carrying around (tokens of) the suffering death of Jesus in the body **so that the life of Jesus will be made manifest *in our* [clay jar] bodies**" [for clay jar diagram see *NA*: 174]. We corporeal creatures are to show the light of God, the life Christ brings to earth, **in our bodies!** (2 Corinthians 4:1–10, v.10).[16]

---

15 Cf. George Steiner, *Real Presences* (University of Chicago Press, 1989); Pope John Paul II (Easter letter to Artists, 1999), and Pope Benedict XVI (as Cardinal Ratzinger), "The Beauty and the Truth of Christ" (August 2002). Cf. also comments by Robert E. Webber on "worship as an art form" in *The Younger Evangelicals: Facing the challenges of the New World* (Grand Rapids: Baker, 2002), 198–199.

16 The apostle Paul refers to the *stigmata* of Jesus' suffering and life showing up on his corporeal existence (Galatians 6:17), a kind of Holy Spirit baptismal mark protecting him and certifying his discipleship of following the Christ, the very opposite of the

So the challenge I present for us evangelical believers is to grow up, grow out of the oversimplified soul-with-body view of humans, and explore the Scripturally led philosophical anthropology of neighborhooded, selfhooded humans as an active bodied terrain where the Holy Spirit wrestles with sinful principalities and powers for the mastery of our corporeal members (Ephesians 6:10–20, v.12).

(3) The blessing of God's institutional holds on society in history. Just as the development movement of a sonata may be the hardest to listen to, my third point may cause some difficulty.

I should like to distinguish and relate the organized church (ἐκκλησία), the body of Christ at large (τὸ σῶμα τοῦ Χριστοῦ), and the Reign/Rule of God (βασιλεία τοῦ θεοῦ) in the world.

I do this with some trepidation because I have been led to believe that especially American christian evangelicals have a weak view of "church," an almost free enterprise idea of church as a volunteer organization you pick and choose to join; you can believe in Jesus Christ without being confined to a denominational church institution. Evangelicals are fissiparous Christians, quite content with parachurch activities, able to talk about "the politics of Jesus," buy into "a church growth program," and be thoroughly charismaticized, all at once.

I believe the LORD God said once upon a time, "Let there be light, vegetation, creepy-crawly animals, and humans; that is, God ordained different kinds of creatures to praise God's Name (point 1). Credo the LORD formed living souls, and saw to it that we specially bodied humans in God's image are generated to keep God's promises in a seamless marvel of irreducible intra-related prime ways (point 2).

I also believe that the LORD God's firm covenantal grip on the neighborhooded peoples of the world has provided society with various shelters, you might say, like a family to protect and nurture the young, like a market place setup for persons to barter and trade resources for their livelihoods. God's got the whole world in God's hands, and the LORD's hands hold us humans in different societal hugs: a tribal or national embrace for being ruled as members of a clan or as citizens; a small-talk network and media communicating embrace for sharing news. God has made room for a marriage bond, a room in society that some people do not enter, and are content with friendships; but God's grip for marriage

---

man-made circumcision mark unconverted Jews thought to be a sign of God's elective favor.

is available. God has set aside, as it were, different habitats to provide for humanity in society—one in which to be schooled, another in which to prevent pain, still other places for economic refuge, like banks, shelters for artists' works, like musea, and so on—multiple societal hostels set up by God for us humans to walk into, live in, maybe even serve as host for!

Just a quick double note on God's providing different kinds of institutional shelters for our human mission on earth:[17] (1) The precise shape of God's holding us institutionally is flexible and can change: tribal elders speaking justice to litigants disputing claims in the village square can metamorphose into teams of lawyers sorting out rights and damages before an independent judiciary; a shaman herbalist curing ailments with leaves, bark, juices, and incantations can be historically replaced by chemically trained medical doctors dispensing drugs in a hospital; time was when the regimen of walking or biking to work in the fields well served physical needs for exercise, but now urbanites drive cars to spa clubs to pay good money to walk on treadmills for weight control and muscle tone. The shapes of the habitats in society change, but are modified within God's institutional provisions, for example, for doing justice, restoring health, and keeping physically fit.

(2) The way we humans respond historically to God's institutional hugs are critical for the well-being of generations. If we treat a family like a court of law—Dad is top cop and the kids are on parole—we denature God's family hug into a jail system. If you think the government is simply a business, you will oppose using government tax monies like "profits" to distribute among the poor for the commonweal. If your city becomes a congested high rise megalopolis world financial center, it probably stops being a city of refuge with neighborhoods and becomes more like a stock market with winners and losers, the condominium elite with 24-hour concierge security and ghettoes with gangs. We humans can develop and deform God's institutional embraces into a warm welcome or into strangleholds and slipknots.

What kind of godly institutional hug is "the church"? What is the evangelical christian track record on "church" compared, let's say, to the Roman/Anglo-catholic sustained view and steady practice of "the one holy catholic and apostolic church" all christian believers confess in the ancient Nicene creed (325/381/451/589 AD)?

I'll sort out just a few stitches of the Evangelical church coat of many

---

17 Cf. C. Seerveld, *Bearing Fresh Olive Leaves* (Carlisle: Piquant, 2001), 42–45.

colors, hoping not to misrepresent what I am beginning to learn of the confusing kaleidoscopic history of Evangelicals in God-bless-America.

One thread in the American Evangelical weave is the conviction espoused by Cotton Mather (1663–1728) that the Puritans in "New" England had come to the wilderness to make of it "the city of God."[18] Another strand in the Evangelical **mentalité** would be solid biblical church doctrine, like the Calvinist theology of Jonathan Edwards (1703–1758). Deep in the very woof of the New World Evangelical lies a penchant for church Revival. The pre-Civil War (1861–65) revival led by Charles Grandison Finney (1792–1875) around the 1830s shared the preaching platform with antislavery abolitionist speakers, including women, and pro-temperance reformers, since for Finney church revival and reform of societal sin go hand in glove.

Post Civil War until 1925 American Evangelicals were on a roll: in 1919 the constitution of the United States was amended to prohibit the sale of liquor![19] Irenic urban revivalist Dwight L. Moody (1827–1899), who earned his spurs as a YMCA street corner evangelist, toured England (1872–1875) and American cities with sentimental hymn writer Ira ("There were ninety and nine") Sankey, to much acclaim preaching the simple gospel of "Love God, and be converted." Self-educated Moody also began in Chicago the Moody Bible Institute (1886) to train up laymen and women in fundamentals of the Bible, a self-help program not tied to a precise traditional church confession.

The soft premillennial focus of Moody's evangelism was overrun, however, by the positively harsh dispensationalist premillenarianism of British John Nelson Darby (1800–1882) and C.I. Scofield (1843–1921), with **his** reference Bible, whose uncompromising literalist-allegorical readings of biblical "prophecies," as if they supplied inductive almanac data, promulgated at many Bible conferences and summer vacation camps a focus that drew evangelical churches away from societal concerns (which preoccupied, they thought, "Modernist" liberal "Social Gospel" nominal Christians). All the time folksy cannonball "Billy" Sunday (1862–1935)

---

18 Cotton Mather's tribute to John Winthrop, governor of the Massachusetts Bay Colony, in *Magnalia Christi Americana, or, The Ecclesiastical History of New England* [1693–1697] (1702) quotes Josephus' Greek epitaph for Nehemiah, who rebuilt "the walls of Jerusalem," and in the Latin paraphrase following the Greek epitaph, to make the comparison of Winthrop and Nehemiah, America and Jerusalem, telling, Mather substitutes *Novanglorum moenia* ("the walls of New England"). Cf. *American Poetry and Prose*, ed. Norman Foster, third edition (Chicago: Houghton Mifflin, 1947), 64.

19 This prohibition amendment #18 was repealed in 1933 by amendment #21.

was mixing showbiz successfully with professional mass Revivalism, and saw to it that in 1914 American patriotism for the war was paired with a xenophobic christian Fundamentalism.

Evangelicals who go Fundamentalist still come in many stripes. But christian Fundamentalism in America began in earnest around 1925 after the 11 day Scopes trial in Dayton, Tennessee, concerning the illegality of teaching evolution in schools, where Evangelical William Jennings Bryan won the battle but lost the war to Clarence Darrow: many Evangelicals woke up then to the fact that America the Beautiful was not going to be the dream city of Conservative Protestant Godliness in doctrine and in life. So what do you do as evangelical follower of Christ in America, especially if your church denomination is going soft on biblical fundamentals formulated, for example, by the General Presbyterian Assembly in 1910, which included "the inerrancy of Scripture"?[20]

You separate yourselves like "a stranger here within a foreign land" (Cassels' hymn, 1930) from what is ungodly and impure. Methodist evangelist Bob Jones, Senior (1883–1968) began his own college in 1927. Presbyterian J. Gresham Machen (1881–1937) withdrew from Princeton and founded Westminster Theological Seminary (1929) in Philadelphia. After Machen's sudden death—he had also just organized the **Orthodox** Presbyterian Church (1936)—Carl McIntire (1906–2002) founded the *Bible* Presbyterian Church (1937). It seems sometimes that when burning faith concerns are deeply frustrated, it does not take much—just a little loss of face—for strong-willed individuals to turn the Puritanic streak in evangelical christianity into a church-splitting sorrow. Then, if your small embattled group of the elect do not throw themselves into worldwide mission work or continue evangelistic crusades to make people rapture-ready, you may tend to privatize the faith out of the public square and fight omphaloskeptically over nice doctrinal points that loom as large as major heresies.

Around 1940 a coalitions of American Evangelical leaders wanted to distance themselves from the clusters of "Fundamentalists" who seemed to define themselves often in what they were against—against Evolution-

---

20 The five "essential" doctrines of Fundamentalism formulated by the General Presbyterian Assembly in 1910 were: (1) inerrancy of Scripture, (2) virgin birth and deity of Christ, (3) substitutionary atonement, (4) Jesus' bodily resurrection, and (5) the authenticity of miracles [alternate 5: premillennial return of Christ]," as cited in George M. Marsden, *Fundamentalism and American Culture: The shaping of the twentieth-century Evangelicalism 1870–1925* (Oxford University Press, 1980), 117. Marsden also notes that Archibald Alexander Hodge and B.B. Warfield already defended the inerrancy of Scripture back in 1881 (113).

ism, against Modernist Intellectualism, against Communism, against Catholics, against Liberalism's worldliness—who often seemed to wait for the Church Triumphant while practicing the Church Militarist. Fundamentalists were Evangelicals who bite. So Carl F.H. Henry (1913–2003), Harold Ockenga (1905–1985), and Billy Graham (born 1918) dedicated themselves as self-conscious Neo-Evangelicals to reach individuals with the gospel of Jesus Christ, bring them together into church communions, and build them up in an intellectually respectable faith and a holy life that again would reach out with a **post**-millennial awareness (harking back to Finney perhaps?) to face issues of societal evil too. George Marsden has admirably documented the struggle of Neo-Evangelicalism and inerrant Fundamentalism for the soul of Fuller Theological Seminary in California (begun in 1947 by Charles E. ["The Old Fashioned Revival Hour" radio program] Fuller).[21] It is typical of Evangelicalism that it took Fuller **Seminary** 25 years to move back to the Nicene Creed (1972) as the standard for teaching at Fuller, and adopted a formal adjunct relation with the Reformed **Church** of America only in 1985.

I have recited this thumbnail sketchy history of American Evangelicalism, as I understand it to date, not to hang out dirty wash, but to suggest its conglomerate nature, which shows certain recurrent "family" traits—Puritanism, Revivalism, Militancy, Premillenarianism, Evangelism, free lance Individualism—that all together over a period of a few hundred years has held an ambiguous relation to the institutional church. When "the church" has not performed its task or has gone lax, American Evangelicals have jumped in to get the gospel job done, and you worry about the institutional niceties later. Evangelicals do not have a fixed, ecclesiastical hierarchical chain of command that can put down disputes, quell unrest, and fix perennial policy with infallible authority. If the evangelism crusade ideal is for it to be truly inter/pan-denominational, does that really mean "non-denominational"? You hold the mammoth Crusade not in a church environs—think about it—but in a Convention hall. Are historic faith traditions and confessions not so important any more in the emergency to preach the gospel of Jesus Christ to a profligate, dying world?

To give a roundabout, probably provocative reply to that question I should like to engage you in a thought experiment:

---

21 George Marsden, *Reforming Fundamentalism: Fuller Seminary and the new evangelicalism* (Grand Rapids: Eerdmans, 1987).

— Needed: Biblical Recovery —

As the LORD gradually unfolded God's will in Older Testament times with the selected seed of Abraham, the people of Israel, the **ark** of the covenant came to be the centering place for God's imminent presence. The ark eventually held the stone tablets of God's Ten Words spoken at Sinai, a memorial pot of the daily manna the LORD had provided God's ungrateful people in the wilderness, and the rod of Aaron, which had miraculously sprouted flowers confirming his priesthood (Hebrews 9:1–5).[22] The holy ark was finally brought to **Jerusalem** captured from the Jebusites to show that God was now going to be resident in the city of David and make it "the city of God," where justice would be done (2 Samuel 6:12–15, Psalm 132). Later young King Solomon built a house for the ark, a **temple**, where God's Spirit presence hovered between the cherubim over the mercy seat (1 Kings 8:1–9).

So God's people, before their exile, regularly made pilgrimages to the **city of Jerusalem** (Psalm 122)[23] where the **temple** was located holding **God's ark** tended by priests and Levites; that is the location where the people made their special sacrifices, prayers, and thankofferings.

In this thought experiment, remember that the **city administration of Jerusalem** did not collapse into **the precincts of the temple**, and that **the ark** of the covenant was kept in the holiest section of the temple.

Now since Pentecost God's temple on earth is no longer a building constructed with stones in Palestine with a veil covering the place of the ark, but is the communion of two or three saints, **the Spirit-filled body of Christ at large**, in which every faithful disciple of Jesus Christ is self a royal priest in the order of Melchizedek, which has replaced the Aaronic privileging of only some to be priests (Matthew 18:15–20, 1 Corinthians 3:16–17, 2 Corinthians 6:14–7:1).

The Jerusalem of the Bible, Zion, the city of God, which shall someday descend from God as a completed **new** Jerusalem (Revelation 21:1–4), appears now and then historically—epiphanies of its glory acoming, you might say[24]—for Newer Testament followers of the Christ there wherever God's will is done in faith: wherever on earth—in the arts, education, commerce, for example, or political sphere of action—**wherever the Messiah's redemptive, rectifying, just-doing Rule takes place**, even by the Cyrus faithless?! **there is a manifestation of the holy *city* of God's ordering.**

---

22 Cf. Exodus 16:31–35, Numbers 17:1–11, Deuteronomy 31:24–29.
23 Cf. Exodus 23:14–17, Exodus 34:21–23.
24 At the eschaton God will make **all** things new (Revelation 21:5), but now in our age the newness begins: a person can become a **new** creature (2 Corinthians 5:17).

The institutional local church congregated for worship—in this thought experiment—is a surprising reprise of the covenantal ark of old, because God's Sinai tables of Ten Words updated in the resurrected deed of Jesus Christ are present in **the sound preaching of the Word**; God's manna is liturgically served in **the eucharistic response of the faithful** restfully celebrating union with Christ; and **those present** who are **captivated by God's enabling Holy Spirit will indeed** sprout buds, **bear fruit**, showing they have been adopted into the priestly order of Melchizedek.

So my proposal for your consideration is a full-fledged trinitarian conception to help us keep conceptually distinct and historically related: (1) God the Father's blessed institutional grip on humans, which channels us confessing our root faith-commitment into a visible body of believers—the synagogue for Jewish believers, a mosque for Muslim adherents, the organized church confessing Christians know. The special internal tasks of ἐκκλησία[25] as a local congregated assembly (*qahal*) of humans called together in Christ (Galatians 1:22) as **a household of God** (1 Timothy 2:15) is to hear God's scripted Word proclaimed, to celebrate the eucharistic manna as a memorial of hope, and to be disciplined, edified (1 Corinthians 14:26), in worshiping God by confessing the Reign of Christ acoming. The chief external task of the institutional church in society is to confess the everlasting Good News of God's redeeming reconciliation in Christ of God's world back to God (2 Corinthians 5:17–21).

(2) Christ is the head of the institutional church, but Christ's body is broader than the institutional church, as was the temple, which housed the ark. Τὸ σῶμα τοῦ Χριστοῦ, the body of our Lord and Savior God Jesus Christ, is not a normal institutional creational grip of God the Father, but is this special sprawling historical communion of the saints that has grown up out of the churchly household of God and become, says Scripture, "a dwelling place of God the Holy Spirit," "a sanctuary in the Lord" (Ephesians 2:19–22), **a people of God.** All who are indwelt by the Holy Spirit—and since Acts 2 and 10 that means **any strangers** on the face of the earth pinioned by the Holy Spirit—you are no longer wandering sojourners, because now "you are a chosen kind (γένος) of person, a royal line of priests! a holy peoplehood, God's own people!" (1 Peter 2:9–10). And since Jesus Christ's resurrection, ascension, and promised coming in

---

25 Scripture terms for ἐκκλησία and τὸ σῶμα τοῦ θεοῦ, like those for σῶμα and psyché are not used precisely, like technical terms, but are not used ambiguously in a given context.

glory, Christ's **body**, God's own adopted **bodied people**, while they repair to the church ark of thanksgiving for en-courage-ment, they are busy daily distributing shalom by spreading the good news of their reconciling ambassadorship, not by preaching and prophesying so much as by **communally** teaching, healing, giving wise counsel, generously lending time and goods to neighbors, spreading joy around, that is, enacting—God helping you—the compassionate Rule of Christ on earth.

(3) The whole point of God's historically holding humans together in institutional bounds, including the church, and Jesus Christ's scandalous, persecuted worldwide body on earth, is their paired witness to the βασιλεία τοῦ θεοῦ, the heavenly (=unearthly!) Kingdom/Reign/Rule of God, which the Holy Spirit is spearheading. "Repent and believe in the good news," preached Baptizer John, "that the Rule of God is at hand"! (Mark 1:14–15). "Whenever you pray," Christ taught his disciples, "Pray, **Your *kingdom* come! Your will be done on earth** as it is done in heaven" (Matthew 6:7–13). And Jesus spent his last 40 days on earth after the resurrection speaking to his befuddled disciples, says the biblical book of Acts, not about the "church" or "evangelism," but about "the Reign of God" and their coming baptism in the comforting wisdom of the Holy Spirit (Acts 1:4–5; cf. John 14, especially vv. 15–17, 25–26). The apostle Paul too filled out the imperfect faith-knowledge of believers in Ephesus by spending months in the synagogues, even years! says Scripture, "boldly speaking . . . conversing and persuading [them] about **the Reign of God**" (Acts 19:8–10)—"the Way" to be obeying the universe-wide Will of God. The Rule of God, the ***city* of God**, which God the Holy Spirit self brings to pass, is not simply "church" work, is not restricted to ark-exhorting and evangelizing; but **God's kingdom, which clergy with laity in Christ's body at large are to seek *first*** (Matthew 5:25–31, Luke 12:22–31), at great cost to their own lives—become childlike eunuchs with respect to power and fame! (Matthew 19:12–15, Mark 10:13–16, Luke 18:15–17)—is the main theme of the whole Bible. (Any would-be christian zealots, however, need to remember God's Spirit sometimes seems to pull into the city administration of the **new** Jerusalem odd characters who are not model believers.)[26]

The upshot of carefully drawing these distinctions—God's con-

---

[26] Next to the pagan Persian Cyrus, who is even called "God's anointed one" to administer restorative justice for God's people (Isaiah 44:24–45:8, v.45:4), there are the riffraff mentioned in Hebrews 11:32. The point of 2 Kings 2–5 is that charismatic prophet and great miracle worker Elisha had to be humbled to learn that God's grace could reach beyond the Lord's "elect" to touch their hated Syrian enemies. Cf. Amos 9:7 and the mystery of Revelation 21:22–27.

-gregated church, the body of Christ at large, and the over-ruling Reign of God's Spirit in history—is to call to your attention in their complex inter-relation the crucial **centering**, focal, but **limited** task of God's institutionally gripped fellowship we call the organized church.

Of course churches should witness to the Truth in the public square. The early apostles did it (Peter, Philip, Paul, Acts 2:14–22, 8:26–40, 20:17–21); Proverbs commends it (Proverbs 1:20–33, 8:1–36); and Nehemiah wisely had the books of Moses read in the Watergate square of the city so that non-Jews could attend to hear God's Word (Nehemiah 8:1–8). The institutional church also does well to send encyclicals to families, corporate businesses, governments, colleges, artist collectives, medical practitioners, calling upon them to respect the biblical injunction to do what is just, keep your promises, and walk humbly before God (Micah 6:8).

> But the church is not to pretend its **ecclesiastic** authority dictates all the norms for the people of God, the body of Christ, whose lay leaders in their institutional callings are directly responsible together *coram Deo* to posit imperatives for making and receiving artistry, for conceiving and nurturing children, for setting professional standards for scholarship, bargaining for wages that will not keep workers poor, for practicing restorative justice that contributes to the merciful Reign of God. And ordained clergy and gifted charismatics (who can sometimes fall into the trap of aspiring to be a site-specific, local pope) must hear the pleas of God's assorted people not to shirk on the resident task of church to discipline all comers with a convicting God-is-speaking-to-us biblical literacy—understanding Older as well as Newer Testament—and to stir up the regenerating joy of celebrating in tough times the justifying LIFE found on earth in belonging to Christ's everlasting body, as God's Rule inscrutably approaches. If the church at worship is not a visionary ferment of deep biblical preaching, God's people will soon be at a loss.

That is why, from my Reformation biblical vantage point, our **church** communion's Heidelberg Catechism answers the question 32, "Why are you called a **Christian**?" with the splendid answer:

> Because by faith I am a member of Christ
> and so I share in his anointing.
> I am anointed to confess his name,
> to present myself to him as a living sacrifice of thanks,
> to strive with a good conscience against sin and the devil in this life,
> and afterward to reign with Christ
> over all creation for all eternity—

The answer does not mention the institutional church! Not because the church is not central, but because the "church" as a hierarchical *magisterium* or specially ordained clergy may not assume, as did imperial Constantinian Christendom, and does not mediate **or** obviate my Melchizedekian responsibilities with fellow laity to the Lord. That much is clear.

In the history of Evangelicalism it is less clear to me, but I detect the tendency in Evangelicalism to erase a definite confessionally bound institutional church, a mysterious ark of the ages **into** which a person is baptized, erase church into a looser people of God understood more as a voluntary association of potential evangelists who have said "I do" to the Savior Jesus, and then **to collapse Kingdom of God activities into churchly tasks performed by the non-ecclesial communion of saints**. So Evangelicals are more likely to have confessing christian business men and politicians hold prayer breakfasts rather than hammer out a political and economic policy that would shame the U.S. government and American weaponry companies into stopping production of land mines. And an Evangelical communion (like mine too)—a Pragmatist christian (or Muslim) Fundamentalist would not be so quiet—but an Evangelical communion would probably prefer to remain tongue-tied instead of comment on the Iraqi War or the momentous declaration in the "United States National Security Strategy" official document (art. 5, 2002) that this nation now stands for preemptive strikes with terrible weapons: "After all, we are church and they are state. . . ."[27]

But such silent impasses and laissez-faire dereliction of christian salting, by church and saints at large, is untenable once one sees the immaturity of such an underdeveloped understanding—as if "church and state" is not a simplistic problematics—of how we bodied humans within God's rainbow of historically institutional hugs are called to be faithful suffering servants following the Christ.

(4) The unhurried Holy Spirited eschatonic priestly task of God's adopted children from every nation under the sun. Imprisoned apostle Paul's charitable comment to the saints at Philippi has always impressed me, although I find it hard to swallow: even if those with a grudge talk about Christ in rivalry, pretentiously, trying to get my goat, I'm still glad "Christ" is getting mentioned (Philippians 1:15–18). Okay, but in the Scripture with which I began I also hear God's impatience with us "He-

---

27 Jesus' wise answer to the tricky Pharisees is often taken amiss (Matthew 22:15–22). To "give to Caesar what Caesar has coming to him" means "Call your government to the godly task of doing what is right, to defend the weak and victims of violence, and institute restorative justice that brings the fruit of peace," not fight terror with threat of terror.

brews" who love to tell the old, old story of Jesus and his love, when we remain milk-suckers after it's past time to be chewing solid food with fiber.

Let me dare offer two critical, loving observations about Evangelicalism before I make my closing remark and show slides of a couple artworks for our times.

(1) There are several basic positions in the philosophy of history that have lasted throughout the ages: there is nothing new under the sun; things are growing better (or worse); and the chiliastic position that seems to tread water apocalyptically, eager to escape our historical turmoil.

Evangelicalism, as I understand it, seems to gravitate toward the perduring **chiliastic tradition**, keen to repeat the mountain-top experience of one's Damascene conversion, certifying **my** personal redeemed status, as Armageddon approaches. The millenarian expectation of imminent rescue is a form of theodicic vindication of one's societal troubles, and sets the stage for periodic sessions of "spiritual" revival. If we can't reform corrupt society, let's at least promote the inner renewal of our spirit—"Revive us again! O Lord."

To a Pentecostal or charismatic premillenarian Christian, if I pick it up correctly, it is so difficult to change course of the large, slow-moving ocean liner of the traditional sacramentally loaded church, it seems better to go surf-boarding in the waves.

As I went to worship with a charismatic Greek Orthodox congregation in Thessaloniki, Greece, on a huge sign across the front of the platform in this converted cinema auditorium stood PEREMENE ENA TAUMA—Expect a miracle!

But after the Miracle Moments, the Hour of Decision, the Week of Revival Meetings, one still needs to return to the plodding ocean liner or to one's surf-boarding club looking for bigger waves, and especially to the polluted ocean water we swim in—unless you sell all your belongings, give the proceeds to the poor, and head for the nearest range of mountains.

I am not saying Revivalism is wrong. Thank God for Spring Harvest Festivals, Greenbelt, and the other regular Cornerstone events in the USA—every follower of Christ can use a shot in the spiritual arm. The question in my observation is this: does a chiliastic stance on history in history—which can sometimes count 1 Corinthians 12 tongue-talk as a badge of the Holy Spirit to be more important than Acts 2 speaking in multiple languages **understandably**—does a millenarian visionary focus give us corporeal humans blessed with God's enriching institutional embraces the prompt to be fully obedient until the Lord returns, or does it arrest our maturation?

(2) The second matter I observed surprised me, and gave me hope for this untidy phenomenon of Evangelicalism. The basic biblical tenets held by Evangelicals from Cotton Mather to Billy Graham remain much the same. The family features I have noted—the Puritan, Pietist, Rigorist, Evangelizing, pre- and post-millennial accents, Social work as rescue mission, Denomination-splitting Protestantism—shift about but are also fairly constant. What I did not expect but think I found is that the spirit at work in American Evangelicalism since after Civil War days, pre- and post-1925, is close to what I would call the Neo-Idealist spirit that infuses "the American Dream," the painterly art of Thomas Cole, *The Voyage of Life* (1839–40), and the hymns of Fanny Crosby, "Someday the Silver Cord will Break" (1893).

There is a New World Victorian gentility in the scholarship of Machen, evenhandedly balancing theoretical and practical knowledge, in the programs of Moody and Fuller and colleagues, an almost Biedermeier stuffed furniture concern for morality, respectability, along with a generous rationality. The **Neo**-Evangelicalism of Carl F.H. Henry and the National Association of Evangelicals (1942) is anti-Revolutionary, filled with the desire to unite the best that has been said and thought in christian sources. As in every "Neo-movement, in Neo-Evangelicalism too, there are atavistic traits: the sense of earlier discoveries being warmed-up, newly seasoned, recovered, but settling down, a domesticated spirit.

If that kind of tempered, wistfully resolute Neo-Idealistic spirit marks Evangelicalism through four or five generations, it seems evident to me that Fundamentalists operate with a quite different **spirit**: Carl McIntire with the American Council of Christian Churches (1941) was forcefully against many things, and Jerry Falwell, James Dobson, and Pat Robertson in the recent past who seem to specialize in single issue politics: their pronouncements—however godly the men—have a point-blank if not Pragmatist spirit, to get things done. The different spirit, it seems to me, separates Fundamentalists from Evangelicalism more than what either stands for.

My thought is: the major biblical tenets of Evangelicalism are sound, but a Neo-Idealistic spirit—which partially accompanied Abraham Kuyper's endeavors too—is out of date, and inhibits Evangelicals from growing up faith-fully and developing **a christian philosophical grasp**

of humans and society in world history. What I find buoyant in the writings and ministry of Stanley Grenz and Robert Webber is their wise coaxing, from within the milieu of Evangelicalism, for Evangelicals to put away childish things, shuck the spirit of "We-have-it-all-together," a Neo-Idealistic spirit tinged with wiser-and-holier-than thou intimations, and go for the more gutsy, down-to-earth matured servanthood spirit of being Melchizedekian priests among bodied humans in a God-ordered institutional society needing signposts of the Lord's Rule acoming in God's glossolaliac world. As the apostle Paul wrote to the Corinthian churches: it's okay to be babes in evil, but **become mature in thinking things through** (1Corinthians 14:20).

That leads to a concluding remark about the biblical call for us followers of Christ, and any neighbors, indeed to become mature. It is a normal matter to move from being naive to growing up in the world, but it displeases the Lord (according to the letter to the legalist-leaning "Hebrews") to decide **not** to be mature, to prefer a hardened immaturity.

One mark of maturity is to realize how complicated things are, and yet know with humble childlike certainty where you stand historically.

A fourth position in the philosophy of history is that the creator LORD God is busy bringing about the glorious Rule of Jesus Christ, and the fulfillment of that redeemed creaturely LIFE will take place at the end (*eschaton*) of God's determining—Jesus did not know when it would be (Mark 13, vv. 32–33), even if he is the only one now who can open the mystery book of history (Revelation 5)—the eschaton is sure, with or without our human preparations.

So God's mature people do not need to be in a hurry or anxious, since the LORD surely works out God's will through generation after generation with God's timing (Acts 1:6–8). We are called simply to take the inheritance of our generation, and with steadfast, patient composure faithfully—God's Spirit working in us both the willing and bearing the fruit, says Scripture (Philippians 2:12–16)—cultivate our heritage: enlarge the place of our tent, hammer in the tent posts more firmly (Isaiah 54:2–3); that is, in the communion of saints at large, in a holy Reformational spirit—the spirit that swept through the conciliar decisions of Vatican II (1962–1965), the Spirit bringing Mennonite workers into the Christian Labour Association of Canada today, the Spirit that stirred up the spirituals and gospel song of the Afro-American evangelicals who have suffered more than enough as a people ever to become Idealistic—

joyfully give away our gifts to the neighbor in Christ's name, with eschatonic hope, not with apocalyptic foreboding.

For God's children "to preach Christ" to disembodied "souls" is an immature parodic charade, because humans are corporeal historical creatures. To argue about what you believe, defensively or aggressively, probably overrates the role of thinking in convicting an other bodied person of our love for them: giving an account of the hope within you (1 Peter 3:13–17)—"evangelizing"—is more mature and persuasive, it would seem to me, if you lay down your corporeal life, or at least a coat or two, **give time and words that show respect** for the poor stranger encountered (Matthew 5:38–41, 11:1–6).

It is also immature, in my book, to "go it alone" as a follower of Christ, a solitary pilgrim, since we must not underestimate the power of corporate systemic evil: a local market for people to exchange goods is a blessing, but MARKET INCORPORATED UNLIMITED WITH MONOPOLISTIC AUTHORITY, so that the internal markets of a whole country are forced to be subservient to GLOBAL TRADE DICTATES, is a curse. Even churches at worship can be seduced by the principality of ABSORBING ENTERTAINMENT, and sell off serious exegetical exposition of Scripture for a mess of anecdotal, homiletic potage. No wonder Scripture admonishes us as a communion of saints to become mature, worldliwise as snakes, but to remain as innocent, as undeceptive and without guile as a dove (Matthew 10:16). Ideologues are worse than liars because ideologues deceive but think they are telling and doing the truth.

The Scriptural injunction for followers of the Melchizedekian high-priest Jesus Christ to become mature in their faith action asks us to follow in his footsteps as **ambassadors practicing right-doing with mercy**. If I hear Jeremiah correctly in the light of "seek the kingdom of God *first*," it means our focus as body of Christ, and yes, the ark of the church too, is that we **seek the welfare of *the city* where we are in exile** (Jeremiah 29:1–14, Matthew 6:24–34), pray to the LORD for the inhabitants of Babylon! Nineveh, Chicago, Toronto, you name it, where "prayer" means "practice merciful right-doing." More exactly, God's people together, in whatever capacity and with whatever authority they may have in trust, are invited to **share God's gift of abundant life with those who have no hope**, and do it non-spectacularly **in deed**, quietly, slowly restore the bodied lives of the hopeless derelicts in the world to be corporeally free in God's world with water, food, clothing, shelter, work, schooling, under the Lord's blessing.

Jan Disselkoen, who serves with the Christian Reformed World Relief Committee in Niger, Africa, has helped a miniscule group of saints called a church in Niamey set up a little credit union for and with poor local Muslims (who were at first suspicious this was a plot to convert them) so that now Salama is begetting micro-loans enabling indigents to make a livelihood and spread tangible hope in the city. No media blitz. Not a "success" story. Just living justice, loving mercy, and letting the love of Jesus sweeten relationships between hostile neighbors.

The angels in heaven probably know about a lot of other Melchizedekian acts which happen even among college students who are wandering around aimlessly despite their hi-tech accoutrements. . . .

This painting by a South African woman artist, Penny Siopis (born 1935) portrays a woman figure that has fallen hard and landed, it looks like, on a scrap heap. Her bare body is an overwhelming blistered mass of semi-distinct scenes of struggle, violence, a transparent quilt of burns and scars. The ground too is composed of a jumble of vignettes—steel girder construction sites, abandoned buildings, mine pits, people walking, working, broken railroad tracks. *Terra incognita* (1991) [*RA* #68] is the title: a woman's body is an unknown continent; the earth, "Mother Earth" also has become unknown to its inhabitants, treated like a blasted junkyard, its original glossolalia become a maze of screaming sirens. Will the fallen woman (who was pushed?), the earth, be given a helping arm to get up? Will we Evangelicals memorize John 3:17 along with verse 16?

Anselm Kiefer (born 1945) ups the ante with *Nero malt* (1974) [*CP* #2]. Kiefer chides artists who like Nero just keep on painting their little hearts desire while Rome, New York City, Baghdad, New Orleans, burn on the far horizon past the killing fields of scorched earth furrows. What filters into our consciousness as we practice our profession, "do" our philosophy?

Britt Wikström's (born 1948) installation of 5 poles and figures for an Amnesty International artistic competition, entitled *Cathedral of Suffering* (1994) [*RA* #31], waits for you to walk toward it in a field: the woman figure is bent to shield herself helplessly from the unstopping attack; the little child, arms raised to protect its face, has its own solitary grown-up pole; the spread-eagled man is crucified between the torture of hanging from two poles; and the empty pole stands waiting for another victim. Evil and sin are insatiable in our society. As you walk away from this poignant artistic testimony to our own horrendous permitting of such terror happening even as I speak—too cruel for earth to bear it, and chillingly unacceptable to the heavens, placeless—it occurs to you that maybe the empty pole is meant for me. (I'll keep showing this maquette at christian colleges until somebody raises the money to site it on a campus, preferably an Evangelical Seminary campus, since I think the abiding presence of this piece nearby might help bring theological reflection biblically down to historical earth and re-set analytic priorities.)

I was speaking at the Rands Afrikaans Universiteit in Johannesburg, South Africa, in 1991. Each graduating class is given a wall to paint in the Student Commons. The graduating mural I saw seemed to eulogize night life, sport, fun, and anything but study; tucked up near the top off to one side, however, was a vivid student critique of American political foreign policy—1991!—where the stars in the Stars-and-stripes become crosses, and the Statue of Liberty becomes the grim reaper [infra #42].

I show this here not to be obnoxious—I am still also a US citizen, and my Dutch wife was liberated from Nazi domination in Holland by Canadian and American troops in 1945—but from what I have read, Evangelicals have been tempted at times to fix Catholics, Communists, or some scapegoat as the Antichrists. It occurs to me that any Christian who is not **self**-critical, especially of the American civil religion that believes right or wrong America is God's country, needs to reflect on Jesus' story told the Jewish faith leaders and lawyers of his day, about the man whose evil spirit left, and after the old man had cleaned house, made himself spic and span, empty! the seven spirits who joined the first one returned were worse because they were now clean, self-righteous devils inhabiting that corporeal human consciousness (Matthew 12:43–45, Luke 11:24–26). With every imprecation uttered in the psalms against God's enemies comes the abject plea: probe **me** deeply, Lord, to see that **I** not be false to you (e.g., Psalm 139:19–24, Psalm 137:5–9).

To end "After Evangelicalism" upbeat I'll show you Messiah College Ted Prescott's *Salt Lick Cross* (1991) [*CP* #60] spiced with sharp steel. Maybe you think Christians are supposed to be the salt of the earth (Matthew 5:13) in salt-shaker fashion: you sprinkle a few salt grains here to preserve meat, and you sprinkle a few other Christians over there to add flavor in society. A more mature reading than the Individualistic grains of salt one is to grasp that followers of Christ are to be a salt lick in God's world, a communal source of life. One cross, "one holy catholic and apostolic church," **one** body of Christ with its many members and institutional constellations united by **one** Holy Spirit (1 Corinthians 12): imagine—after Evangelicalism—us here gathered as being a cross of a saltlick, Christ's one body outside the church door, God's peoplehood . . . in the educational, commercial, political, artistic, health-care worlds, a communal saltlick that leads by serving the interests of others—**one** winsome Melchizedekian royal priesthood with nothing to lose but our self-importance—becoming a vulnerable, veritable salt offering to the Lord, which attracts all kinds of neighbors. (It's a great metaphorical picture, I think, of a christian college—curious students nosing up to lick the tasty salty wisdom off the one philosophically united faculty. . . .)

> It is impossible, you know, for those who once and for all were brought into the light [of God's grace], who once tasted both the gift from heaven and had come to be sharing in the Holy Spirit, that is, who experienced the live [preached] Word of God and the moving powers of the Coming Age, but then stopped short, stepped backwards: it is impossible to stir them again to a radical change of heart **if they deliberately turned away from maturing**, because then they are busy crucifying the Son of God again in their own lives, actually holding up the [the claims of Christ's highpriesthood] to ridicule.
>
> You know what I mean: the earth that drinks up the rain falling down upon the ground again and again, giving birth to plant life suitable for food to those by whom the soil is cultivated, that earthy ground shares in the blessing from God. But earth that bears thorns and thistles is good for nothing and in danger of being accursed [by God], fit for burning.
>
> Even though we're talking tough this way to you whom we love, we are confident that you are on the track of the better things, things which lead to restoration. After all, God is not unfair. God will not forget the work you did and the selfless love you have showed for God when you served your fellow believers, which you continue to do now.
>
> But—and that's the point!—what we passionately desire is that each one of you may come to show the same earnest eagerness you have for brotherly and sisterly love, show that same zeal to reach the full maturity of the [christian] hope, on and on till the end come, so that you don't settle down lazily, become sluggish, callousedly hardened [unmoved by the imperative to become mature]. Instead, start acting like [grown-up] people who through a trusting faith and long-suffering patience do come to inherit the [riches of] what God has promised.
>
> [Hebrews 6:4–12]

Bibliography

Ammerman, Nancy T. "North American Protestant Fundamentalism" in *Fundamentalisms Observed*, eds. Martin E. Marty and R. Scott Appleby (University of Chicago Press, 1991), 1:1–65

Appiah, Kwame Anthony. *In My Father's House: Africa in the philosophy of culture* (New York: Oxford University Press, 1992).

Berger, Peter L. *A Rumor of Angels: Modern society and the rediscovery of the supernatural* (Garden City: Doubleday, 1969).

Berger, Peter L., ed. *The Desecularization of the World: Resurgent religion and world politics* (Grand Rapids: Eerdmans, 1999).

Brun, Jean. *La Nudité Humaine* (Paris: Fayard, 1973).

Buechner, Frederick. *The Clown in the Belfry: Writings on faith and fiction* (San Francisco: Harper and Row, 1992).

Carpenter, Joel. "Fundamentalist Institutions and the Rise of Evangelical Protestantism, 1929–1942," in *Church History*, 49 (1980): 62–73.

———. "The Fundamentalist Leaven and the Rise of an Evangelical United Front," in *The Evangelical Tradition in America*, ed. Leonard I. Sweet (Macon: Mercer University Press, 1984), 257–288.

Cray, Graham, Maggi Dawn, Nick Mercer, Michael Saward, Pete Ward, and Nigel Wright. *The Post-evangelical Debate* (London: Triangle, 1997).

Dayton, Donald W. *Discovering an Evangelical Heritage* (San Francisco: Harper & Row, 1976).

Disselkoen, Jan. July CRWRC newsletter from Niger, West Africa, 3pp.

Ellul, Jacques. *Les Nouveaux Possédés* (1973), translated by C. Edward Hopkin as *The New Demons* (New York: Seabury, 1975).

Evangelicals: What they believe, Who they are, Where they are changing, eds. David F. Wells and John D. Woodbridge (Nashville: Abingdon Press, 1975).

Frankforter, A. Daniel. *Stones for Bread: A critique of contemporary worship* (Louisville: Westminster John Knox, 2001).

Fuller, Robert C. *Naming the AntiChrist: The history of an American obsession* (Oxford University Press, 1995).

Grenz, Stanley J. *Renewing the Center: Evangelical theology in a post-theological era* (Grand Rapids: Baker, 2000).

———. *Revisioning Evangelical Theology: A fresh agenda for the 21st century* (Downers Grove: InterVarsity, 1993).

Griffioen, Sander. *Moed tot cultuur: Een actuele filosofie* (Amsterdam: Buijten & Schipperheijn, 2003).

Guinness, Os. *The Gravedigger File* (London: Hodder & Stoughton, 1993).

———. *Time for Truth: Living free in a world of lies, hype and spin.* (Leicester: InterVarsity, 2000).

Henry, Carl F. H. *The Uneasy Conscience of Modern Fundamentalism* (Grand Rapids: Eerdmans, 1946).

Hervieu-Leger, Danièle. *La Religion pour Mémoire* (1993), translated by Simon

Lee as *Religion as a Chain of Memory* (Cambridge: Polity Press, 2000).

Hunter, James Davison. *Evangelicalism: The coming generation* (University of Chicago Press, 1987).

———. "Operationalizing Evangelicalism: A review, critique and proposal," in *Sociological Analysis*, 42:4 (1982): 363–372.

Jenkins, Daniel. *Christian Maturity and the Theology of Success* (London: SCM, 1976).

Jenkins, Philip. *The Next Christendom: The coming of global Christianity* (Oxford University Press, 2002).

König, Oliver. *Nacktheit: Soziale Normierung und Moral* (Darmstadt: Westdeutsche Verlag, 1990).

Lausanne Covenant. Lausanne Committee for World Evangelization, Lausanne Gathering, 1974. 4pp. http://www.lausanne.org/en/documents/lausanne-covenant.html

McGinn, Bernard. *Antichrist: Two thousand years of the human fascination with evil* (New York: Columbia University Press, 2000).

McLoughlin, Jr., William G. *Modern Revivalism: Charles Grandison Finney to Billy Graham* (New York: Ronald Press, 1969).

Manila Manifesto. Lausanne Committee for World Evangelization, Manilla Gathering, 1989. 9pp. http://www.lausanne.org/en/documents/manila-manifesto.html

Marsden, George M. *Fundamentalism and American Culture: The shaping of the twentieth-century evangelicalism 1870–1925* (Oxford University Press, 1980).

———. *Reforming Fundamentalism: Fuller Seminary and the New Evangelicalism* (Grand Rapids: Eerdmans, 1987).

———. *Understanding Fundamentalism and Evangelicalism* (Grand Rapids: Eerdmans, 1991).

Marshall, Paul, with Lela Gilbert. *Their Blood Cries Out* (Dallas: Word, 1997).

Marty, Martin E. and R. Scott Appleby, "Conclusion: An Interim Report on a Hypothetical Family," in *Fundamentalisms Observed.* Eds. Martin E. Marty & R. Scott Appleby (University of Chicago Press, 1991), 1:814–842.

Marty, Martin E. *The Modern Schism: Three paths to the secular* (New York: Harper & Row, 1969).

———. *Protestantism in the United States: Righteous empire* (1970), second edition (New York: Charles Scribner's, 1986).

———. *The Protestant Voice in American Pluralism* (Athens: University of Georgia Press, 2004).

Michel, Otto. οἶκος θεοῦ in *Theologisches Wörterbuch zum Neuen Testament* (*TWNT*) 5 (1954): 122–161.

Moltmann-Wendel, Elizabeth. *Mein Körper bin ich* (1994), translated by John Bowden as *I am My Body: A theology of embodiment* (New York: Continuum, 1994).

Newbigin, Leslie. *The Gospel in a Pluralist Society* (Geneva: WCC, 1989).

Noll, Mark A. *American Evangelical Christianity: An introduction* (Oxford: Blackwell, 2001).
Padilla, René C. *The New Face of Evangelicalism: An International Symposium on the Lausanne Covenant* (London: Hodder & Stoughton, 1976).
Peck, John and Charles Strohmer. *Uncommon Sense: God's wisdom for our complex and changing world* (Sevierville: Wise Press, 2000).
Ridderbos, Herman. *De Komst van het Koninkrijk: Jezus' prediking volgens de synoptische evangelien* (Kampen: Kok, 1950).
———. *Paulus: Ontwerp van zijn theologie* (Kampen: Kok, 1966).
Sandeen, Ernest R. *The Roots of Fundamentalism: British and American millenarianism 1800–1930* (University of Chicago Press, 1970).
Schlier, Heinrich. *Die Zeit der Kirche: Exegetische Aufsätze und Vorträge* (Wien: Herder, 1966).
Schmidt, Karl Ludwig. "βασιλεία, βασιλεία" in *TWNT* 1 (1933): 576–595.
———. "ἐκκλησία" in *TWNT* 3 (1938): 502–539.
Schweizer, Edward. "σῶμα" in *TWNT* 7 (1964): 1024–1091.
Seerveld, Calvin. "The Damages of a Christian Worldview," in *After Worldview*, M. Bonzo and M. Stevens, eds. (Sioux Center: Dordt College Press, 2009), 55–80. {see *CE*: 105–129}.
———. *How to Read the Bible to Hear God Speak* (Sioux Center: Dordt College Press, 2003).
———. *Rainbows for the Fallen World: Aesthetic life and artistic task* (Toronto: Tuppence Press, 1980/2005).
Spykman, Gordon J. *Reformational Theology: A new paradigm for doing dogmatics* (Grand Rapids: Eerdmans, 1992).
Tamez, Elsa. *Contra Toda Condena: La Justificacion por la Fe desde los Excludidos* (1991, translated by Sharon H. Ringe as *The Amnesty of Grace: Justification by faith from a Latin American perspective* (Nashville: Abingdon Press, 1993).
Tomlinson, Dave. *The Post-Evangelical* (London: Triangle, 1995).
van den Berg, J. H. *Het Menselijk Lichaam: Een metabletisch onderzoek* (Nijkerk: Callenbach, 1962).
———. *Metabletica, of Leer der Veranderingen: Beginselen van een historische psychologie* (Nijkerk: Callenbach, 1962).
Wacker, Grant. "Searching for Norman Rockwell: Popular evangelicalism in contemporary America," in *The Evangelical Tradition in America*, ed. Leonard I. Sweet (Macon: Mercer University Press, 1984), 289–315.
Webber, Robert E. *Ancient-Future Faith: Rethinking evangelicalism for a postmodern world* (Grand Rapids: Baker, 1999).
———. *Common Roots: A call to evangelical maturity* (Grand Rapids: Zondervan, 1978).
———. *Evangelicals on the Canterbury Trail: Why Evangelicals are attracted to the liturgical church* (Harrisburg: Morehouse, 1985).
———. *The Younger Evangelicals: Facing the challenges of the new world* (Grand Rapids: Baker, 2002).

Wright, Nigel. *The Radical Evangelical: Seeking a place to stand* (London: SPCK, 1996).

I am also gratefully indebted to John Franklin for his timely bibliographic counsel.

With John Franklin, Executive Director of Imago,
at the Art Gallery of Ontario, 2012

The Gift and Distraction of Pleasure

In Basel, Switzerland, you celebrate *Fasnacht* (Mardi Gras) **after** the Lenten season has begun, just to show how Reformed you are. Even though the bridegroom is indeed absent (Matthew 9:14–16), why should we follow the millennium-old church discipline of fasting for all 40 days before Easter comes? Many Roman catholics make the tourist trek to Basel too for this second fling during Lent before they sober up for the prescribed church regulations. I must admit it was a lot of fun as student in Basel (Lent, 1956), dressed in my red-and-white striped pajamas for costume, dancing through the winding inner city streets behind the many fife and drum corps, to go sit in cafés to feast on Swiss *quiche* and beer, discussing Barth and Cullmann's theology. Although Lent has been a sometime thing for my Dutch Reformed faith tradition, we usually are pretty sober faced.

Have you ever wondered about God's basic gift of pleasure to us humans, and why so many Christians are afraid to enjoy their sensuous nature? Is there a redemptive way to eat and drink with joy, to relish chocolate, to satisfy one's sexual desires? Or does our evil hedonistic age and the constant atrocities around the world put the kibosh for followers of the Christ on satisfying sense experience?

Creatural pleasure as good

The LORD saw the radiant sunrise and colorful sunset, when God created them, as good (Genesis 1:14–18). The LORD is tickled at watching trees suck up water and grow verdant foliage; God likes the feel of darkness when beasts in the forest stalk prey (Psalm 104:14–23). God was happy to make Joseph good looking; young Joseph had a fine figure, says the Bible (Genesis 39:6). And part of the promise the LORD gave God's people for the time coming when all tears will be wiped away from our faces is that God would serve up choice meat and full-bodied wines (Isaiah 25:6–8).

Appeared first, edited down, with 2 illustrations, in *The Banner*, 26 February 2001, 16–18, under the title "Celebrating the gift of sensuous pleasure."

God respects what is visible, sensible, shapely, and pleasant to the senses [#36].

[#36] Mature Malbec grapes on the vine

Although it was humiliating for God in Jesus Christ to become a Jewish man (Philippians 2:5–8), God became incarnate, embodied, fleshed, as we men and women are. God was not ashamed to walk around on two legs, to eat fish (Luke 24:36–43), to sweat and urinate. That's the good way God created us men and women to be. The fact that Jesus grew up (Luke 2:40), became tired, turned hungry and thirsty, but was without sin (Hebrews 4:14–16), is something worth thinking about. Our bodily processes like digestion, defecation, sleeping, maturation, and aging are normal marvels of the Lord's creative ingenuity. It pleased God to make us not unchanging, disembodied spirits or ethereal ghosts but to bless us to be concrete, tactile, sensing bodily creatures. God even wants to resurrect us **bodily** somehow from the grave (1 Corinthians 15:42–50), so important is our vital corporeal, creatural nature to the redeeming Almighty Creator.

To take delight in the warmth of ordinary sunlight on your skin and to be refreshed by a cool glass of water on one's dry palate is a pure gift from God. To feel the fabric of silk or wool between your fingertips, and to have your flesh breathe through cotton underwear is a wonder of experience often unnoticed, until you lose such sensations. The smell of freshly baked bread and the aroma of a brew of coffee, especially if you are tense, can be like a moment of grace in one's life. Even a stab of pain can be a redemptive warning that your tooth, a muscle, or bone needs to be repaired. Human senses, less acute than the intelligent senses of animals, are veritably a decisive source for situating us smack in God's fantastic world.

It is the actual hug of a mother or father that impresses the child with love, not just a stated intention. It is the pressure of a kiss on lips or cheek and the gentle touch of a caress that signal commitment, restrained passion, and promise. No wonder adolescents want the private caress of very long showers. It is the tone of voice, as much as the message itself, that carries the meaning of compassion or hate implied in words.

The delicate song of a husky alto voice or the bell-like ring of a countertenor touch a person's humor with cheer. The tactility of Barlach's wood sculpture *Das Wiedersehen* [*CP #16*] invokes tenderness that makes one long for Jesus' handclasp of forgiving acceptance. The spacious feel of restfulness in a room where the architect has thought about light sources, ventilation, human proportions, and movement patterns, drastically affects the quality of life possible in its environs. Whenever our sight or hearing is impaired, and if we become insensitive to taste, odors, or touch, then we men and women are more than "challenged": we are deprived of a goodness in God's world, no matter how much we overcompensate. Sense pleasure is a God-given richness and was created to be good.

The devil's gambit
"Has God said you should never drink a rum and coke, or taste liquor? Don't you know that even the Scriptures say, 'Wine is good for what ails you'" (1 Thessalonians 5:23)?

The Satan is a mastermind at corrupting what the Lord God has made good. Satan does it by isolating creatural good, exaggerating its importance. So the devil perverts what God gives us in trust by seducing us into making pleasure into an idol that stands by itself for us supposedly to manipulate. Pleasure then becomes something you live **for**, instead of your receiving pleasure as a gift, an accompanying surprise to normal activities. Once we humans aim to get pleasurable sensations we have walked into the devil's trap, because sense gratification begs for more, and more, especially if your existence is troubled, or you want to escape feeling miserable.

God has set creational limits to our senses to protect us against sinning: the intense satisfaction of an orgasm is relatively brief; at a certain point our taste buds becomes surfeited by sweets; the immense kick of a tobacco high in one's blood gradually smokes out one's lungs; too much alcohol depresses one's spirits and corrodes your liver. If one becomes enslaved by pleasures, one is punished by becoming cruel to one's body or to others in a way that lays our passions waste (Titus 3:3). Sensations wear out, even as one tries to prolong or intensify them. Inordinate pleasure chokes our life to immaturity, taught Jesus (Luke 8:14). When sense satisfaction is indulged disproportionately, it seems to block the development of more complex human delights and tends to reduce human joy to mere enjoyment, and the exuberant wonder of happiness to a dull state of lassitude.

The devil is a maniac, and tries to make us humans manic on pleasure, to go overboard. That's what the principality of Hedonism is all about: you are caught in the power of calculating how to get the most pleasure possible, without suffering a hangover, or worse. Then desire becomes an insatiable craving, things sensuous turn sensual, and one becomes distracted by the enchantment of pleasure as a coveted luxury. The hedonistic man or woman restlessly hyperventilates in the pursuit of sensational revelry. People driven by seeking Pleasure become aggressive, warlike, covetous, blinded by lust (however respectable looking), and therefore become good for nothing (cf. James 4:1–3). God's gift of pleasure is ruined into a distraction.

The Pharisaic ploy
There is more than one way to trick a sinner. If the devil leads us men and women into prostituting pleasure by getting us to worship it, to spend pleasure on ourselves, a kind of masturbation, so we become playboys and playgirls, the opposite evil of long historical standing is to promote a kill-joy spirit.

Ancient Greek and Roman Stoics and Cynics (the "dogs" the apostle Paul said to beware of, Philippians 3:2) believed pleasure was by nature evil. You should steel yourself against being sensitive to whatever is delectable; don't become dependent upon material delights outside the control of your mind, because then you are at the mercy of what is not rational. There is no *veritas in vino*! Physical satisfactions below the belt are not human—that's your animal nature, the source of everything destructive to humanity and society! Flee bodily desire, and shun what is pleasure-friendly if you would be virtuous. If you don't develop apathy, said the Stoics, you will become a pathetic figure.

It was easy for Christians to adopt this pagan "spiritualistic" denigration of what is fleshly physical, because the whole Jewish legalistic tradition in force among the early followers of Christ had localized sin to specific things you should and should not do: don't touch a dead body, wash your hands before eating, don't travel more than a stone's throw on the sabbath, attend worship at the new moon (cf. Numbers 19:11–22, Isaiah 1:10–20, Matthew 15:1–2). But whenever a community issues taboos as a foolproof method to manage evil and to insure its members become good, that group of people is begging to become self-righteous.

The Pharisees of Jesus' day had that problem, looking down their noses at profligate women and tax collectors (Matthew 11:16–19, John 8:3–11), blind to the fact that their own hearts were bigoted cesspools of greed, slander, and murder (Luke 16:14, 18:9–14, 23:13–25). Such authoritarian church leaders who have guilty sexual consciences are terribly hard on others, forbidding the pleasures of marriage, demanding abstinence from certain foods, rejecting sportive activity, and are hopelessly wrong, writes God through Paul to Timothy, because whatever God has created is good if it can be received with prayerful, celebrative thanksgiving (1 Timothy 4:1–10).

The "spiritualism" of the ascetic Pharisee, denying the pleasures given us by God, is even worse than the "materialism" of the secularist who idolizes such enjoyment into a distraction, because we Pharisees pretend to be righteous when we really are only aggressive, selfish, abusive, inhuman (*astorgoi*, devoid of normal feeling), conceited, hardened sinners. Avoid both godless and counterfeit godly people, says Scripture (2 Timothy 3:1–5).

Redemptive Scriptural direction
Beware of scoffers who use the media to wallow in their lascivious passions, laced with impieties (Jude 18). Also beware of the hypocrites who are so uptight about the distraction of pleasure they reject what God made good (1 Timothy 4:1–5).

The Bible sings with approval about the intoxicating sensuous pleasure of sexual love enjoyed by those whose vows of troth are sure (Proverbs 5:15–19, Song of Songs 4:9–15, 6:2–3, 7:10–8:3,6–7). The refrain of Ecclesiastes affirms ever more certainly throughout the book that to enjoy food and drink and have pleasure in one's work (Ecclesiastes 2:24–26, 3:12–13,22, 5:18–20, 8:15), fun with one's spouse, if you have one (9:7–10), is a gift from God one may receive and celebrate, especially when you are young! (Ecclesiastes 11:9–12:1), since such providential pleasures are basic to a life of loving God-service.

It was Jesus himself who demonstrated the need to turn the Pharisaic ethic upside-down by converting the large vats of water set aside to wash and purify one's hands and feet before meals into gallons and gallons of choice wine, better than California's best, to make merry at a wedding (John 2:1–11). Jesus' deed, his first miracle! is not a license to get drunk at wedding parties, but it certainly ends the strain of abstemious kill-joys.

It is not the sensuous pleasure of the taste of fresh sourdough bread, mature Brie cheese, and a glass of red wine by candlelight that makes you impure: it is the ascetic work-righteous, sanctimonious lust in your heart that makes eating and drinking sinful (Matthew 15:1–20). It is not the sexual ecstasy of bodily love intercourse that serves a false god: it is the disparagement of gentle marriage or the desire to possess another person for your own benefit that converts sexual joy into private rape, however legal it may appear.

The LORD created us sensible, bodily humans to enjoy God's gift of pleasure, but we find multiple, devious ways to smear its enjoyment with evil. The prayer of the tormented Augustine in his *Confessions* as he struggled to be both passionate and pure is terribly poignant: "Give me chastity and continence, [O Lord,] but not yet!" (*Confessions* 8.17). Unlike the argumentative, controlling hypocrites who pretend never to have committed murder or adultery (Matthew 5:21–30), the believer Augustine demonstrates the truth of the revelation in James' letter, that the distracting temptation of pleasure can produce in the faithful followers of Christ an enduring, seasoned maturity for receiving the Lord's good gifts (James 1:2–8).

Whether we respond with thanksgiving to our created capability for the godly pleasure, for example, of a healing, reassuring massage [#37], or prefer to forego enjoyment of the Lord's gift of pleasant sensuous gladness during Lent, let us magnify the Lord (1 Corinthians 10:31–33). And I hope, if any of you readers are anemic in pleasure, handicapped by a lack of pleasure, or a world-and-life vision that avoids pleasure, that you will feel invited by our Lord, before, after, or even during Lent—since **Christ's bodily resurrection has taken place** (*Psalter Hymnal* 372, stanza 3)—to join hands with the sense-deprived villagers of *Babbett's Feast* and dance a lovely, sensuous circle-dance of praise to the LORD who created us and our pleasures for us to offer them back to God and "fully to enjoy God forever" (*Westminster Larger Catechism*, question/answer 1).

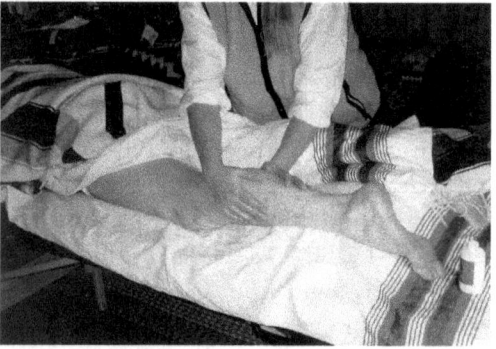

[#37] Author undergoing massage from a Registered Massage Therapist

THE SMELL OF YOUR SCHOOL:
A LETTER OF REFERENCE?

My meditation exposits a few paragraphs of the Newer Testament we call 2 Corinthians 2:14–3:6.

Corinth, you may know, was rebuilt by Julius Caesar and became a major seaport in the Roman empire, halfway between Rome and Egypt; Corinth was the raucous trade capital of Greece in the Roman empire.

If there was any church the missionary Paul "fathered" (cf. 1 Corinthians 4:14–21) that gave him trouble and that he loved and struggled for, it was the people of God at Corinth (cf. Acts 18:1–18). Paul wrote the letter we call 1 Corinthians (after a still earlier letter, cf. 1 Corinthians 5:9) while he was doing inner-city mission work at Ephesus in Asia Minor. There were factions in the Corinthian congregation, and a presumption that the Older Testament writings no longer held for them as Spirit-filled people. Don't let your being educated puff you up to think you are not called to live according to Scripture, to what has been written, says Paul (1 Corinthians 4:6–7, 8:1–3). I preached the simple truth to you people that Christ was crucified for your sins and was resurrected, remember? (cf. 1 Corinthians 15) so that you might repent, not fight among yourselves, and be empowered by the Holy Spirit to know a deep, brotherly-sisterly communion that deals in what really counts: **holy living in God's world**, as you make the forgiveness of sins in the name of the risen and ascended Jesus Christ known to **all** your neighbors. . . .

In the meantime historically, between our first and second Corinthian letters, a group of jealous christian Jews arrived in Corinth to trouble the new Greek believers there. These Jewish Christians called Paul's apostolic authority into question: who's this Paul? He's no apostle—he didn't get into the act until long after Jesus was gone! What does he have to recommend himself? these Jewish Christians murmured. So Paul followed up another troubled letter to the Corinthians (cf. 2 Corinthians 2:4), now from Macedonia, with an **apologia pro sua vita** and his co-pastor, pagan convert Titus's ministry.

Originally appeared in *Christian Courier*, 50:2411 (2 September 1994): 10.

This is the word of God:

> . . . Anyhow, to God be thanks who always leads us around in the triumphal procession of Christ [in the glory of Jesus Christ's ascension, cf. Ephesians 4:7–16], and makes phenomenally clear through us in every place the odor of intimately knowing Christ. That's right, Titus and I are the fragrant aroma of Christ to God among those who are being saved and among those who are being destroyed; so, to some we are a putrid smell and to others an odor of fresh life. (Who indeed is up to such a ministry?) For Titus and I are not peddling around God's word the way a mass of people do: rather, as ones [who live] out of unadulterated singleheartedness, indeed, as those directly from God, we speak as ones [who live] before the face of God in [union with] Christ.
>
> Are we beginning to recommend ourselves again? Do we not need, say, as some do, letters of reference to you [as the Judaists troublemakers furnished], or [letters of reference] from you? No, you are our letter [of reference], written in our hearts, being intimately known and constantly read aloud by all [kinds of] people: you are making phenomenally clear that you are a letter from Christ, issued by us, written down not with ink but with the Spirit of the living God, not engraved on stone tablets but inscribed on tablets of fleshy [human] hearts.
>
> —That's the kind of confidence in God we have through Christ: Titus and I are not able to claim ourselves anything as due to ourselves, but our empowerment comes from God who has qualified us to be ministers of a new covenant, not a covenant of mere letter, but a covenant of spirit—the mere letter [of a covenant] kills, but the Holy Spirit makes [a covenant] alive. . . .

And Paul goes on under the leading of God's Spirit to book the difference between the splendor of the old Mosaic ministry and the more permanent, glorious hope of Christ's ministry, outfitting those who by the mercy of God live to proclaim and effect the worldwide lordship of Jesus Christ (2 Corinthians 3:7–4:6).

The note about smell and the metaphor "letters of reference" are worth remembering since they capture en passant sound direction for us educational leaders who would be obedient to the Lord.

My wife has a sharp sense of smell. God too has a good nose, according to the Bible. The pleasing odor of Noah's animal sacrifices after God's flood had judged the world led the LORD to inaugurate the rainbow covenant with the earth (Genesis 78:20–9:17). And the prophet Amos quotes God's saying God couldn't stand the stink of Israel's special holy days and offerings because their ordinary lives were lawless and their praise was fake (Amos 2:4–8, 5:21–24).

When Paul spoke to unbelievers in Athens about God's determining appointed periods of time and the boundaries of human dwellings on the earth so that men and women might look for God, possibly touch (!) God and find God (Acts 17:24–31), the apostle was carrying on the psalm tradition of reporting the palpable presence of the LORD with us creatures (cf. Psalm 115). And here in the second Corinthian letter Paul claims there be an "odor of intimately knowing Christ" that is fragrant to almighty God, which turns off disbelievers like rotting flesh and attracts those destined to be worshipers of the living Lord as if it be a whiff of fresh air.

Smells foul and fair
What does a person or a community smell like that pleases the Lord?

I have attended meetings where the subtle stench of power struggle drifted through the room; you could sniff the juices of hidden agendas, and the pungent charge of envy and frustrated anger. Evil power cloaked in righteousness has a particularly rank, overly sweet smell. Jealousy is as blatant as hydrogen-sulfide; and a company befuddled by overmuch drink emits the vague foulness of vomit. The biblical word for "vanity" (*hebel*) means "hot air," the stink of passed gas from one's colon—a wonderful exposure of such empty pretension. A selfish person, an aggressive institution, has a manufactured acrid odor like disinfectant—corrosive, efficient, a fast-working sterility for those it attacks. And then there is the odorless carbon monoxide killing of deceit and quiet betrayal.

Against such odors (cf. Galatians 5:13–24) the smells of new-mown hay, an unpolluted seashore, baked bread still warm, correlate with gentleness, self-control, faithfulness, goodness, kindness, patience— When fruits of the Spirit like peace attend a gathering, there is a fragrance of fruit blossoming trees all around.

The first time in my life I genuinely experienced "sabbath rest" was after a Friday evening vesper service among Seventh-Day Adventist believers at a seminar in Collonges-sous Salève, in France: God's sun was just going down as our final prayers and doxology rose; people began to walk more slowly on the promenades overlooking the distant city of Geneva as darkness approached; the pressure of work eased off your shoulders, your neck relaxed, and the smell of garden herbs mixed with God's cool blessing of the evening brought a joyful peace into your nostrils, filled the throat, bathing one wholly, bodily, untensed.

I have attended worship services upon occasion where you didn't need the ritual pomp of a censer burning incense because the expectancy of the faithful gathered to hear the Word of God preached bubbled up like a verdant meadow filled with green trees, wild flowers, running brooks, and a gentle breeze. I have at times experienced the hard smell of shared pain, where sorrow like sweat clung to your skin but was sweet, not offensive—it had the odor of exertion, was intensely physical, like a game of squash, but was muted because something inexplicable and hurtsome, a burden, was being actually borne by another person (cf. Galatians 5:25–6:2). And maybe I have known the subdued fragrance of being forgiven; it smells softly like a forest of pine needles, balsam, and cedar wood.

Odors have meaning
I don't mean to set up a fanciful synesthetic roster of odors pegged to virtues and vices, so you can order the requisite perfume, and no matter your closeness to God or not, come out smelling like a rose. I realize Calvinian Christians of the Reformation smell differently than Mennonites, and Baptist believers have a different odor than Anglicans, and our Lord does not have a one-track smell.

But I am serious about the fact that we Westerners may have Platonized away appreciation of natural body odors and never learned the Eastern sensitivity to the fragrance of oils, and therefore lost—we use "de-odorants"—the creatural richness of good smells, of fish when it is truly fresh, the bouquet of a ripe Persian melon, the exquisite fragrance of a disingenuous act of love, which lightly fills the air and lingers pleasantly.

Paul makes us aware that our odors betray us—jokes at tea break smell delightful or foul (cf. Ephesians 4:25–5:20)—and that we are called **as a communal body** to have the aroma of a living intimacy with the Christ, which will be neither stuffy nor humdrum, probably not exotic, but shall be attractive to those seeking meaning, and offend those who are secretly at bottom stubbornly proud of themselves.

A calling rather than credentials
Paul's defense of his and Titus's ministry among the Corinthians admits

to human frailty (2 Corinthians 4:7; 2:16c; cf. 1 Corinthians 2:1–5), and disclaims the props used by his evangelistic competitors—pedigree CV, upbeat statistics, letters of reference. We are not in the business of selling Christ, says Paul, or of becoming an establishment with vested interests. In our weakness as an appointed diaconate of God's new covenant, which writes the discipline of passionate, selfless love for God, neighbor, and the world on the malleable hearts of Greeks and Jews, women and men, slaves and proprietors, we are only single-minded, single-hearted ambassadors for Jesus Christ, sure of a habitation with the LORD forever, even if we die in our calling, thanks to God's gift of the Holy Spirit (2 Corinthians 3:17–5:21; 10:1–12:21).

The fact that Paul took no credit for the Corinthian congregation's zeal to serve the Lord yet boasted of their confession on his travels (2 Corinthians 9:1–5), strikes me as very close to the way wise educators relate to their students. The Corinthian church was pockmarked with immorality, bickering, disorder, and contentiousness, yet Paul still gives God thanks for their existence (1 Corinthians 1:4–9), and cites them in our passage as being a letter from Christ, transcribed by Paul and Titus, written down not with ink, not engraved on stone tablets [as God self did with Moses; cf. Exodus 31:18, Deuteronomy 9:10], but a letter from Christ written indelibly with the Spirit of the living God on their human hearts.

Spirit-written letters
I shall not try to piece out here Paul's whole polemic with the legalistic Judaists who crippled the gospel Paul preached to the pagans (cf. Galatians), nor show the error of reading Paul as Sadducees and gnostics have, who wrongly pit Spirit-freedom against rule-bound laws. Paul never sets up an opposition between God's law (*nomos*) and God's spirit (*pneuma*), as I read the Scriptures. Paul rejects the self-righteousness of those who think fulfilling the letter (*gramma*) of a covenant gives them credit with God. Paul claims that the LORD God used him and Titus to fulfill the Pentecostal promise made through prophets Joel (2:28–29), Jeremiah (31:31–34), and Ezekiel (36:22–31), that the LORD would write God's laws upon human hearts, put the holy Spirit within human beings (cf. also Psalm 40:8), so that the **law of the Spirit of life in Christ Jesus would set the faithful free** from the "law" of sin and death (cf. Romans 8:2–11).

And that is the challenge the biblical text leaves with us educators: that we ourselves be letters from Christ, in the handwriting of whatever godly mentors we ever had like Paul and Titus, and that we accept the task of transcribing the next generation of our students as letters from Christ, breathing a holy spirit into the script of their talk, thought, diet, art, ruling, use of money, smells. . . .

As the Adventist and Reformational communions of higher education strive to be a letter from Christ in our secularized day of syncretistic license and politically correct legalism, beset by the pragmatist push to become sophisticated technicians and experts short on reflective wisdom, we need, says Scripture, not to live as those alienated from the LORD do (Ephesians 4:17–24), but without grumbling and dialectical calculation; that is, that we without guile hold firmly onto the Word of life, our Lord Jesus Christ, that holy Scripture makes known (Philippians 1:27–2:16; cf. John 5:24–47). If to be an authentic letter from Christ for the neighbor in our lifetime costs us persecution and being forced to the margins of power politics and culture, remember we are simply following the footsteps of the apostle Paul (1 Corinthians 1:18–2:5; cf. 2 Timothy 3:10–17), and need only to pray to be a legible letter of reference for Jesus Christ and a winsome aroma, if we would be found faithful when the Lord returns.

A Christian School Song for Parents and Teachers (PTA)

Christian weekday schools are not "church schools," we say. A christian school education is not "Sunday school" plus reading, writing, and arithmetic. The contribution of a Reformation christian orientation helps evangelical followers of Christ understand that a "school" is not a "family," is not a "church," is not a "state" institution, but is a "school," is a school, is a school with its own specific God-given responsibilities. And a school and a church and a state and a family are called upon to exercise their specific God-given responsibilities toward the other institutions too.

A christian day school is also not a "parochial" school, the way Roman Catholic schools are subordinate to the control of "the Church."

In Quebec, Canada, since confederation, there was a dual setup for schools: Roman Catholic schools under Church control, the Protestant schools under state control. In Ontario, Canada, the Protestant majority wanted the state to control all schools. But the British North American Act[1] made it possible for Roman Catholic schools in Ontario to keep tax monies for their separate Roman Catholic schools and keep a Roman Catholic direction in the teaching and governance. This legal right was later extended to Manitoba and the Northwest Territories.

As the public (considered Protestant) schools gradually became more estranged from "religion," distinctive "**christian**" **day schools** were formed by non-Catholic, Reformation, and evangelical parent societies who were willing to pay extra, in principle, above their regular taxes, for

---

1 In Canada, because public (Protestant!) schools already received educational tax monies from the government prior to confederation, separate parochial Roman Catholic schools were allocated the educational tax monies of Roman Catholic parents by the government, thanks to the British North American Act (1867, art. 93 & 93A), which was Quebec's price for being part of the Union.

A shortened version of this essay was first published in *Christian Educators Journal* 47:1 (2007): 18–19.

schooling that would meet quality standards set by the government, be "Bible"-oriented, but be free from Church control.

Such christian parents elect trustees who at arm's length oversee the faith direction of the schooling. We parents delegate to trusted teachers the task of showing the next generation of children how to follow Christ in performing art, reading books, studying science, investigating society, communicating by speech and internet, professing the rainbow rich lordship of Jesus Christ in God's world.

The price of distinction

Because christian school education is extra costly for middle or lower-income families who want their offspring and neighboring children to have a God-centered education, school teachers, administrators, and boards welcome prayer and free-will offerings from churches, and charitable donations from modest and larger generous philanthropists. Currently various *modi vivendi* have been worked out to get a measure of educational tax money allocations from the government in certain provinces and states, to help the government begin to exercise its proper just-doing rule for all citizens, while parents keep directional control of the schooling, and not let the state imperceptibly absorb the power to determine how we christianly teach the children.

It is sometimes tempting, for expediency sake, to let go of the difference between Church and school if it means we could deduct **all** our tuition and auxiliary educating costs when paying legal income tax to the government. What's a fine "philosophical" point about "christian" or "parochial" schools compared to saving money? to protesting and circumventing societal injustice?

But just as it is important to keep "civil unions" distinct from the institution of "marriage," so it is important to keep "schools" distinct from being franchises of "the state" and distinct from being a quasi-"church" institution (as it is important to keep bona fide, tax-free "church organizations" distinct from "businesses" and "profit-making" enterprises).

If a Christian weekday school is conceived and practiced as if it be a disguised church (comparable to a *madrassa* of a mosque community), then **education** will easily slip into **catechism** and **indoctrination**, since a church rightly has direct **doctrinal** criteria for its teaching, while a school rightly has direct **ethical** and **analytical competence** criteria, and only **indirectly** has **confessional** doctrinal concerns.

To make the same point in other words: schooling leads immature persons to discover (often playfully) God's creational order for the world and the way we are to be redemptively faithful in practicing our many tasks before the Lord's face. This disciplined, **trustworthy leading** (ethical) of children should be conducted by wise, seasoned educators, trained to help the young make mistakes! in school so the youth themselves learn to judge their correctly playing musical instruments, using calculators, telling history, deciding between puzzling alternatives in complex personal inter-relational problems. Good teachers are guidance counselors in studies who let students learn to "bewonder," distinguish, speak about, and practice what is real and relevant for living responsibly in hope and tough love during these complicated days. School teachers should **not dictate** (doctrinal) the right answers. Christian school teachers should also not pretend to be "neutral" and "non-directive," instead of oriented by the Biblical writings and Holy Spirit in leading children to understand God's world.

Much more needs to be said about the implications of **believing** that **a school is not a church nor an arm of the state**, and that each kind of institution is called to serve the other institutions in society by performing its proper task toward them. (A church is not a school either, even though a church has a catechetical function. And the Canadian or American state is certainly not a school or a church, although government does confess and inculcate a "bill of rights.") It is also so that a school does rightfully have a confessional function among its medley of activities—Bible or Qur'an or Enlightenment principle **study**, devotional **exercises**—and is called to do justice to the subject matter it teaches. But I make the point of difference here to introduce **a song-text specially conceived for a school circumstance**.

A school song
When teachers and parents (and school board directors) get together for a school meeting, you need a school song. Not a "rah-rah" school song to accompany a school's hockey or basketball sports event. Also not a church hymn to fit the fact that most of those present also attend church services. And unless you are commemorating a national holiday as school society, the national anthem is not so appropriate either as unifying song. One could use **a school song** to celebrate **a school gathering**, the rationale, purpose, and joy (amid hardships) of what calls us together as PTA or **a christian school society**. (When "home-schooling" families get to-

gether for a meeting, they could use a "school song" too.)

The text I wrote for this christian school song credits God's Spirit for pulling us motley group of people together to guide the young in doing God's will, especially just-doing in the world, with a passion for the truth. Our school society pleads for the schooling going on to be wise in explicating Christ's Rule—that is our mission—as we wait for the Lord's coming again.

The song is a strong melody kept within an octave range, without skips or chromatic difficulties. It is not light and cheery like so many simplified children songs today. It has no modern dissonance, and also not the comfortable sound of nineteenth-century piety. Nor does the song sound like a Methodist hymn of the 1700s with bright emotional clarity. This 1600s melody has the grit and firm determination of a song line that knows what it wants to say in brief compass, and ends with confident assertion.

The melody for this christian school song comes out of a time when schools were still practically an outreach ministry of churches historically, not yet differentiated as independent schools. For centuries people had had the Bible as their primer to learn to read. And the melody has a forthright toughness and directness we middle class citizens of Western countries might do well to learn today, in developing an awareness of the many Christians in the world whose blood cries out to the Lord for redress from evil. We may have difficulty in paying for christian schooling, but our persecution is mild, genteel. Yet there is no harm in having an edge to our school song, since in certain ways we educators who follow Christ are still embattled in an apostate culture.

It would take a little while for "Here comes a fully laden ship of blessings" (that's the name of the tune—"Es kommt ein Schiff geladen") to become an old favorite of PTA societies. But it might be worth a try and a little persistence; this new song, a fresh breeze of Huguenot-like brusqueness, might well prove to be like a resilient fly in the ointment of sweet and happy Bible choruses. In our post-Church world society, it could be time to try to compose and sing **christian school songs** that are marked by age-old vigor and certainty. Young song writers should also start composing **school songs** about wisdom and peace-making in the land. . . .

A Christian School Song for Parents and Teachers (PTA)

1. Your Spirit, Lord, has taken our hearts and formed a root that never shall be shaken, and shall bear much good fruit.

2. Entrusted with the labours to train and guide the young we parents, teachers, neighbours, desire "Your will be done."

3. Protected by God's caring
we seek to lead the youth
in doing justice, sharing
a passion for the truth.

4. Confronted by the great need
to discipline our lives
in though, in word, in real deed,
we ask, Lord, "Make us wise."

5. Conceived in faith and wisdom
our dedicated school
is ready for the mission
to explicate Christ's Rule.

6. As expectation rises,
O Lord, to see your face,
we pray, send us surprises
of your unfailing grace.

Text: Calvin Seerveld, 2002 ©
Tune: Andernacher Gesangbuch, 1608;
harm. Emily Brink, 1985

7676
Es kommt ein schiff geladen

Being thanked for lecturing at a Conference of the Greek Union of Christian Artists by Anestis Petalidis, Phaedon Kaloterakis, Katerine Papadopoulis, at Leptokaria, Greece, 1995. (Poet Anestis, Song-writer Paidon, and Opera singer Katerina later performed *The Greatest Song* under Seerveld's direction, in Thessaloniki, Greece, respectively as King Solomon, the Lover, and the Shulammite maiden, in 1997.)

WAYS-OF-LIFE AND BECOMING ELDERLY WISE

Because a world-and-life-view one may hold can change, or could be at variance with the dominating course of societal history currently in force, the "con-structed" character of anybody's world-and-life-view may not be the right key for understanding what one's whole life, as a matter of fact, means.

> Mijns inziens is het juister allereerst te denken aan 'wegen'. Het is het gaan van een weg die aan het individuele leven samenhang geeft. Ook al is er principieel de mogelijkheid van pad te verwisselen, (v)ast blijft staan dat elk pad afzonderlijk een bepaalde 'logica' kent: op bepaalde stappen volgen andere. (W)e zullen De Hart en De Vries moeten toegeven dat het huidige leven diffuser is dan voorheen. Maar zonder wegen kunnen we niet. In zoverre behouden ook levensbeschouwingen een oriënterende betekenis.[1]

It seems so to me too, that the "way of life" a human creature leads, embodies most surely what that person stands for, suffers, lives through, puts on the record. People who are not philosophically trained, and people who may not be conscious that their pattern of daily life could be articulated in a vision of what they apparently hold dear or have to cope with as priorities, still cannot avoid, if they be sane, **a way of life** which holds together.[2] Even a Dr. Jekyl–Mr. Hyde, Clark Kent–Superman, or the fractured duplicity of a bona fide hypocrite, lays down a concrete track of footprints of one's life journey an investigative observer could trace.

---

1 Sander Griffioen, "Leven in de verstrooing. De kracht van levensbeschouwing" (1996), in *Moed tot cultuur: Een actuele filosofie* (Amsterdam: Buijten & Schipperheijn, 2003), 193.

2 "A philosophy, as I understand it, is similar to a way-of-life and to a world-and-life-view (1) in its encyclopedic, systematic compass, and (2) in its being an out-working of one's underlying faith-commitment. But philosophy has an analytically defined consistency." Calvin Seerveld, "Philosophy as schooled memory" (1982), *In the Fields of the Lord* (Toronto: Tuppence Press, 2000), 86–87. Cf. C. Seerveld, "Skeleton for Philosophy 101 at Trinity Christian College" (1960), mimeo, 2–3.

First published in *Een weg gaan: Cultuurfilosofie tussen west en oost* (festschrift Sander Griffioen) Govert Buijs, ed. (Budel: Damon, 2006), 129–140.

I should like to explore briefly a few different **ways-of-life** which have enveloped us human creatures, and are still **directional options** for any particular person today practically to find oneself in, which one adopts or struggles with as one matures in the dated/located circumstances into which you are born. Since this short piece commemorates Sander Griffioen's exaugural address from the Vrije Universiteit in Amsterdam, "*Een weg gaan*," I wish to bend the analysis toward "growing old." What does it mean to age as a human? Does the particular way-of-life one follows alter the meaning of one's existence? Is the human creature's adding on years imbricated in and telltale of the nature of the world we, with animals, trees, oceans and mountains, inhabit? That is, does how we conceive things at large to be, alter what we actually make of inescapably becoming elderly and "finishing" one's life task, or leaving one's walk "unfinished"? How does anyone judge the worth of one's own way-of-life? As Shakespeare's Jacques epigrammatically put it in *As You Like It* (II, 7):

> All the world's a stage.
> And all the men and women merely players:
> They have their exits and their entrances,
> And one man in his time plays many parts,
> His acts being seven ages....

Do humans face the choice of a fork in the road, like Hercules in the ancient Greek myth,[3] and have to choose between **either** the (virtuous) way forwards **or** the (degenerate) way backwards? Would it be possible somehow to travel **both** the high (slow) road **and** the low (fast) road, since all roads lead in the direction of one destination—sans teeth . . . sans every thing? Are certain ways-of-life virtually dead ends?

Deny aging

The stories—537 novels!—by American Horatio Alger (1832–1899), even though they were considered beneath the notice of literary critics, galvanized and epitomize a way-of-life that fit an earlier Puritan ethic going mercantilist in the nation. Every poor boy from the country in Horatio Alger narratives, who goes to seek his fortune in the big corrupt city environment, by honest pluck, persevering hard work and self-reliance, becomes healthy, wealthy and successful, against all odds. The English William Hogarth's series of graphic engravings portraying *Industry and*

---

[3] This mythic situation told by Prodicus was recorded in Xenophon's *Memorabilia* (II, 1, 21–34). Cf. Diels-Kranz, *Die Fragmente der Vorsokratiker*, 6th ed., fr. 84B, 2:313–316.

Idleness (1747) had puckishly taken a similar line; but Horatio Alger accents the positive, blending the superficial how-to-get-ahead "wisdom" of Benjamin Franklin's *Poor Richard's Almanac* (1732) and Emersonian morality (transcendental "Self- Reliance," 1841) into an underdog picaresque Idealism that was immensely popular and widely published on into the 1920s. This rags-to-riches way-of-life buttressed the Darwinian Capitalistic political economy practiced in the free-wheeling days of New York's Tammany Hall and the "Robber Baron" philanthropist families of Carnegie and Rockefeller as the United States of America became a modern world power.

Today, a North American way-of-life practiced by many more people than yuppies counts the American Dream of affluent prosperity to be worth fighting for, you might say. "Life, liberty, and the pursuit of happiness" (American Declaration of Independence) governs and justifies the incessant striving which characterizes this committed dedication to betterment. Those who practice this busy way of life act in a world whose only constant is change, where the fittest survive. Such a geneticistic way-of-life[4] can have variant emphases, but the crucial point for my focus here is: everybody is too intent upon living and doing, to think of dying.

Since being productive, active in energetically improving one's own existence, that of society or the environment, sets the contours to one's life time, one must try to stay young, vital, innovative, up-to-date, changing with the times like a human chameleon. The influential *Wired* magazine, *Glamor* journal advertisements, tabloid newspapers, and TV sports, all of which often show a crass pragmatistic spirit to boot, reinforce the conviction that continual engagement—never give up!—is critical to your having a meaningful existence. If you cannot drink from Ponce de Leon's "fountain of youth" or take hours and hours a week for an extreme fitness program, and so turn old, a non-productive burden, there is little place for you who are aged, who are essentially dysfunctional—unless like a self-made millionaire you are rich enough to be the consumate consumer cruising the sybaritic seas, a frail, retired consumptive par excellence.

A trouble with this common, attractive, workaholic way-of-life

---

4   The philosophies D. H. Th. Vollenhoven analyzes to be "cosmogono-cosmological" in nature, whether it be a dialectical Hegel, evolutionistic Comte, revolutionary Engels, devolutionary Spengler, or vitalistic John Dewey, as honoring both the genetic and structural composition of things, I prefer to highlight as a "geneticistic" stance, since cosmic structure of reality is really eclipsed and understood by such thinkers to be essentially one of constant change. Cf. K.A. Bril, *Westerse Denkstructuren* (Amsterdam: VU Uitgeverij, 1986), 120). Geneticistic figures often seem to be monistically inclined.

which would deny aging in order to affirm progress, was exposed by Jessica Mitford's insightful, sixties muck-raking book, *The American Way of Death* (1963). If your way-of-life is driven by the constant effort to succeed, your way-of-death should certainly try to hide any failure. That is precisely what the American establishment of funereal undertakers arranges: ornate casket open for viewing the corpse briefly embalmed to look natural, enveloped in costly floral arrangements; then what remains of you is transported to a lovely landscaped Forest Lawn Memorial-Park (Southern California)—public graves in the churchyard have been "upgraded" to plots in privatized commercial real estate cemeteries—where you can die happily for ever after.[5]

Such a Hollywooded non-ending, it strikes me, is a fitting macabre epitaph for the self-serving way-of-life whose **practice and vision** would deny aging, and tends to trust that whatever is new cannot be regressive, **as if we humans produce history** rather than act a bit part in the story of the world.[6]

Death not unwelcome
A quite different way-of-life than the standard ambitious American praxis, which is shared by peoples around the world, of striving for well-earned progress—giving everything a run for its money—is the more composed walk of the ancient Stoic who indeed sees a fork in the highway of life and says one should choose to take the road less travelled by. Not the *carpe diem* route, but the duty-bound, difficult road of public service is the way to go, even if it ends, as it did for Cicero, in assassination (43 BC). Seneca, mentor of Nero, did not practice in daily life what he preached in philosophy; nevertheless, because it was Seneca's conviction that a man's immortal soul is what really counts most, when he was implicated in a plot to murder Emperor Nero and things turned ugly, Seneca at age 69 decided it was the rational time to commit suicide (65 AD). Whether you were born a slave (Epictetus, fl. 85 AD) or became a

---

5 A stanza of Afro-American Countee Cullen's (1903–1946) poem "A Brown Girl Dead" catches the embroiled bittersweet sadness of the poor who have to play this expensive way-of-life-and-death:

> ... Her mother pawned her wedding ring
> To lay her out in white;
> She'd be so proud she'd dance and sing
> To see herself tonight.

6 Cf. Johan van der Hoeven and Griffioen on the matter that humans are called to "disclose" rather than "compose" history, in Sander Griffioen, *The Problem of Progress* (Sioux Center, Iowa: Dordt College Press, 1987), 46–47.

Roman emperor (Marcus Aurelius, 121–180 AD), if you practiced the Stoical way-of-life, you steeled yourself against whatever Fate or (mis)Fortune put in your lap to bear, by hardening your physique in Spartan fashion to withstand pain, and by developing the will-power to remain unaffected, impassive, if not apathetic, toward whatever might disturb your rational equilibrium. *Che sera sera*. Old age fortunately ends the tyranny of desire (Cicero, *De Senectute*, xii, 39–xiv, 47). And death is simply a natural step following up old age which releases your soul from its physical bondage and the strenuous round of civic duties; so take the transition in stride.

When Christians adopted and fortified this ascetic, dutiful way-of-life as a pilgrimage through our worldly vale of tears to the Celestial City, its praxis became more sobering and arduous than Montaigne's limited stoic concern that a man pass the final test of death 'quietement et seurement' (*Essais*, 1:19). Because sin is now a factor in the journey humans make, it is as if Bunyan's "Christian" faces a fork in the road of his *Pilgrim's Progress* (1678) **everywhere**. You are tempted to dally buying wares in Vanity Fair or to step off the King's highway onto a bypath where the walking is easier. But the straight and troublesome pathway demands you bypass doubtful crossroads, shun enticing vistas which bring missteps, and walk finally through the threatening deep river of death by sheer faith.

The non-conformist way-of-life—John Bunyan (1628–1688) wrote *Pilgrim's Progress* during part of the twelve years he spent in prison for being a Dissenting Puritan preacher—has a decisive schematist clarity and simplicity to it[7]: you either walk the suffering way of truth to eternal happiness, or you wander down the lanes of false ease and dissipation. There is nothing new under the sun. So realize, O mortal, that one's lifetime is but the repeated Hour of Decision, a preparation period for death and glory. Old age brings you closer to consummation: *in pace requiescat*.

An antinomy I find within this stoical-puritanic way-of-life is the residual denial of the creatural goodness of human corporeality and God's wonderful, psalmodic world which we do indwell. To live out in earnest that history is a battle between good and evil, and that one must persist in doing what is right, no matter the cost, seems so much more responsible than the self-indulgent resignation of Voltaire's Candide whose categorical imperative of resignation is "*il faut cultiver notre jardin*." Also,

---

7   I call "schematist" those philosophies Vollenhoven orders as being "purely cosmological," like the double Ways of Parmenides, Montanist Tertullian, and "spiritualist" Rousseau, since change and real development are strictly rejected by such thinkers who take history to be imprints of a fixed paradigm. Many schematist thinkers prefer some kind of dualist approach to reality.

the stern Mennonite practice of living like heavenly strangers in a foreign apostate land while doing good to their neighbors held at arm's length, can gentle this severe way-of-life with notes of God-pleasing peace. Yet great Irish poet Yeats is mistaken to request in exquisite, chiseled poetic lines ("Sailing to Byzantium," 1928) that

> Sages standing in God's holy fire
> Consume my heart away; sick with desire
> And fastened to a dying animal.

It is indeed possible that "the next (two-thirds world) Christianity" Philip Jenkins claims is acoming[8], who have nothing to lose but their incredible abject poverty, may rally to this abstemious way-of-life in order to convert their dying under the unjust yoke of indentured resource-trade slavery imposed by rich nations of the world, convert it into an impatient waiting for the glorious heavenly city to come. But for humans to **conceive and practice** their way-of-life to be a purgatory in which **death is not unwelcome** is sadly to miss and preclude, it seems to me, the accent of expectant joy God promises to provide in the very nature of our being creatural.

Fade away

A way-of-life quite different both from travelling the rigorous ascetic journey which rejects indulgence and from the go-get-it *excelsior!* (the motto of New York State, USA) way-of-exertion is the *wu-wei* (non- purposeful acquiescence) of aligning one's becoming being and non-being with Dao.

The ancient Chinese writings *Daodejing* (under the *Laozi* name, c. 500 BC) and *Zhuangzi* (c. 300 BC) present an attitude and project for carrying on human existence that is decidedly non-humanistic. Rather than pursue the canonic Confucian ethic of hierarchical civil order and ritual reciprocity of social and familial propriety and privilege, a Daoist practice of *li* (activity in accord with *dao*) is very pliant, almost plant-like behavior or like going with the grain of the jade or of wood. *Dao* (道) is only an ingenious moniker for the inexpressible primordial, protean spontaneous Generative Process continually birthing and sustaining the universe with its outgoing, receding, far-reaching and turning-back everlasting re-ingression of existences (*Daodejing*, 25, 40). Humans are empowered to be coming *de* (virtuous) when their way-of-life resonates with the undulating waxing and waning of *dao*, including returning to the

---

8 Cf. "The Next Christianity," *The Atlantic Monthly* (October 2002), http://www.theatlantic.com/issues/2002/10/jenkins.htm.

quieting originary, ongoing cosmogonic wholeness (*Daodejing*, 16, 21).

A Daoic way-of-life treats whatever happens as manifestations of a **benign** cosmic "*ewige Wiederkehr*," as if absolute reality is at core an ever-recurring, quasi-sacred occurrence whose indeterminate Re-source is unfathomable, but which one can follow if you be initiated into the gnosis of yielding like water. Nothing in the world is more submissive and weak than water; yet gentle water overcomes the most unbending adamant stronghold (*Daodejing*, 78), to wit, a tsunami. Just as in judo (the gentle art) your **active** passivity lets the attacker harm himself while you remain unhurt, just so let humans flexibly go with the becoming and begoing flow of things, the Way-of-water. Basic living-the-*dao* lies below and occurs before the lingual fixtures of "good" and "evil," and antedates predications of "lawful" and "illegal." War medals are "good" for morale but "bad" for the dead soldier; so "make spring with things galore!" (*Zhuangzi*, 5). The eternal Dao process burdens you with forming things, belabors you with breathing life, eases you in old age, and rests you in death (*Zhuangzi*, 6): one dies of old age and fades away, gone with the wind, completely natural. Good for the traveler who leaves no tracks behind (*Daodejing*, 27)!

The *dao* way-of-life commends itself today to educated practitioners who are fed up with the cultural garbage dump on our hands resulting from three centuries of European *sapere aude* "Enlightenment," gone technocratic. What one could call "California Zen," a life style during the Beat Generation of the '60s, adulterated, bagatellized and popularized aspects of Daoism in the praxis of a pacifist (during the Vietnam War debacle) Woodstock love-in kind of let-it-all-go way-of-life. John Cage aestheticized the way of Yijing (the ancient Zhou era divining Book of changes) in his music performance and teaching. Michel Foucault's (1926–1984) oeuvre is a stellar example of contemporary mythologizing philosophy, to use Vollenhoven's good category,[9] where his arcane reflection proposes to avoid the logocentric predicament by doing an archeology of human cultural achievements, which erases causality and continuity as constants, and poses that our human inheritance "is an unstable assemblage of faults,

---

9 "Mythologizing philosophy" for Vollenhoven and myself designates systematic thought which ascribes to cosmic order genetic finality and simultaneously grasps genesis as everlasting, repetitive order. Such philosophy usually has a more world-and-life-viewy character often attended by a cultic atmosphere. C. Seerveld, "Biblical Wisdom underneath Vollenhoven's Categories for Philosophical Historiography," *Philosophia Reformata*, 38 (1973): 137–138 {see *AH*: 14}. Figures like Hesiod, Plutarch, Basilides, Jung, and late Heidegger (as well as Daoism and Foucault) tend to view history as a virtual diaphonous recurring echtype of a fixed archetypal schema.

fissures and heterogeneous layers" of singular isolated events which recur! with reversals![10] No wonder Foucault's sophisticated post-christian, hardened-heart variation on the ancient, more benevolent Daoist way-of-life ends *Les mots et les choses* (1966) by confidently wagering "que l'homme s'effacerait, comme . . . la limite de la mer un visage de sable."

While the **vision and praxis** of Daoism have a vivid sense of the pervasive, fecundive genesis and decay of creaturely life, and is rightly inclusive of the worthwhile variety of non-human creatures found in the universe, the *Daodejing* and *Zhuangzi* scriptures nature-ize men and women, vaporizing human responsibility to give leadership in making things flourish, and weakens the sting of evil by conceiving evil to be merely a contrary of good, both of which are relative and necessary to the Yin/Yang parallel polarity of the world.[11] That is why I find Wan-Lim Yip's proposal to save contemporary China's culture from being overrun in a global commodifying sameness by refreshing the Watercourse Way of Daoism in China, utopian.[12] Because the Daoic way-of-life lacks an endpoint—**we just fade away**—and knows no impinging compassionate judgment of God, its perpetual becoming and begoing misses, it seems to me, any room for mercy and forgiveness, and thus has little possibility for redemptive start-up action in history.

The differences between the three ways-of-life I have sketched, and a fourth I shall describe, noting their takes on aging,[13] are not "arguable,"

---

10 Foucault, "Nietzsche, La Généologie, l'Histoire" in *Hommage a Jean Hyppolite* (Paris: Presses Universitaires de France, 1971), 145, 152, 159–161; translated by D. F. Bouchard and Sherry Simon as "Nietzsche, Geneology, History" in *Language, Counter-Memory, Practice: Selected essays and interviews*, Donald F. Bouchard, ed. (Ithaca: Cornell University Press, 1977), 139–140, 146, 153–54.

11 A sound hermeneutic key for me to start understanding and relating the encyclopedic integrality of philosophical Daoism within the world-wide historical panorama of human endeavor making sense of things is to read the Dao thought pattern as a pre-Christian mythologizing parallelistic monism. Cf. K.A. Bril and P.J. Boonstra, *D. H. Th. Vollenhoven, Schematische Kaarten* (Amsterdam: De Zaak Haes, 2000), 185, 204.

12 Wai-Lim Yip, "The Daoist Project as a 'possible' metanarrative," in *Chinese Thought in a Global Context: A Dialogue between Chinese and Western Philosophical Approaches*, Karl-Heinz Pohl (ed.) (Leiden: Brill, 1999), 145–170. Cf. also Wai-Lim Yip, *Diffusion of Distances: Dialogues between Chinese and Western Poetics* (Berkeley: University of California Press, 1993).

13 One other major schematist way-of-life I leave unexplored here is the steady trek, as it were, from hell through earthly purgatory to heavenly glory modeled by Dante's (1265–1321) *Divina Commedia*, which gives the Church a special, almost mediatorial role in human affairs. And there are other serious ways-of-life worth scrutinizing, like that of the traditional Canadian Inuit peoples, to see how they faith-read the

are not able to be dialectically melted down and resolved into one best all-inclusive way-of-life, because a way-of-life is not "rationally" determined. That is the misguided alchemical mistake thinkers have often made, pretending to take a neutral, rational God's-eye point of view to settle the differences between divergent philosophies. Philosophies are schooled memories, and memories are selective. World-and-life-visions are orientations, and orientations depend upon where and upon what overlooking point a person stands. Ways-of-life beaten out historically in **varied** circumstances sacramentally sign and seal your communal identity and the direction in which you are headed; a way-of- life is not an "academic" problem to be solved in an armchair. So there are basic unbridgeable differences at the base of conflicting philosophies, committed world-and-life-visions, and plural ways-of-life.

As I see it, the differences in ways-of-life are **contraries**, because **all humans are given the same creaturely reality to deal with**, and our lived, envisioning, and meaning-reflective responses to the meaning of things are constrained by the one triune LORD God's ordinantial embraces and apportioned duration **within which we creatures in common act, change, and beget**. The significant differences we humans hold depend upon the divergent subjective responses made to our begraced creaturely givens,[14] store responses variously marked by ignorance, astigmatic vision, willful obstinacy, faulty obedience and the like, which responses become engrained in human traditions.

Full of years
It is noteworthy that early Christians were known as followers of "the Way of God," "the Way of the Lord" (Acts 18:24-26), which the Jewish people of God called "a sect" (*haeresin*, heresy, Acts 24:14). [Dao 道 stands for the **no-name** "Way."] The Bible reveals there is a Way in which the LORD God calls freed people to walk (Deuteronomy 13:1–5). The "christian" road sign reads "Path of tried-tested-and-true life-giving right-doing" (*tzedaqah chayyim*, Proverbs 12:28) and "Way of abundant peace" (*derek shalom*, Isaiah 59:8, Romans 3:17). The entrance gateway to this "Path of coming-through-with-justice," alias, "the Way of wisdom" (Proverbs 2 and 4:10–19) is narrow, especially for those who are fat

---

given glossolalia of creation and the world of invisible spirits nearby. . . .

14 Griffioen recalls Geertsema's keen designation of many human culturing responses in "het antwoord-karakter van de werkelijkheid" (cf. my glossolalia, cs) as "vluchtwegen voor de waarheid van God over het menselijk leven." H. G. Geertsema, *Het menselijk karakter van ons kennen* (Amsterdam: Buijten & Schipperheijn, 1992), 130, 154 n.98.

with riches, education, and aplomb (Matthew 7:13–14, Mark 10:17–27) because "the Ways of the LORD" are not simply doctrines you affirm or specified cultic acts you perform, but veritably **a way-of-life** that is upright (*yesharim*, Hosea 14:9). The Biblically enjoined *hodos* (Way) is not so much a specific confined route on the earthly cosmic map you tred (to get to heaven) as it is a habit of God-thankful integrity doing justice in the world and society that breathes life and love for the neighbor instead of hatred and death (Psalm 119:1–3, 29–32, 35–37; Proverbs 12:28, Acts 13:1–12, v.10).

Once a person has found the way-of-the-LORD to live, you can go anywhere, without fear. This Way-of-the-LORD, the cheerful Rule of God (βασιλεία τοῦ θεοῦ) which Jesus Christ walked and tried to instil in his disciples (Matthew 10, Mark 1:14–15, Acts 1:3): the all-consuming passion to give relief to the poor and ill, communion to the outcast, saving knowledge to the misguided, sure hopefulness to the discouraged, is the Way-of-life we humans are called by the God of the Scriptures to walk in, enact, crisscrossed by persecution, and prepare for all suffering humanity to experience (1 John 3:11–18, 2 Timothy 3:12–13, Isaiah 40:3–5).

What has marked those who have practiced and fitfully walked in the biblically posited Way-of-life, whether it was Abraham, Job, Moses, Deborah, sinner David, decapitated Baptizer John (Matthew 21:32) or Aurelius (*Da mihi castitem et continentiam, sed nolo modo – Confessions*, VIII, 7,17) Augustine: they all were buoyed by the knowing faith that they did not need to succeed, the outcomes might be deferred, but God would pick up the pieces of their deeds and consummate their obedient efforts with lasting blessing (Ecclesiastes 3:10–15, Luke 12:22–40, v.32, Hebrews 11). This God-trusting way-of-life holds a singular joy peculiar for its walkers among all the other ways-of-life, because those actually walking within the guiding life lines of "the Ways-of-the-Lord" know existentially that the timed and temporal reality of all creatures bespeaks (Psalm 19) and is headed for a winnowed, culminating endpoint. So each creature's life time is an "eschatonic," *einmalige* precious **gift of the LORD**, and not one's owned personal property. Aging is creaturely normal—much as Shakespeare phrased its stages—and not something to be denied, treated as an inconvenience, or venerated but overlooked. Death, however, is a curse. Yet the venerable rite of passage is swallowed up for Christ-followers in the guarantee of the victorious resurrection and new life everlasting, without tears (John 5:24, Romans 8:31–39, 1 Corinthians 15, Revelation 21:1–4).

"Abraham (aged 175) breathed out his life breath and died in a good old age, an elderly man full of years; and he was gathered to his folk" (Genesis 25:8). Old man Abraham was blessed to die in **peace**, says the Bible (Genesis 15:15 – the first time the word *shalom* appears in the canon), "full of years," that means, aware that his troubled itinerant life of faith had been filled incredibly full with God's surprising blessings and was ending now with God's promise to continue to provide shalom on earth through Abraham's son Isaac (Genesis 25:11), a coming generation of faithful ones in the LORD's service. So aging in the-Way-of-the-abiding covenant-keeping Lord-of-everlasting-life, as one becomes bodily worn in and worn out like a good old reliable shoe, and simultaneously as one's frail spirited hold on the hand of God nevertheless becomes ever more firm: aging, becoming old, elderly, can be a good time to realize and accept that one's accumulated portion of treasures dispensed by God's Holy Spirit over so many years has been generous, even gratuitous! and shall be carried on and given away redemptively by others your life has touched, even as your forebears of faith tendered such gifts to you.

Intractable pain—an evil almost worse than death in my judgment—can somehow stymie this elderly wisdom. Incessant bodily pain is demonic, making a person feel corporeally homeless, tearing your very insides out into an unwelcome public stare.[15] Just as fruit becomes most delicious precisely when it turns fully mature exactly before it starts to decay, so a human life is at its ripest when its thankful service settles somewhat and satisfies at a best-before pain date. Biblical revelation allows believers to fight with God against the enemy of pain and "untimely" death, and to grieve the miscarriage of young promising lives ended too soon on earth (Psalms 13, 39, 116). And until one's will to live diaconately is broken by pain, it seems the LORD encourages a devoted follower of the Christ to pray for 80 years rather than 70 as a measure of *shalom* (Psalm 90, especially vv.9–12, Psalm 91, especially vv. 14–16). However, depending upon one's strength and circumstances in "agonizing the good struggle of the faith" (1 Timothy 6:11–16, v.12), whether it be the haunting cry of Job 19 or the exuberant praise of Psalm 16, a person becomes wise en route to the eschaton when one is certain—despite appearances! and the timing of life and death may remain in dispute—that one's troubled labor in the Lord's kingdom has not been in vain (1 Corinthians 15:58). Then one is "full of years" and can sorrowfully leave loved ones of

---

15 Simone Weil puts her finger on a problem close by in distinguishing "malheur" from "la souffrance physique," in "L'Amour de Dieu et le Malheur" [c.1942], *Attente de Dieu* (Paris: Fayard, 1966). "Il en est autrement d'une souffrance physique très longue ou très fréquente. Mais une telle souffrance est souvent tout autre chose qu'une souffrance; c'est souvent un malheur" (99).

the next generation behind, and enter with shalom into a glorious **new** Way-of-everlasting-life (1 Corinthians 15:42–57).

Personal note

The fact that Griffioens have lived for generations on *Rijksstraatweg* ("The Kings Highway") in Loenen aan de Vecht I playfully take as a happy comment on the direction of their chosen Way-of-life: harvesting fruit from trees, teaching and healing neighbors, offering hospitality to untold strangers, faithful *godsdienst*. The colleague Griffioen I know never judged but always respected academic thinkers who held the most divergent convictions, and the humble wisdom he offered had an unhurried, tempered graciousness. Anyone who would take precious vacation time to experience the Trans-Siberian Express train ride from Moscow to Vladivostock and back has learned the meaning of the Arabian proverb: "Slowness is a gift from God; haste comes from the devil."

Doreen and Sander appear to me sometimes like the late self-portraits of Rembrandt, weather-beaten by societal relations and services rendered, yet somewhat more cheerful than Rembrandt's craggy visage because they have become seasoned to the wisdom of Psalm 92 en route:

> De rechtvaardige groeit als een palmboom,
> als de Libanonceder omhoog:
> die geplant in het huis van de Heer
> in de hoven van God mogen groeien,
> maken nog in hun grijsheid nieuw lot.
> Groen zullen zij zijn en vol frisheid.

(Psalm 92:13-15, translation by Ida Gerhardt and Marie van der Zeyde)

My hope for Sander Griffioen, who has borne tasty fresh fruit here and there in the Institute for Christian Studies in Toronto, Dordt College in Iowa, Calvin College in Michigan, Vrije Universiteit in Amsterdam, and at numerous universities in Korea and conferences around the world, is that our Lord will keep him "fris en sappig" as he and his loved ones slowly become "full of years."

Sander and Doreen Griffioen

Import of Biblical Wisdom Literature for a Conception of Artistic Truth

I propose to take a biblically led orientation on the matter of truth, and from that perspectival standpoint try to elucidate the particular glory of imaginative, literary, and artistic historical truth-telling in God's world. I am self-consciously not presuming to present a universal approach, and I realize my tack as an octogenarian academic in 2010 AD is shaped by a certain earthy, philosophical faith-thought tradition called "Reformational," which, with relaxed seriousness, takes Βασιλεῖα τοῦ θεοῦ (the Ruling ordering of God) as a driving focus for communal reflection and action.

Biblical givens on truth

The exclamation "Amen!" perhaps best signals for me a biblical affirmation of when truth happens. **Truth means God's blessing presence is in evidence**. That's why revelation of truth (אמת) in Scripture is surrounded by mention of God's חסד (covenantal love), God's משפט (doing justice), the occurrence of שלום (fullness of peaceful existence), שמחה (joyfulness) and חיים (flourishing life). "True" in the Bible designates what you can certainly trust actually to come through with God's צדקה (justifying mercy) in creaturely affairs.

To catch this guiding idea, let me read you aloud a declaration from the LORD God in a paragraph (abbreviated) found in Ezekiel 18:5,7–9:

> v5 If a person proves to be true (צדיק), that is, enacts justice (משפט) and צדקה [Buber translates the Hebrew as *Wahrhaftigkeit*]—
> v7 does not deal harshly with anybody, lets a debtor get his loan security back, does not rob the unsuspecting, gives one's own bread to a hungry person and covers a naked person with a garment,

---

Presented at the "Truth Matters" conference, convened by the Institute for Christian Studies, August 2010, Toronto.

v8 does not lend to get interest, does not grab for profits, pulls one's hand back from what is deceitful, works at performing reliable (אמת) justice (משפט) in man-to-man affairs,

v.9 [that is,] walks within my providential ordinances (בחקותי) and takes care to keep my justice intact (משפט) by working out what is truly trustworthy (אמת), that is a tried-and-true person (צדיק), one who shall surely **live**, be alive: this is what my Lord, the LORD God declares.

Human obedience to God's multifaceted ordinances and Word result, I hear, in what is true, a deed filled with God's promise to be working blessing. No wonder Jesus Christ could say (John 14:3), "I am the Way, that is, the truth, veritably life!" Recalling Exodus 3:13–15: "I am . . . God's promised blessing present in fleshly human corporeality."

Truth is not presented as a self-subsistent entity or as an abstraction in the Bible, I gather, but **truth characterizes whatever manifests God's on-going gracious, justifying mercy.** If one would understand the inscription over the arch of Victoria University's campus chapel building, partially obscured by vines [#38], "The truth shall make you free," its original biblical thrust is: God's blessing presence (in Jesus Christ, in the Holy Scriptures, in Holy Spirited acts of just-doing and wisdom) will save you . . . from sin! from the Lie that harbors waste, crookedness, suf-

[#38] Victoria University administration building, University of Toronto, c. 1835

fering, and death.

And it is this peculiarly biblical note of sanctifying holiness as an integral mark of truth, I think, that would enrich our understanding of what is at stake in the whole range of human cultural undertakings.

Bonhoeffer's insightful fragment on **ethical truth** argues it is a betrayal of truth to disclose correct states of affairs to those who are evil-minded and untrustworthy (326–334). Goudzwaard/Vander Vennen/Van Heemst have shown how **political-economic truth** bringing a thrifty, generous justice into citizens' lives is threatened by a militaristic ideology bent on distorting "freedom" into a security guaranteed by being stronger in weapons (115–123).[1] Zuidervaart's careful affirmation of **propositional truth** as assertoric correctness notes the decontextualizing role of logical analysis in our human understanding, and hence points up the limits and responsibilities of justifying valid statements in our over-all task of knowing truly what is to be done in the societal matrix we inhabit (2009, 10–12,15–18).

That is, it seems to me, there are various irreducible, inter-related kinds of truth waiting proleptically for us humans to embody as we try to enact or default in passing on the blessing of God's צדקה (justifying mercy) in ordinary affairs.

Biblical writings manifest a defining literary quality
The Bible itself is uniquely true, in the sense I am using the term. The Holy Scriptures are veritably **God-speaking literature**, credo, given to us humans historically in Hebrew, Aramaic, and Greek languages (as Jesus Christ as Jew once walked upon the earth) to compel our hearing by faith the one true story of the LORD's Rule acoming, and providing the contours to inform our task (מצוה) of multiple obedient responses (Seerveld, 1979 & 1980).

My remarks will focus now on the kerygmatic Bible's literary character, and note the significance of such artistic defining quality to mediate notice of God's saving revelation, and then take that prompt, especially by looking at the Older first Testament texts of "wisdom" writings, to elucidate the good creational structure that makes such imaginative disclosure of God's will possible and trustworthy.

As Martin Buber wrote, the Bible asks to be taken as one book in which its different sections are not closed but are open and reverberate with one another (1935, 169). Robert Alter cites as "an intrinsic feature of

---
1 Also cf. Thrasymachus's position in Plato, *Republic*, book 1.

the original texts—their powerfully allusive character" (1998, 50). One could well think of the Bible as **a literary collage of written texts meant to become oral**, to be read **aloud**, **voiced**, a story **told**, and counsel **being spoken** by God to us humans. And the scripted form is not a curse of indeterminacy but is a wonderful, colorful mnemonic with artistic finish and cohesion. The Bible is more like a gargoyled cathedral or a cinematic documentary film edited by the Holy Spirit than like bulletin announcements from Headquarters.

Because the LORD God used an Egyptian university-trained scribe like Moses (Exodus 17:14, Hebrews 11:23–27), pop-song composer and sinful king like David (2 Samuel 11, Psalms 3–41 et altera) and a born-again Jew with a thorn in the flesh like Paul (2 Corinthians 12:1–10) to be God's living ventriloquist dummies, the biblical historical and promising narrative with poetry **stutters**, comments Buber (1926, 28). A very artistic, convicting stuttering of God's creating the temporal world by speaking, selecting a disappointing people to witness to the shalom of obedience, and offering God's own self bodily to act as pivot in history, tempting all readers and hearers to join the motley band of Canterbury pilgrims on the Way to the eschaton (Hebrews 11:32–40).

Alter's many studies document the finely tuned inter-sectional ironies throughout the Bible book that highlight its literary make-up: Jacob deceived by Laban with Leah hints back critically to Jacob's deceit with Isaac to get Esau's blessing, so that later one hears the pathos of Isaiah's quoting God's agonizing reference to the people of Israel in terms of "Jacob" the deceiver (in chapters 40–44, 48–49), which note intensifies the later good news—preposterous!—that **God loves deceitful sinners**! (Matthew 9:10–13, Ephesians 2:1–7, 1 Timothy 1:12–16).

The whole laconic biblical tale from Genesis to Revelation, assembled in over a thousand years, is replete with near repetitions: Ruth's sojourn echoes patriarch Abraham's leaving a home location to become a progenitive link in the Messiah's redemptive role on earth (Matthew 1:5); Judges 19 even repeats sentences of Genesis 19 in describing a typical scene of hospitality brutalized (Judges 19:22–24, Genesis 19:4–9). Joseph flees Potiphar's wife, but Judah begets child with his sister-in-law Tamar whom Matthew puts in the genealogy of Jesus (Genesis 38, Matthew 1:3). The key gospel parable of the wicked tenants of the Father's vineyard (Mark 12:1–12) harks back to Isaiah's song of God's vineyard that produced only sour grapes (Isaiah 5). Hebrews 8:8–13 quotes Jeremiah 31:31–34 to make a literate tie-in, and is not the result of slipshod redaction. Minute details like the Israelite atrocity of cutting off the toes and thumbs of Canaanite king Adonibezek anticipates the similar end of Israel's wicked king Zedekiah (Judges 1:4–7, 2 Kings 25:1–7), and gives literal historical detail to the narrated events. Such exquisite, subtle recurrent connections in the one long story intimate an over-all providential pattern of sin and deliverance, of grace and judgment under God's omniscient authorial eye, that proves the recounting is booked with more than literal fact interest.

The sure literary intensification and configuration of the biblical writings becomes particularly evident in pieces like Proverbs, The Song of Songs, Job, and Ecclesiastes. The dialogue feature of Satan with God, Job and his erstwhile friends, and between Job and God, asks us listeners to discover the meaning **inbetween** the set speeches. And if you fail to catch the import of the LORD's final literary flourish, the tribute to animals! to birds of prey, the monstrous hippopotamus herbivore, the formidable reptilian Leviathan, then you default on the point of God's Word here, which smashes the overly neat universe of rational moral discourse bounded by rewards-and-punishments held up by Job's interlocutors, and miss the good!? news that Evil is as darkly uncanny (suggests the provident God) as the inscrutable, marvelous, and terrible animal world (Popma, 228–235; Alter 1985, 76–110).

The book of Ecclesiastes too is as synoptically composed a chorus of voices as is שִׁיר הַשִּׁירִים (The Greatest Song), and requires a literary intelligence to plumb its meanings in the parry and thrust of radical questions juxtaposed to a sevenfold refrain that bespeaks God's providing care in the deepest shadows of life's failures, death, and cruelty. Even a calculating "wisdom" is called into question by Qoheleth (Ecclesiastes 7:23–29) if the wise person thinks to figure out and resolve the unfathomable meaning of mortal creatures subject to God's mysterious guidance, which reality is best held and confessed in a carefree literary suspension—"Throw your bread out on the face of the water!" (Ecclesiastes 11:1)

And when the book of Proverbs, headed up by the proem of chapters 1–9, is understood to be composed in what I call the "Yes, but" rabbinical mode of teaching wisdom (Seerveld, 1998, 190–193)—not as a list of maxims to be memorized and put into practice—one does more justice to the literary office and focus of the God-breathed, educated court counselors and poets who booked these aphoristic texts. For example, to mine the message of the conundrum found at Proverbs 26:4–5, in the large 12 verse pericope assessing foolishness, one needs to recognize the allusive "Yes, but" catch to its covert literary cast:

> Never begin to respond to a godless fool like a godless fool;
> otherwise you will start to be like a God-damning fool yourself.
> **Yes, but!** [(understood)]
> Answer a godless fool with what befits his godless foolishness,
> lest he seem to become wise in his own eyes.

The directive wisdom presented is this: remain innocent of joining godless foolery, but flummox fools with canny speech. Jesus' updated version was: Be as prudent as snakes, but remain as innocent as doves (Matthew 10:16).

The collocated paragraphs of riddles in Proverbs are not contradictory logical puzzles so much as far-reaching **literary truths** that provide playful, imaginative knowledge for the good of those with ears to hear.

Literary texts assume a creational order of allusivity

The defining literary finish of the biblical writings—whether narrative, poetry, or instruction—banks on our responding first of all believingly to its artistry in kind, with an imaginative receptivity. Otherwise we violate the nature of the biblical texts, which simultaneously protect God's mystery yet issue sound authoritative directives with soft edges for our learning how to live holding onto God's hand. And the ludic, enigmatic quality of the booked revelation is peculiarly apt for disclosing God's gracious dealings with us faulty, sinful creatures, because our potholed history is not straightforward but continues by fits and starts, because guilty deeds and human repentance are prone to irony, and because trusting the LORD whose acts are often beyond our ken begs to be satisfied by only inklings of knowledge. That is, the booked disclosure of God's great deeds among us is multivocal and roundabout as befits literature—you can recite Israel's history by both upbeat Psalm 105 and downbeat Psalm 106 as well as by ballad-like Psalm 78, without being duplicit. **Literary expression can be truly intimate and present bona fide, nuanced knowledge of the deepest sort while remaining elliptical.**

In the Reformational faith-thought perspective of an ordering Word-of-God creational ontic setting (Seerveld 1985, 61–62, 76 n.59), given the existing phenomena of texts with a special literary identity, one can take the cue and posit that there be a specific creational ordering for distinguishing literary scripts from non-literary dicta or expostulations. Literature, like graphic art, poetry, and music, does appeal, in my judgment, to an order in God's world, **a creational ordinance for suggestion-rich allusivity** (as there is an order for promise-keeping, for generous thrift, for assertoric correctness, etc.) that can be approximately discovered, is historically formulated and re-formulated, and will be followed in human acts, poorly or well, and that will mark such cultured deeds and products typically as artworks. **The fact that the biblical writings bear this artistic quality means that truth—God's gracious working presence—can show up also in this particular creatural channel, in what one may call an aesthetic way of being creaturely extant.** And it would be a mistake to try to take this rich metaphor-sparking kind of literary/artistic truth-telling and force its multi-splendored, winsome, if not sometimes whimsical glory flat to a bare residue of non-imaginative deposits.

To work with the philosophical hypothesis (=under-grounding thesis!) of an irreducible creational aesthetic ordinance calling for its own kind of limited prehensive knowledge can correct several misleading ideas. For example, lingual clarity may not always be the *summum bonum* for communicating knowledge: a silent twinkle of a wink with a gentle hug and a lingering kiss may "say" "I love you" more deeply than the sentence could, so you know the troth is certainly true. To think an exact, frontal passport photo—both ears showing—provides literal identification, while a portrait is a distorting, honorific compliment, fails to recognize that a Rembrandt chiaroscuro rendition of his face may truly depict the searing depth of his make-up no replicating description could ever match. To pursue a conclusive argument for the existence of God against which there could be no credible retort, and to suppose that a novel like Dostoevsky's *Crime and Punishment* is merely "fiction," could be a misguided trust in and hope for the power of human reasoning while being blinded to the imaginative truth a novel lays bare about the reach of the Holy Spirit to sanctify sinners.[2]

In other words, artistic truth has its own ontic legitimacy and is not in competition with other modes of knowledge that may also bode epiphanies of God's blessing to those who are busy thinking, speaking, or doing just deeds. Allusive imaginative knowledge exemplified, Paul Ricoeur would say, in parables, like ones Jesus told, with all their complicated, indirect, surprising twists and turns, harbor an arresting potential for telling reliable truth peculiar to its particular aesthetic configuration (54–65).

---

[2] Many in the church have been misled by reading Romans 1:21, as the "King James" translation has it: ". . . but became vain in their imaginations." The Greek, ἀλλὰ ἐματαιώθησαν ἐν τοῖς διαλογισμοῖς αὐτῶν, might more carefully be translated, "but became foolish (cf. Proverbs 26:4-5!) in their **reasonings**."

A true translation of literary texts will be allusive

To give a little more definite substance to the nature of artistic truth I should like to contend that translation of literature is primarily an aesthetic activity in the medium of language, and therefore will be a true translation if the new (home) language version is a faithfully allusive, in-depth echo of the original foreign language piece voiced again. Then God's presence insuring an abiding **imaginative replica** is honored, and the translator's diaconate service deserves praise.

Any language provides idiomatic clarity for a person whose mother tongue it is and has learned the vernacular. But when the connotative element within a language spoken rises like cream to the top of the bottled milk of lingual communication, lacing even the denotative feature of language with a rhetorical accent, the talk thickens to poetry, which is not ordinarily "clear." A text can be a record of speech or be directly composed as a document, like a score for music, blueprint for a building, or a diary to be read. A literary text has a dated/located setting like a speech act, but literary texts seem somehow to bury their authorial historical placement inside the perduring artistic text, which is conceived to invite a free-wheeling imaginative reading. The tricky task for a translator of poetry or literature then is to carry over and transpose, re-create the earlier nuance-ridden text anew in a different set of worded, syntactical language that hosts the source text, and do the metaphorical transference with equity.

Because language, and especially literature, has a different nature than formal logic or mathematics, good translation does not attempt to get isomorphic equivalence, a literal imitative restatement, but attempts to do justice to the earlier piece, better, recapitulate its gestalted body with love—its inimitable nuanceful tenor, purportive thrust, and continuing literate significance. A good translator, says George Steiner, remains selflessly submerged within the original foreign tongue, yet produces a new translucent text in the second language marked by a "deliberate strangeness" (310, 319). The current lingual idiom of the targeted translation deserves to be a little unfamiliar, and could well sport an archaic displacement of the current idiom, so that the foreign import not seem so strange, but sound somewhat like a voice out of one's native past, as if the matter were being remembered (333–353). And you may need dare, adds Buber, in obedience to the task of inventing an allusive reference, to coin new words, which the younger generation will adopt and own (1930, 142–143).

The principle guiding translation of literature is reciprocal enhancement: you give the primary foreign text outreach and afterlife, and vivify your own lingual-literary culture with supplemental knowledge, stretching your home language with unfamiliar rhythms, vocabulary (there are no actual synonyms even within one language), odd emphases, alternative human tempers and tastes. A true translation of literature honors the original fully, letting its unusual light shine on our doorstep but not be dimmed to our current visibility.

Dante Gabriel Rossetti's poetic rendition of Sappho's lyric about "the sweet apple . . . a-top on the topmost twig" is a true translation: poem for poem.[3] I always found W. H. D. Rouse's racy, "holy moly"[4] prose translation of Homer's *Iliad* and *Odyssey* (1938/1937) to be much more imaginatively faithful to the rambunctious original Greek story than Richard Lattimore's (1951) "free six-beat line" sonority. The gracious rolling British English exposition of Tolstoi's Russian garrulity in *War and Peace* by Louise and Aylmer Maude (1942) is also a classic journeyman achievement.[5]

It is easy, of course, to botch translation of a literary text and be unfaithful.[6] A translator may misconstrue the primary text through ignorance, haste, or personal insensibility; and if one diminishes or inflates the meaning of the primary source, or settles for a paraphrase, one has defaulted on the arduous task. The critical guideline, however, it seems to me, is to maintain that translation artistry of literature is true when its struggled-for product redeems the original in kind and resurrects an imaginative hologrammic similation of the piece's spirited slanted insight and is permeated by intriguing obliquity (Seerveld 1987, 50). It is not untrustworthy for the translated piece to present a range of meanings limited by the order of allusivity.

I believe this thesis also holds for translating the Bible and other texts

---

3   οἶον τὸ γλυκύμαλον   Like the sweet apple
    ἐρεύθεται ἄκρωι ἐπ' ὕσδωι   which reddens upon the topmost bough,
    ἄκρον ἐπ' ἀκροτάτωι,   A-top on the topmost twig
    λελάθοντο δὲ μαλοδρόπηες,   which the pluckers forgot, somehow—
    οὐ μαν ἐκλελάθοντ', ἀλλ' οὐκ ἐδύναντ' Forgot it not, nay, got it not,
    ἐπίκεσθαι   for none could get it till now.

4   μῶλυ δέ μιν καλέουσι θεοί, Ὀδυσσειας, 10, 305.

5   Margaret Lesser, "Taking on Tolstoy," *Times Literary Supplement*, no. 5598 (16 July 2010), 14-15.

6   George Steiner's wry comment, "Ninety percent, no doubt, of all translation since Babel is inadequate and will continue to be so" (396) could be; but he at least struggles persistently with the noble difficulty to alleviate ignorance. The Italian bon mot *traduttore traditore* (translators? traitors!) seems to me to be simply a trite putdown.

considered to be sacred, like the Qur'an. Many grown-up Bible readers, somewhat like M. Jourdain in Molière's *Le bourgeois gentilehomme*, who was surprised to find out he was speaking prose (II, 4), will be taken aback to hear that the Word of God they read is booked as literature. But the Reformation dogma on the perspicuity of Scripture does not mean the book is a simple sentence telegram. Even the fisherman apostle Simon Peter complained **in** the Bible! that some of Paul's letters were difficult to understand (2 Peter 3:14–16). The dogma of the "clarity" of Scripture means that its principal message, of the Lord's loving the world so much that God sent the Messiah Jesus to save us from our sinfulness and calls us to thank God together by following Christ's Way of reclaiming and caring for God's creatures till the end (John 3;16–17, Galatians 5:25–6:2): that this truth can be heard and accepted by a childlike faith. Yes! but Scripture is still literature unique for its God-speaking nature, demanding our obedient response.

Martin Buber took the God-speaking oral character of the Bible so seriously that he translated it by having a rabbi read God's Word out loud to him so he could hear the sensed articulation of mouthed words, the breathing pauses, the paranomastic *Leitwörter* sound, the paragraphing of the text, for Buber's interpretation of the Hebrew into German—he was bilingual. Buber's written Hebrew Bible translation is in crabbed, Hebraicized contorted German; but Buber squeezes strictly into the German text the minutest iota shade of meaning the Hebrew original brings into play. **Written Bible translation tries to park and prime activated speaking of the text in a definite nuanced way.**

One could say that Jerome's amazing work in putting the Bible into Latin and the subsequent *Vulgata*, Luther's brusque folk language version, which helped set German writing style, the quietly magisterial "King James" translation birthed by Tyndale (1611), minding with italics what was absent in the Hebrew, the Revised Standard Version (1952), and Buber's contribution are all true . . . with wobbles, failings, weak spots, because each varied imaginative attempt kept the surrogate biblical narrative integrated literately, nuanced within the bounds of an allusive intelligence that knew they were transmitting vital, deep knowledge in a parabolic, symbolical, convicting form true to the core original message couched in and constrained by a rhetorical order.

How would one translate Exodus 3:14 truly into English, אשר אהיה אהיא?

". . . Taking advantage of the ambiguity of Hebrew verb tenses" (Alter 1985, 131) and approaching the amazing burning unincinerated bush episode commissioning Moses to lead God's descendants-from-Abraham people out of Egyptian slavery: with an aesthetically relaxed care for the context and a nose for nuance, I should like to improve on the traditional rather stentorian, Parmenidean "I AM WHO I AM" translation. Buber is correct, I think, to tone down this revelation of God's proper Name— the Bible is not encouraging an exercise in theo-ontology—to "I will be who I was, who I always am"; as the next verse says, the everlasting faithful LORD of your fathers and mothers' generation, recalling Genesis 15 and anticipating Exodus 34:6–7. This revelatory incident, notes Buber, exorcizes any move to make God's Name magical (1929, 341). Moses could tell God's faithful ones, "Was-Am-I-Will-Be-With-You" sent me. Remember? and believe![7]

The tone of reading Scripture can make or break the truth of a translated text, since voice inflection is the primal interpretation of a text. One should not read Psalm 104 as if it be Wordsworthian nature poetry, and an English speaking person should have in mind Gerard Manley Hopkins' sprung rhythm rather than Walt Whitman's rolling lines while proclaiming Isaiah. A person goes wrong too, for example, to think conflicted administrator Pilate was starting a deep philosophical discussion with Jesus in John 18. Pilate, in my reading, said, "What's truth?" the way Hamlet dismissed the verbose Polonius with the line (II, ii), "Words, words, words." The ordinance of allusivity admits a penumbra of "itineraries of meaning," to use Ricoeur's phrase, but not "anything goes."[8] Whether it be formulating the written version of a Biblical translation or speaking it, the operative disciplinary discernment called for is of **an imaginative sort that hones in on precise nuances of the insight that stay aesthetically open.**

---

7 "A direct translator will in a learned and aesthetically appropriate way use the resources of the target language to richly capture the details of the original, even though readers may be challenged by some of the Bible's foreignness." (Van Leeuwen, 2001, 34).

8 Buber wisely rejects "Gesetz" as a good translation of תורה and settles on "Weisung" (1930, 158). A good English translation could be "Guidance." God's תורה (law) is like an embrace to keep us safe, and is not an ominous threat against misbehaving. Edip Yuksel's Reformist translation of the Quran deals with the same problem of nuanced multiple-meaning words, for example, *iDRiBuhunne* in Quran 4:34 (cf. *QURAN, A Reformist translation*, Edip Yuksel, Layth Saleh al-Shaiban, and Martha Schulte-Nafeh, Brainbow Press, 2007, 17–20). If it be so that certain undecidable words are "untranslatable into a single word" (Derrida, 196 n.8), that does not entail that meaning must remain permanently ambivalent.

Summing-up with two implications

My presentation makes two main suggestions: (1) Beginning with a biblical orientation, consider truth to be a gift of God's blessing of shalom experienced temporally, consonant with our historical nature, rather than conceive truth to be an ontic substance or something humans can achieve that becomes eternally fixed, beyond revision;[9] and (2) recognize the enrichment and wonderful credibility of artistic truth with its playful elasticity, providing certain imaginative true knowledge next to other kinds of truth, the argued correctness of analytic truth, or the verified factuality of legal truth.

There are also two implications I should like to pose for discussion. (A) If the quality of being true will stigmatize human efforts that obey God's ordinantial injunctions to be allusive, to be just, to be consequent, to be clear, to be faithful, and the like, that is, to be holy in the whole panoply of modally varied, ordinary living circumstances, then **it is philosophical error to assume truth be a religious ultimate to which we aspire**. Elaine Scarry's Plato-inspired book *On Beauty and Being Just* (Princeton University Press, 1999) epitomizes for me what I think is a misdirected attempt—to pull in James Elkins' deserving project—to re-enchant our post-post-Enlightenment culture with "spirituality" (Elkins 2009, vii–x). Writes Scarry: "What is beautiful is in league with what is true because truth abides in the immortal sphere" (31). And when one pursues beauty, she says, and "other enduring objects of aspiration—goodness, truth, justice—" we "unself-interested"ly enhance ourselves (87). Jaroslav Pelikan's judgment, however, I find more trenchant: humans intent not upon following Jesus' Word in God's ordained world, but keen to relate themselves constructively to the Holy One by affirming transcendentals like Truth, Beauty, and Goodness, (or strive to experience the wordless Numinous of Rudolph Otto,) unfortunately fall into a self-deceptive moralism (80).

(B) If literature and artworks are indeed defined by the quality of allusivity, and their truth is genuine imaginative disclosure of significant meaning, carrying God's presence of blessing, then human responses to literature and artworks should be informed, competent, and well-willing to "read," interpret, and critically judge the dated/located artistic contribution, its structural integrity and import (Zuidervaart 2004, 125–134), first of all imaginatively. **Artistic truth is not confined to God's chil-**

---

[9] This would be my way of understanding "truth is both structural and directional" (Zuidervaart 2009, 10).

dren, since the LORD's grace is not restricted to confessing Christians (or monopolized by sinful saints).

Although I cannot here spell out a complete hermeneutic, I should like to posit that in one's community of aesthetic interpretation, as a person absorbs and comments on a given artwork or artistic event's proffered meaning, one does well to stipple in the spirit and perspective found lodged in the object under scrutiny. And a visual reader, the interpreter with words, or reflective critic, can honor the ordinance of suggestion-rich allusivity especially by comparing the piece at hand to the artist's oeuvre and to other artworks.

For example, Inuit carver John Tiktak (1916–1987) from Rankin Island, Canada, sculpted humans out of stone in the '60s—hardy, ordinary, vital fellows—nonchalant even, hands in pockets? unapologetic mouth. Worlds away from the 1968 Paris student revolution or turbulent Chicago. Mother with child (c.1962) strapped to the back is an ancient rite of workaday love, the figures clothed with respect. Tiktak's *Bent Man* (1970) exemplifies the corpus of his '60s artwork: a sincere expression of the manful, burden-bearing chore that life in the cold North is. But Tiktak's artistic testimony to that truth is not fraught with the conflicted Piqtoukun's sharper struggle lamenting the loss of the Inuit shaman culture and the mythology of polar bear able to morph into whiskered human power. Tiktak's world is not out-of-joint [*RA* #43]: this weather-beaten wizened face may not even be six inches tall, but its indomitable archaic presence has the incredibly dense mass of wise human perseverance. My favorite Tiktak sculpture [*RA* #153], still untouched by any debilitating souvenir commerce, symbolifies the painful joy connecting generations in God's world: the long-faced mother has a vulnerable but strong, bony, mute glory plodding along with her child trundled like a humpback. The piece makes me remember Psalm 131, where the psalmist is humbled and calmed, imagining himself like a weaned child near the neck of God.

Swedish-born Dutch sculptor Britt Wikström (born 1948) produced a plaster cast of a man gently cradling an older sick child in his arms, an image telling with artistic truth that human holding can be healing. Wikström's bronze piece of two wrestlers, placed in a psychiatric sanatorium, show exquisitely how the struggle of patient and mentor, Jacob and the מלאכה אלהים is like a dance where you have to hold on to one another as you seek to prevail and win a blessing. Henry Moore's world-class brown Horton stone *Reclining figure* (1926) [*CP* #38] discloses the quiet Mother Earthy reserve and strength of woman—restive, majestic, alone. Wikström by contrast usually embeds the social dimension of neighbors into her artwork [*CP* #5, 27], like simply helping an older grateful man put on his coat [*CP* #92]—this piece is placed in the village square of Deurne, The Netherlands, commemorating Anna Terruwe's life work of an affirming psychiatry with troubled persons. And it is Wikström's tombstones where the truth of resurrection life, of reuniting loved ones, of triumph over our mortality comes obliquely to the fore [*CP* #15]. The graphic artistic truth of the dove returning with a sprig of olive leaf after a world disaster promises the bereft loved ones a softly cheerful solace, with the grace note of a birdbath of rain water cut into the granite top, to be kind, meanwhile, almost like a lay baptism to the birds of the air who flutter around wishing to be clean.

Quite different graphic artists Tiktak and Wikström both illustrate, in my view, artistic truth. My interpretive reading reflecting with words on their nuanced sculptured offerings tries to honor their true plurisignalic presentation of meaning. I claim my reading is true because it recognizes and reaches down to the committed spirit and visionary faith depth of their artwork, hence invoking its *coram Deo* dimension. Yes, there can be other true interpretations too, just as there can be two good sermons from the same Bible passage. Heidegger's grappling with truth matters as art's providing a temporary clearing in which we humans are ecstatically open to things' showing their being, a kind of ungrounded epiphany hiding! their mysterious Source (Heidegger 1926, 285; 1935–36, 41–44; 1943, 15–19, 25), is at the keyhole of knowledge, I think, but lacks the key. Because the truth of God's blessing presence is real and can be historically disclosed and experienced by artists, interpreters, theorists (and by statesmen, women medical doctors, journalists, and others in their fields of investigation) always in our earthen clay jar fallibility (cf. Vollenhoven in Kok, 233–250, 260–272, 280–290), would-be truth tellers as artists or interpreters need to be humble enough to be not hesitant, not uncertain, but tentative in their production, especially if one's judgment upon occasion must be as severe as the prophetic calls of a Jeremiah.

Because our day characteristically promotes living, said Buber, without any sense of obligation (1926, 14), it does seem to me to be important for more academics, teachers and leaders at large to pay attention to the enriching existence of **artistic truth** in God's world [#39], which not only gives wise direction but refreshes life, to use Isamu Noguchi's phrase, since rightly experiencing bona fide artworks is "like falling in love **again** for the first time."[10]

---

10 Reported by Diana Apostolos-Cappadona in Elkins (2009,239).

[#39] *Bocca della verità,* porch of Santa Maria in Cosmedin, Florence, Italy, 300s BC

Bibliography

Alter, Robert (1981), *The Art of Biblical Narrative*, New York, Basic Books.
Alter, Robert (1985), *The Art of Biblical Poetry,* New York, Basic Books.
Alter, Robert (1992), *The World of Biblical Literature*, New York, Basic Books.
Alter, Robert (2007), *The Book of Psalms*, New York, W.W. Norton & Company.
Bonhoeffer, Dietrich (1955), "What is meant by 'telling the truth'?" in *Ethics*, ed. Eberhard Bethge, New York, MacMillan Co., 326–334.
Botha, M. Elaine (2007), *Metaphor and its Moorings: Studies in the grounding of metaphorical meaning*, Bern, Peter Lang.
Buber, Martin and Franz Rosenzweig (1936), *Die Schrift und ihrer Verdeutschung,* Berlin, Schocken Verlag.
Buber, M. "Der Mensch von heute und die jüdische Bibel" (1926), 13–45.
Rosenzweig, F. "Die Schrift und das Wort" (1925), 76–87.
Buber, M. "Über die Wortwahl in einer Verdeutschung der Schrift" (1930), 135–167.
Buber, M. "Zur Verdeutschung der Preisungen" (1935), 168–183.
Buber M. and Rosenzweig, F. "Die Bibel auf Deutsch" (1926), 276–291.
Buber, M. "Eine Übersetzung der Bibel" (1927), pp. 300–309.
Buber, M. "Königtum Gottes" (1929), excerpt, pp. 338–341.
Derrida, Jacques (2001), "What is 'relevant' translation," translated by Lawrence Venuti, in *Critical Inquiry*, 27, 174–200.
Dooyeweerd, Herman (1935), *De Wijsbegeerete der Wetsidee*, Amsterdam, H.J.

Paris, 2:491–514; (1955) *A New Critique of Theoretical Thought*, translated by D. H. Freeman and H. de Jongste, Philadelphia, Presbyterian and Reformed Publishing Co., 2:560–579.

Elkins, James (2004), *On the Strange Place of Religion in Contemporary Art*, New York, Routledge.

Elkins, James and David Morgan, eds. (2009) *Re-Enchantment*, New York, Routledge.

Gadamer, Hans-Georg (1970), *Wahrheit und Methode*, Tübingen, J.C.B. Mohr (Paul Siebeck), 3A., 1972.

Gemser, Berned (1962), "The Spiritual Structure of Biblical Aphoristic Wisdom" in *Adhuc Loquitur: Collected Essays of Dr. B. Gemser*, eds. A. Van Selms and A. S. VanderWoude (Leiden: Brill, 1968), in *Studies in Ancient Israelite Wisdom*, ed. James L. Crenshaw, New York, Ktav Publishing, 1976, 138–149.

Goudzwaard, Bob and Mark Vander Vennen and David van Heemst (2007), *Hope in Troubled Times: A new vision for confronting global crisis*, Grand Rapids, Baker Academic.

Heidegger, Martin (1926), "On the Essence of Truth (Pentecost Monday, 1926)" translated by Theodore Kisiel, in *Becoming Heidegger: On the trail of his early occasional writings, 1910–1927*, eds. Theodore Kisiel and Thomas Sheehan, Evanston, Northwestern University Press, 2007, 277–288.

Heidegger, Martin (1935–1936), "Der Ursprung des Kunstwerkes" in *Holzwege*, Frankfurt am Main, Vittorio Klostermann, 1957, 7–68.

Heidegger, Martin (1943), *Vom Wesen der Wahrheit*, Frankfurt am Main, Vittorio Klostermann.

Kok, John H. (1992), *Vollenhoven: His early development*, Sioux Center, Dordt College Press, chapter 7.

Lesser, Margaret (2010), "Taking on Tolstoy," *Times Literary Supplement*, no. 5598 (16 July 2010), 14–15.

Loretz, Oswald (1964), *Die Wahrheit der Bibel*, translated by David J. Bourke, *The Truth of the Bible* (1968), New York, Herder and Herder.

Pelikan, Jaroslav (1955), *Fools for Christ: Essays on the True, the Good, and the Beautiful*, Philadelphia, Muhlenberg Press.

Popma, K.J. (1957), *De boodschap van het boek Job*, Goes, Oosterbaan & Le Cointre.

Quell, Gottfried, and Gerhard Kittel and Rudolf Bultmann (1933/1953), ἀλήθεια and אמת in *Theologisches Wörterbuch zum Neuen Testament*, Stuttgart, Verlag W. Kohlhammer, 1:233–251.

Ricoeur, Paul (1981), "The Bible and the Imagination," translated by David Pellayer, in *The Bible as a Document of the University*, ed. Hans Dieter Betz, Ann Arbor, Scholars Press, Poleridge Books, 49–72.

Scarry, Elaine (1999), *On Beauty and Being Just*, Princeton University Press.

Schwartz, David T. (2000), *Art, Education, and the Democratic Commitment: A defense of state support for the arts*, Dordrecht, Kluwer Academic.

Seerveld, Calvin (1971), "The Relation of the Arts to the Presentation of Truth," *Truth and Reality,* Festschrift dedicated to H.G. Stoker, Braamfontein, De Jong's Bookshop Ltd., 161–175 {see *NA*: 219–232}.

Seerveld, Calvin (1979), "Preface" in *How to Read the Bible to Hear God Speak. A Study in Numbers 22–24,* Dordt College Press and Toronto Tuppence Press, 2003, xi–xiii.

Seerveld, Calvin (1980), "A Contribution of Christian Aesthetics toward Reading the Bible," in *Rainbows for the Fallen World,* Toronto Tuppence Press, 1980/2005, 78–102.

Seerveld, Calvin (1985), "Dooyeweerd's Legacy for Aesthetics," in C.T. McIntire, ed., *The Legacy of Herman Dooyeweerd,* New York, University Press of America, 41–79 {see *NA*: 45–80}.

Seerveld, Calvin (1987), "Imaginativity," in *Faith and Philosophy,* 4, 43–58 {see *NA*: 27–44}.

Seerveld, Calvin (1998), "Proverbs 10:1–22: From poetic paragraphs to preaching," in *Reading and Hearing the Word, from text to sermon. Essays in honor of John H. Stek,* ed. Arie C. Leder, Grand Rapids, Calvin Theological Seminary and CRC Publications, 181–200 {supra pp. 101–123}.

Steiner, George (1975), *After Babel: Aspects of language and translation,* Oxford University Press.

Strawson P.F. (1970), *Meaning and Truth,* Oxford, Clarendon Press, 1970.

Van Leeuwen, Raymond C. (1988), *Context and Meaning in Proverbs 25–27,* Atlanta, Scholars Press.

Van Leeuwen, Raymond C. (2001), "We Really Need Another Bible Translation," *Christianity Today,* 22 October, 28–35.

Vollenhoven, D. H. Th. (1926), "De analyse van de kennis," translated by John H. Kok, "The Analysis of knowledge," appendix II in John H. Kok, *Vollenhoven: His early development,* Sioux Center, Dordt College Press, 354–361.

Zimmerli, Walther (1933), "Concerning the Structure of Old Testament Wisdom," translated by Brian W. Kovacs, in *Studies in Ancient Israelite Wisdom,* ed. James L. Crenshaw, New York, Ktav Publishing House, 1976, 175–207.

Zuidervaart, Lambert (2004), *Artistic Truth: Aesthetics, discourse, and imaginative disclosure,* Cambridge University Press.

Zuidervaart, Lambert (2008), "Dooyeweerd's Conception of Truth: Exposition and critique," in *Philosophia Reformata,* 73, 170–189.

Zuidervaart, Lambert (2009), "Unfinished Business: Toward a reformational conception of truth," in *Philosophia Reformata,* 74, 1–20.

Žižek, Slavoj (2000), *The Fragile Absolute or, Why is the Christian Legacy worth fighting for?* London, Verso.

A Modest Proposal for Reforming the Christian Reformed Church in North America

Introduction

My modest proposal for reforming the Christian Reformed church in North America is this: close Calvin Seminary. Disband all denominational boards and standing committees. Strip yourselves of ministerial status; and let the ruling elders in the congregation designate as instructors in the Word whoever can bring the Word of Life from the Scriptures and is practicing a daily walk of prayer and fasting in the spirit of the Gospels.

I speak to you as a grownup son of the Christian Reformed church. I attended already as a bawling baby and as a mischievous, wiggling boy; but I never rebelled against the church because of wise parents and of having had a pastor during the teenage years who preached the life and death of the Word so it stuck in your heart. I increasingly love the confessional tradition of our denomination and have no embarrassment in the least at our Dutch genetical matrix. I am not a first or second generation, nor a sophisticated nondescript internationalist: thoroughly American born, I have been coming to know the riches in our reformed Dutch heritage during my late twenties and thirties. I also have a growing sense of the peculiar strength of the Christian Reformed church, its century of orthodoxy, its remarkable homogeneity because of a baffling network of intermarriage and the mobility of our clergy, schooled at the same seminary,

---

This essay was first presented as a lecture at the Ministers' Institute of the Christian Reformed Church held on 2 June 1970 in Grand Rapids, Michigan. It was published in *Out of Concern for the Church: Five essays* (Toronto: Wedge, 1970), 45–73. The note there, on page 46, reads as follows: My title holds an allusion to Jonathan Swift's essay, "A Modest Proposal for Preventing the Children of Poor People in Ireland from being a Burden to the Parents or Country, and for Making them Beneficial to the Public." In that essay (1729) Swift called attention to the outrageous oppression of the Irish poor, unhelped by those in power, through recommending that maybe they should help themselves, by using their own surplus children for food.

moving around the whole continent on a fairly regular basis. I know our people's godly habit of liberality, meeting quotas, the envy of many non-reformed enterprises; honored even by the Chicago underground a few years back, who systematically robbed one Christian Reformed church's safe after the other there, never touching the Baptist churches next door. I thank God for being raised in this church with grit.

I also speak to you men here a little as an outsider. I spent seven formative years in European communions, in Italy, Switzerland, Germany, as well as in the Netherlands, and worshiped within the Southern Presbyterian confession in Mississippi, for a time. I have no seminary training, have never been an ecclesiastical office bearer; I do not know the inner workings of the denomination nor the political infighting among you members of the cloth. So I may sound somewhat like a naïve sheep at this ministers' institute. Nonetheless, I make my modest proposal with an open heart—it would involve only about 800–900 people—that's not many in a church of 250,000, in a nation with 35 million orthodox evangelicals, in a world with many more millions of Christ-believers.

To get the Christian Reformed church moving biblically as a reforming leader in North America will take an explosively radical, communal act of faith by its leaders—that is what I understand you to be. To that end I introduce my modest proposal for your honest discussion, and perhaps, imaginative action someday soon.

Part I: Analysis before the Norm

A deteriorating cultural situation

If Peter could say on Pentecost, "We're not drunk; it's just the prophecy of Joel being fulfilled" (Acts 2:14–16), then I may say in 1970 *Anno Domini*, "North Americans are not mad; it's just the prophecy of Amos being fulfilled":

> Days are coming, says the Lord Yaweh, when I shall let
>   loose famine upon the land,
> not a hunger for bread, not a thirst for water, but
>   starvation for hearing "words" of the Lord.
> They shall stagger and stumble from sea to sea, roaming
>   around from North all the way to the East,
> trying to lay hold of the Word of the Lord . . .
>   but they shall not find it at all! (Amos 8:11–12)

That kind of restless chase for a revelation of what life means and the direction society must take to find *shalom* characterizes the crisis of our day in North America. Woodstock, Berkeley, Uppsala, Selma . . . in different ways testify that men and women of good will, or of bad will, all are serious in finding some new "word" that shall spell the anagram of human existence right. Because the old patterns set by christianized Humanism, which served Western civilization so well for centuries, from feudalization of men through industrialization: those old societal patterns, the values of the Silent Majority—courtroom decorum, diplomatic niceties, cardinal Newman's university gentlemen—no longer hold today. They are disintegrating.

> . . . anarchy is loosed upon the world,
> The blood dimmed tide is loosed, and everywhere
> The ceremony of innocence is drowned;
> The best lack **all** conviction, while the worst
> Are full of passionate intensity. (Yates, *The Second Coming*)

You don't need to be a Dooyeweerdian to realize we are in the twilight of Western thought, in the throes of something big going to pieces: the religious dynamic that has propelled our civilization is being found wanting! It does not have the healing power needed by a frustrated, urbanized, mechanized humanity. So it, and its civilized embodiment, is passing away!

Meanwhile, men cannot live by the dollar alone. That fact is why the prophecy spoken by Amos to Israel before its imminent captivity reaches out to us today. God made humans to respond to God's Word, God's creational Word, understood in the light of the inscriptured Word as well as the incarnate Word. When a generation of people ignore the true Word, they necessarily—they are built that way—look for other authoritative "words." And they are legion when a culture breaks down.

SDS Weathermen get their "word" from Mao Tse-tung. John Birchers accept the "word" of the Pentagon. Many thousands of intelligent, secular students expect the "word" to come in Zen buddhistic rites, horrible drug experiments that blow their mind, or from some occult magician or yogi. Ten thousands of more respectable people wait for the evening "word" from Walter Cronkite, as if the oracle of Delphi is headquartered at CBS. Others rise and fall by the "word" of GMC management; and a myriad number regularly get the best negotiated "word" from the AFL-CIO as to their daily bread. But these "words" are not the Word of the Lord, and those who religiously live by them follow the Lie.

AP dispatches from Viet Nam, *Time* color photos of Russian artillery, the headlines of *Chicago Today*: it is packaged, prefabricated, hiding the truth that we of North America as a whole are on the way to revolutionary Death because we operate outside the Word of Jesus Christ. Anytime violence is presented as a commonplace in reporting, you have the Lie. Anytime covetousness is propagated under cover of benign progress, you have the Lie. And hundreds of thousands of North Americans grasping for "words" of the Lord are receiving a steady diet of lies, are embracing Baalim, taskmasters, principalities, and powers of darkness that ruin their created lives and run our compromised culture into the ground.

A loose strand in this ferment, I should mention, is the present state of official christendom. After World War II Tillichian theologies helped secularize the Judeo-Christian hegemony on confessional life in America. During the 1940's and 1950's Jewish, Roman catholic, and Protestant concerns gradually entered the lists of secular cultural causes, while any secular group that felt intensely enough about some "ultimate concern" passed cultic muster. The net effect was that long-standing walls between faith-traditions seemed to become movable partitions, and the line between conventional belief and unbelief grew fuzzy. As Martin E. Marty succinctly wrote recently[1] during the late '50's, during the pontificate of Pope John to be exact (1958–1963), there was a centripetal convergence felt within the major divisions of the organized church, a sense of revival, a pacific, conciliatory trend toward concordance (New Delhi, 1961 and *Pacem in Terris*, 1963). But since 1965, says Marty, the movement has been centrifugal, dispersive. The uniting Kennedy symbol was assassinated; the Six Day War of Israel against the Arabs got fought; Russia invaded Czechoslovakia, and dialogue between Western and Marxist theologians stopped; Pope Paul's encyclical *Humanae Vitae* (1968) affirmed the old birth control stand. The National Council of Churches is no longer stage center, and the many denominational mergers are bogged down in church polity machinery. It seems as if a fragile opportunity for inter-faith rapprochement historically has gotten waylaid . . .

I might add that Second Commandment Christians—those armed with proof texts from Matthew (25:31–46) and 1 John (4:7–12, 20) who argue that loving your neighbor is loving God—are simply overwhelmed today by the worldwide societal disaster on our hands. They cannot cope with it—if money, expert advice, and Peace Corps love get no response, what more can you do?—they are honestly, sensitively overwhelmed, so that (I agree with Robert McAfee Brown)[2] the direction of the future for

---

1 Martin E. Marty, "The American Situation in 1969," in *The Religious Situation: 1969*, ed. D.R. Cutler (Boston: Beacon Press, 1969), 25–43.
2 Robert McAfee Brown, "'Secular Ecumenism': The Direction of the Future," in *The Religious Situation*, 395–422.

World Council churches is "secular ecumenism," humanizing world relief, rather than trying to engineer ecclesiastical realignment. Lamentably they have the wrong handle to a right problem, and if such a program persists it cannot help but denature the instituted church.

Our church hypocrisy
But first, how do we stand before the norm of God's Word in this 1970 of a situation? Confronted by the cosmic evil powers of Lie and Violence, while the ecumenical movement is typified more by committee work than élan, what marks our deepest drives? I mean us in the larger context as an orthodox, evangelical-reformed, Christian community, but have in mind especially the Christian Reformed church. What gets at the heart of our in-the-world existence today? And the answer is not blowing in the wind, I'm afraid, but with few exceptions is: hypocrisy.

By hypocrisy I do not mean just the usual insincerity of men, nor even the dissembling of righteousness to cover up one's sin—something we would all immediately own up to—part of our dogmatics. By hypocrisy, as what typifies our communion as a whole, I mean the searching indictment Christ made to the people when he said, "You know how to interpret what's going on in the heavens and on the earth; how come you can't tell what time it really is? (Luke 12:54–56) Why do you ask for a miracle straight from God's throne before you will be convinced only my Word is the way? (Matthew 16:1–4) You expect the Messiah, practice the law, debate with doctrines, but miss the Truth—unaware of what's up right in front of your eyes—hypocrites!"

Hypocrisy, according to the Scriptures, is first of all: living in the neighborhood of the Truth but being unaware of what the score is. There is evidence that the wonderful people of the Christian Reformed church by and large are hypocritical, *that is*, are unaware of what time it is, living as if we are not in the last days, in crisis, under the judgment of the Lord for letting God's kingdom pass by right in front of our nose! The faithful and less than faithful of your congregation, I dare say, do not generally have existentially in their consciousness a realization that the whole world is going to hell because the Word of God is not formative in its vision!

Our kind of people can read the stock market page and invest wisely; they know how to interpret do-it-yourself instructions for assembling stereos and household gadgets; even riots, the war, and the weather are closely watched on TV, but they do not understand what they read and see in terms of the coming of Christ's kingdom, it all is kept at a comfortable, spectator distance. At most they are affrighted by the lawlessness, offended, mystified—"cut your hair! stop that foolishness and get to work!"—they do not *know* it, know what is at stake with an intimate heart knowledge or it would shatter their tidy world. They do not really care, because they do not believingly understand, because they have not been told with authority that we are living in sin unless, as Paul puts it (Ephesians 3:8–10),

— we are showing unbelievers the incalculable richness of Christ and making clear to all men the mysterious way, hidden for centuries, God,
who created everything, how God sets things up.
— we live in sin unless we are doing this
so that the rainbow-rich wisdom of God be made known now by the Church to unearthly ruling principalities and powers (of the age).

Orthodox, evangelical-reformed church members are by and large stamped with hypocrisy, *that is*, act unaware of what the true score is historically—with unseeing eyes see hunger, fear, sexual perversion, racism, respectable godlessness, and pass safely by on the other side of the road, on the way to a missionary rally (if I may overstate the case): we carefully orthodox, Bible-confessing regular churchgoers are fundamentally hypocrites because the discipleship of Jesus Christ and the Kingdom vision of Paul and the prophets has not been proclaimed with power, ingrained in our minds and hearts by our pastors. Whenever the shepherding clergy have spoken out to rouse the faithful, it has usually been against the wrong enemies.

That is a second basic ingredient of hypocrisy according to the Scriptures: fighting the wrong enemies, in the name of all that is holy. Fighting visible enemies of flesh and blood, hewing the line of doctrine and ethical life as if your salvation depended upon it, scrupulously condemning external transgressions: but letting the evil spirits of the Age roam about uncontested among believers and unbelievers like angels of light.

I am talking close to home. Our evangelical-reformed communion as a body is in general sympathetic to crusades against international Communism, but you get in trouble quick if you challenge what I once called American Communityism[3]—something practically any Christian who has made good in the system has had to practice—but which is squeezing biblical life blood as surely out of our societal framework. I know,

---

3   "The Christian School in American Democracy," address to the National Union of Christian Schools Convention in Kalamazoo, Michigan, 11 August 1964, published in pamphlet form by NUCS, *Convention Addresses* (1964), 2–19.

Darwinian American capitalism is not repressive like Soviet totalitarian statism, but our common idolatry of success is the same, and our materialism is the same (plus, we are the liars, trusting God on our dollar bills). The point is not to debate evils, but to say that spending Christian energy crusading against the specter of Communism may be misplaced; where is the cry for Christian action that breaks with all-American Communityism? because this pragmatic, leveling, democratistic ideal shall have killed us Christ-believers inside long before Russia or the Chinese forced a showdown outside.

Or, to be more specific: We have our exhortations for Sabbath observance and our polemics against dirty books. But where is the Word on the weightier matters of the law, for Monday through Saturday observance, that goes beyond moralisms and directs employers to administer justice and mercy concretely to their helpers, and searchingly questions whether the AFL-CIO local "brotherhoods" are not a mark of the secular Beast on believers' foreheads? Is there preaching support for learning how to Christianly read dirty books so that we will not have blind leading the blind? And there are sermons on stewardship and meeting the budget, but who counts the costs of having a $25,000 building used less than ten hours a week? Preposterous! today.

Matthew 23 is the Word of God and must be heard by our church and its leaders. After he paraphrased Micah 6:8 there Christ said ironically, "It would be good, all right, to do what's just, compassionate, and be a man of faith; but don't forget to add up your precepts, dice ceremonial P's and Q's, and hammer away at the tithe!" (Matthew 23:23). Those sermonic darts about "church hopping" and "oncers"—"You hypocrites!" says Christ, "You strain gnats out of your wine but swallow the American, suburban way of life whole, like a camel!"

Do you see what I am after? God's Word heard in faith as norm can be relentless in scalpeling through to what we would rather hide from analysis, *our* mean *selves*. But we cannot afford to deal with surface phenomena. I learned that from Schilder[4]: You must not judge by making comparisons, however tempting, like pitting carpeted consistory rooms against ghetto homes without screen doors, or black-topped church parking lots versus lack of plumbing on a mission outpost. That method of evaluation is actually pharisaical, weighing externals. You do not get a *biblical* analysis by looking at what is seen in the mirror, because then you congratulate yourself on these things and do a little plastic surgery

---

4   Klaas Schilder, *Gereformeerd Farizeïsme? Zijn de Gereformeerden de Farizeeërs van deze Tijd?* (Delft: W.D. Meinema, 1925).

on those things, and never get at the heart of apostasy yeasting in the church. We must test the spirit, the gut of our churches, and then come clean before the Lord if we expect to be blessed rather than cut out of the Tree of Life!

Pharisee/Sadducee ping pong polemic
Let me press the analysis all the way home for a minute.

It can be shown, I think, that this hypocrisy accounts for the culturally formative immobility, the unholy disarray of our orthodox, evangelical-reformed communions in North America. Because we breathe hypocrisy we cannot lead. Because we are actually largely out of touch with what is really going on in God's world and are busy fighting the wrong enemies, we simply cannot set the direction making known the rainbow-rich wisdom of God, which has what it takes to captivate and transform God's people on this continent into a spirited power bringing the Word of healing for the total cultural life of our disbelieving neighbors. Hypocrisy ruins that and kills churches so they become good for nothing.

That is the predicament of our Christian Reformed church.

Evidence for the fact that our church is all but dead as a genuine community alive to biblical reformation is the continuing presence of obvious polarization into left and right, "conservative" and "liberal," freer thinking/tightly scholastic, *Torch and Trumpet/Reformed Journal*, Bonhoeffer and Barth/Bavinck and Berkhof, Dordt/Calvin, heads up-front/heads turned-back, ping pong, pong ping—

In other erstwhile, orthodox confessional bonds you will find the same pattern at work, in varying stages of frustration (the arbitrary proper names will be different). What we have on our hands is the old sterile, mesmerizing polemic between Pharisee and Sadducee, left/right, "conservative"/"liberal" etcetera—which dilemma kills the obedient freedom men have anew in Christ, where you may be a joyful proprietor producing both new things and old ones out of the Scriptures into the excitement of your life (Matthew 13:5). But No, this polar fixation spells death for joy; it has evil constrictive wrenching to it that tries to force everything and everybody to identify themselves in terms of its mismanaged, categorical frame-up: choose sides, between being "progressive" or "traditionally" oriented.

But this age-old, polar setup of factions that dominates our church life is a sign of decay, because *both* alternatives are thoroughly hypocritical, that is, fail to do *combat* with the secular spirits of the Age. Therefore, it is a framework of stifling hypocrisy. It kills communion in the very name of dialogue. It is as immobilizing to budding, biblical reforming consciousness as an old-fashioned case of cramps and diarrhea.

I shall not spend time now probing how each wrong faction paralyzes biblical reformation. My study on Numbers 22–24 in *Understanding the Scriptures* shows how the Sadducee "liberal" is poison in the blood of a church; they belong to the double-dealing house of Bileam, the Nicolaitans, who maintain a somewhat distinctive theological theory but *in praxis* mate with the godless culture, seducing along with them especially the young.[5] Given time the Sadducee "liberals" will neo-orthodox you to death. While the Pharisee "conservative" prototype follows those nameless, small-time theologians and confessional leaders who pestered Christ with rationalistic quibbles and exacted such a killjoy, hidebound piety from their disciples in the name of holiness that our Lord finally told them, "You leaders seem to be more intent upon keeping the doors to the Kingdom of heaven shut rather than open!" (Matthew 23:13, Luke 11:52). Pharisees interpret the Scriptures according to our human confessions, and are fervent in casuistically making what is written and what is our tradition rhyme. . . .

The *Association of Christian Reformed Laymen* ("that's the bad one") is not completely stupid. They smell something putrid in the church. The ping pong, pong ping business is confusing in the absence of great preaching with large vision and reforming conviction. They see no leadership from the seminary that they can understand and trust; so they go "conservative." When the layman on the street is not led, he stands still; he becomes a "conservative." When the "conservative" then is isolated and laughed at a bit, he becomes conservatistic. And our conservatistic laymen have hard heads even without hard hats.

But the shame, the deeply troubling irony of the situation (not even counting the rent in Christ's body) is this: should Conservatists win many influential control posts in the denomination, within a generation the Christian Reformed church would be predominantly "liberal" because Conservatism is consolidated to a past, is anti-historical, reactionary in makeup; it cannot direct and open up new developments of the now-generation for the church. So it cannot succeed in setting the course today, despite its Christian concern, unless it emigrates with the Amish to a commune in a remote plain of South America.

---

5   A. H. DeGraff and C. G. Seerveld, *Understanding the Scriptures: How to Read and Not to Read the Bible* (Toronto: Association for the Advancement of Christian Scholarship, 1969), 88–92. Today Seerveld's words from 1969 are available in a newly expanded edition: *How to Read the Bible to Hear God Speak: A study in Numbers 22–24* (Dordt College Press and Toronto Tuppence Press, 2003), 51–56.

Does that mean a loosening of the moorings, that the flirting lead of the Sadducee wing in the church is inevitable? Can we not continue to muddle through with inconclusive compromises, trying to stay as close as possible to dead center, holding our breath that maybe the tension between left and right will go away after some synod or other?

A combination of slow poison and hardening of the confessional arteries is no choice a person freed in Christ can live with! And God, who is longsuffering, does not swallow hypocrisy indefinitely. God spits.

You all know, I suppose, better than I, what winds of uneasiness or under-the-carpet-sweeping are blowing through Christian Reformed consistory rooms on this continent in response to the ping pong state of the church. One thing I detect among our people is a growing—what shall I call it?—"congregationalism." You expect that naturally whenever there is a crisis in leadership of an organization, a power vacuum, a habit of tactical compromise: the power of leadership reverts to a smaller, tighter, atomic unit so that no matter what the "confederation" does, at least our individual survival as a certain kind of entity is more assured. Selectivity in payment of quota items, doing your own liturgical thing, careful caucus on trios—not every Christian Reformed minister fits in every Reformed pulpit these days—are straws in the wind.

Paired with the "congregationalist" tendency, if I detect rightly, is an unhappy opening—maybe it is regional—toward what you could call less-than-reformed, revivalist fellowships. For example, we are largely simple folk in Chicago, unacademically trained. We know in our bones the church is rather dead on Sundays. We don't want to bother with all that modern theology stuff. Moody is simple, safe, and biblical, plus they have something we are missing—feeling! Therefore, before you know it or can say WMBI[6] (and few detect a difference!), in principle, you have sold your reformed birthright for a mess of Bible-believing, emotionally spiced, world-flight pottage. It may be Christian (I am not knocking Moody), but it is not reformed Christian—Christian *Reformed* church—and it is inadequate for the cosmic task God has given us in North America. But it figures. If you don't get meat, you at least try to get milk of the gospel.

When my wife and I in 1961 were counselors for the Billy Graham crusade, which Chicago classes[7] had decided we could not officially sanc-

---

6   The Chicago AM/FM station WMBI is owned and operated by the Moody Bible Institute in Chicago.

7   A "classis" is a group of churches within a geographical area. It has the authority to deal with matters that concern its churches in common and its decisions are binding on the churches in its region. There are 47 classes in the Christian Reformed denomination.

tion as a church, sometimes at McCormick Place it looked like Christian Reformed layman's night at the ball park, counseling, ushering, singing, directing traffic—an unarticulated attempt to escape from the ping pong deadness in our church.

If "congregationalism" and "revivalism" gain momentum in our circles so that they threaten—more than a stray *Banner*—established denominational functioning, there will be, I suspect, a corresponding move by those who administer the machinery of the church to strengthen hierarchical control. Whenever an institution is threatened by disintegrating factors, to maintain its administrative operation, proportionate to the lack of leadership and loss of respect for its defining character and direction, there must come a proportionate increase in centralized, bureaucratic control (Seerveld's Law of bureaucratic creep). But that would loose upon us a host of evil spirits like "synodicalism," "anti-clericalism," "parochialism," and all the brutal violences and lies that go with maintaining the institutional form of godliness while lacking the power thereof, in propping up a church whose candlestick is being removed by the Lord because there has been no Word of healing spoken to the world in which God instituted it. If the polarization into left and right is openly joined by the tension of up and down, it will probably be too late for more analysis. Then the Christian Reformed church will hardly be a viable instrument of God's Grace, but will have metamorphosed into a collection of impotent believers full of guile playing games with themselves. It is possible for us in this room today who are almost too old really to make any drastic change in perspective. . . can we look at ourselves, the church, before the norm of God's word? The wages of hypocrisy in a church, according to the Scriptures, which do not lie, is also death.

PART II: ACTION UNDER THE SPIRIT

What must we do in order to be saved from ourselves and our pernicious, stymieing hypocrisy as a church? How do we escape from the many other dead end alternatives? Especially the dead end of saying, "Yes, you've got some good critical points; we need to be more aware of what's going on, of the space age we live in, not always just talking isolatedly to ourselves; we need more love and unity. . . ."

No. We do not need more democratic tolerance and handshaking congeniality, pious adoration of God in heaven, and information about technology. We do not need theoretical agreement with an analysis (that is why I asked Bill Kieft to sing the "Brotherly Philippic" to break down theoretic distance): we need repentant action as a church under the Holy Spirit!

We need to feel in our blood how little we count. God does not need the Christian Reformed church. God got along quite well, thank you, before our existence, and God will get along very well without us too, if we go the way of all denominational flesh. What we must know is that *the Kingdom of God is at hand*—that is what's really going on—and unless we are "poor in spirit," pride-broken, humiliated in all our ecclesiastical trappings, we shall not be blessed with a hand in Christ's rule upon the earth but shall stand foolishly outside the door, blocking the entrance of others.

Our church hypocrisy can be cleaned out only by a fresh act of faith followed by biblical wisdom. That means a fresh act of faith—I make no apologies for saying it—especially on your part, because you are by definition not fit for the job of teaching elder called to preach, says the Scriptures (cf. 2 Corinthians 2:14–17). And I don't mean to encourage pseudo-modesty or the compounded hypocrisy of rationalizing defeatism. In the name of the Lord, get with it! as the "angels" of our churches, and let the Scriptures humble you to see what in the world our church is to be and what message must be preached that has a center that holds people and things together in creation reconciled to God.

The instituted church, confessional fellowship with a limited, central place in society

There are a few biblical givens about Church that are so foreign to our way of thinking, because of the individualistic, rationalistic, American Protestant traditions we have absorbed by osmosis as it were, that to mention them, even here, may be confusing, sound almost like glossolalia. But these few, fundamental givens, and how to read them, are critical for the fresh act of faith needed for bringing reform to our Christian Reformed communion.

1. The Bible reckons with the people of God, not with loose individuals. The Word of God was spoken to Israel through leaders like Moses and later the prophets, and the New Testament letters were writing mostly to congregations of faithful believers, not conceived as God-communication person-to-person. The saving work of Jesus Christ, justification from sin and restoration to sonship with the living God, is received by a man or a woman through faith enacted by the Holy Spirit, is received by a person not all by himself but when he or she is grafted into the body of Christ, symbolically initiated and sealed into it by baptism. That is, according to the Scriptures, there is a one people of God, a grand body of chosen loved ones—whether old Israel or the New Hu-

manity—whose head is Christ, which is a worldwide, enduring, messianic community, a community of saints that has a corporate character, is not a collection of separate individuals but is a single, large communion into which people whose hearts are changed by the Holy Spirit enter as members. This is the holy catholic Church, which I confess especially when I eat the bread and drink the wine festively in Chicago—cheers for the Lord's return!—knowing I am celebrating it with Harry Boer in Nigeria, Seraphimedes in Greece, Mrs. Neuerburg in The Hague, Smit in Japan, struggling students in Florida, Washington, Toronto, together confessing this glorious, corporate Body to which we all sinfully belong.

2. The ἐκκλησία reported in the early chapters of the post-Pentecostal Acts of the Holy Spirited Apostles reveals a confessional union with a broad range of communal activities. The beginning church sounds most like a commune, with their κοινωνία of voluntary sharing material possessions, abiding by the *didache,* the bylaws, drawn up by the apostles (a kind of Christian *torah?*) to keep order among the more than 3,000. They met regularly to share monies, participate in ritual-like meals, and to pray—not in the synagogue(!) but—in a colonnaded section of the temple, so that it got on the old guard, Jewish leaders' nerves: these followers of the Way are attracting adherents! But respected Pharisee Gamaliel said, "Let them alone. Political (!) movements like this have petered out before."[8] That is, important to notice about the congregated church is that from the start there was an apparent full-orbed, total life—political, business, and welfare, as well as liturgical activities—shared by the communion of saints. As the new Israel, their "temple" worship took place within the rainbow-rich field of many other faith-shaped activities.

3. An organized, confessionally delimited church life does not exhaust the Christian life. Christians are people so overpowered by the Holy Spirit they become living letters of Jesus Christ (2 Corinthians 3:3), acting out in thankfulness the βασιλεία τοῦ Χριστοῦ Christ has delegated to them as task because they have been incorporated into his working body (Luke 22:29). But βασιλεία, the "Kingdom of God," better "God's regime," has cosmic dimensions, which spill out, over and beyond its realization within the confessional bond of faithful church worshipers. The church at Jerusalem and the churches in Asia Minor happily recognized this, the Scriptures show, and specially appointed Paul, Barnabas, and others to go out and proclaim that the reconciling Rule of God in Christ is begun coming upon the earth, emphasizing what Christ him-

---

8 T.W. Manson, "The Earliest Christian Community" in *Ethics and the Gospel* (London: SCM, 1960), 69–86.

self said he had been sent for (Luke 4:43): the "Kingdom," the Regime of God is what men and women must seek (cf. Acts 28:30–31, Matthew 6:33). That is, according to the New Testament witness, a church is called to preach βασιλεία and is itself to show the presence of βασιλεία τοῦ Χριστοῦ within its particularly defined fellowship if it means to be true rather than a false church; but genuine ἐκκλησία is not identical to βασιλεία.[9] Also, while a Christian naturally breathes within a church communion, being a Christian is not adequately satisfied by being a faithful churchman or woman. *It is significant, biblically very correct, that the Heidelberg Catechism does not mention churches when it answers the question, "But why are you called a Christian?"*[10]

These three biblical givens–

1. the corporate body nature of the holy catholic Church,

2. the full-orbed life manifested by the early undifferentiated church communion at Jerusalem, and

3. the fact that Christian life encompasses more than organized church life because God's Regime has cosmoscopic kinds of interests and assignments not portioned out to a congregated, confessional, manifestation of Christ's Body (not portioned out to a historical, institutional expression of what Paul sometimes, especially in Ephesians and Colossians, grandly calls "Church").

These basic, biblical givens are the main directives we have to work with for determining what our church is to be and is to be doing in the world today.

Do I need a parenthesis on method here to make explicit (so you can more easily challenge it) my assumption that you can not go to the Bible and pick out exactly what the structure and primary task of the Christian Reformed church communion should be today, but that those matters must be discovered from the way our Lord has ordered things in creation and provides for their historical development understood *in the light of the Scriptures*?

That means, for example, Acts 2 (:42–47) and 4 (:32–37) do not prescribe the normative pattern for an institutional church today in our specialized world; otherwise we should be holding daily prayer services, voluntarily selling off goods to wipe out the poverty-stricken circumstances of underprivileged brothers in Christ around the world, and have

---

9 Herman Ridderbos, *De Komst van het Koninkrijk* (Kampen: Kok, 1950), 288–308.

10 "Because by faith I am a member of Christ and so share in his anointing. I am anointed to confess his name, to present myself to him as a living sacrifice of thanks, to strive with a good conscience against sin and the devil in this life, and afterward to reign with Christ over all creation for all eternity." (Answer 32 in Lord's Day 12).

only twelve apostles sanhedrinizing operations. But already in Acts 6 (:1–7) it is reported, because of logistical needs, the Jerusalem church ordained seven Spirit-filled men as quartermasters, and later on when the churches needed emissaries and gifted men to evangelize in foreign countries, they singled out those kinds of specialists; and the point is, the developing needs of established, instituted churches did not stop at 100 AD. So the Bible does not have the complete word on everything ecclesiastical, any more than it has the complete word on things ethical and dogmatic. It has the final, authoritative, guiding word, yes; but the Bible, also on "the church," is not like a bag of timeless ready-mix cement that you slit open, pour out the texts, add a little watery logic, and have something you can build on. That way you more likely get a dead weight that burdens man and ox alike.

We all know you may not read prescriptions and proscriptions right out of the Bible as if it were a rule book, but we are all still easily tempted to trade proof texts like lefts and rights to the jaw for our pet ideas to get *ex cathedra* answers.

To use a better metaphor: the Bible is not like Instant Nescafé. Right, you read Acts 2, 4, 6, and the rest of the book filled with wonderment at how men and women in action under the Spirit can speak the Word of God with such boldness that it frees others from demonic powers and from the yoke of circumcistic traditions to raise up an army of world-shakers (Acts 4:31, 15:8–11); and you remember Christ's ascensional benediction that opened the door wide for his disciples to teach all peoples to do all the things he had laid upon their hearts about the Regime of the Lord (Matthew 28:19–20); and you recall Isaiah's apocalyptic prophecies about the coming Rule of *mishpat* and *shalom*; you hear the antiphonal psalms of worshiping hallelujah; you catch anew the terrific Word-revelations of Leviticus on holy, communal living because Yahweh is our God! (e.g., Leviticus 19): you are reading Acts 2, 4, 6 . . . and you do not stir-and-serve. You let all the passages—Acts, Matthew, Isaiah, the Psalms, Leviticus—percolate. Percolate while you study how institutions develop specialized officers for fulfilling complications of its task, and you study how in the unfolding of institutions certain functions assumed by it in the initial stages gradually differentiated off and take on a semi-dependent and then independent interrelated status. All the while the Scripture is percolating, percolating till the canonical wisdom, the guiding directive, starts to filter through on what these special Christian relationships called churches after Pentecost are and appropriately should do. . . .

The Christian Reformed church, like any instituted church begun in time, is a confessional fellowship, that is, a group congregated from among men and women not because they are friends, blood relatives, with the same minimal academic competence, ethnic background, or geographic proximity, but a group congregated with a (denominational) identity because they hold to the same, specific confession(s). *Credimus* is what types us structurally as a church institution and keeps us distinct from being a business, state, or school institution. Naturally we have our church finances (mission budget), church courts (consistory, classis, synod), church schooling (catechism), simply because these are inescapable aspects of our institutional confessional operations; but such church business, church government, and educational activities are thoroughly permeated and normed by the peculiarly churchful, confessional concerns. If something other than confession dominates our churched togetherness and deeds, then we become denatured as a church institution.

Oftentimes on the mission field, where the first and only presence of Christian consciousness shows up in the organized mission work of some church, that church may need to assume kinds of duties it is not particularly cut out for. A mission church may need to serve as employment agency and marriage bureau for converts ostracized by a pagan culture; in ghetto circumstances a given church may need to improvise as law protection agency for some of its parishioners against kangaroo court proceedings or criminal gang reprisal, offer civilizing language instruction, welfare or drug rehabilitation programs. When you preach Christ and his kingship and a woman gets born into new life, it affects her whole existence: the faith cannot stay closeted in a creed. So when a church is virtually alone in bringing the gospel somewhere (cf. the early church communion of Jerusalem described in Acts), it quite properly lends a hand for various sorts of churchly extra-mural concerns because those life-matters are so vitally important to that woman, who is a whole person, brought into its confessional fellowship; but the institutional church also makes haste slowly, historically, to turn these temporarily sideline services over to groups of mature believers specialized in those tasks so that it can concentrate on its own defining activity: confession.

The chief task of a church is to initiate, nurture, exercise, open up the confession of men, women, and children. That means that our church, and any congregated fellowship confessing of Jesus Christ as Lord of the universe and that we are his followers, co-workers for the coming of God's Rule, confessing that we want to obey his Word for our lives because we are members at large of the New Covenant: that means that any true, instituted church committed to propagating and developing biblical confession among the people shall always recognize its key work to be proclamation of the very living Word that effects and establishes such confessional, responsive fellowship. As a true church enjoins and enriches liturgically, catechetically, diaconately, the believers' confession, and stands ready with judgments ruling on its contours, disciplining those who overstep its bounds, the dynamic focus to all this characteristically ecclesiastic, church action will always necessarily be the preaching of the Word of God.

I must firm up this point about instituted church before we pursue the remark about preaching because right here is a spot that hurts. Right here is a pressure point that calls for that fresh act of faith, especially on the part of you leaders in our denominational confession, that shall make or break reforming action in our church under the Holy Spirit today.

In the light of the three biblical givens I tried to formulate, it must be made clear that the Christian Reformed church communion is not identical to the holy catholic Church and therefore may not be idolized by exempting it from probing, frontal critique. The Christian Reformed church is only a historically earthen vessel; and we are a confessional institutional manifestation of Christ's universal Body of believers only if our churchful practice is spirited and biblically normed by the revealed givens. We may never glory in the Christian Reformed church, it is not our "mother": only in Christ may we exalt and hallu Yahweh (2 Corinthians 10:17–18).

Furthermore, and this may be the first test of whether there will be action under the Spirit in this church I love—not even preaching elders may think more highly of themselves and their office than they ought to think (I know, it takes sterling faith to pull oneself humbly back into line): we must understand, become thoroughly convinced, and then practice the significant fact that in our complex world of differentiated institutions and specialized vocations the Christian Reformed church, and any instituted church at work in the pale of North American civilization, rightly has *a limited, central place* in our society. Because of its defined confessional nature our church has a special position nonetheless relativized among the many institutions circumscribing our lives.

One's "confessing" activity has a recapitulating, celebrating richness to it, revealing so fully one's underlying faith commitment, that is not so explicitly developed in any of one's other activities; but we are more than a confessing people. One's confessional ability also seems to be pivotal, depending upon its makeup, for constricting or fructifying one's emotional life, thought life, trust relations, and what not, deepening such acts with certainty of impoverishing them uncertainly.

Now if human "confession" is creationally ordained to be so prominent, since the instituted church has as its special province tending to human confessional life, then our church has the very critical responsibility of directing and fortifying that confessional life so that it helps all other areas of our life flower according to God's ordinances rather than be stunted. A (true) church is one way the corporate Body of Christ shows up concretely in history, although it is not the only way. (A believing Christian family or Christian schools are expressions of Christ's body, but they are *not* churches.) The ministry of a church, however, has special formative leverage in society because it feeds and matures, or ruins(!), our confessional life, which in turn, like a stopcock, regulates the élan or fin de siècle weariness to our total life style.

But this specifically central task of a church to nurture, exercise, and open up the confession of believers in no way entails some unlimited prerogative: no church has a monopoly on making God's Word speak just because it gives proclamation a priority, since that is the key to its peculiar institutional task; and no church authority is unlimited—despite its terrible power for banning someone from fellowship with saints eating and drinking to the Lord's return—no church officialdom can ever pretend to be popes and consign someone to Hell through censure and excommunication (cf. our form for readmission to the fellowship). No instituted church, and that includes the Christian Reformed church, may act as if it be the ark of God in North America today. Our one hundred year old communion may be thankful indeed if candlesticks of the Lord still reside with us and you who are appointed to the office of lighting them, rather than covering them under bushel baskets, are made aware of the awful burden to light them obediently. Today too the Spirit is speaking to those with ears so that they may hear and overcome the dragon, or be snuffed out.

Prophetic Word of the Lord to be preached: become grownups at work in the coming of God's Regime

Exactly how the instituted Christian Reformed church is to relate to what is going on outside the walls of our confessional fellowship in the culturally deteriorating situation of North America and the twentieth century world, and exactly what our message is to be to fellow believers and secular disbelievers is no mean thing to say. But there is a biblically simple directive for it and for curing our hypocrisy: prophecy!—a prophetic declaration of the coming of the Lord's Regime, βασιλεία τοῦ θεοῦ! Preaching is not the answer to our troubles. More and better preaching is not the answer if you mean gifted eloquence, original delivery, contemporary language uncluttered by "thee's" and "thou's" that sound like Latin to our youth, or if you mean good ol' pulpit pounding preachers saying "beloved" to fellows in their 20's with crew cuts or long hair. Desperately sincere or methodologically improved preaching does not make it "relevant." Preaching done with a learned scribal, scholastic veil over the eyes, a social-concern or passion-for-souls or some other fashionable veil over the eyes of the preacher hinders ears from hearing the prophetic word of God and comes no further than the tintinabulating gong of 1 Corinthians 13. On the other hand, you can have mediocre preaching that is prophetic, because it knows what is going on and does battle with the powers of the Age—that is what counts!

But how can the confessional church preach prophetically, proclaim the Word of God so it applies to all of life without certifying, in God's Name, some political program, economic measure, or peace move that turns out later to be disastrous? And if you have differences of meaning in your congregation about race, Cambodia, homosexuality, the lodge, how can you preach concretely without disturbing the peace of the church?

Indeed. How do you pray in the Sunday worship service during the Vietnam War? "Keep our boys safe" . . . and let it hang there? No guts, no horror, no outrage! Helplessness pleading before the God of the nations! Is it not more often like a pastoral filibuster to fill out the "long prayer" (which Christ said should be short, in public)? To personalize with a name still avoids the issue of this ugly war.

Is that the choice for preaching? Devotional, ethical, doctrinal introspection plus a sterile permissiveness on everything else (the Pharisee tack), *or* you proffer "the church" answer to the Indochina struggle as a just war or as an atrocious field-technology training for the graduates of our national military academies (Sadducee penchant)? Is there no alternative to *either* preach your ethical-theological knitting, shutting up about the rest, *or* wage war with contemporary issues, bolstering your considered opinion by standing behind a pulpit and wearing ecclesiastic dress?

The only way out of this double dead end trap that shall stir the people of God from their frozen, hypocrite lethargy and offer lasting *shalom* to the misled mindless of the nations is prophecy that recovers proclaiming the "whole counsel of God" in no uncertain terms to whoever is in front of you.

Preaching the "whole counsel of God" does not mean you make certain you treat all doctrinal loci or touch base on every book of the Bible during your ministry or have worked through the Heidelberg Catechism at least once in three years or balance-off devotional homilies for the aged with practical tips for the young. "All the counsel of God" means, says Paul (quoted in Acts 20:25–27): preach the kingship of Christ, the Regime of God, that *all* life belongs to the Lord—not just church life, home life, personal life, school life, but—*all* societal life patterns and relationships. This is the core of the gospel and the only Spirit-enriched framework that shall not falter into elliptical balancing acts of competing interests—which are fine for circuses and the tedium of theologistical schoolmen, but has no place in giving forceful direction to those hungry for the Word of the Lord.

We must not be conformed to the patterns of this evil-spirited age, but by the re-formation of our consciousness be so changed that we can begin to discern what God's good, pleased, *full* Will is for life (Romans 11:36–12:2). We have been given the ministry of cosmic reconciliation! What's old goes—yes! Things become new (2 Corinthians 5:17–19); things on earth as well as in heaven are to be reconciled newly back to God through Christ (Colossians 1:16–20). And people are called to salvation as people-in-relation, to neighbors, to country, to roads, toys, and postage stamps! The ministry of reconciliation comes not first of all to us as souls and secondarily then to bodies, but it is slipped like a wedding garment over our shoulders as whole earthlings, formative in many kinds of (institutional) associations, called to be sons and daughters of God in joyful action. . . .

This is the temper of prophecy! Anathema to Sadducees who kill its love-of-Christ constraining power by emasculating it into a theoretical principle . . . one should certainly affirm! Disruptively unpleasant to a Nixonic audience of comfortable suburbanites who are content with normality of daily life, purity of doctrine, and evangelism committees. Prophecy! —

Are you saying we should preach "Christian organizations," lest we be less than faithful to the richness of God's word?

The scriptures say, if preaching does not lead to Christian action—and that does not mean *churchy* action!—that preaching is in vain, a dumbshow.

What is "Christian" action? Christ-body action! —

How firmly are you church leaders committed to the oneness of Christ's Body, the corporate nature of our one, holy Universal communion? Do you reduce Christ's body in your mind, churchify it? Or even denominationalize it? How permanent and pervasive is that Communion of the saints? And to be openly professed? Does it stop as soon as you have two or three Christian carpenters gathered together? Or a handful of Christian voting citizens? Should evidence of Christ's body then go underground?

Do not be faked out into thinking I am talking up a Dutch import, the special interest of a Canadian pressure group, a Kuyperian hobby of the *Doleantie*, which our Christian Reformed church, begun earlier in 1857, is under no obligation to pick up (although *Afscheiding* pietism *intensified puritanistically* would have to be considered just as much a European import). The prophetic Word about communion of the saints does not get lost in legalistic structures or quibbles about strategy and contingencies. It simply presses home to the hearts of God's people the truth that communion of the saints is more than a statement of fact: it is a blessed gift and program for action! An economy (*oikonomia*) of God, the way God ordained for things to be done on earth.

You do not need to require "a Christian school sermon": just ask for the convicting Truth of Psalm 78 to be bared to the congregated faithful. No one should feel threatened into "preaching for Christian labor unions": if a pastor can read contemporary history with biblically informed eyes, holds to the corporate nature of Christ's body on earth, and lets the normative vision of Paul's witness to the Ephesians (6:5–9) and Colossians (3:22–4:1) and James' letter (4:13–5:6) loosen his tongue, you will have prophecy from the pulpit! There should not be requests for "Christian patriotism sermons" or "Christian pacifist sermons," pitting Romans 13 against Revelations 13: let the message of Isaiah 40 and 1st and 2nd Chronicles for today be heard to still men's proud hearts from tumult of conquest so that their self-righteously bloody swords get sheathed.

Again, the way to end the hypocrisy of our church is to prophesy, that is, in the name of the Lord to call believers in the pew from every vocation, out of every nation, race, and clime, to join in working out communally our Lord's Regime in the world. The instituted church must not itself meddle churchily in politics, labor, art, and mores, judge their trends and lipservice solutions—at best that way you still must react amateurly to what and where and how the secularists locate the problems. But neither may our church try to commit cultural suicide, flee from the world to shadowbox and fight papier-mâché enemies—our church communion inescapably witnesses to extramural life, when our catechumens go to war or refuse to go; and if the Christian Reformed church is pastorally silent at its formal meeting about the *confessional* implications of our rising American standard of living versus the rest of the world or on the *confessional* perils hidden in the higher level of unemployment, that pastoral silence sounds deafeningly in heaven before the throne of God.

That is, our Christian Reformed church is in the twentieth century, secular, cultural world, and the only answer our instituted church can give that will bring leadership to the disorganized believers of North America and challenge the secularists with "a center that will hold" is the vision and message of Christ's kingship, which does not stop somewhere halfway. (Christian schools are halfway houses and make no biblical reforming sense unless they lead historically to a Christian art institute, Christian world relief warehouses, Christian political reflection groups, and more, battling professionally deep in the contemporary bog against the powers of the day.) Our instituted church answer must be the prophetic Word, which girds the faithful confessionally strong and stirs them to become grown-up believers, mature in the fullness of Christ (Ephesians 4:12–16) so that they flourish Christianly as his body outside the instituted (denominational) church fellowship wall too. As an up-to-date Christian political manifesto puts it:

> While recognizing the church's calling to proclaim the message of the Word of God as it applies to all of life, the Anti-Revolutionary Party believes that Government and people must learn to understand on their own, in the light of the Holy Scripture, what this message means for the political life of every age.[11]

This tenet, multiplied by many more Christian cultural organizational undertakings, is what our church should say "Amen!" to, so that by humbling its own confessional, institutional ambit, it may exalt the grand Body of Christ and let God's Grace bless freely all other kinds of human activities striving to be obedient to the Word of the Lord.

The surprising result of giving centrality to the message of Christ's total lordship—and surprises always come when God's ordained setup is obeyed—will be seeing our church's ability to concentrate powerfully on its confessional mission task, freed from adventitious cares, and simultaneously seeing the instituted church's becoming a veritable proclamation hub for all other societal activities; the rallying place where fighters hungry for the Word of life come to be confessionally heartened, reproved, corrected, comforted, and instructed in Christ's righteousness. If our

---

11 Article 2 from Statement of the Principles and General Political Program of the Anti-Revolutionary Party drawn up by the meeting of Deputies in Utrecht, The Netherlands, 10 June 1961.

church were to prophetically proclaim that "Blessed are those undergoing persecution for Christ's Name's sake in the world of secular labor, business, government, education, art, and mass communication," the central significance of its limited task for our actual, concrete lifetime would be overwhelming!

Our congregated church should not coax along Mr. and Mrs. clubs with speakers and amateur after-recess programs, once a month, but should say, "Mr. and Mrs. couple, go discover the Lord's Regime coming in higher education; enter the program of the Christian college of your choice." And our struggling Men's societies in the church—is it not historically time, especially in urban settings, for them to differentiate fraternally off from church sponsorship and become full-fledged debating societies or service organizations, become a local of the Christian Reformed Laymen's League or of the Christian Action Foundation? There is no competition between instituted church and the other society life *if both are manifestations of Christ's body*, getting their different, limited authority to work at their specific task from the unction of the Holy Spirit, which outfits every believer (1 John 2:20, 27).

Not to move this way, under the banner of Christ's total kingship, is to be anti-historical. For the Christian Reformed church to stifle such an outworking of God's Regime, write it off as an upstart movement rocking the ecclesiastic boat, or try to leave it in the realm of talk, is for our church to have been weighed in the balance of biblical prophecy and to be found wanting. Then the Christian Reformed church cannot help but remain hypocritically high and dry.

Do you realize the terrible irony of our church hypocrisy, its utter poverty of leadership, as I speak to you today? While the mighty revolution of Violence and Lies, Luxury and Hate sweeps down upon us like an avalanche in 1970, we have organized *church* softball teams and leagues, but have not had a viable, reformed *Christian* political association organized in North America.

INTENT OF THE PROPOSAL

Part of the reason for beginning my modest proposal with what must have sounded like a whimsical, bludgeoning suggestion—close Calvin Seminary—is the agonized, playfully wrestled dismay at not knowing how do you get the reformation we need as a church moving! The more I speak outside our circles, the more I become convinced we have a store of riches simply unknown to many, many other Christian communions, and a legacy of biblical grit and thoroughness that could win the grudging implacable hatred of the most influential secularists—which would draw the issues right for a change—but, instead of showing reforming leadership in North America, we sit on our Body of Christ hands. And now we have got to get action under the Spirit of God within our Christian Reformed communion if we are not to perish ourselves; we who once tasted the good Word of God and experienced the powers of the Coming Age of Glory but who have fallen away from the earnest, in-your-blood proclamation of Christ's total lordship that we are called to work out concretely as a communion of saints! So, like a naïve sheep, I headed for the center, the quiet eye of the ping pong tempest in our teapot, the Seminary.

And wondered: should Calvin Seminary be moved away from its idyllic environs to an abandoned warehouse near the ghetto heart of Chicago? Or should we start another one there? Not to firm up factions in the church, but to invigorate its whole climate, give a new locus for its theological mentality to form—should Calvin Seminary as it is have a kind of monopoly on where all Christian Reformed ministers come from?

But No, actually we do not need "seminary training." We need *Christian* training. By that I mean: theological studies should be pursued in the immediate, encyclopedic context of all the other sciences, in a university setting, to help stop the theologian from losing a sense of his limited, integral place in the whole cosmic enterprise of reconciliation. True, training our pastors in a university setup might greatly secularize the church, but not if that universe of scholarship be genuinely Christian, a complex of graduate scholarship where there is *a common Christian, biblically reformational mind operating*. We do not need "pastoral psychology" so much as a network of Christian psychiatric insights prepared by a department of psychology; we do not need "theological" contemporary literature courses so much as Christian literary critique developed in departments of comparative literature and aesthetics; we do not need personal and social ethics tailored for preachers so much as Christian sociologists and Christian ethicists working communally at their disciplines, illustrating their analysis from the whole burly girth of human life. Theology demands specialized study, yes, including an in-depth knowledge of Hebrew and Greek, German and Dutch, philosophical prolegomena to theology, and historiography of the confessional meanderings of our churches throughout the centuries, but theology must not mean isolated study. The conception of a seminary-by-itself can already be a step toward secularization, ivory-towered self-sufficiency, and softly polish-up the age-old, evil idea that theology is the discipline that must supply all the Christian answers to the multiplex problems of our existence, rather than see them grappled with in a community of like-minded, living Christian scholars knowledgeable in various, specific fields.

Also, what the instituted church rightly expects its seminaries to do can hardly be done in our schoolmasterly encrusted fix of lectures, notes, and rounds of tests. Our church wants the seminary to be a school for prophets! To take intelligent, dedicated young men [and women] and deepen their confessional sensibility by preparing them in the competencies needed for opening the Scriptures prophetically to God's people and anyone with ears to hear. But no theological schooling can guarantee to effect prophecy. And it does not take much—only one whiff of lingual positivism can poison a whole seminary—it does not take much of anything to make theological science seem arid and removed from life, because wrongfully wonders(!) are expected from it; and that leaves the disenchanted theological students often misthinking thorough analysis is bad for the faith, so they cast about for fieldtrip "experiences" that make Christ's love seem real or something. But such a wrangle derails any attempt at both a sound theology and a rich confession.

The least we could do: Mastering Berkouwer's balanced compendia is not the best study for knowing what and how to preach, is it? Devouring Tournier's little gems of books is little help for bringing the Word of God's merciful judgment upon us sinners for the Bible, is it not? The least we could do is begin to work prominently, concertedly, incisively, out of and beyond the tradition of S. G. de Graaf, B. Holwerda, A. Janse, J. C. Sikkel, M. B. van't Veer, C. Veenhof, Klaas Schilder, C. van Gelderen— what seminarian can be worth his reformed salt in the pulpit who has not worked through writings of these men!—because this tradition of Old Testament and New Testament exegetical scholarship breathes deep learning, intense urgency, and a reformed confessional focus; exactly the kind of spur to reform that our preaching elders need who *must be concerned* that *ecclesia reformanda*, and simply must get up out of the dogmatic trench into the line of fire against the invisible powers and authorities of the Age and kerygmatically pass the ammunition.[12]

Considerations like these led me to make, for your imaginative reaction, the wistful, savage, helpless, withal serious first remark of my modest proposal.

---

12 Cf. the important doctoral thesis on this very matter recently published: S. Greidanus, *Sola Scriptura: Problems and principles in preaching historical texts* (Kampen: Kok, 1970).

As for suggesting disbanding the boards and standing committees our church is starting to grow like long, long hair: I mean to extend it as an unresearched, intuited feeler, like litmus paper, to see whether it shows up any measure of guilty conscience.

I have been led to understand that synod, which is the governing body of our communion, is a two-week event, during which the consciousness of the Christian Reformed church gets expressed. And that it, after exercising its formative control on the confessional matters before it, goes out of existence till the next year, leaving behind only a few designated folks to answer official correspondence. Such regular cohesion for decisive acts, yet absence of administrative management, strikes me as soundly in keeping with the kind of fluid, continuing, open-ended, congregated fellowship Christ meant for the instituted church to maintain. Any move toward substantializing needed committees into ecclesiastical commissions or giving semi-permanence to pockets of power able to make key appointments and policy decisions would be anti-normative; turning church into something more like a state. And whenever a church acts like a political entity, it has lost its confessional savor.

Should we not now already beware, and searchingly ask: Are our large denominational boards exhibits of wisdom and stewardship? Or is it, under cover of the democratistic dictum to honor a grass roots' responsiveness, not some kind of spoils system; a spoils system that feeds bureaucratic creep (instead of doing things, appoint a committee to talk) and leaves manipulating things to a few insiders nevertheless? Would not the glamor of broad travel diminish, and the effective dispatch of its work proportionately increase, if each participating member were expected to pay at least half of those expenses?

Just a piece of litmus paper to test those in the know. Deathly important, because we may not be found putting our confessional money and time and stamina wastefully into a hole in the ground!

The intent of my modest proposal becomes most clear in the last clause, which asked whether or not you men would lay down your ministerial status and let the ruling elders in the congregation designate as instructors in the Word whoever can bring the Word of *Life* from the Scriptures and is practicing a daily walk of prayer and fasting in the spirit of the Gospels.

I do not want to encourage the congregationalistic disorder I spoke against. Nor does the suggestion say to stop ministering, or that we dissolve clerical ordination until we know exactly and certainly what it should mean. The idea is just that you give up ministerial "status," give up ruling by the authority of human investiture, ruling by pulling rank as being scribally learned-in-the-Scriptures or warming the seat of Moses, rather than leading church members charismatically by the respect won because of continually holding up biblical wisdom.

We all know the day is past when the educated dominie always had the last word. Fear of dethronement from that position, however, of stepping down to be among *ho laos* of God (although you have to be *laity* to be saved!), or not knowing how to do it without becoming a buddy-buddy preacher that has lost his character of overseer, this is contributing, I am afraid, to the establishmentarian petrification that sooner or later starts to settle in upon a church, and cannot help but be threatening our hundred year old communion too. So my appeal to you now is take the lead, set an example that will reverse the trend of supposing we have established ourselves; that is, concretely tackle our church hypocrisy in your post of service, as I should in mine, and be willing to forsake all to follow Christ, including your prestige; be willing to lay down your life, your professional life—ministerial status—for the faithful in our churches, your brothers and sisters, so that they and you may hope to gain the Life that never fails or ends.

There are, of course, all kinds of possible, imaginative ways to implement such action. A young bachelor of divinity(!) might not, at the drop of a graduation hat, accept being capitulated into acting like president of the corporation, so to speak, right away as chairman of the consistory, but wait a few years till he has been weathered by congregational life. The preaching elder in a very large congregation might seek approval for a group ministry with others there (like you have responsible group practice in medicine and law today, the better to cope with complexity in our differentiated society); *if they are of one confessing mind*, sensitive to one another's strengths and weaknesses—why should all our clergy be general practitioners?—you could have a glorious time of it under your ruling elders initiating new and multiple worship services rather than holding just the two at the sacrosanct morning and evening hour, that is, hear the Word and celebrate the resurrection newly (—This might be a way to avoid the appearance of spendthrift evil occasioned by relocating, or duplicating, in an expensive building within five motorized minutes of another Christian Reformed church building, what is only a sentimental entity or an outdated, ruralized concept of "church"). . . .

But enough—the point is not at all that pastors might be more modest or that we could experiment institutionally with care. And the point is certainly not that we should just think up some bright ideas, make our resolutions, and take a new lease on life as a denomination. No. That in no way would get at the crux of healing the ailment of our communion.

The crux is that we need somehow a communal faith-act on the part of our preaching elders in the Christian Reformed church so that powers of the Age the Lord calls us to fight, which are thwarting the lives of the faithful and the unbelieving world at large from sharing in the laughter of the New Age, be challenged by marked men, prophetically filled by only the Holy Spirit—because these demonic powers of Violence and Lie, Luxury and Hate, can be exorcized only, as Christ once put it (Matthew 17: 19–20), by spirited faith-action secured through prayer and fasting.

There is an Asherah on every green hill, beside every pile of magazines, inside every TV box; Baalim are worshiped left and right, and read "Right or wrong, my country," "The inalienable right to own and use your own gun," "You've come a long way, baby"; there is flagrant idolatry of becoming middle class and overweight, of polite hatred of the next race, of the Big Lie of newspapery news—all these Powers in the air slave-rule ten thousands times ten thousands, decimate the Christian community, and have invaded most surely even our oh so protected church life. The point of my proposal then is that we simulate persecution as a church, really adopt the lifestyle of prayer and fasting faith-action, live a much less settled, less possessive, yet firmly confessionally rooted life, so that we be driven back as a communion joyfully to hear and follow only those who speak with the Spirit-filled authority of the Word of God for this evil hour, and disregard or be rid of the talk of those whose mock authority is like that of the scribes and Pharisees. (If the Holy Spirit does not power the words of the preaching elder, what good is it but wind?)

Prayer and fasting does not mean an ascetic, pious show, the way the Pharisees organized it. It may mean, how can one preach from the prophet Amos while living in a (usually) most comfortable parsonage—even if you say it right, who would believe you meant it? But Christian prayer and fasting faith-action means that with a singleness of heart and a consequent intensity of purpose that cuts *everyone* here down to size, we be found fervently trading our talents *together* for building up the Lord's Regime. Prayer and fasting means—in everything I have been led to say today, there must be no comfort for the ping mavericks among us or for the pong watchdogs who aim to hold the bridge at all costs and then go down with the ship—if anyone has difficulty in changing their minds or loosening up their sensibilities in response to the full Word of God because they might lose face: prayer and fasting, before God I tell you!

means we have got to lose those funny faces we make at one another, take off the masks of pride that break the communion, and get the passionate love that is done with dissembling (Romans 12:9), and implore the Lord with ripped open hearts for the convicting Grace and Power to preach the full counsel of God! that is, to prophesy in the name of the Lord so God may haply revive us again as a convenanted communion. Otherwise, we perish as a church.

There is mostly a hole in my life for the past decade (if I may oversimplify a little and lament out loud), and it goes by the name of Sunday worship. It is not a private grief. I have met with old men who cried because there was no stuffings to the proclamation in our Christian Reformed churches today compared to what they remembered in days gone by, no meat!

I am certain, formerly, that rationalism, cluttered with Dutchisms, oversimplifications, and who knows what else not provincial, hindered those sermons of yesteryear from being homiletic showpieces; but I like to think they were biblically straight on the key things and above all, where Kuyper still was read, had a vision—maybe it was only a vision—of our Lord's kingship over all of life (what used to be called "Calvinism"). Today that central message is *generally not believed as a norm to be obeyed by saints in communion* but is kept at arm's theoretical length as a rational principle or historical exhibit, part of our heritage wares. Yet only "the whole counsel of God," the Good News of our calling to work out the Lord God's cosmic Regime, preached on Sunday without pulling any punches, can start bringing relief from our church hypocrisy and initiate reforming action under the Spirit among us. Only because I preached you God's worldwide kingship, Paul told the Ephesians on farewell, stops your blood from being on my hands (Acts 20:24–27).

If there is blood on our hands, and no explosively radical, communal act of faith forthcoming to do what Paul did, then the Lord says to us "Woe to you. Woe to you preaching elders of the Christian Reformed church. Woe to you, instead of *shalom*."

Background Material
Berton, Pierre. *The Comfortable Pew: A critical look at the church in the new age* (Toronto: McClelland & Stewart, 1965).
Calvin, John. "De nessecitate reformandae ecclesiae," in *Tractatus Theologici Omnes* (Amsterdam: J.J. Schipper, 1667), 37–64; "The Necessity of Reforming the Church," in *Tracts Relating to the Reformation,* translated by Henry Beveridge. Vol. 1 (Edinburgh: Calvin Translation Society, 1884) (Grand Rapids: Eerdmans).

Conversations with many faithful Christian Reformed Church members, ecclesiastical office-bearers, and also disaffected believers, across the continent in the last five years.

Cullmann, Oscar. "Authorités," in *Vocabulaire Biblique*, ed. J. J. Von Allmen (Neuchâtel: Delachaux & Niestlé, 1954), 28–31.

De Graaf, S.G. *Kerkelijk Besef* (Zutphen: J. B. van den Brink, 1925).

DeGraaff, Arnold H. "The Church and its Ministry," in *The Educational Ministry of the Church: A perspective* (Delft: Judels & Brinkman, 1966; and Nutley: Craig Press, 1968), 56–88.

DeMoor, Henry. *Theology: Its nature, place, and task*. Presentation to the *Theologia Reformanda Est* Club of Calvin Seminary on 27 January 1970, dittograph.

Gibbs, Mark and T. Ralph Norton, *God's Frozen People* (Philadelphia: Westminster Press, 1965).

Harrison, Paul M. "Religious Leadership in America," in *The Religious Situation: 1969*.

Kromminga, J.H. *In the Mirror* (Hamilton, Ontario: Guardian, 1957).

Kuitert, H. M. "Het Spreken van de Kerk," *Anti-Revolutionaire Staakunde*, 39:12 (1969): 341–355.

Ridderbos, Herman. "The Church and the Kingdom of God," *International Reformed Bulletin*, 9:27 (1966): 8–18.

———. *Paulus: Ontwerp van zijn theologie* (Kampen: Kok, 1966), 364–441.

Roxburgh, Robert L. *Pattern for Change: A handbook for church renewal* (Seattle: Benrocks, 1969).

Schmidt, Karl Ludwig. "βασιλεία," in *Theologisches Worterbuch zum Neuen Testament*, ed. G. Kittel. 1:579–592.

Schrotenboer, Paul G. *Man in God's World* (Grand Rapids: Reformed Ecumenical Synod, 1967).

Seerveld, Calvin. "The Meaning of Silence for Daily Life and Sunday Worship," *International Reformed Bulletin*, 10:30 (1967): 6–19. Reprinted in *In the Fields of the Lord* (2000), 294–307.

Smith, M.C. *Cultuur en Heil* (Amsterdam: A.G.O.R.A., 1959).

Stringfellow, William. "The Case against Christendom and the Case against Pierre Berton," in *The Restless Church* (Toronto: McClelland & Stewart, 1966), 11–25.

Vanderkooy, T. P. *Maatschaappij in beweging* (Kampen: Kok, 1967), 69–82, 163–172.

Vander Stelt, John C. "The Church in Society," *International Reformed Bulletin*, 11:34 (1968): 15–36.

Wilckens, Ulrich. "ὑπόκρισις," in *Theologisches Worterbuch zum Neuen Testament*, ed. G. Friedrich. 8: 558–571.

Zijlstra, Bernard. "The Place of Christianity in our Times," *International Reformed Bulletin*, 13:41 (1970): 24–28.

A Snake and Dove Policy for Redeemer Graduates

The gospel according to Luke reports the following:
> When the impure spirit goes out of the fellow, it wanders through waterless places searching for a place to rest. Not finding one it says, "I'll go back to my house where I came from."
>
> **Coming back the impure spirit finds it swept clean and redecorated [Matthew's account adds, "up for rent"]. So it goes and recruits seven other spirits more perverse than itself, and gaining entrance they set up housekeeping there.**
>
> **The final stages of that fellow become worse than the first.**
> (Luke 11:24–26)

Now I know that Jesus told this story to warn the new generation of hearers not to be like the Pharisee and Sadducee leaders of God's people who, once they got rid of their singular lust for an indulgent life became a repository of sevenfold self-righteous demons: they loved money but gave a double tithe (Luke 16:14–15, 18:9–14); they followed the law God gave Moses but treated its statutes as their savior (John 5:39–40, Matthew 19:16–22). That is, in biblical terms, their faith and vision slipped a notch and they became antiChristlike: they showed the semblance of piety and orthodoxy but lacked the goods of a joyful, self-sacrificial walk in giving away help and healing to their (undesirable) neighbors (Matthew 23:23–24, 25:31–46).

It would be quite a stretch to apply this story *tout court* to Redeemer University College's 1999 graduation circumstances where you as faculty, students, parents, and administrative staff are celebrating the first graduating senior class to have your holy spirited years of study given

---

Graduation convocation address at Redeemer University College, Ancaster, Ontario, 29 May 1999.

the regular BA and BS degree names recognized by the government of Ontario and the secular employment world. Unlike a rose, some things by other names smell sweeter. And I should not like to exemplify a kind of "Reformed" crotchety streak that often seems to have to temper its joy with a little admission *sub voce* that there are still a couple of filthy rags in our back pocket. Why can't you just be happy once, and thank God together, without leveling it off to congratulating yourselves?

So I'd like to give heartfelt voice to that by saying, "Thank you, God, for blessing these patient, praying, working servants of Jesus Christ with good fruit on their labors of 18 years! Thank you, LORD, for having your Holy Spirit convict strangers that the education in this institution consecrated to the Rule of Jesus Christ on earth has as good a consistency as the food served up elsewhere at Nebuchadnezzar's court (cf. Daniel 1:5–16). Thank you, God, our Lord, for coming through in this definite way during our lifetimes, so we may carry on the testimony of your covenantal faithfulness to us often short-sighted folk who belong to you, and tell it experientially to generations not yet born!

Matthew 10:16. What remains now to be said on this festive, celebrative occasion, marking with ceremony the gift of exchange between a teacher and a student generation in the presence of parents and friends? As you walk off this platform with your certified degree and go on to graduate studies, professional training, unpaid employment, or commercial service with wages, the responsibility of your academic mentors gradually fades away into **your** taking credit for the mistakes and insights. Is there a word from Scripture that would not have me pontificating clichés, but offer something worth remembering?

My gift to you graduates today and to Redeemer is this wisdom our Lord Jesus gave his followers:

> **Look, I am sending you out as sheep into a pack of wolves.**
> **So you all become worldliwise as snakes and (remain) innocent as doves.**
>
> (Matthew 10:16)

What does this homely, mixed animal metaphor mean? That the past Harris government has been a pack of wolves in society? that Redeemer graduates are to become snakes in the grass of the unsuspecting church? that you spend the next few years cooing plaintive sounds or frequent the upper ledges of corporate buildings as pigeons?

My uncle who taught me to play chess taught me that when you recognize an obvious line of attack by your opponent, look around for a more concealed plot, like a covert rook attack after the next turn; if you see a good chess move for yourself, first double-check other better possibilities, maybe with your fabulous horse-jumping knight.

Could this Matthew 10:16 proverb be Christ's take on how sheep play chess with wolves? Act like a snake/dove combination?

Our wolverine context 1999 AD. I am going to assume Scripture is right, even if you don't think so, that when you leave the sheepfold of Redeemer you will be at large in a wolverine culture. You have formed a community here nurtured by the Spirit of God, God's Word, and prayer; and I know, trust, and deeply respect a large number of the good shepherds you have had in your various study disciplines. Redeemer has not been a sin-free environment any more than the church is, but its overall bent has not been seeking whom it may devour, but has been assiduous in equipping you to be savvy to the world and able to act with a redemptive quality.

North American society, however, is running on a different generator, in my judgment, and is caught in a monstrous dynamic that is intrinsically rapacious. It is so that lots of wolves have manners, and Scripture exposes the kind that dress up not in Red Riding Hood grandmother's clothes, but wolves that prey on people in sheep's clothing!—false prophets (cf. Matthew 7:15–20). I don't want to malign the real wolves in God's world, for we are talking principalities and evil powers that are God's enemies, not flesh and bloody persons (Ephesians 6:10–13). Scripture is saying, don't be fooled into supposing that our secularized post-christian culture is a normal human setup, for it is truly twisted, crooked in this generation: humanitarian Canada bombing the former Yugoslavia in an undeclared war as the NATO means to achieve the end of human rights for Kosovars, we are told. Tax cuts! Ontario tax cuts are trumpeted as something desirable, while the poor who can't pay taxes are treated like outcasts, untouchables, a tumor in the body politic. The endless varieties of packaged cereals filling the shelves of your local food "chain" store "supermarket" witness to the colorful, bursting competitive careless superfluity in our economic system, where the bigger companies squeeze out the smaller ones without compunction. . . .

It is also true that there are lots of nice people everywhere, including us. But the point is: the framework of North American society, where we live, whose systemic network is bigger than any person or even clique of leaders, is carnivorous. The secularized, fast-paced North American way-of-life consumes people's lives the way wolves eat sheep for breakfast. Not only women and children, but men too, who want to succeed. People try to survive, but don't know how fully to live before God's face.

This is the world, I believe, you and I have been living in during your full-time service for God studying at Redeemer. After graduation you will miss this protective communal matrix and its leisure of being busy in academic reflection, and you will face the wolfish milieu full-time on your own.

A common danger is that you become co-opted because the office routine you enter is set, the professional training you sign on for has its requisites fixed, the housing you can afford situates you in a neighborhood with its particular mores, and you fit in more or less, without the time or the wherewithal to examine every *quid pro quo*. Even if you form a makeshift christian fellowship in your good-natured wolverine work community, the outcome is moot. Rap music began in the New York '70s as the self-respecting, identifying music of a disenfranchised young black minority that figured this music at least could not be absorbed by the dominant white cultural system; yet by today *TIME* magazine has done a cover story on crossover hip-hop culture (8 February 1999) whose gansta rap and glamorous Lauryn Hill exemplify the capitalist Money-making culture their initial lyrics and rhythms rejected! It makes me wonder whether a **successful** Christian in our society is not a phantom.

Next to the danger of co-optation, a common temptation for bright young Christians starting out after finishing formal education is to isolate your faith, keep it safe in church, home, and school, but don't get it dirty where the cultural action is, in broadcast media, health care policy, professional entertainment. It simplifies one's life, it seems, to restrict obedience to the Lord where you can manage it, and not introduce the upsetting notion of normative practice and doing what is just for helpless people where things are out of your control. Such a fallback tactic pours energy into parenting, christian school boards, becoming a good deacon or elder in the church, while you, of course, perform your workaday job with integrity. Such a domesticated christian faith has commendable features, but tends to close down with tunnel vision your communal possibility to turn the evil abroad upside-down! to exorcize evil that plagues your neighbors. Such reduction of faithful societal engagement to one's in-house concerns also leaves a major portion of your maturing lifetime out of the house "up for rent."

A snake and dove policy. The direction for Redeemer alumni sheep to take that Jesus recommends, it seems to me, is different: become worldliwise snakes together and remain innocent as doves.

A curious selection: a dust-bound animal usually detested, sometimes dangerous, associated by Scripture with the historic fall into sin by Eve and Adam (Genesis 3); and an airborne harmless bird Scripture says finally brought Noah a sign that God's punishment of the world with the flood was over (Genesis 6–8), and a bird the Holy Spirit used at John's baptizing Jesus into communion with repentant sinners to attest God's approving presence (Luke 3:21–22, John 1:32–34). Is that really our guideline? Worldliwise snake and innocent dove—!

Metaphors are not meant to be pinned down with logical precision, in my book. Their truth lies in the nuanced ambiguity you ferret out intuitively but leave hanging, tantalizing you imaginatively. One can still delineate, however, finely tuned meaning in a given word-picture.

Jesus' snake, Matthew reports, is wise (*phronimos*), circumspect, "worldliwise," I translated it. This snake is alert, wary, knows which way the wind is blowing, and anticipates what the score will be because it has the *savoir faire* to know what time it is as it slithers concertina-wise over a large warm rock (cf. Proverbs 30:18–19). The Bible story about the five virgins with oil in their lamps are called snakily wise (*phronimos*) because they were ready, prepared for whatever might come (Matthew 25:1–13). In another Bible story, the man who knew to build a house on rock-bottom foundations showed he was *phronimos*—prudent, discreet, wise to what goes on in the world (Matthew 7:24–27). As I read Scripture, a strong peripheral vision, timing (cf. Matthew 24:45, *en kairo*), and being subtle (if short of "sly") is the tenor of the worldliwise snake Christ held out to his disciples.

The virtue of snake-wisdom—"prudence"—has an illustrious, contentious philosophical history that is not proper to rehearse on this occasion, but I'll just mention Machiavelli's slant in order to sharpen up what the Bible means. Machiavelli boldly tells leaders to appear to be good lawful princes, but like a centaur, be ready, when it's in your own best interests, to let your bestial component kick in: "be a fox to recognize traps and a lion to frighten off the wolves."[1] So, dissemble human integrity, bully at will, and act foxy, because your ends justify any means.

Machiavelli presents the antithesis of what Jesus enjoins in the snake

---

1 "Bisogna adunque essere volpe a conoscere e' lacci, e lione a sbigottire e' luppi" (*Il Principe*, chapter 18, p. 180). Cf. "...ma la prudenzia consiste in sapere conoscere le qualità delli inconvenienti, e pigliare el men tristo per buono" (chapter 21, p. 218).

and dove instruction. Holy Scripture asks those who would be followers of the Christ to meld with their snake-like foresight and "cunning" the innocence of a dove, that is, a nature and demeanor that has purity, is undefiled, unsophisticated, simple, untouched by evil, as it were (Romans 16:19). The dove stands for a person without guile. It's very close to the biblical notion of being "without a blemish" (Ephesians 1:4, Colossians 1:21–23, Jude 24), the kind of doves and lambs the LORD required in the Older Testament for sacrifices and thank-God-offerings (Deuteronomy 17:1). And the context of Matthew 10 follows up the Lord's proverbial direction to be snake and dove disciples with sobering talk about "sacrifices," that is, persecutions coming, trouble, in-fighting—the dusty snakes who are clean doves may get badly hurt. But be glad about that, says Matthew earlier in the gospel (5:11–12), because God will stand by you persecuted for Christ's sake with everlasting blessings.

So Christ's injunction to be worldliwise snakes and innocent doves is metaphorically precise: be suspicious but without guile; be as flexible as a snake but as uncalculating for advantage as a dove; sense the battle lines and imminent animosities but be making peace; be salt that has a seasoning bite to it **and** a gentle light for your neighbor's pathway (Matthew 5:13–16); keep your *Gereformeerde voelhorens* (Reformation snail antennae) testing the air (the way canaries are sometimes sacrificed deep in coal mines), but respond gently to anger and giveaway your life, in perhaps tough places, become a living sacrifice doing what pleases the Lord (Romans 12:1–2).

When my wife labored as a social worker with the Salvation Army in the red light district of Amsterdam years ago, trying to help *des filles de joie* to a different life, she was in snake and dove training. When a young christian actor portrays an undesirable character with rough language or lascivious desires in a theatre piece that reminds us of how **we** sinful humans can struggle to find meaning in God's world, that is training in Christ's snake and dove approach. The Lord does not invite us to be prim people who see no evil, hear no evil, and never talk about what is evil. The apostle Paul puts it clearly:

Don't be children in your knowledge of things: you can even be babies in doing evil! but become mature in your knowledge of things.

(1 Corinthians 14:20)

—snake-mature (*phrésin teleioi*) but childlike-dove (cf. Luke 9:46–50,

Matthew 18:1–14).

This is Jesus Christ's handshake for you graduates, whatever field you enter—parenting, business, nursing, laboratory work, teaching literature, policing, artistry. . . The "snake and dove policy" is not meant as a shake-and-bake formula to make things pleasant. I don't know whether you can work as snake and dove for Microsoft Corporation without gradually being eaten alive. I don't know, if you become pastor of a congregation or work in christian circles later, whether you will be tending real sheep or simply people dressed like sheep. I don't know, if you go on for christian or unchristian graduate studies, whether you will be seduced into cynical sniping at the fleas in Christ's body and let the excited vision of your childlike faith be eroded or not. But I do know it is wise not to be "up for rent" to the legion of principalities looking for housing in our culture. Instead, please God; walk away today from your Redeemer College graduation filled with the Holy Spirit intent not to become successful and genteel, but to become a body of worldliwise snakes and innocent doves joyfully serving in the coming of Christ's Rule on earth.

I close with God's letter Paul wrote to the Philippian Christian believers, echoing ironically Moses' graduation speech:

> . . . **especially now . . . with awe and trembling** [=in deep humility] **continue working out your salvation because God it is who is working in you both the willing and the bringing forth results to God's satisfaction. Do all the stuff without grumbling and clever arguments, so that you may remain blameless and innocent children of God without blemish smack in the midst of a crooked and perverse generation, among whom you will shine like stars in the cosmos, holding up the word of life, so that in the day of Christ's** [glorious return, your Redeemer profs, staff, and administrators] **will be mighty pleased that they did not** [teach] **in vain, did not labor so hard in vain.**
> (Philippians 2:12–16; cf. Deuteronomy 32:5ff).

A few sources read for this address

Barth, Karl. *Erklärung des Philipperbriefes* (Zürich: Evangelischer Verlag A.G. Zollikon, 1947).

Campolo, Tony. "Time to Meet the Challenge," *Third Way* 22:4 (May 1999): 15.

Goudzwaard, Bob. "Tussen de klippen door," in *Bewogen Realisme: Economie, cultuur, oecumene*, eds. Herman Noordegraaf and Sander Griffoen (Kampen: Kok, 1999), 5–27.

Johnson, Sylvia A. *Snakes*. Photographs by Modoki Masuda (Minneapolis:

Lerner, 1986).
Kittel, Gerhard. "ἀκέραιος" in *Theologisches Wörterbuch zum Neuen Testament,* ed. G. Kittel (Stuttgart: W. Kohlhammer, 1933), 1:209–10.
Machiavelli, Niccolò. *Il Principe* [c. 1517–19/pub. 1532] *e altri scritti minori* (Milano: Ulrico Hoepli, 1924).
Rang, Lloyd. "BA and Common Sense: Michel Foucault, Mike Harris and my Mom do lunch," in *Redeemer Images* 13:1 (Fall 1998): 8–11.

Graduating to Glocal Martyrdom

The wise person in the Older Testament biblical book of Ecclesiastes answers the question "Is a deathdate better than a birthday?" by saying, "Yes! Entering a home touched by grief is better than walking into a house toasting champagne, because death is the conclusion of every man and woman, and when the living (face it), they have to take it to heart" (7:2).

Is a graduation day from Trinity Christian College better than the day you entered as a freshman or fresh woman?

It depends, let's say, on whether one faces what is happening to you today.

Georges Rouault's bittersweet print, "Il serait si doux d'aimer" (1914–48), "It would be so sweet to love" [#40], shows a mother tenderly gesturing with her extended arm outward to where the nestling child needs to go, to places where the protecting love of the older generation is traded in for circumstances less safe, where you cannot, it seems, be your childlike self, love and be loved, without getting trampled to competitive death.

[#40] Georges Rouault, *It would be so sweet to love*, 1948

I do not mean to do a variation on the old commencement bromide of "Okay, fellows, now you are go-

---

Commencement convocation address at Trinity Christian College, Palos Heights, Illinois, 14 May 2011 AD.

ing to go out into the **real** world!"

No, the real world of opportunities and failure, of disappointments and acts of kindness, has been present inside your Trinity education too. You do not escape sin and blessing in daily action by going to a Christian college. However, if you have been an actual student, instead of majoring in extra-curricular affairs, you have enjoyed the wonderful gift at Trinity of an "academic" fix on your activity.

That is, you can err in a biology lab dissection experiment without killing somebody; you can be wrong in a theology class without being declared a heretic; you can do musical, mathematical, basketball exercises before you face the test of execution; you are given time to "practice" teaching and not be fully responsible yet for the lives of young learning children. **The college years are a wonderful time to make mistakes**, because they can be corrected by teachers in this "academic" training setting of trust.

There is less leeway for bad consequences in botched trial-and-error raising of your children, in a failed medical diagnosis or surgical activity, or in implementing unwise commercial decisions. The protecting cover of an "academic holding position" (like a circling airplane needing to wait to land at O'Hare) goes! when you graduate from Trinity. (That's why anybody who continues on to "graduate" studies must be wary of doing so just to avoid facing direct life responsibilities of landing, because "academics" can dry up and be good for nothing in God's world, unless they envelop their research and pick priorities with a holy spirit of Wisdom.)

So, you are graduating, prepared by Trinity's solid educational program in the tradition of the historic christian Reformation of Martin Luther and Jean Calvin, and you are called by God, I propose, to "glocal martyrdom."

What does that mean?

"Glocal" is a fairly new English word that combines "global" and "local"—"glocal." Biblically formed followers of Jesus Christ, from whatever christian tradition, develop a cosmic **global vision** and a humbled sense of **local responsibility** in a united (bifocal) **glocal perspective and task**. "God did not send God's Son into the cosmos in order to condemn the cosmos, but in order that the whole cosmos (=environment, plants, animals, society of humans) be saved by God's Son" (John 3:17). And, said the resurrected Jesus to his prospective disciples, "You will receive power when the Holy Spirit comes upon you all to be witnesses of me, (of my bringing in the Reign of God, both locally) in Jerusalem, all of Judea, Samaria—that is, Chicago, mid-Western USA—to the very ends of the earth—Europe, Ecuador, Asia, Australia" (cf. Acts 1:8, 3).

Glocal martyrdom: we do not have to save the world. The triune God fully revealed in the historical Jew Jesus Christ with the Holy Spirit will see to that. We who are "Christians" in more than name only have to be faithful, obedient witnesses locally first of all, **actually practicing, living the Lord's merciful just Rule acoming over the earth**, be bringing shalom to all creatures on earth under the sun. Μαρτύριον in Newer Testament Greek means "witness." Martyrdom means "giving a testimony . . . that could cost you your livelihood, your life."

Is that my recommendation to you who will be graduates within the hour?

Scottish poet Robbie Burns, you probably know, has that famous poem, "To a louse, on seeing one on a lady's bonnet at church." In the last stanza are the lines:

> O wad some Power the giftie gie us, / To see oursels as ithers see us!
> Oh, would some Power give us the gift to see ourselves as others see us!

From his pew sitting behind the lady decked out in her Sunday best, the poet noticed a dirty "ugly, creepin blasted wonner" of a louse crawling over the fancy fine clothes—

> How daur ye set your fit upon her— / Sae fine a lady?

But the moral the poet settles for is that if we could see ourselves with others' eyes, it would free us from many a blunder, foolish notions, fashionable airs in dress, way of life, and "ev'n devotion!"

Do you know how others in the globalized world see us educated, graduated Americans?

In 1967, just before the so-called "Seven Day War" in which Israel swiftly demolished Egyptian military forces and took over the Sinai peninsula, my wife and I were traveling in Egypt with a German archaeological group, speaking German, passing for Germans, since Americans were not loved during that time of Secretary of State Foster Dulles. Our Egyptian guide, at the Aswan Dam site that the Russians were now building since America had abruptly pulled out, apparently told a group of young Egyptian men hanging around, "There are a couple of Americans here." So they came over, faced us: "Why you no like Nasser!?" As we talked, they asked to see our American passport. I showed it to them; even let the leader hold it for a brief moment. I saw from his fixed, fascinated stare what that American passport meant to him, even though we were an enemy: Power! Prosperity! Work and Happiness! practically unimaginable for his stymied generation. And he was holding this pure gold ticket in his hand!

That American Dream of ivory palaces in the sky was brilliantly pictured by Thomas Cole's four-part series, *Voyage of Life*. Image 41 is the soul of *Youth* (1842) setting out to reach the holy grail of life, liberty, in the pursuit of happiness guaranteed by the US Constitution, blessed

[#41] Thomas Cole, *Voyage of Life: Youth*, 1842

by his guardian angel on the shore. The Idealist aspiration colors much of American cultural history, and resonates with peoples throughout the world. Jules Breton's sentimental *The Song of the Lark* (1884) [RA #77] was the most popular painting at the Chicago Art Institute during the widespread depression of the 1930's, probably because it gilds the barefoot working poor with a halo of sunrise light and imagined, inspirational bird song—an utterly unreal escape for the urban unemployed or those "blessed" with menial assembly line drudgery.

An underside to how others see us with an American passport is this mural [#42] painted by graduate students on the wall reserved for each graduating class at the Rands Afrikaans Universiteit in Johannesburg, South Africa, which I photographed in 1992, almost 20 years ago. It depicts student hijinks, but up in the far corner is a sad comment about us and the Viet Nam expedition and subsequent military interventions where the stars in "The stars and stripes forever" march slide down into crosses on graveyards and the Statue of Liberty becomes a stalking Grim Reaper. Without making a political comment about the invasion of Iraq and Superpower America's embroilment in the killing fields of Afghanistan and Pakistan today, I am just showing you how certain others see the lice on our well-cut and Idealistic clothes.

[#42] Rands Afrikaans Universiteit student mural [detail] (1992)

The Trinity registrar wrote me that you twenty year old graduates are "ready to take on the world." If your eyes are open glocally, you know the world at large is distraught and speckled with violent abuse. Not just God's earthquakes and tsunami's in Japan, Chile, Haiti, Indonesia—California and British Columbia are still due—but human wars over clean drinking water and boundaries, life-and-death questions like "Can we dispense **generic** drugs to the poor who are sick unto death? Who has the right to pack a gun? Can **anybody** immigrate into 'the land of the free and the home of the brave'?" What will your Trinity Christian College graduate glocal witness be in (American) society?

Trinity art professor Dayton Castleman gives a good imaginative example when he witnesses in an old God-forsaken stone penitentiary outside Philadelphia with a very thick steel pipe that threads its up and down corridors and right through stone walls surfacing out into the prison exercise yard where it finally scales the impassible wall: once over on the other side, the blood red pipe (not a silver lining!) multiplies into a seven-fold set of organ pipes trumpeting a "Hallelujah! Freedom!" chorus [#43].

[#43] Dayton Castleman, *The End of the Tunnel*, 2005

I find this site-specific art piece called "The End of the Tunnel" (2005) to be a fine corrective to the insatiable ambition integral to achieving "the (Idealistic) American Dream," because the bright red pipe expresses a more humbled search, through obstacles, with a patient hope for finding the Way to become free . . . to praise, and thank God. The glocal martyrdom the Lord God calls us to, also you graduates as well as your parents and friends here present, is to give hope in service, not rise to success, to heal the world, not bomb it—sometimes I wish I were a Mennonite—to rehabilitate prisoners, not neglect them into incorrigibility, to give priority to the handicapped, not push them aside. The task

Scripture clearly posits is: "**bear one another's burdens, and in this way you will fulfill the law** *of Christ*" (Galatians 6:2).

I do not know you students, but I know personally many of your professors in philosophy, sociology, art, theology, literature, psychology, communications, chemistry, and I know they have articulated and embodied, along with their colleagues, the Reformational heritage Trinity stands for—"capturing every notion (and practice) to make them obedient to Christ" (2 Corinthians 10:4–5). That is how you students have been trained. And my final point is that that yoke is light! It fits well over your graduating shoulders, even if it makes you feel maladjusted in our Darwinian survival-of-the-fittest society. Glocal martyrdom is not a "downer": **with the worldwide vision of this being God's world, to which Jesus Christ will return! joyfully give away your life to enact locally the peace of the Lord.**

You see, I have eaten in the Trinity cafeteria; the amazing surplus of good food there is staggering, available for the taking (once you have paid the piper). How can anyone who eats this luxuriously daily ever understand, I asked myself, what "hunger" is? I heard an earlier Trinity graduate, Elvia Rodriegez, say last month in a meeting here, that when she first came onto Trinity's campus, it seemed like an "Enchanted forest." Well, I hope you graduates will have the eyes to see that Chicago itself is . . . a burning bush where God says, "Take off your shoes and make my presence known on the streets here, and to the uttermost parts of the earth."

When you business graduates walk past this city street [#44], resolve again to open up thrifty commercial deals to the liberating profit of generosity for the neighbor. This mural-decorated building in the Pilsen district downtown (photographs taken by Professor John Bakker) is a hostel for the homeless—no home to go to!—for the unemployed who are hungry, destitute, who are losing their human dignity, while across the street a non-Trinity-graduated real estate developer has built a colorless, pricey condominium building looking like a formidable, unfriendly bunker.

When you Education majors become teachers, or even principals, persist in giving the difficult or autistic unruly child in class, the extra mile of love, though it wear you out.

When you nursing graduates become overworked hospital caregivers or serve in an African village without adequate medical supplies, remember this sculpture by Britt Wikström called *Caritas* (2006) [#45] (which Professor Michael Vander Weele along with another Trinity grad-

[#44] Homeless shelter in Pilsen district, "HOPE Respect JOBS," Chicago

uate, Dr. Nicholas Vogelzang got commissioned by the University of Chicago hospital downtown; it stands in their cancer ward waiting area) where a younger man simply helps a more feeble older person put on his coat, for which the elderly fellow, as if he were Jesus (cf. Matthew 25:31–46), gives a look of quiet, bewondering gratitude.

Your graduation day from Trinity, I dare say, with Ecclesiastes, is better than your matriculating entrance day, because your profs, as a community, have spent endless hours protecting you by faithfully correcting reports and exams, so that you are now more readied to accept the glocal martyrdom of disciplined living and embodying the compassionate holy spirited rule of Jesus Christ that **is** acoming.

May you joy in this day, graduates, and go in peace.

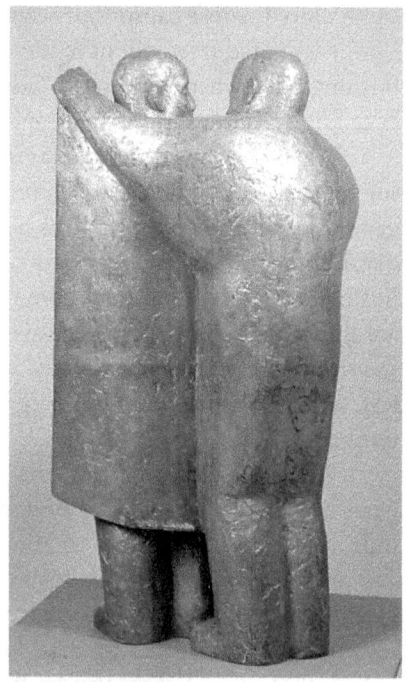

[#45] Britt Wikström, *Caritas*, 2006

REFORMED INSTITUTIONS IN TRANSFORMATION

I am a non-immigrant, American-born fellow who, thanks to H. Evan Runner, went on to the Free University of Amsterdam after Calvin College and the University of Michigan to do a Ph.D. in philosophy and comparative literature with Vollenhoven (including a foot-loose *Wanderjahr* in Basel and a glorious first married year studying in Rome, Italy—which have provided good insurance against parochialism and forged an abiding respect and gratefulness for the Reformational faith-life-and-thought tradition I came to know).

So I'll tell a few anecdotal vignettes to highlight certain points I remember as important, with hindsight, at least in my life, especially with the Institute for Christian Studies (ICS).

In 1961 I hitchhiked with Rev. Paul Szto from Queens, New York, to the ARSS (Association for Reformed Scientific Studies) Unionville Conference and met Gerald Vandezande for the first time. In quick succession I was trusted enough to speak at the conferences in Unionville and Banff (1962, 1963). At this time I believed in the need for christian philosophy, christian schooling, christian artistry, but had not been convinced by Runner and meetings of the Anti-Revolutionnaire Party held for American students in The Hague that you needed christian organizations in other societal areas of ordinary life.

Speaking for the ARSS Unionville conference in Canada, I stayed with Gerald and Wynne Vandezande. A key event happened there. Gerald happened to be on the telephone with a *Toronto Star* reporter trying to explain the CLAC (Christian Labour Association of Canada) to him. "Get on the extension," said Gerald. So I listened in. The *Star* reporter said, "You mean—like the religion has to come up out of the background into the foreground?" "Yeah, yeah. That's the idea," I heard Gerald say.

It was very exciting for me to experience this kind of direct, un-

---

Presented at a small working conference, organized by Carroll Guen, "Reformed Institutions in Transformation" in Bolton, Ontario, in June 1998.

sanctimonious witnessing to secularized people. I wanted to be a part of a community sharing the Rule of Jesus Christ this way. So that simple event convinced me of the full orb of Christ's claim the way Runner and AR Party's arguments had not been able to do.

Gerald gave me a dozen books to read, in Dutch, that were written by reflective practitioners, theorists, and theologians: at that time I was much helped by Harry Antonides' writings about a third way between Capitalism and Socialism. That book reading led to *Christian Workers, Unite!* (1964), *Labour, a Burning Bush* (1965), and the polemic later with De Koster, "Christian Camel Drivers, Unite?" (1966).

So I was brought as a naïf into the orbit of Canadian Reformational organizations by (1) Gerald's personal witness (prepared through years of study with Runner, Vollenoven, Zuidema) and (2) by reading Kuyper, A. Janse, Van Riessen, Van der Kooy, Habermehl, S.G. de Graaf, De Gaay Fortman, Goudzwaard, and others. Because I was literate and educated I could become a voice for these wild Dutch immigrants in Canada labeled "triumphalists" by their well-established North American antagonists.

During my early years as teacher at Trinity Christian College, Chicago (beginning 1959), I was voted in as a trustee of the Association for Reformed Scientific Studies (ARSS). My first introduction to the trustees is emblematic of the climate, I think, I entered:

I was picked up at the Pearson airport by Rev. Jonker and driven—we were late—to the trustees meeting in Rehoboth church. As we entered the church building I heard shouting. We walked toward where the shouting was coming from and finally opened the door to the room: there were Runner and Peter Speelman with angry red faces fiercely shouting at one another.

After being a trustee I was appointed to the curatorium and chaired that group of academic bishops for several years, during which time Henk Hart, Bernard Zylstra, and Jim Olthuis accepted appointments and came to Toronto. Meanwhile at Trinity with Bob Vander Vennen we were developing a faculty that included Arnold de Graaff, C.T. McIntire, Martin Vrieze, Harry Cook, Arie Leegwater, Rockne McCarthy, Emily Brink, Bill and Gloria Stronks, Phil Holtrop, Peter Steen, Richard Russell. . . .

During the late '50s with our Chicago Social Action Seminars we invited Gerald and Bernard Zylstra down to debate with AFL/CIO bigwigs on "closed shop" and "christian political parties"—heady stuff—and later flew Jim Olthuis down regularly one semester to teach a course in ethics with me at Trinity. The radicality of Trinity faculty largely integrated by "the Kingdom vision," combined with evening events of a societal-political nature breathing the same spirited perspective, led, I believe, to unusual blessing in the lives of many students and parents during those years in Chicago.

Up in Toronto as ARSS curatorium we rode herd on a different bronco. I remember one meeting when we met with a delegation of students, Robert Carvill and Horace Baker. It seems their practice was to walk into church at the last minute with their large Jerusalem Bibles ostentatiously visible, sit in the front row of the worshipers, and then after the service at the exit door engage the minister in heated discussion about the faults of his sermon. This was causing some problems in Public Relations. As Robert told Jack Vos, Remkes Kooistra, Paul Schrotenboer, Peter Jonker, and myself why the churches were a mess if not apostate and we should start another one, Paul Schrotenboer asked why they thought theirs would be any better.

That is, I remember the early years at Unionville and 141 Lyndhurst as in fact visionary, not to say ecstatic (graced by "chocolate milk"), combative, stepping on toes, in which a Kuyperian biblical vision embodied live in certain frisky people united almost monastically to do the obedient thing before the Lord's face, calling upon a dedicated band of committed, sacrificially giving supporters, kept going against all odds (*gewoon doordonderen*) with the élan of a Holy Spirit-led movement. Institutional organizational matters were handled by dedicated amateurs: we will do this our uncharted way.

To sum up this first stage of ICS history, let me tell of a fateful two day meeting at Knollcrest, Grand Rapids, where a delegation of myself as curator chair, director John Olthuis, and staff Henk Hart met with Calvin College President Spoelhof, Henry Stob, Lester De Koster, board member Andy Kuyvenhoven, and a couple others (Runner was not invited to be there, as I remember), to try to clear up the reasons for our "graduate university" experience in Toronto, which Calvin College felt was muscling in on their educational territory.

During the conversational babble of a coffee break there came an unexpected pause during which unintendedly Henry Stob's clear voice was heard to say to his neighbor, "That's why the ARSS must die!" (The argument during the meetings was: the CRC community can support only one university, and it should rightfully be an extension only of Calvin College and Seminary). That unrehearsed remark by Stob gives an idea of what this little Canadian "christian university" faced in the early days.

A second stage of the ICS as I experienced it came in 1972 when I as an inside outsider with family moved to Toronto to become Senior Member in Philosophical Aesthetics at 229 College Street West.

Regular graduate seminar courses became *de rigeur*. The curatorium asked us profs to pull back somewhat from our itinerant philosophical forays into the hinterlands stirring up the faith on controversial matters, and to do some serious academic work, interact with secular university associations, publish professionally, give rigorous theoretical grounding in certain fields worthy of the M.A. and Ph.D. degrees that we were fighting, with the help of Citizens for Public Justice (CPJ), to receive government recognition for, and to turn this l'Abri-like haven for disaffected brilliant intellectual castoffs from other institutions into a bona fide academic graduate institution that would teach Aristotle's poetics, Hegel's phenomenology, the aesthetics of Cassirer and Mikel Dufrenne, Gadamer and the theology of Karl Rahner, along with Dooyeweerd writings.

John Olthuis called this step, if I remember correctly, "consolidation" of our task. Those '70s and '80s were painfully sweet years of building up a new generation of gifted students to think biblically and to go on to culturally formative service in many places in the world; a cloud of witnesses today, it seems to me. Despite the sin and lack of money and the organizational ineptitude—Senior Members hardly brooked any supervising administrator in-house—God blessed the ICS richly.

External relations improved: Bob Knudsen set up a meeting for Westminster Seminary faculty and ICS Senior Members to talk for a day at a church I knew lay precisely halfway between Philadelphia and Toronto. At that meeting, after asking, "What's the Institute's doctrine of God?" and receiving a blank response, the Westminster faculty for the first came to realize the ICS was not a seminary (and therefore not a competitor). Authorities at Calvin College gradually realized that despite the rhetoric, ICS was not planning for a full-fledged university campus (and therefore was not a serious threat). Regent College of Vancouver and ICS held a symposium together at the York University campus on "Creation and Christian Philosophy" (1975), and around this time Jim Houston said publically that it seemed to him ICS was no longer throwing stones at their neighbors' windows.

These are the banquet years of *Vanguard* under the editorship of Robert Carvill, Bonnie Green, and Bert Witvoet, which did reach a non-Dutch readership too. This is the time of the fierce, ugly debates at Wedge Publishing Foundation on whether to publish university press tomes like

Zuidema's *Communication and Confrontation* (1972) or popular booklets. This is also the brief decade of the Patmos flower, where we found out that the "vision" for christian art garners support easier than when you have an actual imperfect opening of artworks at 561 Richmond Street West basement, which were not little masterpieces. (Designer Willem Hart, I should like to mention, is an unsung saint, I think, who was incredibly important in the development of almost all the Canadian Reformational institutions in existence, not only Patmos, especially these years).

During this proliferation of Toronto-based cultural activity, also because ICS was learning to concentrate on its specific task of graduate mentoring and scholarship, individuals discovered you can't attend everything—events at ICS, at CLAC, CJL/CPJ, Patmos, local christian school society meetings, be in Western Canada as well as Ontario, serve as deacon or elder in the local congregation; and if you try to show up everywhere you become frazzled. So ICS Senior Members did come to operate at more of a remove from the supporting non-academic community. Visionary language doesn't go very well at the secular Learned Societies meetings, and it takes time to think and communicate redemptive knowledge in another universe of discourse than that of our supporters.

Willem Hart, artist, art designer, mainstay of former Patmos Gallery, key graphic communicator for Reformational outreach in Toronto, 1960s–present

And then there were always the internal jealousies and personality tensions that afflict close communal christian organizational activity. During these years, behind the scenes, I experienced in-depth communion of the pig-headed saints with my colleagues that mediated God's grace in amazing ways. Prayer and hugs at bottom held us broken people together in a ministry that was bigger than we were as persons.

I remember one ICS retreat at which Junior Member Marcille Frederick initiated us into the healing ritual of foot-washing, which we incorporated into a concluding worship service. At a certain point Bernard Zylstra was given the towel and opportunity to wash someone's feet. He went into the praying congregation and touched Henk Hart for him to come forward. Then at the basin of water Bernie quietly washed Henk's feet, and there was peace, the apostle John might say, in heaven for the space of a half hour.

So for about 20 years, it appears to me, (1) the graduate Institute for Christian Studies came to focus on its particular, specific ministry of building a quality, graduate academic researching and teaching institution that was consciously Reformational. A younger generation of scholars was shaped by the ICS program and have distilled its redemptive vision all over the world in ways that can only be credited to the Lord's blessing and the faithfulness of many trusting people.

(2) There was a close-knit bond of persons-in-community articulating a heart-felt vision of Christ's Rule in our increasingly secularized society, surrounded by a cluster of other christian Reformational institutions, all dealing with complicated problems that admitted of no simple solutions but wherein one tried to discover a more normative way to press Christ's claims of redemption on human societal life.

A third stage of the Institute for Christian Studies began around the early '90s, I think. Since I do not feel as if I have been so deeply involved in what is current there as a new generation sets direction, finds its footing, and ramifies programs, let me close with a few general and perhaps debatable thoughts germane to this gathering on "Reformed Institutions in Transformation '98" which, I take, is minded to carry on anew the blessing of redemptive living, including redirection of education.[1]

First, a few "christian principles" for sound leadership I picked up and distilled over the years ("Principles" for me are beginning guidelines, not legal rules, not timeless rational dicta, not even ethical norms, but are posited injunctions, appels, callings to wisdom):

(1) Propose first of all something positive rather than begin with negative critique [Vollenhoven]. Critique is usually reactive and can be cheap: it takes selfless wisdom to suggest what openings should be pursued.

(2) If a christian organization is out to maintain its own cultural power base rather than make the redemptive peace of Christ tangible in service to the neighbor, it is really antichristian

---

[1] Cf. for background "Footprints in the Snow," *Philosophia Reformata* 56:1 (1991) 1–34 [academic version] {see *CE*: 235–276}; *Philosophical Aesthetics at Home with the Lord: An untimely valedictory* (Toronto: ICS, 1996, 31 pp.) [professional version] {see *NA*: 259–284}; and "The Informal Fantastic Life of a Believing Fishmonger's Son," in *In the Fields of the Lord* (Carlisle, England/Toronto: Paternoster/Tuppence Press, 1998), 23–37 [popular version].

[Van Riessen on third-generation "christian organizations" in the Netherlands]. Power struggles within an organization signal decay.

(3) Make friends of your antagonists: then they will more likely listen to your faith-insights and vision [Peter Steen's method of exporting christian philosophy]. Be winsome rather than combative: giveaway your treasures without thought of return rather than try to get *quid pro quo*.

(4) Be glad when there is a controversy or crisis: use the difficult matter to make a redemptive point to the media [Gerald Vandezande policy of being ahead of reactionary responses]. The gospel provides reorientation and patient, savvy long-term paths to follow more than short-term answers to questions arising from bad problematics.

(5) If the institutional/societal mess before you seems impossible to correct, take a small redemptive step, and then the LORD will surprise you by opening up further possibilities for healing [Goudzwaard]. God is Lord of historical time and process as well as of current impasses and tiny victories.

(6) Yes, "by their fruit you will know the health of the trees"; so if, as professor, laborer, counselor, merchant, political activist, you are not also building up the congregated churchly faithful, you are barren, clad only in the rhetoric of fig leaves [a thoughtful Bob Sweetman thinking aloud]. If there be no psalms and hymns astir in the mouths of "Reformed institutions" (the way South African blacks massed in the streets sing, or Italian peasants as they wait hours for the Pope to appear in San Pietro), if there be no "spiritual songs" with verve and bite, scared hope and victorious joy on our lips, then something is amiss, I believe. Do we still have communal songs of sturdy faith in our throats?

From where I sit behind a study desk, emeritated, I might raise the following three matters for starters:

(1) Each Holy Spirited institution and organization has its own specific task that it should exercise faithfully before the Lord with the other christian institutions in view—which may not, however, define your institution's task—as well as be geared to bring healing to the neighbor.

That means for me, ICS should not become a think-tank for CPJ; CPJ political policies are not necessarily to be those of labor-organizing

CLAC; *Christian Courier* (CC) is not to be house organ of CLAC or CPJ, but a "free-standing" weekly paper; the CRC (Christian Reformed Church of North America) goes wrong if it would try to dictate what is kosher for ICS. Yet each specific institutional member of Christ's body at large has the office to enable and fortify the other christian organizations' mission.

It was meet for me to have Patmos and the CRC Psalter Hymnal committee as my "aesthetics lab," but my philosophical aesthetics seminars were rightly conceived to be graduate level theoretical investigations, not workshops for artists to overcome the bohemian idea of artistry, or popular lectures to correct the marginalization of art and "dumbing-down" of song in middle-class society—you may do that too, but "extra-curricularly."

It is good for Redeemer and the King's College to hold up the profession of mental health counseling as a worthy occupation for which they institute Psychology majors, indirectly supporting Shalem [Christian Mental Health Association] and Christian Counseling Services (CCS). Since the CLAC is non-adversarial in policy, they would be proper mediators in a dispute between christian school teachers and governing boards of parents, provided the non-business nature of schools is honored. CPJ expertise rightly aided ICS's brief to obtain a charter from the government, but CPJ's struggle for aboriginal rights is closer to its mandate. CC is expected to do investigative reporting that will publicly broadcast the struggles for justice CLAC and CPJ undertake. CRC pastors should teach congregations that officers of CLAC, CPJ, ICS, CC, CFF of O (Christian Farmers Federation of Ontario), CCBF (Canadian Christian Business Federation), CCS, and Shalem are also "missionaries"! and worthy of tithes (but that they are not "para-church organizations").[2]

That is, the guiding principle of an institution's specifically limited task inextricably exercised in concert with neighboring christian institutions encourages confederation rather than a dominant organization that calls the shots. And one should not expect organizational unity to bring about a united witness, for it is only, in any judgment, a living single-minded, biblically shaped *community* envisioning Jesus Christ's compassionate Rule over the world that can effect such genuine inter-supportive care.

(2) It is easier, I believe, to start a christian organization than to keep it

---

[2] As apparently designated by Ray Elgersma, "Reformed Institutions in Transition," 1998, typescripts, p. 1.

going well once the élan of the first generation has spent itself and the second generation's sins and mistakes start to catch up with you. It is crucial both intra-institutionally and inter-organizationally, I think, to reiterate for each succeeding generation the founding biblical vision so it kindles the centering Holy Spirited passion of our variegated communal christian service.

Many christian school teachers today, I am told, have no habit of thinking Christ's Rule embraces the very contours of teaching their subject matter, or what that might mean beyond good morality. Many pastors have little sense of how to bring the full counsel of God to bear on actual daily life in a liturgically moving way that shows Older and Newer Testament scripture together proclaiming hope and direction for those in the pew needing emergency treatment in finding lasting meaning for their lives. Many workers/business people and citizens like us are so fascinated and frustrated by the insidious commercialistic Mammon standard of living we inhabit that "sacrifice" is an unintelligible foreign word, so we miss its balm. Many intelligent students are so taken by Derrida, let's say, rather than traditional Rationalism with its short black/white answers to complex affairs, they flirt with the skeptical fire of *différance* (deferred differences of possible positions) rather than undertake the difficult pointing of their thought toward a destination with positive analytic wisdom.

So, as Mekkes always practiced, somebody in your organization, is my thought, must keep on articulating afresh, with contagious accents, the old, old story of the blessed Rule of Jesus Christ over every inch of cultural existence. Not as shibboleth "doctrine," not as "emotional motivator," not as mantra of "our peculiar Kuyperian heritage," but as the very meaty directional call of the LORD to be obeyed by the communion of saints at large, which convicts the new generation by bringing actual offerings of its blessing into various zones of human activity. Otherwise we face the pain of punishing dispersion of our descendants, if not extinction of "Reformed Institutions" in God's secularized world.

(3) A third-generation[3] Reformational christian organization usually either goes stale in its traditional tracks, metamorphoses through synthesis underneath into something hardly recognizable though by the same name, or renews its vision and reconfirms, newly translates, its founding service more precisely and winsomely, "transforming" (I personally prefer "reforming") itself to be more conformable to God's will for its task in

---

3   Cf. my "Third Generation, *Calvin College Chimes* 46 (2 May 1952): 2.

this generation (Romans 12:1–2).

Given the hardening of mega-corporate secularity in society and the distrust among thoughtful christian leaders for Utopian projects (because our culture thinks "the one constant is change,"[4]—which thesis I do not believe; as Sander Griffioen says in his recent article "Cultuuromslag aan de VU," change is not unstoppable![5]): given what seems to be our straitened cultural predicament today, I sometimes wonder whether "Reformed institutions" will not fall into the temptation of settling for what one might call "the 'little-story' solution": do your own individual thing for Christ, brightening the corner where you are, being instrumental in the conversion of persons who possess the power to change certain things, and lobby hard for and against selected ethical flashpoints.

With Paul while in prison I would say that if the compassionate judgment of Christ is proclaimed, even from inadequate or false motives, praise God (Philippians 1:12-18). But what I hope will not get lost among those who would provide leadership in the rising generation are the rich horizons and buoyant holy spirit to the endeavors here represented, which convicted me to become Reformational in the ICS[6]:

(a) A radical biblical faith-vision of Christ's Rule out of which we **communally** live and stay faithful—breathing hope to God's folk as a **peoplehood** is critical—and not be geared to success [Patmos ended in 1979, but it did not "fail."];

(b) Living immersed in the Reformed (French, Dutch, German—European) faith-thought tradition by reading the founding writings so that you become evangelical-Reformational in your

---

4 So Ray Elgersma, *op. cit.*, 5.

5 S. Griffioen in *Vinden en Zoeken, Het bijzondere van de Vrije Universiteit* (Kampen: Kok, 1997), 75.

6 "I have used this term since 1959 to catch several related meanings. 'Reformational' identifies (1) a life that would be deeply committed to the scriptural injunction not to be conformed to patterns of this age but to be re-formed by the renewal of our consciousness so that we will be able to discern what God wills for action on earth (cf. Romans 12:1-2); and (2) an approach in history to honor the genius of the Reformation spearheaded by Luther and John Calvin in the sixteenth century, developed by Groen van Prinsterer and Abraham Kuyper in the nineteenth century, as a particular christian tradition out of which one could richly serve the Lord; and (3) a concern that we be communally busy reforming in an ongoing way rather than standing pat in the past tense (*ecclesia reformata semper reformanda est*)." Quote from my "Understanding the Scriptures: How to Read and not to Read the bible" (1969), published in an expanded edition under the title of *How to Read the Bible to Hear God Speak: A study in Numbers 22–24* (Sioux Center/Toronto: Dordt College/Tuppence Press, 2003), 39, n.

historiographical blood—our working perspective did not just drop out of heaven—seasoned by hard choices, and not be just a fellow-traveler who knows the slogans [a bibliography is tell-tale of one's adopted communion of the saints]; and

(c) Deepen one's institutional service with time-consuming, professional diligence that remains geared to tough love for the body of Christ and neighbor at large, rather than adopt the omnivorous efficient factory model of producing "christian" products for sale.

I know, the difficult moot problem of deciding priorities is not exactly a reflection of the quality of one's faith in our Lord, but which priorities one does choose for an institution is somehow related to one's committed faith perspective and sense of task and timing. Isaiah 54 would give me my lead:

So, people, make the place your tent covers larger:

Let the tent tarpaulins where you have settled down be stretched out farther—don't hold back!

Lengthen the tent ropes you have, and hammer the tent stakes in more firmly!

That's right: You will be spreading out both to the right and to the left,

And your children's children will come to rule over nations;

They shall come to dwell in the cities people have deserted. (vv. 2-3)

A couple of my priorities would be: ICS should take the ten years it needs to understand the many Chinese Christians in Toronto and humble itself to recruit them gradually as Junior Members. Canadian Reformational institutions should free themselves to prospect more for committed money in the USA.

And leaders of the various "Reformed institutions"—perhaps in this very room—amid all our talk of "organizational strategies" might do well to find occasion to wash each other's feet. When my feet have been washed by one of my colleagues, a Junior Member, or a stray letter, it has been a moving human occasion for me humbly to thank God and carry on light-heartedly what the Lord has given to do together in us earthen vessels.

BOOK REVIEW

Reading Ecclesiastes: Old Testament Exegesis and Hermeneutical Theory by Craig G. Bartholomew. Analecta Biblica no. 139. Rome: Editrice Pontificio Insituto Biblico, 1998. Pp. vii + 319. $ 39.99.

This book has scope and depth, and is written with the lucid style of the author's having mastered the topic. The footnoted documentation bristles with good articles for follow-up, while the main text reads like a fascinating historical novel. A pastoral concern always permeates the scholarship.

How main commentators understand Ecclesiastes is made a test case for investigating the relationship between Old Testament exegesis and the (often-covert) hermeneutical theory governing a given exposition. Bartholomew also shows that every theological hermeneutic depends on certain philosophical decisions regarding the nature of history and the character of literary texts.

Bartholomew's historical survey of the many interpretations of Ecclesiastes before and after the Reformation, during and after the Enlightenment, and on into our postmodern times is simply brilliant. Seldom does one meet a discussion of difficult thinkers and complex issues with such focused precision, not oversimplified, yet elucidated with conversational ease.

Chapter 3 is a thorough exploration of the historical-critical method that has long dominated Old Testament study (c. 1750–1914). Bartholomew goes behind Wellhausen and Gunkel to show how their Romantic Idealist philosophy of history and prejudice for treating the "inner life of great individuals as the key to history" (88) reduced biblical hermeneutics to a critique of sources, which adherents of the method pretended to carry out without any philosophical bias. The result was a focus for interpretation on "reconstructed texts" rather than on the biblical text given us as canonic by the church.

First published in *Calvin Theological Journal* 34:2 (1999): 443–45.

Chapters 4 and 5 describe the corrective the Bernard Child's canonical approach brought to reading Scripture and how the theory and practice of "New Criticism" and "Structuralism" brought the literary nature of the Bible to the fore, challenging the Positivist prejudice that trusts only propositional fact as knowledge. Bartholomew demonstrates how these new orientations in A. G. Wright (118–22) and M. V. Fox (143–46, 154–57) lead to a close reading of the Ecclesiastes text, with special attention to its poetic structure and narrative features, and how a crucial decision on what genre Ecclesiastes is affects reading this section of God's word. Bartholomew also investigates at length (158–70) Fox's analysis of the epilogue to Ecclesiastes (12:8–14) because how one relates the epilogue to the main body of the Ecclesiastes text is a crux for one's interpretation.

Chapter 6 is a deft, clear treatment (no mean feat) of Derida's program for writing, and Baudrillard's notion of the hyperreal world of consumerism on our hands, and how such worldview affects the reading of Ecclesiastes. Bartholomew shows how postmodern skepticism of metanarrative can at least call into question (178–80) the hidden agenda of "neutral" scholarship in academia for doing Old Testament studies. However, the "imperialistic pluralism" that denies "there is a correct way to read such texts" (202, 260) would be simply another tyranny.

In the final chapter, Bartholomew puts together a hermeneutical method shaped by a Christian perspective distilled from studies by Thiselton (*New Horizons*), Wolterstorff (*Divine Discourse*), Sternberg (*Poetics of Biblical Narrative*), W. Booth (*Rhetoric of Fiction*), and work by Fishbane, Ray Van Leeuwen, and others that honors literary features of the God-breathed Scriptures as clues to the message of the text. Bartholomew's "communicative model" (with similarities to speech-act theory) values texts as interpersonal communications, not as disembodied texts (219 n. 39). Therefore, texts are accorded rights "to be heard and criticized *objectively*" (220); the reader is obliged to pay attention to what was indeed said (215), even though each reader brings his or her own baggage to the interpretation (225-26). Bartholomew favors a "bibliotropic" exegesis (203, 210, 226).

Bartholomew's reading of Ecclesiastes as "a developed wisdom form of the royal testament or fictional autobiography cast in a frame-narrative" (228) is thorough and convincing. He examines (with Fox) the irony of key matters like *chokmah* and (with Ogden) the structured repetition of the joy passages with the *in thob* formula ("there is nothing better than . . ."). Qoheleth is trying empirically to find out an answer to the root problem of what you get from all your human toil (241–44).

Bartholomew's argument is that these signal repetitions (which I would call refrains) leave the implied reader hanging between (1) life as an enigmatic misery and (2) daily joy as a gift one should receive. These repeated contradictions "under the sun" are finally resolved by the Ecclesiastes periscope 11:7–12:8: remember your Creator *before* you encounter death (250–53). Therefore, the proverb of Ecclesiastes 11:7 indicates the final positive step that Qoheleth takes in the tension of life's facing vanity, and the epilogic frame (12:9–14) underscores this orthodox affirmation.

To put it briefly, Bartholomew concludes that "Ecclesiastes is addressed to third or fourth BC disillusioned Israelites who were in danger of succumbing to Greek skepticism. Ecclesiastes is an ironical exposure of an empiricistic epistemology which seeks wisdom through personal experience and analysis without the 'glasses' of the fear of God. . . . The resolution of this paradox is found in the fear of God (rejoicing and remembrance) which enables one to rejoice and apply oneself positively to life in the midst of all that one does not understand, including and especially death" (268).

So refreshing about this scholarly study is its forthright, biblically Reformed intelligence that asks only to be heard and taken seriously today, in dialogue with interpretations of Ecclesiastes by other hermeneutical communities of quite different philosophical stripes. Bartholomew is asking for a biblical Christian hermeneutic voice in the secular postmodern academy/university (181, 212). He shows that taking (from Sternberg, 139–42) the literary (aesthetic), historiographic, and ideological (confessional) aspects of biblical text as structurally integral to a believing Christian standpoint produces a reading of Ecclesiastes that is illuminating, compelling, and can afford Christian public truth.

Bartholomew's book challenges Old Testament theological hermeneuticians to probe their philosophical underpinnings rather than pretend they have none (178), and encourages biblical theologians "to become more theologically literate" (181 n.36, 269) if they would exegete the full counsel of God. Seminary training, whose specialty is "*church hermeneutic*"—you need to come up with the approved dogmatic reading—may be "in danger of short-circuiting the philosophical scaffolding of a [Bible-true] hermeneutic" (209 n.9, 268).

While I might phrase certain matters a bit differently, Bartholomew's reading of Ecclesiastes seems right to me and gives a full-orbed interpretation that helps one see the self-uncritical blind spots where most other major expositions of the book run stuck. Yet Bartholomew has the friendly knack to credit the most disparate exegetes with insights that contribute to his own particular, integrated exegesis of Ecclesiastes.

My hunch would be that comparison of Ecclesiastes' message (formulated precisely, 263) with apocryphal wisdom writings might strengthen the brief that Ecclesiastes (and Job) are not so distant from the earlier biblical wisdom tradition of Proverbs as is sometimes thought (255–60). The wise of the intertestamentary period and the scribes of Jesus' day would indeed make the faithful examinations of Qoheleth immersed in the weal and woe of society look like the search of an empiricist.

That the Vatican's Pontifical Institute chose to publish this excellent, reader-friendly Reformed scholarship is a cause for thanksgiving. Old Testament introductory classes at college or seminary would benefit much if they were assigned to study a couple chapters of *Reading Ecclesiastes* to set their sights by. A fresh, holy spirit blows through the work, and makes one glad to be a Christian confessing God as Creator *inside* one's Old Testament hermeneutic and reading of this powerful, most relevant book of the Bible.

Carlos Martínez Mime Actor

Perhaps the most important mime in Europe these days is the Spaniard Carlos Martínez. He has performed for more than 25 years in over 30 countries. Gesture is practically a worldwide language, and mime speaks without the strain of verbal translation.

Recently Carlos had put in German words his personal reflections (*Desde el camerino*) about the art work of performing as a mime. Carlos quietly talks about painting on the mask in his dressing room before a performance, speaking without words to his cosmetic tools on a red towel as silent friends, as the tension of stage fright mutates into waiting time to step out onto the stage. Together they are going to make invisible realities visible.

[#46] Carlos Martinez, mime artist

The mime's **mask** is like the white gown of a bride dressed for the wedding ceremony. The mime's mask distances a person for the occasion from one's ordinary life and appearance, and gives the facial gestures, especially the outlined eyes, white-gloved hand and nimble feet, the focused presence of forthright symbolic meaning.

It takes a concentrated hour in the privacy of his dressing room to put on the exacting pantomime mask. After the performance it is Carlos' practice to wipe off the mask with his red towel in front of the audience, in ten seconds, to show he is also a normal person. In daily life persons often wear masks they cannot wipe off in ten seconds, reflects Carlos.

Pantomime artists are not "**hypocrites**," but turn ordinary body language into suggestion-rich knowledge, and make it available to anybody.

Posted at http://www.artway.eu/ in November 2010 and later published in the Christian Courier (10 January 2011), 10.

Nobody is illiterate in watching pantomime. The artistically crafted silent gesture of the mime helps an attentive audience hear the many unspoken voices in the reservoir of silence: deep misery, whimsical joys, human cunning, sudden surprise.[1]

Carlos has a program called "Human Rights," another program on "My Bible," another program on what is "Hand Made." Of course we will practice being mimes in heaven, Carlos once told me with a smile. "What else could it mean in Revelation 8:1, '. . . there was silence in heaven for about half an hour'"?

This little book by Carlos Martínez, *Desde el camerino*, is a publishing artwork: generous white space framing black print with red subtitles; close-up color photography by Bernd Eidenmüller, with aphoristic comment.[2] The whole product is gentle, ingenuous, and very wise. It reminds me of Jun'ichiro Tanizaki's book of years ago (1933), *In Praise of Shadows*.

---

1 A supplementary reading can be found in C. Seerveld, "The Meaning of Silence for Daily Life and Sunday Worship," *In the Fields of the Lord: A Seerveld reader*, ed. Craig Bartholomew (Toronto Tuppence Press, 2000), 294–307.

2 Its excellent translation into English by Ryan Jacob, *From the Dressing Room: Reflections on the (silent) art of mime* (2011; ISBN: 978-84-614-8359-4) is available at: www.carlosmartinez.es/#/en/catalogue/.

A Worship Service Where Two People Walked Out

Recently I was leading a church worship service, and a middle-aged couple walked out. Maybe they were offended at something, I thought.

After the worship service I found out their names and was told how to find their home. I drove there and found three couples sitting together outdoors.

"Did you walk out because you were offended?" I asked one man.

"No, but I wanted to walk out," he said, and his wife nodded agreement. "*He's* the one who walked out," pointing to the other older couple.

"Yes, I was offended," the other man said.

The younger couple said nothing.

The couple had walked out of the service before the sermon because I had asked the congregation to read Psalm 115 responsively, the way one did it in Old Testament times. Not mechanically, every other verse, but more like cantor and congregation. I would read the first half of verse 9, "O Israel, trust in the Lord," and the congregation would finish the verse, "He is our help and our shield." The same way for verses 10, 11, and 12. After the final "Praise the Lord" of verse 18, we would stand up to sing a rousing, complementary psalm.

The two who walked out, and the two who wanted to walk out but didn't, felt that this responsive reading was not reverent in God's house. Maybe somewhere else would be okay, but not in a worship service. This responsive reading business was just part of all the changes going on—Singspiration books, elders rather than ministers teaching catechism, evangelization programs instead of visiting the wayward covenant youth who leave our church, and before you know it we'll have guitars for entertainment and people clapping in rhythm in church. . . .

The younger couple didn't say anything.

By this time, I had been invited to sit down.

First published in *The Banner* (19 January 1981), 8–10.

"It upset me," said the woman. "Things have been building up; the consistory knows we don't like it, and tonight it just was too much."

"Did it upset *your faith*?" I asked. "Was *your faith* weakened by what happened? That's where biblical 'offense' comes in."

"It just upset me," she said.

The mosquitoes got too bad; so, we all went inside for a cup of coffee.

"That's the way it started in Holland," said one of the men. "The sermon gets shorter; the extras get longer. One thing leads to another—"

"Why do you have to do it!" asked the woman. "Our fathers never did it, and our grandfathers never had it, and they're in heaven!"

"Why can't things be the way they used to be?" said the man.

"We need to know," I said, "what makes a church worship service right. Preaching the Word is central. That's what we come together for, first of all—to hear the Bible expounded so God speaks to us."

"It was a little too long," said the woman who didn't walk out.

"And we gather in church worship," I said, "to confess our sins and to hear of the Lord's forgiveness. The third thing is to praise God with thanksgiving and shouts of joy. Somebody said 'amen' after the sermon tonight, and it made me glad."

"I know who that was, but it strikes me as showoff," said one.

"Only the minister should say 'amen,' as a representative for us all," said the other woman.

"But, as Reformed people, we believe in the priesthood of *every believer*," I said. "It would seem to me very appropriate, too, for an elder who is gifted in praying, for example, to lead the congregational prayer sometimes in the worship service. The minister is not a pope. He shouldn't always have to do everything."

"The Bible says that if you want to pray, go into your inner chamber; don't pray in public like the Pharisees," said one of the men.

"That's true," I answered. "If you want to wrestle with God about something particular, do it at home, struggling alone or with a friend, not for show. But that doesn't mean every prayer in public except the minister's is for show! And it doesn't mean that everybody who says 'amen!' at a worship service is insincere."

The woman of the house served coffee, and I told of how my father, who has been an elder almost for life in our Christian Reformed church, has inspired me, and of how years ago I trailed along with him when he went as a Gideon to Gideon prayer meetings and we all got down on our knees to pray and people would say "Yes, Lord!" and "Amen!" during the prayer session while other people were praying. Although I found it a little strange as a Christian Reformed teenager, I knew in my heart it was utterly sincere before God.

"But that's emotional," said the woman, as we drank coffee.

"God wants our emotions too," I said.

"But we're Dutch," said the man. "We give God our emotions too, but not that way."

"And this responsive business in the worship service can split up families," said the older woman. "Some of the younger people like it, but it hurts the parents. We never did it that way. As young people we went to services twice, no questions asked. Why is the younger generation different today?"

We were sitting around the dining room table. I pointed to the huge TV in the shadows of the darkened living room. "That's why our young people are different today," I said. "We live differently."

"Before the time of your grandfather who is in heaven," I added, "people read psalms responsively in church worship services. It's thoroughly biblical. You simply can't read Psalm 136 right in public unless a congregated chorus of voices says the response, 'for his mercy endureth forever.' That's the way it was used in the time of Solomon" (cf. 2 Chronicles 7:1–3).

"But that's Old Testament," said the woman of the house. "I'm not sure we need all that history, the fighting of all those kings—do we need that today?—Solomon and all his wives! I don't respect that much!"

'You're not one of those 'fundamentalists' who walk around with just a little piece of the New Testament for your Bible, are you?" I asked.

"No, I believe the whole Bible," she said, "but it's not all straight from God. Paul says it's better not to be married, and God made us to be married. Where would we be if nobody married!"

"God didn't write the Bible," said the husband. "He inspired men to write it, and they gave their own opinions sometimes, like Paul who said this is not a commandment of the Lord—"

"No," I said. "Paul never spoke against marriage. But, there may be times when, for the good of your Christian testimony, it may be better not to be married."

"I had a minister in the Netherlands once who could preach on the dimensions of the tabernacle in a way that you knew that *every word* of the Bible, including all of Pauls' letters, was God's Word, given for our edification. You've got to know how to read it."

"We can't argue with you," said the other woman. "You know too much."

"If responsive reading was Reformed for worship services long ago, why did we lose it?" asked the man who had not walked out of the service.

"Pietism—the kind of Christian faith that is a little mystical—" I said, "mixed in with the Reformed faith and the Reformed sense of worship and made people think that almost the only way to be reverent is to be quiet. We've lost a sense of full-bodied joy and laughter in worship, and the call to use the gifts of everyone of us priests when we celebrate Christ's resurrection every Sunday."

"You hammer away at that priesthood of every believer pretty hard," said he. "The minister has more education. If I'd be asked to pray in the worship service, my knees would knock and I'd shake all over. But I can pray at home all right."

"I respect that," I said. "It's not the idea to get everybody into the act; but surely you can read half a verse in the Bible with everybody else of the congregation to give a sense of a communion of the saints at worship!"

"That's why I came here after the service," said the son of the father who had walked out, "to set Dad straight. When Pastor So-and-so at the evangelism chapel asks me to read the Scriptures for the service, I do it. No problem."

"But that's a different setting than our traditional congregational worship," said the father.

"You see, we don't tell our children what they have to think," said the mother to me.

"It really bothers me, though," said the younger married son, looking at his father, "that my wife and I feel so differently from our parents about this matter."

I didn't want to get involved in a family quarrel, because that's when most outsiders get hurt. And I was deeply touched by the honest hope the younger fellow had just expressed in the simple statement of his troubledness. So I changed the topic.

"I work for the AACS," I said.

"We know," said the other woman.

"That's why it was important for me to take away any offense I may have caused," I said, "because we do not stand for *secular* changes when we stand up for reform from secular educational philosophies. So much of our Christian life *has* been changed, for the worse, and lots of people think it's normal. That includes our worship service. People enjoy their 'Singspirational' songs because they've found our services dull, and they think it will brighten things up. But I know—I've studied music a little—so many of those tunes are *cheap music*. What we need are the Genevan melodies, the Dutch psalms, sung in tempo . . . and responsively—"

The woman of the house looked at me and got up from the table.

"I knew you didn't like those Singspirational books," said the other woman. "I could tell from the way you announced it."

"What you people need to do," I said, "is learn to sing the Genevan psalms leaving the church doors in procession, singing the psalms together marching through the streets so that the unbelievers get scared, like in the old days, and say, 'What's going on? Is the end of the world coming?' And for that you'll need trumpets and cymbals and bass drums!"

"There you go again!" said the woman of the house, and she left the room and went into the kitchen.

"I think I'd better leave," I said. "My wife will wonder whether I've had an accident."

"Will you accept my apology for any offense I gave you?" I said to the man who had walked out.

"It was good of you to come," he said.

"Here is a peace offering," said his wife, returning from the kitchen. With a smile, she handed me three long cucumbers.

I turned to the man and woman who had not walked out but had wanted to. "If I am ever invited to lead your worship services again," I said, "I will not ask for a responsive reading from the psalms, at least not until you have died."

"It was good of you to come, Reverend," said the man of the house.

"I am *not* a 'reverend'!" I almost shouted, playfully. "Do you realize the kind of burden that puts on preachers' kids at school?"

We shook hands all around, almost like at a consistory meeting.

As I rode home alone in the late night hour with my cucumbers, I thanked God for the great time I had had. This middle-aged husband and wife who had walked out of a Christian Reformed church worship service along with their serious friends and their son and daughter-in-law were solid, believing people who were rightly afraid that the daughter of Zion was like a besieged city in a garden of cucumbers (cf. Isaiah 1:8).

There was just one mistake I had made that particularly bothered me. I should not have said I wouldn't ask for a responsive psalm reading in their church until he had died. I should have said I wouldn't do it there until he and his wife could see that a Christian Reformed church congregation can read a psalm at a Sunday evening worship service, responsively, and nobody would *want* to walk out.

Say "Amen!" Somebody:
On Gospel Singing and Joyful Worship

Say Amen, Somebody should be seen by every sourpuss in the Church. It is a 1983 documentary cinema directed by George Nierenberg on the origins and status of Gospel song in North America, and a eulogy of Thomas A. Dorsey [#47] who nursed its beginnings in Chicago. The singing of his protégé, Willie Mae Ford Smith, and a celebration joined by the Barrett Sisters and O'Neal twins, with vignettes of the life-situations in which this christian music grows, makes for a colorful film and a feast of sound. It shows joy in worship. The film does not idealize the Black song unhistorically but catches and transmits its holy laughter that is in force today.

[#47] Thomas A. Dorsey, Gospel song-writer and performer

Thomas A. Dorsey was a player of the blues and band leader for Ma Rainey, but he was converted around 1926 from that laconic, gutsy kind of playful bitching to an upbeat, bright, happy sound. People accused Dorsey of bringing rhythm and blues into the church, but as a matter of fact it was rhythm and laughter. And Dorsey and Willie May Ford Smith, as well as the generation of Gospel singers they have spirited and led throughout years of conventions, believed in being anointed to sing Good News. "It's sickening to hear people singing who don't know what they're saying." Gospel song is good news! and Gospel singers have to sing from belief and for convicting, but not for show.

Dr. Dorsey wrote his famous "Precious Lord, take my hand," when he was suddenly confronted by the death of his wife in a child birth; the child also died. The song is written in the "long meter" Mahalia Jack-

---

First published in *Calvinist Contact*, 6, 20 July and 3, 24 August 1984.

son loved to sing too [#48]. So very slow the tempo, long held notes and drawn out syllables, letting singers embroider the tones, roll the sound around in one's palate and reservoir of cheeks and throat, luxuriating in the glory of human voice, a form of glossolalia really. The worded message is simple and as direct as the prayer of "Abba" (Romans 8:15–17) to the LORD. No one is looking at a watch to see how long the stanza takes, because your whole being is embodied in sound raised in praise to the only One whom you can trust in hard times.

[#48] Mahalia Jackson practices with Thomas A. Dorsey

Dorsey, Smith, and their cohorts are masters of body language. Whether Dorsey sings himself or directs others in song, his aged face pouts and winks, grimaces with understated exaggerations, totally serious and totally relaxed at the same time. Dorsey captures your heart because his mimicry is self-effacing and focused completely on the song, as if in the very presence of God. Willie Mae Ford Smith too, near the end of the film does a crippled dance, as it were, of simply walking with a beat and hallelujah across the front of the church, beside herself with happiness, content to expire. The best Gospel singers literally throw themselves into their music.

The Barrett sisters laugh while they sing, and it's contagious [#49].

[#49] The Barrett Sisters

It's not a performance gimmick for the camera, because the same pulsing vibrancy breaks things loose in a storefront worship service too. "You gotta get the Spirit movin'," says the preacher, "And turn yourself over to Jesus." The bel canto singing is as virtuoso as that of any operatic star. The difference is that the facial expressions of these Black gospel singers is homely, ordinary, festive, and happy. The enormously stout O'Neal brothers in their expensive suits know the difference between revival singing and commercialized performance for $8-a-head ticketholders. Worship is about "saving" people in song: entertainment is something people pay for.

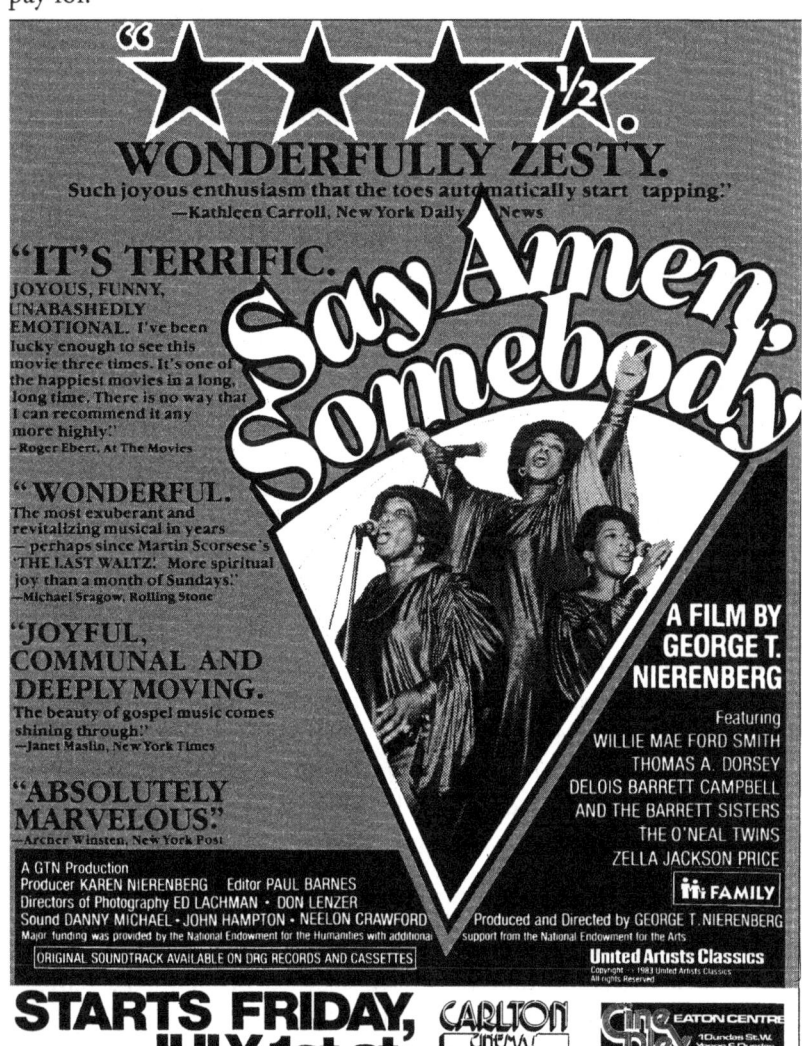

Say Amen, Somebody is a saga about Black Gospel song, how it comes out of the kitchen and washing dishes, how it lifts especially women out of the humdrum of frying sausages for their husbands into positions of ecstasy, because praise is no respecter of persons. The love of ritual—draping the room in white to purify it before the convention opens, consecrating singers for the coming year by applying a spot of oil to their foreheads, processionals and choir members swaying in tune to the beat—is the mark of mature church worship, even if it is fraught with danger. The fact that people cry during the Gospel singing, overcome by joy and sorrow, is a beautiful sight. No wonder the LORD keeps his people's tears in a bottle (Psalm 56:8–11)! [#50]

[#50] Mahalia Jackson (1962)

*   *   *

When I was a teenager, my Dad was president of the Long Island regional chapter of the Gideons. At a Bible study and prayer meeting in our house I attended, everybody got off their chair, kneeled on the floor, each facing his own chair, and we prayed together. It felt strange to me since I had never seen grown-up people in that posture before. I thought it was something only kids did before you went to sleep at night.

Our West Sayville Christian Reformed Church led the service at the Bowery mission in New York City every fifth Monday of a month (about three times a year—we had to drive in the 60 miles). One time as Senior in high school I was asked to give the message, and my brother Harold would play the trombone for special music.

During my message a warden with a broom-stick pole walked around to poke the bums in the small of their back, jerking up their heads, if they seemed to be falling asleep. It was only when my brother played a simple hymn tune that I saw a flicker of life in the gathered indigents (who had to attend the service if they wanted a supper that evening).

When the mission director, who knew a good thing when he saw it, asked whether the men wanted to hear the music again, slowly most of the beaten men there carefully and silently put up their hands. And the mellow trombone tones filled the air and touched the hearts of those lonely men once more. Sometimes, I thought reproachfully to myself, words can't do what music can.

* * *

In the old, early days of Trinity Christian College, when we had only about 50 students, I wanted to expose us WASPs to the history of black song. So I made an appointment with Thomas A. Dorsey and went to visit him on the South Side of Chicago. At his home I was ushered into the living room, spic and span and full of mementoes, with the brand new furniture (it looked like) covered over with heavy duty, see-through plastic (visible in the film, *Say Amen, Somebody*). It reminded me of the *pronkkamer* in old Dutch family homes.

Dr. Dorsey told me his story and agreed to come to the college with a few choir members. In fact he wrote a paragraph the MC could use to start off the performance, which ended, "—and now, introducing Thomas A. Dorsey!" The old showman was still alive.

They came in an extra-long, black limousine taxi, and swung up to the clubhouse entrance of Trinity with a flourish. The five women and Dorsey were all dressed in black. I had wanted a *conversation* between Dorsey and me on how Gospel song developed historically, illustrated by stages of songs. But these black folk had come to *sing*.

So they sang to our small gathering, standing around the piano, and it was a special evening. We ended by his directing us all in "Precious Lord." I'm sure our sincere response was truly mediocre by their standards. Hardly anybody said "Amen" all night long, although we did politely clap.

* * *

When Hans Rookmaaker and I visited Mahalia Jackson in the '60s, we also worshiped at the Salem (Jeru-salem) Baptist Church on Chicago's Southside, which had been her training ground. [#51]

There were three choirs of women in the worship service: the young girls on the front left sang rhythmic, bouncy songs of praise; the women still in their twenties and thirties together on the front right sang syncopated hymns of a more intricate nature; the older women singing from behind the pulpit did anthems as staid and as predictable, working up

[#51] Mahalia Jackson and two deacons from Salem Baptist Church in Chicago meeting Hans Rookmaaker (1961)

toward climax, just like the ones you'd hear in a Christian Reformed Church.

During the service one middle-aged woman in the congregation went rigid with praise. Two big ushers carried her out, stiff as a board, their hands under her neck and ankles. A half hour later she returned under her own power, calm and glad, and walked back to her front seat. "That wasn't fake," Mahalia Jackson told us after the service, "People come here to shuck their troubles, and get hope for a new week."

At 43rd and Wabash, Chicago, is the huge building where the First Church of the Deliverance meets, upwards of a thousand people [#52]. The first time our family worshiped there we put the children in the nursery, back among the stove pipes and heating ducts of the furnace room. About three hours later we retrieved them; we hadn't known the worship service lasted so long.

At offering time, everybody walks around the side and then down the main, red-carpeted aisle to the front where the deacons stand in a semi-circle and watch everybody throw their dollars down in a pile before the pulpit, ready to make change from large bills, if necessary.

And at the evening service, held from 11 p.m. to midnight, which is broadcast on the radio, it was always an unforgettable experience. I don't remember the name of the preacher who preached there in the '60s, but I remember the wizened face of the aged woman who always read

Scripture in a halting, singsongy voice of utter conviction and finality, like a matriarch or prophetess raised from the dead to bring us the living Word.

And I remember Ty Cobb's choir, a hundred or so men and women ranged in bleachers up across the whole front of the church, dressed in white robes and black tuxedoes; two electronic organs, a grand piano, two string bases and an electric bass guitar stood ready to pick up the beat. When the director pumped his arms, the sound took off, and it rained exhilarating paeans of Gospel song, cascading sound and rhythm and joy, so that you were lifted up (*sursum corde!*) into a world of heartfelt exaltation.

[#52] First Church of the Deliverance on the Southside of Chicago

* * *

A couple months ago my wife and I were taken by a friend to the evening worship at the Greater Grace Temple of the black Apostolic Church in Detroit. We came in while they were warming up and didn't leave until it was over, three and a quarter hours later.

There were testimonies from people about how God had helped them during the week, when their son was picked up by the police, when a fire had burned out the kitchen and living room—"Jesus is all I got left, and he is all I need!"—when somebody's broken leg was healed. I couldn't hear them all, but the thousand people present listened patiently and offered their Amens and "Praise Gods" sympathetically.

The men's choir at this kick-off service for a two-week, every-night revival worship series knew how to sway and sing out with power. Their succession of lead singers pitched the song closer and closer to a rock beat, belting out the Jesus-lyrics into a microphone. The preacher for the evening was a woman from Brooklyn, and her text exposited on Elijah and Jezebel.

She delivered the message of God's faithfulness to down-and-out Elijah at Horeb with the intensity, rapidity, and short, staccato sentences of an auctioneer, so that your attention was riveted by her voice. There was no way to get away from the amplified prophecy of her storytelling sermon. You were chastened and comforted, pushed and pulled and caressed by her insistence until you finally submitted and said, "Amen!"

* * *

Also in Detroit I was asked on the spur of the moment whether I would preach from my Reformation perspective in a Pentecostal church. "Sure," I said, and we sped away, arriving after the service had started.

After I was introduced as Brother Cal, I immediately engaged them in response. "Can you take it, for me to read a *whole* chapter from the Old Testament as my text?" I asked. "Yes, Amen!" they said. "Do you know young king Solomon acted like the mayor of Detroit?" I asked. "O no! Amen" they said. And that's the way it went the whole service.

When I came to the prayer at the end, I could hear them shift into higher gear, as it were, hanging onto my pleas to the LORD; and I experienced myself building on their expressed responses, so that it all became a glorious jumble of us *together* entreating the LORD for his blessing on the Word preached.

When the amateur rock band of young people from the church led us in a simple doxology new to me, projected on the front wall by an overhead projector, I too, like their preacher standing next to me, found myself gently rocking side to side, hands and arms uplifted. What does this mean, I thought, for worshiping in Willowdale CRC?

* * *

Once upon a time a few years ago, one evening, when I was exhorting in my home church, Willowdale Christian Reformed, as I left the consistory room behind the elder of service, I spied from the side one of our most faithful, elderly people in a front pew, still singing the last song of the pre-service hymn-sing. It happened to be an uninspired sing-spirational chorus that had turned up in our "Green folder." It made me sad. Here was a seasoned believer, a brother immigrant from the Netherlands who knew our Genevan psalms by heart, could sing verses learned from memory in Christian grade school in the old country, now reduced to the dinky, catchy phrases of a one-line chorus, his confession and praise cheapened by the melody into a trite slogan.

Another time at a combined Reformation Day service in Calgary, exhorting from Isaiah, I knew that the most fitting response after the message would be the solid Bible song from Isaiah 51:11, "Therefore the redeemed of the LORD shall return, and come with singing to Zion! and everlasting joy shall be upon their heads!" You needed a guitar, not an organ for it; and I made sure I clapped as we sang, so people would think it's all right to join in, making a happy noise for the Lord. (I must admit that several persons whose musical judgment I normally trust think that this Bible song is weak, more like a handicapped child who needs special love and treatment.)

What makes one Bible song superficial, and another Bible song's expression of simple praise rich? And an evangelical Black church has so much fun worshiping God; why can't we sober-sided Dutchmen and *burgerlijke* reformed women have holy spirited joy in church without becoming sucked into emotionalism? Is there any way to help us be creaturely human in church worship, tenaciously reformed, and simultaneously lifted up and charged for the coming week as adopted children of the King, kids of the kingdom? When is the last time you were moved to cry or laugh out loud in church worship because the Grace of God was getting through and overwhelming you through what was happening during the service?

I'm not going to *argue* here that the norm for Sunday worship is to have God speak through the preached Word responded to and surrounded by the praise, confession, thanksgiving, and supplication, in joy, of God's people. Simply read the psalms; go and do likewise. God wants his people happy when they gather expectantly to hear the Lord speak, and then shuck their burdens at God's feet, and rejoice that the Lord rules the world and its history! One should not misread Christ's correction of the Samaritan woman who thought that as a Jew Jesus believed you could only worship God in Jerusalem. Worship God with a holy spirit, genuinely grounded in the Christ, and you can worship anywhere, is what John 4:24 means. "In spirit and in truth" does not mean bodiless and purely mental. 2 Chronicles 5–7 and Acts 2 point toward liturgy of a more impassioned nature, as pleasing to God.

But there is excitement and there is excitement in worship. The exuberance of Black Gospel song and worship is qualitatively different from sing-spirational whoopee achieved by a song leader getting you to hold a high note. The one is sustained, earned by sweat and skill, born out of racial persecution and full of awe for the miracles of the Lord in our daily lives. The other is facile, follows a formula, is simple and neat, and does not cost you anything. Similarly for what is truly Pentecostal and what is imitation-Pentecostal. The one is loose, natural, winsome, and relaxed, with its own kind of learned patterns. The other has the uptightness of emotionally weak people who need to feel good before they are sure of themselves, certain that they are praising God; so they manufacture enthusiasm by adopting certain mannerisms.

I have no doubt that the American Black Gospel tradition has a biblical fiber of whole-bodied praise our Christian Reformed communion needs to be enriched by. Black Gospel has its own problems today, trying to remain unadulterated by staged commercialism that makes pop stars. (Another current film called *Gospel* shows what happens when *Say Amen, Somebody* slips over the fine line from an authentic biblical spirit to one of show biz.) But when Dorsey's second-generation of Gospel singers can turn "Jesus loves me" into the amazing hallelujah chorus of joy it is near the end of *Say Amen, Somebody*, then you know you can tell when song is spiritually true or not. What we Christian Reformed folk need is to catch the substance of Black Gospel song and not its manner. We need to be truly filled with the Holy Spirit at worship, have the Spirit in our blood, so to speak; that means, become wise and joyful, breathing love, and not stereotypically pentecostalistic the way some people pick up on Oxford accent.

Black Gospel song represented by Thomas A. Dorsey is kin to an oral tradition, which seems looser and less educated to us who are schooled in written tradition, synodical fights, and doctrines formulated in detail.

But one must indeed discern between what is biblically deep, pure, gutsy, insightful, and what is imitation-inspiration. As we reformed people learn to worship reformationally, modifying encrusted practice, we need to keep before us what pleases God and what is edifying for the long, historical haul.

* * *

When is Sunday worship mature?

Answer: when believers can say, "Thank you, God, for your special presence. This is the way revelation and response will be on the new earth!"

What makes a Sunday worship service mature?

Answer: when the Scriptures are made to speak God's compelling Word, directing all and sundry on the Way of Life, and when those present taste joy in a communion of saints and are able to share the well-meant offer of salvation in captivating ways to neighbors and any strangers.

Not only Hebrews (5:11–6:8) tells us believers to get our worship (services) mature, but even Christ asks for nothing short of a consummate exercise of praise (Matthew 5:48).

There are several things one can work at to develop meaty worship services.

(1) **An educated clergy is normative.** Any preacher must be filled with the Spirit of God, and those who know Hebrew and Greek well, history and languages, cultural settings, and human philosophies down through the ages, have context for understanding and presenting the Scriptures deeply. But they must be Spirit-filled, educated leaders who can preach in a storytelling way that makes the Bible come alive with meaning for daily life.

If your preacher can size up people and speak Good News to their heart, and hardly crack a book in doing it, that preacher will wear thin after a while, no matter how colorful his contacts remain. Preaching that goes beyond milk takes thought, comparative learning, consecrated struggle with texts and commentaries, imaginative formulation, prayer, and fasting. It's not the (memorized) oratory in the pulpit that counts, but the preparation and decisions in the study that are needed. It's so that a striking illustration or graphic image may make people think it was a good sermon when it really was only pedestrian exegesis, and it's true, people are sometimes fed by God in spite of the exposition of a passage.

But preachers are acting responsibly only when they have mastered a portion of Scripture in the context of the whole Bible, in consultation with the host of witnesses who have also grappled with that text, and then find an ordered, skilled way to make it speak to a twelve-year-old boy or girl. Intellectually fortified clergy may prove to be duds, and it's possible that unlearned seers may sound prophetic, but if the biblical writings do not remain central to a worship service, administered by those trained as masters in the tools of their trade, with the whole counsel of God coming through, then your Sunday worship service will lack reformed grit, and suffer from immaturity.

(2) **A professional ministry of music is normative.** Any church musician must be filled with the Spirit of God, and those who have trained hands and feet and voices, know the organ, piano, and choir repertoire for church music throughout the ages and what is current, have the resources to lead the church praise of God's people into richness. Every professional musician begins as an unpaid amateur, but if you try to get joyful singing in a worship service with poorly trained musical leadership, it's like trying to have a good bike ride when one of your tires is flat.

I've met excellent pianists who can't read a note of music; they play by ear, and know how to stir a congregation to sing until the rafters ring.

I also know musicians who play all the difficult notes right, but come through as formal and distant as a metronome block. Again, the LORD does amazing things with the singing of his children, no matter how well pumped-up the tires be. But there's a difference between a ninth chord and a wrong note, and it takes Levitically skilled, consecrated musicians to *lead* the singing *unobtrusively*, so that you forget there are performers and are carried along solely by the song, voices face-to-face with God together.

In the Black church system of musical training, you first become an apprentice to learn the instrument; then you graduate to learn notes; then finally you are ready to play music. No good black church musician I know plays *notes*. He or she *plays* the *piano* or *organ* and knows how to modulate, improvise, blend with registration into what's happening at the moment, soar, whisper, dance. Under their hands the instrument becomes just that—an "instrument" to lift people up into a marvelous variety of sensitive praise. If the playing becomes manipulative or exhibitionistic, the gift has been prostituted; but the exuberance of musical mastery is quite different from what is evil.

In our churches I'm afraid we often settle for less in our musical offerings to God. That's one reason why an outstanding musical performance in our church gets picked up as "special music" and an interlude of "entertainment." Immigrant organists from the old country normally know their task, and although the lead-off tone usually slows down the singing these days because the beat of the psalm has been lost, the *tussenspel* (interlude) shows there is a believer at the organ who knows her craft, at work in the house of the LORD.

But how little have we encouraged the dedicated souls who practice for decades? When have we paid for sheet music? offered to upgrade their skill by providing lessons? given them as much say in the liturgy as is their due? The Christian Reformed Church, St. Matthew's in-the-basement, Toronto, is a model on this score: for years it has never paid those who exhort. Exhorters, like St. Paul and Sunday School teachers, do it for free. But they put a sizeable item in the church budget to salary a liturgete who does homework on songs for the services, composes, directs the band, arranges pieces for the recorder trio accompaniment, teaches the congregation new songs, works hand in glove with the weekly liturgical committee; and the homegrown results, while not trouble-free, open up the possibility of church-musical maturity. Everybody should know that it's not forbidden by the Church Order to pay your local church musical leaders.

(3) **A congregation exercising its Spirit-filled gifts at Sunday worship is normative.** There must be order in a public worship service, and there is an (arguable) right time for everything, for the act of confession and forgiveness, for collecting the monies so it fits in a thank-offering (sometime *after* the Word is preached) rather than as a form of paying dues (before you've heard the sermon), for celebrating the sacraments; but if the believers are expected just to sit there like row upon row of empty jam jars waiting to be filled, you are bound to have an immature worship gathering rather than a festival of responsible praise to the proclamation of God's Word.

When God says through the preacher, "You are sinful!" "You have been saved by the blood of Christ!" "Be grateful this week on the job!" haven't you ever felt tongue-tied sitting there in silence? Was it stricken awe on your part? or the comfortableness of realizing nobody could tell how anemic your confession is? Not that *you* would have to do it yourself, but can you sense what it would mean for a worship service if a publican stood up and with chaste modesty and integrity, confessing sin, asked for congregational prayer? If an old believing person is happy with the birth of a grandchild (Psalm 128:5–6), is it not good to hear that praise quaveringly voiced by the grandparent rather than have it printed in the bulletin?

We don't ever need a variety night kind of program on Sunday—that should be done at church picnics—and there is no place at all for persons in the pew to get in their two-bit crack to stump the preacher, born out of the '60s democratistic movement challenging all authority. Those are immature acts of a do-it-yourself liturgy. But especially in the "catechism teaching" service, there should be place for responses to the Word. It's even the way the rabbi Christ our Lord did it, following the old "wise man" tradition of Israel. It's not a "discussion session" but a *response time* after the sermon, for edifying questions, clarifying answers, multiple voices on the same preached point, to get the richness of the communion of the saints operative.

Our pastor in Willowdale is not afraid to admit he doesn't know the answer to a hard, relevant comment, and asks the elders present to help out. That takes guts, and it encourages the priesthood and prophetic wisdom of every believer. Those who think "the minister should do it" all, removed behind the pulpit, are immature, and may be following a Roman Catholic more than a Reformed idea of worship. To develop a mature congregational response, the preacher needs to take them seriously, and make his text available at least a week in advance, so people can prepare to come to worship the LORD and hear God's Word with their whole consciousness.

(4) An openness to liturgical reform and biblical amplifying of our own particular confessional tradition is normative. When a worship service is cut back to the bare bones, for fear of "trappings," it may be purist pure but it is not mature. When a worship service is an eclectic potpourri of various, valuable items but lacks integrality, it also is immature, like a rack of doo-dads. Rich, mature worship comes when what is biblically sound from any background is woven into an integral pattern.

In our churches there needs to be a unifying, biblical reformed structure of preaching-and-response that absorbs and melds a wide-ranging hymnody (pre-Reformation tunes, German Lutheran chorales, Isaac Watts and Wesley originals, Zinzendorf, Great Awakening melodies, Black Gospel, contemporary dissonant harmonies) and psalmody (from Genevan jigs to the current British Psalm Praise).

We need to recapture some of the Old Testament rambunctiousness of dancing and noise, outcries and hallelujah! We need to be struck by the language of gesture (at least some splashing water at baptism, raising the cup high as a toast to God at the Lord's Supper), movement (processions of the four and twenty elders into the church, men and boys singing responsively with women and girls), clothes (church is neither the opera nor a baseball game), and the treasury of ritual (opening and closing the Bible, *kurie* and *gloria*) as well as informality (time for children to be told the message, and for kids to pick songs) and so on.

Why should only the believers in false gods have fun before their idols, while we are often so formalistically uptight before the living God?! At Sunday worship we tell God we love Him, and it's a mature thing to tell somebody you love them in a kaleidoscope of ways, rather than in the same old, straitjacketed phrases.

Worship responses don't have to be complex to be mature, but whatever gets done needs to be worth doing, and worth doing and hearing again sometime. Short Bible verse songs of strong melody need to become so well known that when something the minister says triggers the thought, somebody says, "You are worthy, O LORD," and that brief song gets sung impromptu. And the rhythmic Genevan psalms get learned in their new English text and syncopated beat so that somebody says in response to the message, Psalm 33, stanzas 3 and 5, and then everybody stands up without a book and lustily sings in unison:

Blessed is that nation, every generation,

> *for whom God is LORD.*
> *Bound to him forever, nothing can sever*
> *God from his people!*

And you've got an "Amen!" going that even beats Dorsey's Gospel song.

I've experienced mature worship services in dozens of ways, from Dr. Harry Boer's preaching in a bare Austrian ski lodge bunk dormitory to a motley crew of young skiers who then prayed together, all the way to our congregation's acting as a choir with our *liber usualis* chant books open, led by a monk, in worship at St. Anselmo outside the walls of Rome.

And as a circuit-riding exhorter you are privileged to be buoyed by God's people in many different kinds of settings: the congenial informality of Meadowvale Community Christian Reformed Church, the quiet, winning *trouw* of Holland Marsh, the excellent organ sounds of First Hamilton Christian Reformed Church that overwhelm you on the pulpit so you wonder, "Can I bring the Word so it will match such praise?" and the open-throated singing of First Barrie, overpacked into their old, too-small building where the booming organ deafens you at times.

There are many, many good ways to be quiet and to be boisterous in preparation and praise response to the central preaching of God's holy Word. Maybe it's time for more somebodies out there in churches, when they have been touched by the living, two-edged, preached word of God, to set their tongues loose and to say happily under their breath or laughing out loud at God's goodness, "Amen"! That's the truth!

Longing to Lament: A Conversation between Michael Card and Calvin Seerveld

Seerveld: The great gospel singer Mahalia Jackson is reported to have explained why she never sang the Blues: "Because I'm not down in that pit hollerin'." I understand that sentiment as a firm statement of saving faith. On the other hand, the biblical Psalms apparently approve of steadfast believers in the Lord voicing their unstinting complaints to God. They lament sickness and the threat of untimely death, enemies, and even God's silent treatment and severe punishment for sin. Doesn't that tell us that we too need songs the faithful can sing that have a beseeching, weeping "blues" character before God? As a church elder I learned congregation members were not really so happy-go-lucky as they appeared in Sunday-morning services. I think that inside and outside church buildings we need popular songs that give vent to the genuine sorrows of our lives and of the world—songs that still allow the grit of a patient faith in our Lord to come through.

Card: I agree. After 9/11 you pointed out to me that the church has no such songs to sing. That pierced my heart and forced me to look at biblical laments. The literature states that anywhere from 30 to 70 percent of the Psalms are laments. As you suggest, they range from struggling with disease and death to the victory and prosperity of the wicked to downright disappointment with God.

First published in *The Banner* 139 (September 2004): 34–38. Background: Shortly after 9/11, Calvin Seerveld began a conversation with well-known singer/songwriter and author Michael Card about the church's lost language of lament. Seerveld had previously written "A Congregational Lament" for use in worship (supra pp. 58–59) and as a result of their interaction, Card began developing both a book, *A Sacred Sorrow: Reaching Out to God in the Lost Language of Lament* (NavPress, 2005), and *The Hidden Face of God*, a CD on lament (Discovery House Music, 2006).

I've noticed also that Job provides a wonderful paradigm for one who longs to lament, to cry out to God, but whose "friends" advise him that such speech is inappropriate. His friends reduce the vast mystery of the way God works in the world to a simple formula of retributive justice. But Job discovers their formula doesn't work.

Those of us who long to be honest enough to speak to God through Scripture-ordained laments find ourselves surrounded by similar friends who try to theologize away our pain, or the world's pain, thereby confining God to a formula. I don't know about you, but the Father Jesus introduced me to is no such frozen theological entity. He is a God who is moved by my tears.

Seerveld: What happened to people in New York City and elsewhere on September 11, 2001 was evil. Can one sing a lament about such atrocity that does not propose powerful vengeance (and pre-emptive war) but repentantly mourns the evil that we ourselves also do in God's wide world?

Card: I believe, if the Psalms are truly a paradigm for us, that there is even a place for an imprecatory response to 9/11. The psalms that cry out to God to take vengeance on our enemies have a deeper purpose than simple revenge. They tell us that it is appropriate, indeed vital, that we take everything to God—even our hate. Confessing that I have enemies and that there is darkness in my heart toward them is precisely the place to start moving toward obedi-  ence to Jesus' difficult command to *love* my enemies. Lament represents a reversal of denial. Most Christians cannot love their enemies because they deny they have enemies.

I believe Daniel Berrigan's book *Lamentations: From New York to Kabul and beyond* (Sheed & Ward, 2002), which connects the situation of Jeremiah in Lamentations to ours regarding 9/11, is the best attempt so far at moving toward a confessional understanding of the part we each played in 9/11. This is another lament or series of laments that needs to be written. In the psalms, most pointedly in Psalm 51, we hear the desperate cry of one who has come to the horrible realization that all sin is sin against God: "Against you, you only, have I sinned" (v. 4). It seems to me that not until we gain this perspective will we begin to move toward the Lord with lament on our lips.

Singing Psalms

Seerveld: Songs in the marketplace rightly cover a larger terrain and have a wider ambit than songs fit for congregational Sunday worship. Both kinds of songs can be either redemptive or bad news. To save the rising generation from an escapist mentality in church, we could learn to sing honestly and regularly more of the psalms in church. Without politicizing into songs of protest, they introduce the reality of laments about the pitiful plight of the destitute in God's world and the horror of "collateral damage" in war. It's through psalms that God's Holy Spirit led the guild of composers and pop-song writers like David, Asaph, and Korah's descendants to bring their joys *and* their sorrows into temple and synagogue worship. Do you have any thoughts about such a liturgical reformation, about re-instituting the earlier Christian church practice of singing whole psalms?

Card: Because laments really are a door to reality, we need them now more than ever. The church is "asleep in the Light," as Keith Green wrote years ago. I believe laments help wake us up. Reintroducing the lament psalms would be a wonderful place to start. Beyond that, like you, I believe artists must move into their own interior suffering and respond to God by all the various forms lament can take: poetry, congregational and individual song, dance (an especially powerful medium for this), and your favorite field, fine art.

Lament, after all, is nothing more than humans doing what we've seen God do in Jesus. All lament centers on two themes: the presence of God and the *chesed*, the "covenant faithfulness," of God. When God responds to our laments, be it Job's, Jeremiah's, David's, or even Jesus' (who laments at the moment when God is most using him), God rarely fixes the hurt by merely waving a magic wand. Often the cancer remains, the rubble of destruction remains, our aching loneliness remains.

What God does and what he surely did in Christ is to actually enter into our suffering alongside us. God's deepest desire is simply to be *with us* (Immanuel). Jesus enters the world as the Man of Sorrows who is acquainted with our grief. Jesus is the presence of God for us. He came to incarnate that defining characteristic of God, *chesed*. So when we lament, we do what Jesus did—we enter as fully as God allows into our own or someone else's suffering. The most exciting part is that during those mysterious forays we encounter God and worship—all of the lament psalms, except Psalm 88, end in worship.

Crying out with creation
Card: Calvin, you coined a wonderful term, "hallelujahing," to describe creation's response to the beauty and presence of God. You made the point that we're called to participate through our imagination in this joyful response to God. I say a hearty "Amen." At the same time, based on Romans 8:22, can we make a case that creation is also lamenting? And if so, are we also called to participate in this groaning through biblical lament?

Seerveld: Yes. Because of the accumulated polluting sin of humans, the trees of the fields are *not* clapping their hands or dancing today. And the apostle Paul continues on to say that if we humans have the beginnings of the Holy Spirit in us, we will *groan inwardly* because the redemptive bodily deed we yearn for is not yet forthcoming (Romans 8:23–25). That is one New Testament biblical directive that charters lamenting in faith. We groan because we see how we are ruining the praise God's environment is created to bring to the LORD. It hurts to pick up oil-slicked birds and dead fish washed onto beaches.

I remember James Ward's rollicking *Creation* song, "The heavens are telling" (1970s), which is composed in the certain hope of Isaiah 55:12–13. It's true, we need a companion song that cries along with the diseased grasshoppers and the little girls in sweatshops who no longer sing (Ecclesiastes 12:1–7). As God says a little later to would-be followers of the Christ: "Rejoice with those rejoicing, and weep with those weeping" (Romans 12:15). Maybe we Christians do not respond so well to these Scriptural appeals to groan and weep in our songs because we don't hear nonhuman creatures groaning or our human neighbors weeping.

Card: I'm afraid that some in the church will dismiss this idea of lament as merely good psychology. "It's good to get stuff off your chest," they might respond. But isn't there much more at work here? I want to say that lament is the road to genuine worship, but is that too narrow?

Seerveld: I would rather say that the kind of lament the Bible enjoins is the in-depth cry of seasoned believers who trust the LORD all the way. Immature believers miss out on the psalm laments.

God also hears the wailing of helpless Iraqi, Palestinian, Israeli, and Sudanese mothers for their freshly killed children. (Woe to the murderers!) But the kind of lament the Lord wants us to utter is the cry of outraged faith in the LORD of *chesed*—which your questions rightly highlight—pleading with the covenantal LORD God of reliable mercy to come through *now*: Why are you destroying my life, God! At least treat me with a little hospitality before I die (Psalm 39)! My God, why have you left me in the lurch? The evildoers like beasts surround me for the kill (Psalm 22). O God, devastate those who systematically murder the innocent! End the lives of those driven by evil principalities to desecrate us faithful who are in terrible need (Psalm 69)! Why do you have to punish us so drastically for our sins, O God?! Jerusalem is *your* city, LORD—we are *your* people, O Redeemer—what will the disbelievers say about *you* if we are destroyed (Lamentations 2–3, cf. Exodus 32:7–14)?

Biblical laments are intercessory prayers by God's children who experience their helplessness to set things straight in God's world. I too believe God is moved by our tears of faith.

Biblical laments are also sometimes the obedient response of praying *for* those who persecute the weak. Terminate their evil-doing, Lord! Do so for our sake and for the evildoers' sake too, since what you made good should not be wasted.

Card: Berrigan says that 40 million people die every year from hunger. That's like the crashing of 320 jumbo jets every day. Likewise, the persecuted church is seeing more martyrs today than at any time in the history of Christendom. These numbers represent enormous reservoirs of lamentable suffering. Closer to home, innumerable tragedies surround us: abused and abandoned children, hopeless addicts—each a microcosm of suffering. What difference does/could our entering into their pain make? Why would God require this of us?

Seerveld: Near the core of the Christian life is growing the eyes of faith to experience the suffering of those around us, to concretely enter their pain in ways more real than a TV screen allows. The book of James is so clear it's painful to read. Anybody who thinks he or she is scrupulously religious but prays, "Thank you, Lord, I'm not bad like those crooks nearby," is self-deceived. To visit orphans and the bereaved *in their affliction* is what "pure religion" is all about (James 1:26–27).

If you can't visit orphans in Romania, if you can't get permission to visit lost souls in the penitentiary, if you're unable to listen to the lonely in rest homes, if you lack the credentials to minister to a distraught student, take it to the Lord in prayer—in a song! Laments for suffering outcasts, if made by one who is doing right in God's eyes, "avail much" (James 5:13–18).

The laments of the faithful, like the entreaties of Job, are not bootless cries in the dark. They are acts of love toward our neighbors before God's ear. The Bible warns that we can fulfill the law of Christ only if we bear one another's burdens through passionate laments (Galatians 6:2). We need song composers to school us in singing laments of faith also as exercises for humbling ourselves from vanity, power trips, and indifference to God's care for the poor.

Card: I believe that, given the perfection of his life, Jesus alone provides the final source for our understanding anything meaningful. He is the perfect paradigm. I flee to his life when I need understanding. So when I looked at lament I knew—or believed or hoped—that at some point I would finally find myself back at his feet. After a lot of reading and meditating on the subject, I want to say that Jesus incarnated the only two answers to lament that God ever offered in the Old Testament, God's presence and God's *chesed*. When John says "the Word became flesh," I've begun to wonder if the "Word" wasn't *logos* but, somehow, *chesed*.

When you look at the life of Jesus of Nazareth, do you see anything like this? Does Isaiah's understanding of the Man of Sorrows mean that lament should be seen as a major category in Jesus' life? And if the advent of Jesus is the penultimate point in our journey of lament, where do you see the Bible speaking about the end of lament?

Seerveld: God's Son, Jesus, came into human flesh to save the world and all its inhabitants from the wastage of our human sin abetted by devils (John 3:16–21). Since the wages of sin before God is death (Romans 6:20–23), in our stead Jesus Christ had to suffer and die. I find it illuminating that Jesus had Psalms 22 and 69 alive in his memory on the cross, as the evangelists tell it (Mark 15:33–37). Jesus' laments were born out of steadfast faith, not out of disorientation or severe doubt. Even when "his sweat was like drops of blood" in Gethsemane, Christ, in pain, was driven on by the solid conviction to do God's will (Luke 22:39–46).

So imitating Christ or the apostle Paul (1 Corinthians 10:31–11:1) does not mean that I should use them as models so much as that I am to be instructed by their obedience (see 10:1–13). I may holler at God for letting bad things happen *because* I know in faith, love, hope, and deep residual trust that, thanks to Christ's obedient sacrifice for us, all things shall indeed work together for good to those who love the Lord (Romans 8:26–28). So why put it off, God? Save us and the neighbors from ourselves and from enemies so we may shout about your *chesed* in the congregational meeting place (Psalm 22:21–31, 69:30–36)! It's true, a service of praise choruses with nary a hint of sorrow is cheapened grace. Laments and praise of God go in tandem. When the Lord comes back, then there will be no more tears and no laments (Revelation 21:1–4).

A delicate affair
Seerveld: Thank you for your thoughtful responses and searching questions on lamentations. For us affluent believers to offer laments to God that will not be a false show condemning ourselves may be a delicate affair. A lament will reach the Lord's ear, I believe, only if it embodies intimate admission of *our* sin and is uttered in faith when we are *helpless* before evil. It's as difficult for a person or the church or a country that has power and riches to offer an acceptable lament to the LORD as it is for a tank to go through the eye of a needle.

In the culture of hatred, deception, fraud, and violence enveloping even the worldwide body of Christ today, God's children must never forget that even armed human enemies are our neighbors. Only *God* may wreak vengeance, *not us* (Psalm 137:7–9, Romans 12:19–21, Philippians 4:4–7). And laments will come through best, I think, in liturgical settings where the person lamenting is a voice of and for a community of faith. So your idea to cradle the new laments we need in themed services seems right to me. Lamenting is wrestling with God in communion on behalf of others, not a freelance protest business. My prayer, Michael, is that you songwriters will reach down for the utterly sober trust in the Lord it takes and that you will receive the grace to sing us awake to the tough love of laments we will need in the coming years. May our Lord and God's angels go with you, and may you be filled with the Holy Spirit.

The path to praise
The Scriptures are filled with lament. Of the major categories of psalms,

lament is by far the most numerous. With the exception of one psalm (88), each lament turns eventually to praise, revealing an important truth that has been lost: lament is the path to praise.

The importance of lament is especially seen in the life of Jesus. At every turning point of his ministry, Jesus pours out his heart in lament—when he enters Jerusalem for the last time, when he experiences his final meal with the disciples, when he struggles with the Father in the garden of Gethsemane, and most important, when he endures the suffering of the cross. Jesus reveals that those who are truly intimate with the Father know they can pour out any hurt, disappointment, temptation, or even anger with which they struggle.

With all that and more in mind, I am working on a book of meditations built around a Bible study on the subject, as well as producing a series of recordings that I hope will help reintroduce this lost aspect of worship to the North American church.[1]

In the end, I have several aims:

- to help Christians become more thoroughly connected to the process of worship by integrating their emotional struggles and disappointments into the content of the lyrics
- to reintegrate into the church those who are hurting but have felt disenfranchised by feel-good, "lamentless" worship
- to equip worship leaders with new materials, both music and meditations, that will aid them in leading congregations in lament
- and to help introduce a new dimension to missions, whereby North American Christian missionaries around the world might connect with other believers, many of whom have not lost sight of what it means to lament.

While thankfully biblically imaginative and Christ-centered worship music is still being produced, the bulk of what gets marketed as "worship music" these days is often shallow and self-centered. No doubt there are many reasons for this departure—the influence of commercialism, the impact of a self-focused culture, a slipping away from biblical study. However, I would like to suggest that a primary reason for the denigration of worship in North American Christianity is that we have lost the ability to lament.

---

1   *Voicing God's Psalms*, with accompanying CD (Grand Rapids: Eerdmans, 2005).

The Rule of God

The Slow of Heart (I)

> "O you thick-headed fellows! So slow of heart not to believe all that the prophets have spoken!" . . . Jesus said to them, "It's written that the Christ must suffer and be raised from the dead . . . so that repentance toward forgiveness of sins could be proclaimed to **all** nations." Luke 24:25, 46–47

> Jesus showed himself to his disciples to be alive . . . and allowed himself to be seen by them for forty days in order to keep on telling them all about **the Rule of God**. Acts 1:3

Jesus' disciples were woefully ignorant of what Jesus' death and resurrection meant. "We had hoped," said the couple from Emmaus, "that Jesus was going to redeem Israel from our subjection to the infidel Romans, that he was going to become the God-appointed King in Jerusalem! But it fizzled out."

Luke writes at the end of his first book that it was reported that Jesus had tried to show that the law, the prophetic writings, and the psalms about his coming and his victory over lawlessness, injustice, and even death on earth had been fulfilled in his crucifixion and resurrection. Redemption had now been achieved for believing-Israel! The Rule of God was historically instituted as never before. But in his second book Luke writes that Jesus spent forty more days on earth to drive home what the Rule of God was like (Acts 1:3)—because his followers were so obtuse, so "slow of heart."

The Rule of God Is Like a fungus creeping through dough yet worth more than a bank account of six figures. Christ's disciples couldn't figure how the Rule of God Almighty on earth could be like both. How in the world could the Rule of God grow explosively like a mustard seed

---

Seven meditations first published in *The Banner* (4, 11, 18, 25 April and 2, 9, 16 May 1988).

and yet remain like a little child? Even seminary professor Nicodemus was confused.

The Rule of God was nothing like Christ's disciples had expected because they didn't listen to the thrust of *the whole Bible*. They dipped into the Scripture for proof texts or listened to it with one selfish ear, just enough to "inherit eternal life." They had a superficial devotional knowledge of Moses, the psalms, and the prophets. They used the Bible as a kind of legal benediction on their hopes for a better life, political liberty, and pursuit of happiness. They had mislaid the key of knowledge to God's will, and Christ's closest disciples were at times "so slow of heart" they gave our Lord stomach cramps and tears.

Don't you understand, said Christ, that the victory of the woman with child over the hateful serpent has been won? That the star has indeed come out of Jacob and has dispossessed the warlords of the earth? That the shoot from the stump of Jesse has flowered and vividly made visible the fruitful Rule of God, under which people forgive their enemies? Don't you understand that I sacrificed myself for you while you were still sinners?

Slow of Heart. We have a hard time getting a heartfelt grasp of the Rule of God on earth because we tend to believe "you only get what you pay for," and we are normally intent on hanging on to something for ourselves. But Christ took his befuddled disciples through the Scriptures to teach them the truth. The *liberating Rule of God is free*. And the Rule of God is something you don't hoard for yourself; you *give it away to your enemies*. You are now free from hating the Romans, says Christ, and you are empowered to rule them in a godly way, that is, to serve them by telling them that because of my resurrection their sins are forgiven.

This was unwelcome news, really, to Christ's followers, whose hearts were sluggish. Christ's disciples and their relatives were anticipating posts at the top of the new kingly administration and they would not be above settling age-old political scores with the Samaritans, who had collaborated with the enemy troops centuries before.

Christ's dull-witted disciples wanted to *restrict God's Rule* to those who were *kosher* and to use God's rule for their own advantage. That's what to be "slow of heart" means. We hear only a partial gospel, not the full counsel of God. We don't pay close attention to the story of God's slowly ongoing, historical fulfillment of the Lord's promises because we suppose the Rule of God will drop out of heaven promptly for us. Our faith is too sloppy to hear Scripture say that if we sacrifice our lives for the Rule of God, we will receive it again many times *in this age, with persecu-*

tion, and that *the Lord creates strength out of weakness.*

When the veil of the temple was rent on *Good* Friday, the tradition of "Jews only" (and the tradition of "whites only" or "males only") was ripped to pieces. The holy things of God were now openly available to Samaritans and women, to Ethiopian blacks and Italian army sergeants, and to people who believed in the Rule of Christ but remained physically uncircumcised.

Since Christ arose from the dead, it is time that we rip to pieces the veils over our hearts when we read Scripture so that we are not slow of heart but wide open to the quickening Rule of the Holy Spirit. *God's topsy-turvy Rule of just mercy for all kinds of people is coming in history.* It'd be too bad if we as a virgin church were too slow getting oil in our lamps and missed the coming wedding celebration.

Job's Friends (II)

> Yet I know for a certainty: the One who always comes through to set me safely free (redeem me) is the living God!
>
> And as the One who always finally comes through, this God will be standing up there on the earth (to vindicate me).
>
> Even when my very skin is destroyed so that I be completely without any flesh, I still know for a certainty, I shall see God there in front of me!
>
> Whom I shall see on my side, myself!—my own eyes shall see God—not the eyes of some stranger. . . .   Job 19:25–27

Job's intense confession about the redeeming Rule of God was torn out of him by the harping criticism of his oh-so-proper friends. Job's heart-rent affirmation that the living God would go all the way for him and put him back on his feet to see God—even if the worms shredded him bodily in death—is precisely the kind of fervent testimony that Jesus after Easter asked his disciples to proclaim worldwide. But the Jews' idea of the "redemption of Israel," which the couple walking to Emmaus was interested in, missed the exuberant God-focus that Job expressed. The Jews more soberly expected Israel's "redemption" to be released from Roman domination, as something simply due them as their inheritance as sons of Abraham who were following a messianic king.

The Redemptive Rule of God. Although Job sometimes blamed God for his troubles (of which he later repented), the sterling insight of

Job's bottomless faith in his Redeemer was that *God forgives sinners.* God makes good for those who are not good and who *cannot* make good for themselves. That's what *Redeemer* means in the Bible.

Isaiah calls the Lord God the *Redeemer* of Israel. God Almighty assumed the shame of Israel, repented of being momentarily angry at their godlessness, and then forgave their sin and released them from captivity! When the Holy One of Israel acted as Redeemer, God paid ransom for the kidnapped people of God, who had sinfully sold themselves into hock! The God of Jacob redeemed God's favored people generously, unconditionally (out of pure grace), and repeatedly, from Egypt, from Babylon, from "traditions of men." That's *my* God, said Job.

Job's Friends. But the living God who redeemed undesirables was not exactly the God for Job's friends. God's Rule of giving undeserved redemption gritted in their teeth like gravel. Job's friends believed you basically had to make good for your own sins: God forgives you because you repent and stop sinning.

But Job's friends had God wrong, says God. Their pitch obscured the redemptive Rule of God and adulterated the biblical revelation of God's forgiveness for sinners.

In the first place, sinners are not forgiven because they repent, but *because Christ has made good for them*—us. And, second, God's redemption is not conditional upon our not sinning anymore, as Job's friends implied. Who then could ever withstand judgment? says the psalmist (13:3–4). Sin wrestles with the Holy Spirit in our concrete actions, like thinking, talking, imagining, and feeling, for as long as we followers of Christ breathe (Galatians 5:13–26). That's why the good news of Scripture is that *the Lord's redemption is unlimited for God's adopted children* (Psalm 130:7–8).

Is Scripture soft on sin, then? Maybe Christ could stop the stoning of an adulterous woman by self-righteous churchmen because Christ could see through to their hearts. Maybe Christ could save the skin of a murderer, redeem the man at the very last minute, simply because Christ was God. But does that mean we should adopt a permissive attitude toward sin?

Certainly not. A "permissive attitude toward sin" is simply the posture of a legalist gone softheaded. But Job's friends stood in the way of the coming of God's Rule upon the earth, because they lacked forgiving, compassionate hearts.

If Eliphaz had had a hemophilic child who couldn't go straight, Eliphaz would have put him or her out of the house, would have scratched the name out of the family Bible—period. If Bildad had had two friends who came to a divorce because the husband beat the wife and children, Bildad would have laid down the law of Mark 10:2–10 and would have read the sinner out of the church. If Zophar had had a colleague who became an alcoholic and messed up on the job, Zophar would gladly have forgiven him three times (as rabbis recommended), maybe even seven times, as the apostle Peter generously proposed—but countless times?

Job's friends knew how to remonstrate with sin. Like Pharisees, they brought all kinds of antidotes after the person had taken poison, but they didn't offer much in the way of wholesome food for people who needed nourishment. "Be merciful to me, my friends," Job pleaded. "Be merciful!" Yet except for the initial commiserating silence when they were struck by his brokenness, Job's friends let their indignation at his sins get the better of any merciful counsel. Making good for Job never crossed their minds.

That *Christ has made good for us, redeems us as sinners* is a crux of the gracious way God's Rule takes place (Revelation 5:9–10). And *Scripture forcefully calls us to be redemptive on earth among our neighbors.* The book of Job makes clear that God's redemptive Rule is not our normal way of doing things; we try to even scores and come out ahead. The redemptive Rule of God is the Holy Spirited humbling of sinners to open their hearts for receiving and giving away the mercy Christ's resurrection affords. That Rule of God is filling the earth, despite its confounding, suffering weakness (see 1 Corinthians 1:18–2:5).

Common Sense (III)

Prick up your ears—all of you!—and pay special attention to what I am saying:

Does the farmer just keep on plowing day after day after day if he wants to sow grain?

Does he keep harrowing and disking his field all the time?

Isn't it so that once he has made the earth level and smooth, the farmer then starts to sprinkle dill and sow caraway seeds and then starts to plant rows of wheat, marked-off squares of barley, and rye around the edges? God, the farmer's Maker, gives him this teaching experience. That's right!

Dill is not to be threshed with a big threshing instrument, and the sharp wheel of the threshing wagon is not supposed to be rolled over and over on top of caraway plants. No, dill gets beaten out with a strong stick, and the caraway seeds are harvested by hitting with a rod. Wheat and barley-corn are meant to be ground into bread, but you don't keep on threshing and thrashing the grain forever—when you set the horses going and threshing-wagon wheels churning, you take care not to crush the grain to bits. Do you get it?

Also this kind of technical knowledge originates with the LORD God of the angels. God's deliberate way of putting things together is amazing! God's wise way of working things out is truly magnificent!

Isaiah 28:23–29

The "common sense" people have is always loaded. In the Kuranko tribe up-country in Sierra Leone, it is common sense for women to push and to keep pushing during the birthing process, even if it doesn't help (and exhausts the mother). It's common sense in Western civilization for people to settle differences by rational discussion, although argument seldom changes differences in basic conviction (and instead often engenders heated debate). People who live by common sense are following what Paul calls dated "traditions of men" (Colossians 2:8).

Faded Vision of Life. It is common sense in the Anglo-American variety of "common-denominator sense" that makes the Rule of God seem particularly squint-eyed. This North American common sense (that is, the sense everyone democratically agrees on) assumes, for example, that education leads to a better life, that to have more than enough money is good for you, that the stronger survive in war and peace, and that basically we are honest people. That's common sense.

When such (humanistic) common sense is beaten like flour into the milk of a biblical faith, the batter doesn't make for a good cake. *Common sense* dulls your existential awareness of God's closeness in daily creaturely life and tends to distance God. It reduces creaturely activities to "common, everyday occurrences" minus the depth vision that creation was and remains an act of God's grace, the grace that underlies the grace needed for our salvation. Common sense subtly gets one to ignore the truth that when we deal with ordinary creatures, we are in the presence of the merciful living God today.

The Uncommon Rule of God. Isaiah's parable makes plain that a farmer doesn't do the same thing all the time. Sometimes a farmer roughly churns up the ground; other times he tenderly plants a seed; other times he harvests the grain by striking off the husks. And it is God who teaches the farmer experientially the complicated know-how one needs to produce fruitfully. Tilling the soil, waiting for growth, reaping food, each according to its kind, are fascinating happenings, says Isaiah, full of wonder, of uncommon ingenuity, revealing God's gracious, minute, imaginative care.

The Rule of God is indeed *uncommonly* remarkable. That green leaves—on trees that only God could make—turn all colors of the rainbow before they drop off and sail gently to the earth to die is an amazing turn of events.

God's way of ruling also shows that education is not the salvation of anything but generates a dominating cruelty unless it be humbled by obedience to the Lord. Loving money is the root of evil—not of well-being. The meek rather than the strong are inheriting the culture of the earth. People since Adam and Eve's fall into sin are at heart corrupt unless they become changed by the holy-making Spirit of God. And that Almighty God, in order to save corrupt persons, should be born as a baby, helpless between the legs of a woman, is simply not rational or commonsensical.

God's Rule on earth is always distorted or denied by the creed of common sense.

The placement of Isaiah's parable in this context reaches out to us with a still deeper message on the uncommon Rule of God. Isaiah told this parable in about 725 BC, when the superpower Assyria was poised to rub the ten tribes of faithless Israel off the map. Isaiah is telling the decadent, scoffing leaders of Judah not to put their trust in the other superpower of the day, Egypt, and not to presume they are safe in their sinful common sense. No, the Lord, hints Isaiah, may be wisely biding the right time to reap the ones faithful to God from among the husks of those in David's line who trust in armed might.

This means that God's people feeling safe in the Bible Belt granaries of the United States and Canada should not think, "It can't happen here." The Lord may send God's reaping angels to our land as God finally did to Judah (586 BC), because God is the Lord of Soviet military force and American missiles and dollars today. Nuclear war like Black Monday can happen here.

But with the warning of Isaiah's parable about our needing to take the uncommon Rule of God seriously comes also deep comfort: if the Lord so cares for kernels of grain that they not be crushed by the sharp wheels of a threshing wagon, will not the Lord God even more gingerly protect us small-time believers who nevertheless are faithful to God's Rule, save us through the refining fire of his chastening anger at the godless common sense of us as a people?

Overcoming Evil (IV)

> Do not be conformed any longer to the lifestyle of this world, but keep on being transformed by the renewing of your consciousness so you can come to discern what is the good, pleasing, and complete will of God. . . . Let each of us share the differing gifts given us by God's grace. . . . Let the underlying selfless love be truly genuine. . . .
>
> Speak well of those who make life hard for you. Invoke God's blessings on them; don't curse them. Be joyful with those who are rejoicing and lament with those who are weeping. . . . That's right; if the one who hates what you stand for is suffering hunger, at least give him something to eat; if the one who works against what you live for is in thirst, go ahead and give her something to drink. Giving sustenance to the enemy who is hurting is like tending an open wound with a poultice of cleansing iodine. Don't be conquered by what is evil. Instead, overcome what is evil by doing what is good.
>
> Romans 12:2, 6, 9, 14–15, 20–21

Paul has spent three-quarters of his letter to the Romans arguing passionately with orthodox believers who want to live by the common-sense idea that God justifies you on the basis of your good deeds. No, says Paul, God's Rule is different. You are saved *only* by accepting, in faith, God's free gift of the death and resurrection of Jesus Christ. That's the way it really is (see Ephesians 2:8–10). And if you want to participate in the blessing of this new order in history, then (1) break with the lifestyle of this world by giving away your *charismata* (gifts of grace) and (2) help the enemy when he or she is hurting.

God's Rule: Our Sharing Our Gifts. I've never forgotten my neighbor who at three o'clock in the morning got me some pills to kill the gut-wrenching pain of a severe gallbladder attack and then sat by my bedside drowsing in the lamplight while the pulsing contractions gradually subsided. We didn't talk much, and he couldn't undergo the hurt under my skin, but I experienced his quiet readiness to be close by as a simple strengthening act of love.

I know someone who was once vilified by a close colleague. Instead of defending himself against the slander, this man quietly said to his friends, "My accuser does not have a very easy life." With the blameless innocence celebrated by Psalm 15, this saint continued to honor his resentful colleague with a genuine love.

Such firm, gentle conduct is a far cry from today's lifestyle in a world that is going to pieces (1 John 2:15–17). People today often satisfy themselves at the expense of others and "go for it"—whatever *it* is—no holds barred. That's why constant turmoil, hatred, and cutthroat bitterness flourish wherever people breathe (James 4:1–12)—except where God's people exercise the Rule of God by giving away God's gifts, made holy by the Spirit.

Patient, selfless, encouragement-breathing prayer nurses peace in God's world. A willingness to forgo bitter debates and to *not* speak "the truth" with self-righteous "love" is a holy act of self-control that usually goes unnoticed. Such forbearance is often a key to promoting a genuine communion of the saints. And *calling one another to repentance with forgiveness* rather than simply "tolerating" the other's deeds—how can the world of humanist morality know the gratefulness and bonding such grace brings?

God's Rule: Our Loving the Enemy. God doesn't make it easy for us to love our enemies. The Lord asks us self-protective people to initiate God's Rule even among people who will bite the hand that feeds them. God lets the sun rise on criminals as well as on us and provides rain for blasphemers as well as for Christians—but does that mean I have to be undiscriminating in loving my neighbor?

Break the bread of life especially for the ones who hate what believers stand for, says God through Paul's letter to the Romans. That doesn't mean we are to shove the Gospel of John down their throats while we have our foot on their necks. The *enemy* is anyone who attacks the saints' faith, livelihood, and service. The "persecuting evildoer" is anyone—inside or outside the church—who undermines, obstructs, or ruins that which builds up God's Rule and hurts faithful little ones with deceit, willful foolishness, or malice. And to such evildoers belongs your ministry of tears, smiles, and supportive care, says Scripture.

When people cry or are in need, they are most vulnerable, most open to being changed in their course. When those who trouble your walk with God are off-guard or down, surprise them. Surprise them with your selfless enjoyment of their gladnesses or with an outgoing compassion that gentles their cries. Fill the need of people who hate you. Let the LORD remove their evil ways or harden the heart forever. But *you* do what is good, just, and true to the Rule of God.

The Rule of God is hampered when God's children act as though they were God—raising up and putting down disobedient people, inflicting guilt, judging hearts, and meting out rewards. Scripture tells us, instead, to give away our special gifts of the Holy Spirit to one another, to our neighbor, and to do good things even for our enemies. That may not seem to our advantage. However, such action does enroll us in the coming of the Rule of God, because then we will know experientially the hope and joy of living out of faith, out of a conviction in the Lord's *promises* (Hebrews 11:1).

THE DEVIL'S BROKEN BACK (V)

> Clap hands hard, all you peoples!
> Shout to God with a jubilant loud voice!
> Yes, the LORD God, the most majestic One, is awesome,
> great Ruler over the whole earth! . . .
>
> **God has ascended to the shouting of victory!**
> The LORD God rose with the blast of the sophar.
>
> Sing to God! Sing and make music!
> Sing praise to our royal Ruler! Sing and make music,
> for God is Ruler of all the earth!
> All of you, sing to God versified songs.
> **God has become Ruler over the nations of the world** [*goyim*]!
>
> Psalm 47

Some Christians will gather on a Thursday evening in spring after a hard day's work to recall Christ's ascension. They realize that the next day—early—will still be a regular Friday, and sometimes they find it hard to understand the meaning of Christ's going to heaven to sit at God's right hand. Psalm 47 is one of the best commentaries on the ascension of Jesus Christ. Christ's ascension is not just an encore, an extra, sandwiched in forty days late after the rousing climax of his resurrection and ten days short of Pentecost Sunday. Christ's ascension into heaven is a special completing victory! It was a new historical development in the Rule of God and clearly calls for rhythmic clapping, shouting cheers, time off to celebrate, lusty singing of newly composed songs, the blasting of trumpets, and dancing.

God's Rule Over Unearthly Powers. When God exalted the risen Jesus Christ, then in some important way the principalities and powers, angels, and unseen evil authorities referred to as demonic creatures all became subject to Christ in a more controlled way (Philippians 2:5–11, 1 Peter 3:18–22).

Christ's sojourn on earth was not a cut-and-dried affair; Jesus really suffered temptation (Hebrews 4:14–16). Only after Jesus had *withstood* the devil's official, crafty offers of free power did Christ say he saw Satan fall like a lightning bolt from heaven (Luke 10:17–20). Only after Jesus had fearfully sweat blood in Gethsemane and had *submitted to God's will* for the ordeal of criminal charges, accusations of blasphemy, and the torture of the cross did he trustfully quote Psalm 22 (Matthew 27:45–54) and commend himself into God's care. Only after Jesus had been *raised* from the powerful clutches of the grave and death (Colossians 2:8–15) did he tell his still doubting disciples that "*all power* in heaven and on earth has been given to me" (Matthew 28:16–20). And only with the *victory* of Jesus' ascension to stand next to God is the messianic dimension of Psalm 110's promise fulfilled—that Christ may now "rest there" while God makes a footstool of the Lord's enemies (Hebrews 10:12–13).

So, Ascension Day is the anniversary of *Christ's historical enthronement to worldly Rule*, recognized also by the "prince of this world" and the devils, who did their worst to prevent it (John 16:4–11). Therefore, Psalm 47 is a liturgical celebration of the Lord's *ascending,* amid the victory shouts of God's people (Psalm 132:8–10), to the place of holiest glory. Here God sits in spellbinding majesty, with his feet on the "mercy lid" of the ark, God's footstool (1 Chronicle 28:2). Indeed Psalm 47 is the right setting and emphasis for the festivity of Ascension Day. Every power against God has its back broken by Jesus Christ's ascension!

Exorcism and the Rule of the Ascended God. True, worldly powers have always existed only as creatures subservient to Christ (Colossians 1:15–20). And the final banishment of evil awaits Christ's return. Meanwhile, Scripture is clear: we adopted children of the risen Lord are not called to fight against people but to battle the very powerful evil *principalities* that subvert God's Rule on earth (Ephesians 6:10–20). Their backs are broken, but they still captivate and enslave many persons and often pose as "ruling protectors" among the nations (Revelations 13).

The *fact* of Christ's ascension, however, and the point of the exuberant Psalm 47 are that we who belong to God and confess that Jesus is Lord shall never be separated from the love of Almighty God. Also we should be casting out the devils that rule and ruin family time. Wherever elemental drives like curiosity, skill, pleasure, and power assume proportions of demonic enslavement (Galatians 4:1–11) and subtly turn people into frenzied dominators (especially those who hold positions of educational, media, commercial, or political command in our secularized society), the ascended Lord asks and empowers Christ's body on earth to humble such disobedient "guardian" rulers (2 Corinthians 10:3–6).

To cast out devils the way the Pharisees and fakers did—for show or gain on prime time—is to be a practicing anti-christ. But to get the devilish nature out of human actions—which normally takes intense prayer, a fasting concentration, and deep godly wisdom—is our inheritance and our mandate from Christ's ascension and is to be exercised in the strong, quieting power of the Holy Spirit (Ephesians 3:14–21).

"Resist the devil, and [it] will flee from you" (James 4:1–10). So shout your thanks and clap your hands hard, all you people!

Daughters and Sons (VI)

> Later on this will happen:
> I shall spill my Spirit upon every body!—
> so that your daughters as well as your sons prophesy,
> so that your old folk dream dreams and your
> energetic youth experience revealing visions.
> In those days I will spill my Spirit
> even upon slave boys and slave girls!
>
> Joel 2:28–32

Joel's prophecy was inaugurated at Pentecost. The Holy Spirit, arriving on earth in person, so to speak, flabbergasted believing Jews who were in Jerusalem from many parts of the world. Peter preached the good news of Joel, of Psalm 16 (Jesus' resurrection), and of Psalm 110 (Christ's ascension). The text from Joel was precisely what Peter needed to set the agenda for the newly forming church, because Joel connects the outpouring of the Holy Spirit with intimations of final judgment.

No Restrictions. The Holy Spirit stormed into Jerusalem with whirlwind sounds and fire and stirred the Galilean disciples to testify in many languages. The day had come, said Peter, for which Moses had prayed, that *all* God's people, not just certain leaders, might become prophets.

This was the day on which the Lord made a *new* covenant with his people. Now, through this covenant, the least important as well as the prominent have God's law written on their hearts. Now they are able, without prompting, to speak about the great deeds of God, in, with, and through Jesus Christ. We can now celebrate, said Peter, that the kingship and priesthood of believers, the anointing to teach, and the prophetic office, are no longer restricted by sex, by age, by position, or even by Jewish blood!

True, Peter personally had some reservations on the extent of God's Rule. God's inclusion of the *goyim* (Gentiles) as the Lord's people was hard for a *kosher* Jew to swallow. It took a while for Peter to practice the Joel he had preached—Peter was "slow of heart." The Pentecost text from Joel, however, on how completely wide open the reception of God's Spirit Rule is meant to be, remains the true, upsetting Word of God for us even today.

Apocalypse Now. Acts 2 reports the initial downpour of the Holy Spirit after Christ's ascension. Christ had promised to equip his followers for ruling in the world by preaching "repentance toward forgiveness of sins . . . to *all* nations." The outcome of this outpouring of the Holy Spirit was exactly that: in language strangers could understand, *every body* spoke about the mighty, saving works of God!

That's what being prophetic is all about: to articulate the compassionate Rule of God for your neighbor and to practice God's Rule of blessing by doing what is good. The Holy Spirit is not something you tuck away in your heart. The Holy Spirit radiates wisdom throughout your whole body, makes your speech about Jesus Christ winsome, and encourages you to dream wise dreams for the next covenant generation. The Holy Spirit is also "no respecter of persons" (Acts 10:30–48) but enters the hearts of girls as well as boys, young as well as old, those in debt as well as those with money, and he sets everyone free from manmade restrictions on service.

Therefore Pentecost becomes a judgment day for those who act as though it didn't happen. We cannot deny the prophet-making Holy Spirit's presence in men *and* women, poor *and* rich, Gentile *as well as* Jew (Galatians 3:26–29) upon their repenting and being baptized. Whoever deny this reality are called upon by Joel to rend their hearts, not their garments (Joel 2:12–17).

One is not home free with Pentecost. If we respond obediently to the ascended Christ's gift of the Holy Spirit on earth and hear God calling us by his Word, then there is blessing and excitement *for all.* If we remain cold and unmoved by the outpouring of the Holy Spirit upon *all flesh,* we face judgment.

Think of the children, for example. Christ's first disciples thought children were marginal to God's Rule in Christ. Wrong, said Jesus. Or think of Timothy. Paul told Timothy not to let older people disparage his church leadership because of his youth.

Christ's early disciples also found it difficult to consider women equal partners in affairs of God's kingdom. But woman's place is not in the kitchen, said Jesus; it is far better for women—just like men—to gain knowledge and understanding of God's Word (Luke 10:38–42). Peter, with the authority of God's Word from Joel, also proclaimed at Pentecost that one does not need to be a male to proclaim prophetically the Word of the Lord (Acts 2:16–18).

To set man-made policies that would restrict anyone gifted with the Holy Spirit from proclaiming the message of Pentecost would be to resist the Holy Spirit (Matthew 12:22–32, Ephesians 4, Hebrews 10:19–31). We must not let the idea of sexual privilege in serving the ascended Lord become one of the principalities God's people need to combat today. Let us, as church, reform our traditions of men (Colossians 2:8–15) on this score and hear the call of God to follow the Word from Joel and the reality of Pentecost.

SEEKING, NOT HIDING (VII)

Prophet: You really are a God who is concealing oneself,
You, the God of Israel, who is busy setting free! . . .
Lord God: No, I have not talked in secretive ways. . . .
I, the Lord God, speak what is tried and true. . . .

Come, gather yourselves, get closer together, all you survivors of the nations. . . .
All you to the ends of the earth,
turn yourselves in my direction, and let yourselves be set free! . . .

Believers: Only in the Lord God have I found, it shall be said, deeds of sound restoration and sure strength...
—Isaiah 45:15–25

The context for the Scripture here is this: the Lord has decided to commission Cyrus of Persia to set God's people free from their captivity in the Babylonian Empire. God "anoints" this pagan king as his "shepherd" to liberate God's people for building up God's holy city. All this, even though Cyrus does not recognize God as the Lord.

This shocks God's people. Why should the God of Israel stoop to use *an unbeliever* to get God's work done?

So Isaiah wrestles with the believing protesters: no clay dish challenges the potter. The Almighty Creator of every creature does not have to answer to fastidious *you* for his great deeds in history. Besides, the Lord chose the world conqueror Cyrus (no credit to Cyrus) to do God's will so that human creatures everywhere on earth might come to know that the LORD alone is the only God.

Present in Apparent Absence. The amazed prophet then confesses, "O, you inscrutable Redeemer of Israel! You seem to hide yourself in history."

"Not at all," says the LORD. "I am working in the world even when you people cannot see me. From Sinai on, I have always said clearly to my chosen ones, 'Obey me, and you shall live; follow idols, and you will disappear.' That call to choose shalom or destruction is the basic law that holds for all history."

God then openly appeals to the non-Israelite "survivors of the nations," the dispossessed refugees of all the turmoil of war. God calls to the unsaved people in central Africa, Java, Tibet, Patagonia—the ends of the earth. "Turn to me, and be set free from your bondage to things made by human hands; do not lag behind, for every race shall join my people! Every tongue shall sing my praise!"

We need to hear this invitation and pledge by God about worldwide conversion so we do not think more highly of ourselves and our missionary efforts than we ought. True, Paul exclaims rhetorically, unless Christ be preached to the nations, how shall they come to believe! (Romans 10:14–21). But God is not bound by *our* particular faithfulness any more than God was tied to the sometimes obedient works of Israel. That's the whole point of Romans 9–11: God works in mysterious ways to harvest God's people. God may even use political powers (like Cyrus) to free people from captivity to idols, to become God's people. Much more is going on in God's redeeming Rule than is dreamt of in our Western suburban theologies! God's Rule is beyond our ken, will be completed worldwide, and is utterly sure.

Absent in Our Present Life. What does this mean for us who "do mission work" as a church?

First, our planting the gospel by the whisper of radio, a shot of penicillin, or a psalm sung in a thatch-roof meeting place smells sweet to God *only* if we do so unselfishly and with joyful thanksgiving because we are forgiven sinners. Mission done for credit on God's ledger or because we think God might depend on us is a monstrosity.

Second, the testimony that a restored life and lasting power are found only in the LORD will be worked by the Holy Spirit. The Spirit will work it into the lives of people who are antagonistic to God and in the lives of children of believers who have suffered through God's "absence."

We also need to confess that God is often hidden behind the smokescreen of our own idols. *We believers are Christ's body on earth,* and if our neighbors abroad think Christ comes in a Western three-piece business suit, we have obscured Jesus the Savior.

Isaiah's constant warning against manufacturing idols should encourage us to admit that Christian mission to non-Western lands has often been a mixed bag of gospel and household idols. (An idol is anything fashioned by human beings in which one finds false security.) Even today we are tempted to export the gospel in cost-economy efficiency units and growth tables, as if a human life redeemed can be counted like an industrial product and as if bringing Jesus Christ must be tested by management-accountability techniques.

North America is also part of the world, and therefore a field of World Missions. Let us be free to celebrate the Lord God's restorative Rule in the land, making plain that God is not hiding but is compassionately seeking those who have lost their way.

LONG-RANGE MERCY FOR AFRICA: THE CRC IN SIERRA LEONE

After two weeks in West Africa, I understand a little bit of the joke Jan Disselkoen told Inès and me as she took a gnat out of her cup of coffee: When a first-time missionary finds a fly in the cup of coffee, he or she throws out the coffee. A fourth-term mission worker, when the cup of coffee is served without a fly, puts one in before it is drunk.

The moral of the joke is this: Africa has a stolid way of molding foreigners who bring the gospel of Jesus Christ into realizing what has priority and what is only superficial. (Sometimes now I begin to think the church should ship all those who from their armchairs swat flies in so many paramilitary churchly papers, ship them to inland Africa for a while for them to bring Christ to the multitude of beautiful people there, who are desperately afraid of real devils and whose children have malformed bellies burning with fever and hunger. It would be good for the church-related papers.)

The lay of the land

You have to imagine mountainous, hilly country 200 miles inland in Africa where there are no roads. There is also no postal service, no telephone, no electricity. The few cities in Sierra Leone do have paved roads, a post office, telephones, and local generators of electricity (which break down). The cities have banks, stores, multiple-storied buildings, and luxury hotels. But upcountry you move into the West African bush with villages of mud huts and thatched roofs [#53] or (upper-class) cement

---

These essays were first published in *Calvinist Contact* in 1987: 6, 13, 20, and 27 February, 6, 13, and 20 March. Seerveld was invited by the Christian Extension Services (CES) field workers of the Christian Reformed World Relief Committee (CRWRC) and CRC World Missions in Sierra Leone to lead their annual Spiritual Conference in the capital of Freetown during October 1986. Afterwards, he and his wife were invited to visit either the Kuranko team at work (inland up North) or the Krim team (coastal work in the South) for a good week.

[#53] A home in Alikalia, 200 km inland, Sierra Leone

houses with corrugated tin roofs. Upcountry you have only sunlight, moonlight, candlelight, and sometimes a kerosene lamp.

As you drive paved roads inland, at a certain point there are 70 miles to go, and you find only a path of beaten dirt tracks, ruts, crevices, sharp jutting rocks, marshland, and sharp, thick, tall elephant grass bending over your way. There is no road to speak of. No wonder—on the return trip to "civilization" we drove 69 of those 70 miles without seeing any other moving vehicle.

Upcountry you *walk* the miles to the next village. You walk the distance to your rice field or down to the riverside to do the family wash. Only white Christians and the government's army have truck-vans. Only the national African CES workers, and a few traders, have Hondas. Children walk, wives walk, men walk, even the Iman (Muslim leader at the mosque), and tribal chiefs walk. The villagers begin walking to their plots of rice, sweet potatoes, cassava, and peanut mounds before dawn, and they return after sunset, often in the pounding, pouring tropical rains. When you ride on wheels upcountry, as we did, also over tree-trunk "bridges" that straddle the streams [#54] and average 15 miles per hour, you are making excellent time.

No hours, no miles

But that last statement misses the lay of the land upcountry in the

[#54] Roadway bridge of tree trunks
over an inland stream, Sierra Leone

Kuranko tribal territory of Sierra Leone. The countryside does not exist to be driven through at so many miles per hour. There are no miles and no hours there. There is only the *next* village, and a *long* walk. There is *tomorrow* and "the hungry *season*" (the moon-months before rice harvest and after the rice of last year's crop is all eaten).

I listened to CES worker Rowland Van Ess from Foria try to set the time for returning "the big men" (chief, iman, Foria village committee) to Foria he had brought to Alikalia for inspecting the new health center CES had gotten built in Alikalia. The Foria chief and Rowland both looked at their watches. "A half-hour from now? an hour? It makes no difference," said Rowland. "After I greet my friends in Alikalia," said the Foria chief.

Time does not mean money in the West African bush. "Time" as a concept does not exist. There is only the slow-paced quality of activity one is doing: walking in the dark to go pull weeds or hoe sweet potatoes, hauling wood to make a fire, luxuriously greeting one's friend you have not seen for a while, sitting in silence together while the moon rises, waiting for rains to end, panting and resting as the baby is born between your squatting legs. Seedtime and harvest and day and night shape the lives of upcountry villagers in the Sierra Leonen bush, but the long continuous stretches of those everlasting rhythmic rounds are not measured in bits and pieces. You just keep going on doing something, or stop it.

That different sense of duration may be one reason, I thought, why it is *so hard to start something new* in the African bush. Things have always gone on the way people remember things having gone on. Why change if Allah is in charge? The bush dweller does not suffer from the secularized curse of American cost-time efficiency experts who quantify acts of love and care and education out of their proper quality and "manage" such deeds into an assembly-line production.

But the African bush villagers were handicapped, it seemed to me, by having a veil of tradition-bound routine over the eyes, which stopped them from recognizing that there are different kinds of time available to humans—an opportune time for initiative, a bad time to wait, a proper time for speaking up, a time to be brief, and so on. But the only time there is in upcountry Sierra Leone is the never-ending unchanging ages.

Dangerous beauty

Nonhuman creatures in the West African bush are fascinating to a Western visitor. The myriad greens and textures of the foliage—from the huge leaves of the banana tree to the elegant, pointed fronds of the oil palm, the svelte leaves of a cola nut (used for tokens of friendship), to the delicate tendrils of blood-red, wild flowers—make you feel small and humdrum next to such magnificence. The sun at midday can be bewildering, pressing down on your head as if the light had weight; and the quick darkness of night after sunset comes warm and friendly, surrounding you with peace and a quiet blanket of night sounds.

It is the animals, I think, that make the beauty seem ferocious and dangerous. Especially when on your

[#55] A God-sent angel who saved Angie Hoolsema's life from the viper's lunging strike

first day in the bush you see a giant Gabon viper killed before your eyes, 10 feet away, by a man with a machete, and then go home to read from a book that it is the biggest poisonous snake in Africa, whose two inch fangs act like hypodermic needles under the victim's skin "against which first aid is not very effective" [#55].

Tropical animals have an exorbitant lushness and secrecy about them: driver ants whose march *nothing* stops (except kerosene); certain flies that bring "river blindness" if the swellings they induce are not treated; tiny female mosquitoes whose prick in your blood brings malarial fever. Even an ordinary cockroach I saw, whose four inches! of reddish brown glittered into the beam of my flashlight, made you realize this is not a romantic dream or a zoo.

These animals are alive in their mysterious existence and aura of strangeness. No wonder the LORD told Job the animals gave God joy as creatures of God's hands, long before humans existed (cf. Job 38–39). The uncanny power of animals certainly puts humans in their place—a humbling experience denied by centuries of Western Humanist culture.

What does the lay of the land in upcountry Sierra Leone mean for bringing the gospel of Jesus Christ?

* * *

We were eating supper in Alikalia on 17 October 1986 with Angie Hoolsema (CES health officer and nurse) and Jan Disselkoen (CES literary office and assistant Kuranko team leader). It was a full moon. We heard children chanting, women shouting, and drumming going on at the other side of the village. Let's go see what's happening, we said.

It was an eclipse of the moon, and people were fearful. The men had been summoned to the mosque to pray. "The cat's got it!" said various people, pointing to the circular shadow obscuring the full moon. "It is not evil," said Jan to the people in Kuranko. "This is the way Allah made the world." And she explained how the earth got in the way of the sun's lighting of the moon, with her flashlight and a hand.

After the eclipse was past, there was rejoicing. We watched the young men do a rope-dance outside the mosque in luminous moonlight, while the three drummers gradually increased the rhythmic tempo in an exciting beat. Everybody was now having a good time.

The spiritual geography of Sierra Leone
A deep layer within the spiritual make-up of the Sierra Leonen bush villager is what an African theologian would prefer to call "traditional Afri-

can religion." Secular books will call it "animism." From what we learned from the CRWRC and World Mission workers, it might best be understood as a pagan fertility-cult faith, moderated by the tradition of ancestor worship, and tied to disintegrating tribal rituals akin to totenism.

The most important event in a Kuranko person's life is being initiated as a member into manhood or womanhood. The women have their own secret society (Segere) into which adolescent girls are accepted by way of an extensive ceremony involving special foods, dances, and the blood rite of circumcision[1].

The men have their own secret society (PORO) in which boys are initiated in order to become men. When men hold these ceremonies with costumed devil dances, fires, and complex rites, all the women of the village must hide themselves. Married men and married women would never even think of revealing different secrets to the other. What the secrets are Westerners do not know exactly, because *that* they are secret is even more important than what the secrets are.

Every fear has a remedy
So your life deep down is dominated by the fear *and ecstasy* of living near taboo (what is sacred, holy, untouchable, power-giving). Yet the Sierra Leonen bush villager does not live in an existentialistic state of anxiety. His tribal faith is not secular, post-Christian; but his taboo is pre-Christian, in ignorance of God's way (cf. Acts 17:16–34). For every fear there is a remedy.

If the devils are strongest in the bush on Mondays (that's when most "accidents" happen, we say), then you make certain your fetish is in place on Mondays. If our child has a strange fever, you call in the sorcerer—who is not a Barnum Bailey con-man, but who is a veritable shaman figure who can and *does* exorcize illness and evil spirits by incantation. When your old, old grandparent dies, you quickly organize the cortege with the proper dress and dances to scare away the devils, as you march into the "sacred forest" for interring the remains. Only after the 40-day ritual (a kind of private "Lent") and a concluding ceremony of throwing more dirt on the grave, have you laid the ancestor spirit so jealous for attention, to rest.

The pagan fear is always dulled by a shroud of prescribed practices, exercised in communion with others, that ward off from you the evil presence, which is unknown but threatening. And this sense of evil beckoning near, death, a quietly malevolent power, runs like a hidden, under-

---
1 Cf. Jan Disselkoen's article in *Calvinist Contact*, 12 October 1984.

ground river beneath the Sierra Leonen traditional villager's life.

Muslim mores

The Muslim faith has a strong hold on Sierra Leonen life too, especially in the urban areas. Money, presumably from Saudi Arabia and maybe Iran, is flowing into the country to build mosques everywhere [#56] and to set up Muslim schools where Arabic and the Qur'an are taught. In the bush practically every village will have a mosque, even if it's a simple shack with a drum to issue the call for prayer. The faith spread by Muhammed has come to shape the basic pattern of much African life. It is not considered a white man's religion either.

A key trait of the Muslim way of life that struck us was its pious acceptance of whatever happens. Greet anybody in Kuranko land with *I na wali*

[#56] Native children gesticulating before a large mosque in Makeni, Sierra Leone

("You and work"—how are you?) and the answer comes back, *Alla tanto* ("Thanks be to God") or in the Mende language ("There's no fault to find in God")! A kind of passive resignation seemed to characterize the Muslim village life we met firsthand. This was not the sharply militant Shi'ite Muslim faith that took American political foreign policy by surprise a few years ago, ready to convert by force, veil women, and reject Western culture. This Muslim life in the bush was somnolent, dull, an accommodating, nondescript brand of Muslim orthodoxy: do good works, give alms, pray regularly, trust God, and honor Allah's prophets who teach Qur'an.

Such Muslim faith gave a dogged, moderating, work-to-righteous-rule cast to everyday life. You praise Allah easily since Allah is distant and final, and has made known oracularly and supernaturally in the Qur'an what we must do if we want to enjoy heaven someday. So you dumbly do it, without complaint and a lot of questions. The Muslim faith does not teach a biblical sense of sin, personal guilt, Christ's historical death and resurrection, with our living a life of *giving thankfulness* in response. The Muslim way of life promotes the status quo of moral rectitude, without necessarily, however, inciting the typical Western calculating vice of *self-righteousness*. If you have three wives, the Qur'an says you must love them *equally*. That's a tough assignment—sleeping with them in rotation, not showing partiality, providing scrupulously the same gifts to each one—but a good Muslim does what is asked, so that he may live in peace.

Muslim life is religion

Again, a devout Muslim is not a secularized Christian. An orthodox Muslim is *ignorant* of what atonement means, has *no conception of* what conversion from the state of sin might be; the living presence of the comforting Holy Spirit is not possible within the Muslim conception of God. But the Muslim has a solid grip on community that puts many a Christian congregation to shame; and a good Muslim prays regularly, the way we harried North Americans plan to do when we retire.

Also, the Muslim mores dovetail with their underlying Muslim faith the way we Christians of the Reformation only talk about. It seems to me that this is important for us people *at home*, in the Western world, to understand if we want to become prepared to know how to support those who will be presenting the grace of God in Jesus Christ to Africans in Sierra Leone.

You could say, roughly, that the Muslim faith dominates the daily life of those in the hinterlands of Sierra Leone, and the traditional secret societies' pagan faith practically controls all the high points of a person's life (birth, puberty, death) and one's fundamental acceptance into society. So the only way to make the full, biblical counsel of God intelligible for them is to end the ignorance by truthful word, by faithful deed, that *shows* a completely different, biblically-directed way of life, also with a genuinely biblical grasp of festivity for the crucial events of human life.

Imported materialism

There is no doubt that greed springs eternal in the human heart since Adam and Eve fell. There is also little doubt that the hedonist form of greed that drives affluent Western materialism is a particularly hardened form of a corrupting faith in pleasure, and power to do whatever you foolishly will. This secularist faith has also entered the spiritual geography of Sierra Leone.

Sierra Leone as a country with a modern identity received a special birthright, as it were, in the late 1700s, after a few false starts, when British philanthropists helped freed American slaves, later recruited especially from Nova Scotia, Canada, to form a "Province of Freedom" in Africa. Sierra Leone's history from a British crown colony in 1808 to an independent sovereign state in 1961, whose constitution of 1978 instituted a one-party system of government is worth knowing.

But its relatively unrevolutionary story is nevertheless marked by profiteering officials who have used political power to become wealthy. As a letter to the editor in a recent newspaper (*The Observer*, vol. 3, 17 October 1986) I bought on a street corner in the capital of Freetown bravely put it: "The official government price inspectors (meant to cut out corruption) are really bribe collectors" (institutionalizing corruption all the way down the line of authority, even reaching village chiefs in the bush). The newspaper pleaded respectfully with the current President Momoh to serve especially the poor people of the country and stop the exploitation of Sierra Leonen natural resources by foreign businesses and unscrupulous nationals in the government.

The curse of an opportunistic elite is sadly evident. A wealthy Briton at the airport on our flight out of Sierra Leone, in the waiting room *after* you have passed customs, bragged to me by showing the gold bracelet and diamond ring he had bought his wife with hundreds of unmarked 10-pound notes from a Lebanese entrepreneur in the luxury hotel circuit. "It would have cost triple the price in London," he said. He had passed customs with a mere 20 leone bribe (about $1) and gloated over his other deals. "The Lebanese (refugees) run this country," he said with satisfaction.

Anything Western is Christian
And the crass ruthlessness to make a buck, which marks the empire of so many Western businesses, can be seen by how Western tobacco "reaches out for new markets" with its tasteless sign planted in a village unable to protect its children from water polluted by feces. When you see get-rich young men upcountry, who walked into Kuranko territory from far away because there's a gold rush on, smoking cigarettes, or watch boys in shanty-towns who don't have good food but are puffing a drag on a Western, then you wish you had the purity of faith to sing the imprecatory psalms, and plead with the Lord to stop such vicious commercialistic faith from infecting this people who are important to Jesus Christ.

I'm not saying smoking tobacco is a "mortal sin." All I know is that when survival of the fittest runs any worldwide multinational corporation and is combined with corrupted, local government authorities, the resulting damage to the helpless people under that regime is pitiful. This imported materialism complicates bringing the biblical message, of redemption of life by following Jesus Christ, because many Africans think anything Western is "Christian"! Then how do you bring what counts of Jesus Christ's healing turnabout from sin without tarnishing it with our secularized Western packaging? (Certainly you don't smoke—?) May you sleep on a bed rather than on a mat on the ground, without proclaiming your Westernness as part of the change the biblical faith entails?

White Christianity
Good British high-Anglican and low Methodist missionaries were busy with Sierra Leone as soon as Britain used the country as a base to frustrate the slave trade. Fourah Bay College was established in Freetown in 1827, the oldest, most prestigious college in West Africa until recently. This Sierra Leonen college was meant to give a Christian education to bright young Africans. I checked its library holdings: the complete set of John Calvin's commentaries on the Bible in English were among its respectable theological sources. It had a good history of philosophy collection too. Early on, foreign missions like the Missionary Church Association, United Brethren in Christ, American Wesleyan delegations, made their well-meant offers of Western Christianity—church and school—and left it there. Good Roman Catholic medical mission stations seem to have been in the country permanently.

In the last generation a United Christian Council ministries has evolved from various indigenous church denominations, and has tried to develop and give leadership in policies of justice in society, as well as run mission schools and coordinate churchly outreach. There have also always been a smattering of hit-and-run evangelistic efforts, where the white man comes in, gets the converts, baptizes, reports the statistics to head office, and then leaves the area, without counting the relapses or having helped "the little ones" know what comes next struggling through the discipleship of Jesus Christ on earth.

But the genuine help the church of Christ has given Sierra Leone has been largely sound, although often weak. It has not been rigorous enough one might say, concerted enough. Its patience and long-suffering sacrificial deeds of charity have needed a larger vision and a tougher awareness of the *totality* of changes needed in personal life and societal patterns, which submission to the Lord of scriptures revealed in Jesus

Christ must bring about if we are to be counted as faithful to the end, rather than have been only agents of godliness, cleanliness, and a better standard of living.

The CRC in Sierra Leone, there only since 1979, has an important and lasting contribution to make to the Christian witness in that country, I believe. But first there is one more important complication to mention.

* * *

My wife Inès, myself, and our host Jan Disselkoen walked through the village of Alikalia in which Jan and Angie Hoolsema live, greeting people at the openings of their huts or houses. Any new *tababu* (white person) is unusual this far inland. Young women of the village joked with Jan in the Kuranko language. "With how many feet did you sleep last night?" they asked her, laughing at me and Inès. (To "sleep with two feet" means you slept alone. To "sleep with four feet" means you slept with someone else.) Any man with a little extra means has two wives. Because they knew Jan was single and chaste, they could joke this way. The Kuranko never make the joke with anyone the whole village knows is sleeping around.

No Kuranko man sleeps with his wife while she is breastfeeding her child. Mothers breastfeed a child for two years. This cultural pattern helps space a woman's children, but it does encourage promiscuity among the men. When a white missionary mother's milk dried up and she stopped breastfeeding her child, the African women were certain that the husband had commanded her to stop breastfeeding, so he could sleep with her again. No Kuranko woman could ever believe that a mother's milk would dry up or that she would stop early giving her child milk. It is simply inconceivable!

A different, developed Kuranko culture
Because we Westerners do not know how to think African, it does not mean the African does not think. Because a Sierra Leonen adult in the village bush is illiterate, it does not mean he or she is unintelligent. What we were meeting firsthand was an oral culture. There is no newspaper in the Kuranko language; nobody could read it. The "newspaper" is the news people *tell*, walking from village to village, and it broadcasts as well as daily newsprint.

There are no law books to consult, no statutes written down that lawyers could misinterpret: the chief *speaks* justice when the complaints are brought to his residence, and each villager tells his side of the trouble to the chief on the open porch. History is what the older people *remember* and *recount* to their children in the dark and long evenings.

In this tradition of oral activity proverbs and riddles play an important role. Proverbs are vivid, *oral* ways of learning, remembering, and passing on wisdom that gives shape to one's life. Jan Disselkoen is gathering Kuranko proverbs from her African national workers, to use in the literacy programs they are developing, so that the beginning adult reader will have a cultural tie-in to his or her background and not be subjected to "Dick sees Jane" types of sentences. It was great hearing her and her three co-workers tell the meaning in English of some of these riddle-proverbs they have written down for their primer.

"Small drops of water fill up the river."

"An old man who steals will not trust a young boy with a big bag."

"A short man should not laugh at a short child." (Don't pooh-pooh small beginnings of something, since results on your own work may be even less.)

"You should put your hand on wet mud so that when it dries there will be a handprint there."

"If you are to be bitten on your bald head, it is because you removed your head-tie" (hat). (When you get intimately hurt, it is because you made yourself vulnerable.)

At a large conference held in Rotterdam recently to discuss problems of "third world" literature, a Cameroun African finally said, "Why do you Westerners keep on asking us why we don't read? Why don't you tell stories!" That made vivid to me how stupid we would look to an illiterate Kuranko if we use notes for a lecture or a teleprompter for a TV "appearance"—don't we know how to speak out what we know? Maybe we should learn the strengths of an oral culture—its person-to-person directness, its homely, human way of being together by word-of-mouth—even as we try to educate others in the important advantages of having a written culture that has records.

Storytelling a celebration
The Kuranko tribe has storytellers. A famous one, who is blind, is called "the Cat." When "the Cat" comes to a village to tell stories, accompanying himself on a small hand-made, 10-stringed instrument, he is honored and feted as if he were royalty. It's a celebration, and "the Cat" tells stories for four hours or more at a stretch if the hundreds of townspeople gath-

ered around him behave.

It's a kind of festive assembly where the lead storyteller singsongs his way into holding their attention, eliciting short response songs from the audience at times, to lighten the narration, often humorously. Gradually he builds up the characters of the story, who are frequently animals (like Aesop's fables), intensifies the suspense by adding opposing figures and ingenious complications, weaving all the new events into the whole by repetition of earlier motifs. And you can almost hear the people pitting their wits against the storyteller's craft—how will it end? who will outwit whom? who or what is the culprit in the twist at the end?

The only thing in our experience I could compare "the Cat" to was the time when big Fred Tamminga, with drummer(!) Matt Cupido, toured Canada in a van during the early 1970s, and the bard Tamminga read and chanted his ballads to clusters of Dutch immigrants who wanted culture different from the secular stuff on TV.

The storytelling of "the Cat" and his colleagues is kindred to Christ's telling parables: an engaging way of teaching people how to live. Such storytelling really goes back to the tradition of the wise men and wise women in biblical times, like Jotham's fable (Judges 9:1–21), the wise woman of Tekoa's charade before David (2 Samuel 14:1–24), and descriptions like Proverbs 7:6–23. The storied wisdom—that includes the Kuranko proverbs and riddles—are dramatizations of wisdom with responsive audience participation, along very definite, conventional lines, full of whimsical fun and poetic devices that gives evidence of a rich cultural tradition and sensitivity. It is all *oral* and story*full*.

"The Cat" does not give dogmatic maxims, like Ben Franklin's *Poor Richard's Almanac*: "A penny earned is a penny saved"; "Early to bed, early to rise. . ." (This way of didactic maxims is how we often misunderstand the living biblical proverbs too, I think.) "The Cat" enthralls his listeners; they hang on his words, they catch a vision from his graphic, time-consuming way of telling the story, and are buoyed up by the imaginative and artful form in which he slowly makes the points that count, so they stick in your memory.

Music for praise
Close in function to the Kuranko storytellers, as folk leaders, are the "praise-singers." They are the ones who make musical instruments like the siraman (a stringed instrument) and *balangi* (xylophone using gourds for resonance), and who compose songs to praise the chief, to honor an important guest, or to introduce a special celebration. The "praise-

singers" are like David's corps of Levites (1 Chronicles 15:16–24), people with the skillful gift of making music. And the training is passed on within families for generations. Pa Konkofa in the village of Sumbana Bendugu is an expert maker of *balangi* [#57] and comes from a long line of praise-singers. He played the instrument for us like the percussion piece it is, vigorously striking its wooden bars in tonal combinations strange to our ears, melodious and dissonant simultaneously. Marvelously quick grace-note runs counterpointed by a sturdy lower line of tones: it was all done effortlessly, with the nonchalant seriousness of a master.

[#57] Praise singer playing the *balangi* he makes, in Sumbana, Bendugu

Imagine this musician with others in procession approaching the paramount chief (superchief) to sing his praises, and you get an idea of what Kuranko church worship will be like, God willing, in the next generation. And it will be God, not the tribal chief, receiving the special glory.

Telling the Gospel

It struck us as a culturally sensitive way for CES to obey Christ's injunction of Matthew 10:16, introducing church services in Alikalia as story-telling time. The CES evangelist tells the Bible story in the open pavilion in the main village square on Sunday mornings from around 7:30 to 9:30. The section-chief often comes, various important Muslims, a couple of men who are without guile in trying to do good for the village life, and the most are a motley group of people wholly ignorant of Jesus Christ.

The Sunday we attended there were about 100 people present, many women and barefoot children. A couple of older boys were drumming complicated rhythms with sticks on home-made wooden boxes, which stopped when the evangelist asked us to pray. Then he led us all through several songs, sounding out a line, and everybody chorused the response, along with much hand-clapping. The people's body movements were relaxed and happy. Someone read the scriptures.

Then the evangelist told the story of Paul in Acts, and the story went back to Abraham, Jerusalem, Bethlehem, Jesus, and then Paul's being shunted from bureau to bureau to get justice until Paul finally had to ask to go to the top at Rome. When the evangelist mounted the two steps forming a kind of podium in the circle of us people, at the King Agrippa scene, I was hoping he'd give the "Almost Persuaded" pitch to the audience. But you are beginning at scratch here. People don't know what to be persuaded about. Christ's Jewish apostles had the Lord teaching them daily for three years, and they still thought they were going to knock off the Romans rather than *suffer* for the coming of God's Kingdom (cf. Luke 24:21, answered by Luke 24:46–48, Philippians 1:29, 1 Peter 4:12–13)! People can't know in a few months of Bible storytelling what it means to "follow Christ." A lot more has to happen too.

That was an important lesson Inès and I learned during our intensive stay in Sierra Leone: when you start from scratch in bringing the gospel of Jesus Christ to people, you are not telling the Bible story to people who are blanks. The Kuranko African has a developed oral culture that needs to be respected as well as refined.

Sin needs to be wiped out. (And sin shows up in each of the four strands in Sierra Leonen spiritual geography.) But the Kuranko love of children, their gift in storytelling, their praise-singing and rhythmic body movements, the keenness for riddles, and sturdy directness (that makes the Kuranko the best police when they "go to the big city" or into the army), needs to be treasured and reformed. To ask a Kuranko church service to refrain from clapping would be like asking us who are Dutch not to be doctrinal when we study theology.

A Kuranko Christian hymnody, if it is given room to develop, will be different from Genevan psalmody, Scottish quatrains, or Anglican anthems. It takes a Holy Spirited wisdom and seasoned historical knowledge for a mission worker to know what is a seed of wheat, and what is chaff among those to whom he or she brings the way of the Lord.

It became clear to us, however, that it would dishonor Christ's Name for a Western missionary to parachute in, as it were, size up what needs doing from the Western point of view, draw up the regulations, convert a couple of bright Africans, give them Hondas and the cookbook manual for Christian living, and helicopter out. Christian mission work without humble cultural knowledge and patient nurturing is irresponsible.

* * *

I will tell you a true story as I remember its being told to me firsthand.

In the Kpanguma area of southern Sierra Leone, near the delta and coastal area where the CES Krim team need to use a fleet of little boats to do their missionary and CRWRC work, stealing had become a major problem by March 1986. Not only cement and building supplies would disappear, shovels and portable items, but fuel was being persistently stolen. It would bring good money on the black market. No matter how tight you were on security, the thieving went on. It made the construction work very difficult, disheartening. Finally, a particularly severe robbery of diesel fuel, siphoned out of the main CES launch, happened, and the thieves botched the job and let a lot of fuel spill into the boat in a very destructive way.

You can go two routes: (1) the Sierra Leonen (national) police, or (2) the tribal route with the (paramount) chief. If you go to the police, they will send in a truckload of officers, terrorize the village, put a couple of people in jail, whether they were the real culprits or not, and then CES has an enormous public relations problem with the villagers it is trying to help. If you go the tribal route, the chief will call in a sorcerer who will lay a spell on the thieves in the name of evil spirits, and likely nothing will happen. What should be done?

Use biblical means
The CES Krim team of Stan and Barbara Drenth, Bill and Jacki de Kuiper, Brenda vander Schuur, Pat de Vries, Dirk and Joanne Booy, Bert and Ruth Adema, thought about it. Can't we somehow just lay this matter before God, do a *biblical* thing, and bring a message to teach this village to be responsible to God's law for human life? That's certainly more important than trying to get compensation for robberies. The Qur'an says, cut off the hand of the thief. Can't we go to the people with the Bible in hand and say, God says you must not steal!

So the whole CES Krim team stopped work, and called a meeting of the whole village; all the local leaders came. Through a Mendes translator they held a public session with the Bible in hand, and said clearly and simply:

> God is a righteous god. God forbids stealing. The living God will curse a village if its thieves are not punished. Stealing harms relationships. It breaks down love. Your village will be known as a thiev-

ing community. We are all thieves, really, taking glory away from God. We need Jesus to turn us away from thieving. This is what God says. Now it is your turn to respond as a village, before God brings judgment on the thieves and those who hide them.

Everybody went back home.

Two hours later one thief was brought forward. The next day the other thief, an accomplice, confessed. They were both fined and made to work several weeks of labor as punishment.

The stealing from CES has stopped. Someone told Pat de Vries later on CES didn't need to lock things up so carefully anymore. "We [the whole village] decided to stop thieving."

(1) Apparently the Sierra Leonen African villagers have very little or no sense of guilt. (This is hard for me as a Calvinian Christian to believe, but we were told this repeatedly and confidently.) These Africans do have an exquisite sense of shame; however, stealing or committing adultery is not wrong if you are not caught. Once your thieving or promiscuity is found out publicly and you are exposed, shamed, then you are indeed an outcast, and it is hard to become accepted again within the community.

It seems to me the CES Krim team had a pure heart when it got angry. They did not want to take punitive vengeance, but simply wanted to have the stealing stopped and point to God's good word for living human lives. The straightforward public (imprecatory) appeal to have God punish the thieves directly, struck fear in the hearts of these villagers, so used to having sorcerers put spells on them, and shamed them, because CES, whom everybody knew as selfless people working for the good of the village, were frustrated doing good. So they turned from their evil way and produced the thieves. The CES action reminds me of the wise woman from Abel Beth Maacah's rescue of her village from General Joab who threatened to raze it to the ground (2 Samuel 20:16–22).

Within the envelope of evangelism

Evangelism is the overriding purpose of a Christian presence in a non-Christian setting: make the shalom of Jesus Christ's rule convicting and palpable to those who are ignorant of the Lord or who are lost in their evil ways. But "bringing the good news" is like an envelope. If it has no stuffing, no content, no body, then the message of the envelope is empty. Or if what is inside the envelope is porous or irrelevant, ambivalent or makeshift, then your evangelism is full of holes in vain.

I happen to believe the Reformed way of evangelism is the most biblical way to bring the gospel: the *full* counsel of God for *all* of life is what is developed. Reformed evangelism does not adapt to what is current somewhere and say, "That's not too bad for starters, but we've got to *add* a spiritual dimension to life so that heavenly concerns complete your earthly needs. God is concerned for your soul as well as your body." No. And Reformed evangelism, as I understand it, does not come into a (pre-Christian) situation and tell everybody, "You are all enemies of God headed for hell unless you decide here and now to choose for Jesus, be baptized, and do exactly what we say the Bible says if you want to get to heaven." That's certainly not the way Paul talked to unbelievers (e.g., Acts 16:16–34, 17:16–32; cf. Romans 5:6–11), although that's close to the kind of judging confrontation Jesus had with the *hypocritical* believers! (Matthew 23). Again, not that way.

Reformed evangelism *accepts* the unbelieving people *as neighbors, challenges* the *sin* of disobedient pride in our own as well as in the neighbor's heart, which is enmity against God, and *calls* everybody with ears *to a changed way-of-life,* God's way-of-life, by *showing* slowly and historically to your neighbor what a holy life and the shalom of the Lord means on earth.

I think the Krim team dealt with endemic stealing as Reformed evangelists. I also want to give a second and a third illustration of the CRC Reformation witness in Sierra Leone.

(2) The George Brook neighborhood of about 7,000 people is a shantytown of poverty on the hillsides of Freetown, the capital of Sierra Leone. There are seven mosques, two churches there, and less visibly present is a CES project headed up by Steve and Carol Nikkel and their national counterpart, Bob Sam-Kpakra, who together with the local churches, the United Christian Council in the city, and with the approval of certain (national) governmental agencies, are doing development work among these hill-side dwellers.

Responding to concrete needs

The CES arranges loans to groups of people who have a thought-out project that will perform a good service in the community, and give themselves satisfying work. One group of young people opened a "coffee shop," a ramshackle counter with a roof, behind which they heat coffee on an outdoor wood "stove." They also serve slices of fresh bread; buttered is extra. Another person was interested in printing. So he now has a place that prints the cheap exercise booklets of lined paper every child who gets into school needs to do his work in. The "coffee shop" also sells those inexpensive exercise booklets. A tie-dying enterprise for coloring shirts and blouses is in the offing [#58]. All these projects are channeled through committees of the local United Methodist Church and the more

[#58] Tie-dying entrepreneur in Freetown, Sierra Leone

independent Ministry of Hope church in this hillside town. CES plans things in the background, arranges, counsels, judges, but wants to leave the daily administration, when possible, completely in the hands of local church people organized in separate-from-the-church-but-related committees of wise followers of Christ.

In our interview with Pastor and wife Sheaka (UMC) we discussed whether they should help unbelievers escape poverty too, no strings attached? And what if people join the church just because they smell development money? How do you set priorities between immediate needs of starving malnutrition and a long-term policy to build up steady employment? Problems abound.

The sociological jargon that secular funding agencies name this kind of activity is "income-generation" projects. In my book, *the whole package* when it is done *in the name of Jesus Christ* (and that doesn't mean perfectly or without mishaps) is Reformed evangelism in action. Inside the message of "Repent from sin and believe that Christ is the Lord of life" is the concrete grit of learning how to do business justly, ministering to what are real needs of one's neighbors—food, clothing, schooling—and learning to make a living and to do it with hope and joy.

(3) One night after dark we rode for an hour over the jolting rocks

and crevices called a road in the upcountry bush to a neighboring village Nyanwulia.

There the Kuranko national CES team that Jan Disselkoen is training was going to introduce—after much preparatory work, they were now asked to come—their offer to teach anyone who would try, to learn to read. Everybody in the village is illiterate, and even the question of *why* learn to read had probably never entered their minds. The paid town crier had announced through the village there would be "cinema" tonight in the main street.

It was pitch dark, and the lovely African sky was filled with stars. The CES team raised a portable screen and attached a slide projector's wires to the van's battery. A large crowd of at least 300 people had gathered in the open air. We waited for the chief to arrive. One of the CES staff introduced themselves. A prayer was made. Then Sam *read* two simple short stories in the Kuranko language from their primer, his face and text illuminated only by the beam of a large flashlight, and the crowd of men, young men (the most forward-coming recruits so far), women, children, and babies, listened raptly, with amusement, waiting for the twist at the end and the point. Then Augustine *read* a few riddles from a booklet, such as, "If the little child has a big mouth, what about the mother?" Different persons in the audience responded with ingenious and humorous answers. Then Kuranke told about the literacy program by commenting on the colored slides that were now projected on the screen.

The gift of self-respect
First, there were pictures of the famous "Cat," the singing storyteller everybody in Kuranko land knows. Then came slides of people—chiefs, mommy-queens, young people in past reading classes, seriously writing letters of the alphabet on a blackboard, and later on receiving their diplomas. Whenever the crowd saw someone they recognized on the screen, they murmured approval. Especially the women I could see standing near me beamed all over at the women in the pictures. They had never seen "cinema" before! And suddenly I understood the mercy that was being given away by CES this evening: to see ordinary people they knew in color on a screen, just like the famous storyteller, "the Cat," gave each one of them more self-respect and maybe even the motivation to try "reading" stuff too. My heart went out above all to the women whom I saw responding with such an intense eagerness and joyful expectancy. They are worked like beasts all day in the fields, often carrying their youngest, and are still expected to prepare food for the family in the evening (since

certain activities are women's work). I'm not suggesting the men are slackers—the women are normally bought and sold in marriage, often younger ones to older men who have the money and it is hard for them to see their beauty without a glass mirror or showing back in someone's eyes who loves them. Here they were recognizing how lovely and respected and assured they as women could be.

It became plain to us that night in Africa how a literacy program wisely done in the name of Christ can be a long-range act of love. Not just that the Kuranko will be able to read the Krio New Testament (which became available, published in October 1986—Krio is the lingua franca of Sierra Leone), but the CES would be arming them against the secular bullies who take the illiterate's money and write them a wrong receipt they cannot read. *Numeracy* is a first step in literacy! And although the Kuranko couldn't know it yet, literacy is not simply a technique to get a better job in a modern world, but literacy does lead to *records*, which call speakers who go back on their word to a just accounting; and records are a gateway to *history-keeping* that outlasts a forgetful idealizing memory, and makes a *cumulative culture* more accessible. . . .

I saw the Kuranko bush villagers respond somewhat uncomprehendingly but nevertheless hoping—responding to the CES offer of learning to read as if it were good news! The CES literacy program is indeed cradled within a gentle love to provide those often unfortunate neighbors of ours clothing with which to bind up some of their wounds, and prepare them for the secularizing world encircling them. Whoever could have seen the faces of those African people shining in the light of an old slide projector that evening would know that Reformed evangelism is so wonderful and happy-making, that everybody should do it!

* * *

Government corruption in the one-party state of Sierra Leone is discrete but—from what I read in that brave newspaper, *The Observer*—continues to eat away at the vitals of the country. CES is in Sierra Leone not for politics, but for good evangelism with road-building, health-care, literacy programs, and church planting. There are real-life stories, however, (which cannot be told now) of how upon occasion CES nationals have been willy-nilly pulled feet over head into political machinations and crossfire.

During one incident God knocked down a tree over a roadway on which evil men were busy abducting a couple of workers. The same night further along God knocked down another large tree across the roadway, which led to the escape of the prisoners. Those in charge thought other CES workers had laid the roadblocks.

God's miracles are as real as *two* inexplicably felled trees. But the mission workers still have troubles and persecution that hang on for no good reason, which makes life fearful. That's a problem.

An example of a different kind of problem: Angie Hoolsema has dispensed medicine for five years in Alikalia and trained midwives (the two best have become Christians). Before she came, tribal practices, local "medicine," and salves could not stop half of the babies from dying in birth. Now perhaps one in 20 still dies at birth, but infection of the cut umbilical cord and tetanus have been greatly reduced by the hygiene Angy has introduced. She also became active in pushing and pulling the village leadership into building a medical treatment center in Alikalia, instead of just using her private house. At a certain point, the chief reneged on finishing the building. So Angie said, "No more medicine for the village until the center is finished."

Miracles and problems
Soon after, a close friend of the chief received a very bad snake bite and cut, and was rushed to Angie for treatment. "I said no more medicine because you didn't keep your word," said Angie. The chief pleaded for his friend, and promised to get the center finished immediately. (Angie had no anti-venom medicine anyhow, but figuring that the bitten man had survived four hours and would probably live, she accepted the chief's renewed pledge, took out her hypodermic needle and gave the snake-bitten man a placebo.) Talk about Christian nerve! But now the four-room medical treatment center of Alikalia is finished—another miracle, knowing the odds against its having happened—and behind it is a spacious birthing room with a roof. The government has appointed someone trained to dispense medicines, and a German agency has dropped out of heaven to agree to stock it with equipment and drugs so long as they receive receipts for everything dispensed. The village supervisory committee, including Angie and the two Christian midwives, want to make certain the drugs will not be stolen but will be sold at subsidized, fair prices to the needy; so they shall have to be watchful.

Angie has also arranged for a polio-stricken boy in Alikalia, and for two in another two villages, who could only drag themselves over the dirt or stay misshapen in a corner of some hut. She got them into a good mission hospital that straightened out their legs somewhat, provided braces and crutches and there Kekura is! [#59] The brave smile on his face the Sunday we were there ("Kekura" means "new boy") when he "walked" all the way to the church service on his own (¼ kilometer), helped you understand the joy Christ must have had in healing the lame, the deaf and dumb, the blind, and those tormented by evil spirits.

One evening we went out for a walk in the cool air to get exercise and to greet people returning from their fields outside Alikalia. On a solitary path in the bush we met a chief walking back to his nearby village. The women bowed low to greet him respectfully. He graciously called Inès "Madam," and exchanged names with me. Would CES also come to his village to work? he asked. And they had a boy in their village too, struck by polio, a good boy; would CES help their boy to walk like a man too?

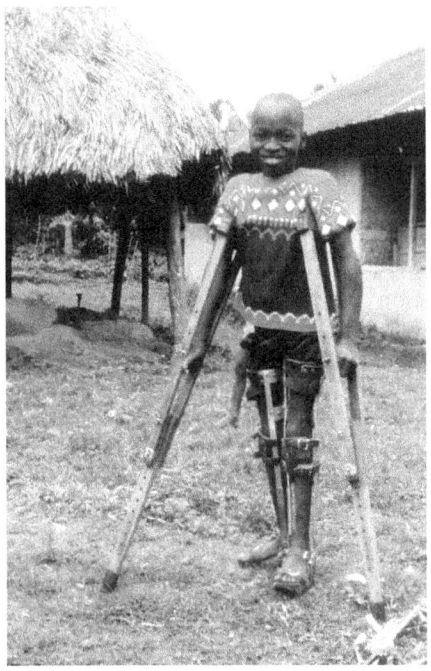

[#59] Kekura, enabled to walk by the love and skill of a christian community

He was a good chief, looking out for the welfare of his people. But that's a problem: as you gradually build up a reputation for doing good in Christ's name, how many places can so few CES workers in the Kuranko bush oversee, and still be responsible?

Promises and mission policy

The problems of the creaturely limits to our given abilities, time, and resources—not even mentioning our sin—will always be with us. God's miracles, the ones we notice along with the ones that go on day and night, which we happen not to see, will also always be with us until Christ comes again. And the troubles of weighing priorities within our main purpose is something that comes with our human task on earth. In weighing priorities there are no simple answers; the Lord only expects us to judge wisely the options we pursue.

As visitors we were disconcerted by the incessant press on Angie and Jan's time, not only at their offices but also at their home, from before breakfast until late at night. (That's a problem the colonialist mentality solved by putting missionaries off by themselves, to live in a compound somewhere away from the village where you worked, violating the basic principle of identifying with those whom you serve.) I was amazed at how Angie and Jan could, at a certain point simply say, "That's it," close the door, and not answer the calls and knocking.

As a CES presence in Alikalia, the only white people for miles around, you are where the medicine, money, and motorized transportation is. That means you are like the hospital, bank, and bus station, all rolled up into one doorstep. No wonder you are besieged by everybody's *needs*. And when the request is important and persistent and real, do you say, "I'm only here to train nationals to do my job in literacy and in health services"? That's like telling Lazarus who asks for a cup of cool water to soothe his fevered frame, "Sorry, fellow, we're only into *preventative* health care." No, naturally if you have any compassion in your bones at all, *you have to do both, somehow.*

* * *

Next to inescapable problems there is one problem that has no right to exist on the mission field, I believe: ambivalence on how serious our committed presence is in a given place. I say this because I think our mission workers in Sierra Leone don't always feel that their mission work has strong priority and staying power with us back home, with us who pray in our armchairs. So all of us need to become utterly clear, certain, and glad about the vision that Christian mission work in foreign territory is there to stay, for at least a generation or two, God willing.

Reformed evangelism is not out to save disembodied "souls," but is committed to seeing *whole human lives changed* by the leading of the Holy Spirit. And not only individual personal lives, but also *the cultural patterns of society* need to be conformed to the will of God. And for Western Christians to train new, first-generation Christian Africans to be indigenous Christian leadership who will themselves train the next generation will take at least a lifetime.

Only an eye and ear
"You had better be careful, Seerveld," somebody says: "What do you know about foreign mission policy? I thought you taught philosophical aesthetics." That is so. And nobody who has ever lived years on a foreign field and drunk the flies in his coffee, stuck in the loneliness *and* lack of privacy that goes with it, helpless heart aching to relieve the utter human

misery and darkness you are wholly enveloped by, should ever think of setting foreign mission work policy.

So I only write as an ear and eye witness to what my wife and I experienced—an immersion course—as I led a concentrated band of 20 mission workers in exploring how the pilgrimage psalms are God giving us blessing and joy for hard times. And then we lived in the African bush village of Alikalia, exposed for 12–15 hours each day to what missionaries go through. We learned much more from the mission workers than we could ever have taught them.

As an educator, however, I know that forming a Christian way of life is not a short-term project. It's never like making a cup of instant coffee, where you boil the water, pour in the powder, mix, and serve. Nurturing a Christian vision and way of life could certainly not be a short-term project when it comes to helping a first-generation of African Christians find their own Christian style of life.

No piecemeal solution
If your best African Christian evangelist in a given place turns out to have two wives, what do you do? Sack a wife? Go for second-best? Move to the norm next time? God through Paul seems to say it may take historical time in places to do what God wants done (cf. 1 Timothy 3:1–13). The Muslim-oriented polygamous blight on the Kuranko people is not the secularized serial polygamy of the West (one *after* the other). But "wives," like the single-parent mothers in the bush villages who thank God they have a growing boy who will keep them from starvation, are tied into the whole economic web of things. It cannot be treated piecemeal. (As I recall, Nigerian pastors came to a Christian Reformed Synod in the '60s with the problem of polygamy: some converts had found out there was an Older Testament in the Bible too, with polygamous patriarchs who were men of God, and what does that mean for today. . . .)

The first-generation African Christian becoming a leader needs someone schooled in the scriptures, especially the Old Testament, which is close in setting to their tribal society, who can repeatedly give counsel nearby in the quiet of an evening, not as to a child but yes, as to one who is a "little one in the faith" (Luke 17:1–4, John 21:15–17, cf. 1 John 2).

No short-term help
If the best person you have found to become health officer in the bush village of Foria and surroundings, replacing Mary Kortenhoven, is a mild-mannered woman named Agnes, what do you do? Sell her a Honda

on credit terms [#60], teach her the basic ropes, and then say, "We'll pay for you from faraway?" Kuranko women are not supposed to ride Hondas over rough terrain, dispense medicines, and sit on councils with men to decide policy!

[#60] Agnes, agent of hope, delivering medicine for CES in Sierra Leone

Even her Christian national CES coworkers who are men have a difficult time imagining her to be wholly equal in authority.

Agnes should be able to expect the word of encouragement in her ear, the steadying hand when she is too bone-weary to stand, and wise advice directly on problems of life and death nobody can foresee—she should expect that from us who put her where she is, for a long, long time. The personal and cultural change she is undergoing *for Christ's sake* is gigantic. Our help must not be thinking short-term, with the result that we would leave behind spiritual orphans: our policy, attitude, and practice should be as long-suffering as the Holy Spirit deems necessary.

Doing it right

You see, the Christian Reformed Church in 1979 decided to go to the most remote areas of Sierra Leone, where no other Christian agencies had ever been, to where ignorance of Christ, where desperate poverty and sickness were epidemic, you could say. It was like going to the Auca Indians. Synod set up a World Hunger Fund and specified it for Sierra Leone in 1979. We are going to do this right: carefully pick a little place in the world in which to be faithful to God with the full package of Reformed evangelism, the biblically-integrated Christian missionary relief effort.

Now it is 1987 and with all the ecclesiastical reorganization going on in CRC World ministries, as I understand it, the *synodical World Hunger Fund* is no longer going to be reserved for the work begun in Sierra Leone.

But let nobody think that hunger in Sierra Leone or in Africa generally can be phased out the way Ethiopian starvation faded out of the secular newspaper headlines, or can be cleaned up the way debris from a hurricane hitting Texas can be cleaned up. Hunger is endemic in Africa, and certainly in the remote bush country of Sierra Leone so long as Christ's redemptive hold is missing on . . . earning a living, *job* formation(!), which is interdependent upon *roads* you can travel on to get produce in quantity to market, which is tied in with being able to *read* records, all of which depends on reliable *health*, by enough of those who as confessing, born-again Christians love mercy, trade justly, and walk humbly with our God.

* * *

"I didn't know Reformed evangelism was so complicated." Well, it is. The good news of redemption, from a biblically Reformed perspective, is as wide as God's creation. And if the church did massive, concerted Reformed evangelism in Washington, D.C., or Ottawa, we would find out, it seems to me, that the complications are not restricted to Sierra Leone.

For at least one day every month in upcountry Sierra Leone, the national CES evangelists, the literacy team, health workers, helpers, whoever can be spared, take pick ax and shovels and go to the spot where with Norm Baker they form a Christian(!) road gang. They are trying to grade the jutting rocks and holes of beaten path into a road linking villages, so transportation will be possible for the market Norm has interested several villages in beginning together.

That monthly act demonstrates, I believe, the kind of integrated, shared life of love for one and all. It illustrates the biblically Reformed seriousness that moves the CRC presence in Sierra Leone, because those "roads" are going to need repair after every torrential rainy season for as long as the earth lasts. We mean to be in there pitching together in the dirt as fellow believers.

Integration of life not information
That is what so deeply impressed us on the field in Sierra Leone. *The Sierra Leonen CES mission workers ARE integrated.* Their life and witness

depend on it! And my fervent hope is that our large bureaucracy now in place back home not make a mistake of thinking its task would be to "manage" or "insure" the practical integration of our biblically persuaded, Reformed world-and-life-vision with deeds, and slips into defining integration to mean "streamlining information" for accountability and "planning done by hierarchical decision-making after receiving inputs."

We as a church, in any of our churchly activities, need to pray to be saved from such "corporate mentality" that can quietly, like radiation, infect the most well-intentioned Christian efforts.

I now ask God for a miracle. I'd like to see the CRWRC and CRWM double-backed board of directors and large superboard of the CRC fuse—as in a vision Ezekiel might have had—into a little band of poorly-clad servants agonizing on their knees in prayer for the hard-pressed families of mission workers struggling in the fields of harvest.

There was a time when being missionary was a life-long calling, and not something like a Peace Corps stint. There was a time when mission workers did not need to fill out monthly reports ("How many adults and children attended Bible stories this week?" "What percentage of babies died this month?" "Did you meet your objectives of people expected to pass the exam?" and so on). Such reporting can be needlessly frustrating when you are trying long-range to decide whether even to dispense medicine in such and such a village, when you want to write the catechism people study, not report on their marks.

And I think I saw how distressing it can be on the field if the home-office feels itself compelled to think too narrowly in terms of getting church organizations in place, period, baptize and move on, because in your report to Synod you have to cite numbers of successes rather than tell stories of heartbreak. I began to wonder how fussy we need to be in checking up on (semi-annual) "progress."

Projects or missions?
For years, I remember, people used to say, "All the money we have spent on Indian missions in southwest U.S.A.—no results!" But suddenly in 1982 there is a Classis Red Mesa represented at Synod. Classis Red Mesa did not come as a result of a two-week Crusade. It came because our church was faithful for a generation, and God blessed our often myopic efforts. Again, because we were on location in Africa we have been moved now to pray harder that ways be found to do things in orderly fashion and to ascertain on faithfulness without hurting sensitive, committed people in bureaucratic short circuits.

The crux of the policy decision, I think, is this: does the CRC go with its highly-dedicated, carefully-selected, professionally-trained mission workers "to bring Christ" to a culture as a "project," with limited goals and quantifiable results, or go with a commitment "for life," with the unoverseeable implications of Reformed evangelism beyond Sunday services, for two, three, or more generations? Unclarity or double-mindedness on this fundamental vision can only confuse the supporting churches and demoralize the workers on the field.

What needs to be constantly held up before all of us, I believe, who yearn to bring the liberating Rule of Christ to the peoples of the world, is to hear from the leaders of our church agencies[2] in mission: hear from their lived experience on the field that our firmly-set policy of Christian mission includes road building, nurses, literacy officers, community developers, teaching teachers, and whatever an integrated team in a given culture most need to have. That is the way Reformed Christians do mission work: raising signposts of a biblically-directed way of life so that others with changed hearts may make a godly way of life out of their traditions.

One could possibly decide just to teach reading as a transferable skill in a short-term project to help national Africans acclimatize themselves to modern methods, and that would be an honorable thing to do. One could decide to bring supplies and medicines to a foreign situation where they are desperately needed, and try to minimize the black-market profiteering that is bound to go on as a matter of course, so the goods reach more needy people, and that too would be a worthy thing to do.

But worthy projects are not Reformed evangelism, and could miss the heart of Christian mission: nurturing a Christian way of life among those who are incredulous that there is anything new under the sun. Mission work of bringing full-orbed, long-range mercy and hope to Africa is not a short-term project of several years, but is a shared life. And it is "Kingdom work," not just getting people on church rolls.

To undergird
Inès and I feel greatly privileged to have seen how an integrated CRC operates in Sierra Leone, by the CES workers who are often literally bowled over by persecuting troubles. I have written out of thankfulness as a testimony to their faithful love for our Lord and their services on our behalf.

I have written also maybe because of the way a fully seven-months pregnant Joyce Baker quietly hugged me goodbye after having travelled

---

2 As William Van Tol did so well in *The Banner* of 3 November 1986.

for two hours to Alikalia for a fellowship supper, and now faced being driven another jolting two hours back, in low four-wheel drive, to their home in Badela.

I have written also because of the way Bert Adema said goodbye to me in Freetown, with weary determination and fire in his voice. "It's not the work that gets us down, or the difficult living conditions. What gets us down is not knowing whether we are understood and fully supported. Whatever you do, please keep praying for us."

Christian Extension Services of the CRC in Sierra Leone [#61] not only needs prayer for its full-orbed, long-range, integrated program of mercy and hope for Africa. It also needs prayed money, and a reaffirmed understanding policy that this integrated CRC effort of Reformed evangelism is going to go forward on all fronts for as long as the CRC lasts, or until the Lord returns.

So that our mission in Sierra Leone does not get lost in the cracks of reorganization, take out your checkbook in this new year of 1987 and send some of your tithe marked to CES, Sierra Leone.[3]

[#61] CRWRC Jan Disselkoen and Francis Saion Kamara before the CES literacy office in Alikalia, Sierra Leone

---

3   For more about the Christian Reformed Church in Sierra Leone today, see: http://www.crcna.org/pages/crwm_CRC_Sierra_Leone.cfm.

WE ARE NOT PILGRIMS: WE ARE CALLED TO BUILD TENT CITIES IN GOD'S WORLD

I believe that this world belongs to God who created it (Psalm 24:1–2, Job 40:6–41:34). So as a human creature I am at home in God's world of marvels, from the eclipse of the sun to the birth of a baby (Psalm 145–150).

And I believe that Christians, as God's word of Ephesians says, are "no longer strangers and sojourners" on earth but are "the intimate household of God"— the very place where God the Holy Spirit hangs out (Ephesians 2:19–22) till Christ comes again!

That's a core of what I believe.

Before I formulate two injunctions that follow from my being at home here in God's creation while facing the North American culture of Mammon—expectant of the Lord's return to end my sin, the cruelty of neighbors to strangers, the tears and pain of cancer, injustice, greed—let me say something about the biblical idea of being a "pilgrim."

Biblical Note on "Pilgrim"

Before Exodus in the Bible comes Genesis, and after Peter's pastoral letters in the Bible comes John's *Revelation* of what's finally going to happen. To note that booked order of the Bible about the beginning and ending of history is important so we not define our human meaning as being one of exodus and pilgrim, as strangers passing through a foreign land.

If you think that the Bible starts with Exodus you are likely to exaggerate liberation from the evil powers of the "Egyptians' establishment" and promote historical subversion or fervent prayer to get to heaven and out of here.

The fact that Genesis is first and establishes that the human generations are here to cultivate the LORD's garden (even before sin laid us

---

First published in *Christian Courier* 53:2545 (12 September 1987): 10–11.

waste, Genesis 1:26–31), takes away any obsession for us to have to go somewhere else than the world where God purposely placed us, man and woman.

The inspired fisherman-turned-evangelist, Peter, refers in his letters to the persecuted Jewish Christians dispersed throughout Asia Minor as exiles sojourning, resident aliens in godless lands (1 Peter 1:1–2, 2:11–17). But at the same time he reminds them that they are really "a royal priesthood" with "an indestructible inheritance" Christ is bringing back from heaven (1 Peter 2:4, 9–10, 1:3–5).

And that return-to-earth theme is the very resounding climax of the last book of the bible, reaching beyond "the Hebrews" who missed the promised patrimony (Hebrews 11:13–16, 39–40): the holy city of God shall descend from heaven and God self will live among God's people fully restored from every nation under the sun, while rulers of the earth bring their cultural treasures purified into this celebrative feast for the Lamb on the new earth under an unpolluted sky world without end (Revelation 21:1–4, 22:1–5).

No strangers to earth

As I searched the Scriptures to prepare these remarks I discovered, to my surprise, it is less than biblical to think of the self as one in the vocation of "pilgrim"! We who are in Christ, children of God, Creator of this world, are not wandering Jews, not Muslim pilgrims, not secular nomads.

Sin and godless culture may make us feel sometimes like aliens and exiles. But humans are not cosmic strangers in God's world, and the Holy Spirit-filled body of single professional nurses, mothers and fathers of families, lawyers, bankers, garbage collectors (now called "solid waste disposal and recycling specialists"), teachers or unskilled laborers: we humans are defined by the task to tend obediently to the earth with the gifts the Lord who is a-coming gave us (Psalm 115:16–18, Matthew 25, Ephesians 4:1–16).

It's true that Scripture says we humans do not own anything outright: everything "in our possession" is on loan from God, held by us in trust, including our precious lifetime of 70 or 80 years. That's why the Lord God forbade the Israelites selling any land "in perpetuity" and instituted sabbatical years and the Year of Jubilee, so rich "Christian" nations could after a while forgive two-thirds-world peoples of their debts (Leviticus 25).

Fixed on Christ

A world-flight policy, however, is wrong-headed, says our Lord. Anybody willing to give up what is valuable to him or her for the sake of God's redemptive rule will receive it all back a hundredfold in these days (with persecution!) as well as in the coming age, which shall endure forever (Luke 18:18–30, Matthew 10:16–33, Colossians 2:8–23).

Therefore, dear reader, if you already enjoy a heavenly citizenship (Philippians 3:20–4:1), keep your orientation fixed on the ascended Christ, who indeed has the power to rule human culture now, engaging us as apprentices (Colossians 3:1–17). Keep that eschatonic vision of Christ's triumphal reclamation of culture coming vivid in your consciousness as you weather the tussle of history in your generation.

I know, there is a long-standing habit of ascetic Christianity, from John the Baptizer's disciples who did not pick and eat corn on the Sabbath or drink wine at weddings, to Non-conformist Puritan John Bunyan's solitary Pilgrim named "Christian" who resolutely left the City of Destruction and slowly progressed to the Celestial City on the other side of the dark rolling river. I respect such serious pilgrims.

But it is wrong, I think, to make an ascetic pilgrimage the norm for Christian living. It is not the full counsel of God, as Paul puts it (Acts 20:17–27), to order life negatively in God's world, denying oneself things, making constant sacrifices, since "everything created by God is good, and nothing is to be rejected provided it be received with thanksgiving, for then it is made holy by the word of God and prayer" (1 Timothy 4:1–5).

Creational injunction

Be joyfully thankful for creatural gifts. It is the amazing grace of God that elicits wonder from children who at a seashore discover the laughing pleasure of having mud ooze between your toes and of feeling the unexpected slap of God's wetness on your bare back flung from a tumbling wave. It is a gift of God to go fly a kite and receive the nuanced knowledge of the wiggle of wind and the tug of air currents.

And the Lord is glad for us to find out that trees are sexual, that butterflies grow out of caterpillars, and gorillas in a normative zoo chewing on carrots are looking at us too. It is a great blessing for us humans to realize God's sand, water, plants, and animals are co-creatures with us and, like the sun, praise God more faithfully in their way than do we (Psalms 8, 19, 104).

The good creation

I'll never forget the lighting and people movements around where I lay sprawled between the kitchen and the dining room in my childhood home when, precisely at 10 minutes past six o'clock on Saturday evening, September 5, 1936—as I was following the large print in a book before me, perusing it on the floor—I suddenly discovered I could read.

"I can read! I can read!" I hollered, and ran to my mother doing dishes in the kitchen, and she had to stop to listen to me haltingly read. To make sense suddenly out of mute written marks on paper seems almost like a miracle to the illiterate.

It may take a while after a girl develops breasts and a boy experiences an erection to become at home in your sexual corporeality. But the erotic solar plexus of shame and intimacy and mutual troth is an exquisite, playful place in God's creation rich with poetry and caresses. It is a great privilege to enter and inhabit that place.

Picking strawberries or wild huckleberries, fruit of vine and bush, free in the fields; or not being blind to that soft incandescent sunlight after a supper hour when green foliage turns golden and shimmers like a bewitching hour; or the ability to weep quietly after someone you love has been inexplicably, deeply hurt: God sees all these creaturely affairs, and it is still good (cf. Genesis 1).

Be at home

So, to bypass daily creatural realities provided us personally by God as if you have to get somewhere else for a special blessing or an oracle—to Delphi, Mecca, Lourdes, to "do" Jerusalem as a tourist, or even to ascend to heaven—is to be ungrateful to our saving Creator Lord.

Therefore, being fundamentally at home here as human creatures in God's creation entails a way of life focused in a joyful thankfulness to the Lord for all God's creatural gifts. This orientation is basic to a reformational Christian worldview.

The whole third part of the *Heidelberg Catechism* (1563) affirms this position by expositing the Ten Commandments and the Lord's Prayer as what structures the gratitude that believers evidence after becoming holy-spirited redeemed sinners in God's world.

Redemptive imperative

Because the North American way of life is so deadly, God's redeemed people should not go on pilgrimages; they should be building tent cities of refuge instead inside the Babylonic Empire. Communal redemptive cultivation of the earth constitutes bringing the Good News of Jesus Christ to your neighbor.

That's the way it always happens: in whatever area of culture Christ's Body does a no-show, that cultural arena understandably goes to hell. If parents don't like the movies and videos available for their children to see, has it ever occurred to them to pray for us to ferment conditions where, over time, a body of informed, professionally competent young Christians could together eventually produce cinema for their great-grandchildren and neighbors? Cinema that would be more than travelogues to Golgotha for showing in church basements or general audience flicks with Hollywoodish happy endings.

Jesus himself prayed fervently to God (John 17) not to take his disciples out of this world but to keep them from succumbing to the evil one as they went into the world to bring healing, the gospel of forgiveness and redirection in cultivating shalom.

The long haul

To work communally at a redemptive culture in our secularized age sounds unreal unless you have a convicted, full-orbed reformational biblical vision of God's sovereign rule over every bit of creation, and a biblical patience for the long haul.

If you wanted to reform the scatological cabaret of *Second City* in downtown Chicago, or at the *Doofpot* in Amsterdam, it would take at least a generation to develop a repertoire of redemptive jokes that could catch the secularist off-guard and draw a puzzled laugh.

Many evangelical Christians want to get you saved, brother or sister, but after you've made the decision to stand up for Jesus, how do you then live in God's world?

Achievable goals

I don't have something esoteric or idealistic in mind with "post-Pentecostal tent cities of refuge," but something as down to earth as a healthy diet set up by parents for their children where you eat more and weigh less so that junk food wrapped in plastic tastes counterfeit, like something overly sweet.

A Christian philosophy that humbles theoretical thinking and can integrate encyclopedically emotional, social, ethical, and economic facets of life is a welcome refuge of meaning at the over-specialized secular "multi-versity." Such a philosophy can sort out mis-formulated dilemmas and locate good openings for analysis.

A collection of short stories like Hugh Cook's *Cracked Wheat* (1985), George Langbroek's viscosity etching *Home* (1996) [*RA #25*], Peter Maxwell Davies' "Eight Songs for a Mad King" (1969), can be places for discouraged unfortunates to take shelter for the time being, get their bearings, to be gentled by wry critique and trenchant insight so that he or she recognizes, thank God, that evil and power-mongering shall not prevail over the meek.

If the worshiping church gives only lip service to its confessing members who are struggling to serve the Lord in a Christian labor union, in a motley community of artistic saints reaching out to passersby, then that organized ecclesiastical communion should be ashamed of itself. Such church leaders who may make pious pronouncements are still false to the godly calling of being persecuted along with God's people who suffer discrimination in our secularized daily life.

Anointed agents of the Kingdom

For me the most biblical, root metaphor for human lives that would be obedient to the LORD is for Christ's followers to be not pilgrims en route to heaven but a remnant community of royal priests in the order of Melchizadek (Psalm 110, Hebrews 4:14–8:13). We must build tent cities of refuge in the very citadels of secularized culture for the outcasts God still wants to save and sanctify (cf. 1 Timothy 4:6–10) through our ministrations, as we wait expectantly for the Lord to return to complete Christ's rule of creation.

Our daily work of parenting, journalism, nursing, buying and selling, or whatever it be that keeps us busy, fulfills the law of Christ, says Scripture, only if it is a channel of loving your neighbor, bearing their burdens (Romans 13:8–10, Galatians 5:22–6:2), not nitpicking whether the "t" in your own particular orthodoxy and orthopraxy be perfectly crossed or not.

So the only "pilgrimage" we royal priests are asked to make is to the worshiping church gathered on the weekly day of celebrative rest (Hebrews 10:19–25; cf. Psalm 122) where we may hear God's sure Word proclaimed about the little stone not cut by human hands that shall someday shatter the godless kingdoms in this world (Daniel 2:1–45). And we may feast on the Eucharist—thanksgiving!—while we sing, particularly, the medley of Psalms 120–134 as we gird up our loins for daily life where the joy is still tempered by tears.

We are not fugitives on the earth, not undercover agents, but "anointed ones" of the Holy Spirit (cf. *Heidelberg Catechism*, Q/A #32), called to build Spirit-filled tent cities of refuge even as we suffer being laughed at because of the sin that still captivates us and wastes our thanksgiving.

We look forward to the cataclysmic return of Jesus Christ, when right-doing shall indeed finally be completely at home in God's world (2 Peter 3:8–13). And we adopted children of God are assured by Psalm 23 that the Lord will give us what we need—even in the presence of enemies—to stay faithful, preserved in the hope of our Lord's coming.

Tent-makers in training, Inès, Cal, and Luke Seerveld, California, 2010
(photo by Jan Seerveld)

Bastards or Sons of God?

You have not yet stood up, fighting against sin, till it cost you blood, have you?
And have you entirely forgotten that *comfort* spoken to you as sons:

> My son, do not belittle the teaching of the Lord that hurts,
> And do not lose heart when you are soberly corrected by God,
> For whomever God loves the Lord disciplines;
> *Everyone the Lord adopts as a son He gives hard knocks.*

So you are undergoing forming that hurts? God is treating you as sons (what son does a father not discipline). If you are lacking the forming that hurts—what characterizes all believers—then you are bastards and not sons.

> The earthly fathers we had disciplined us, and we respected them. Should we not even more so submit to our heavenly father, so that we shall live? Our earthly fathers straightened us out for a little while according to what seemed best to them: our heavenly father shapes our lives with the result that we take part in God's own holiness!
>
> Although all disciplined training seems to hurt at the moment rather than make happy, later on it affords those exercised in its forming the sweet fruit of being right before God.

So then, we too, practically surrounded by a crowd of witnesses [Abraham, Moses, Gideon, Samson, David, and thousands more]: *let us too, patiently struggle in the fight ahead of us,* sloughing off everything that hinders, shucking our own weaseling sin, sight fixed solely on Jesus, the one who originates and completes trusting faith.

> Jesus took it—a cross!—careless of being ridiculed, in anticipation of the happiness ahead of Him: and now He is established at the right side of the throne of God.

Written and printed in 1967, slightly modified by request in 2013.

Take careful note of what came of His having stood up to the obstructing tactics of the lawbreakers ranged against Him so that you, becoming tired out by the strain, do not weaken.
(Hebrews 12:4–11, 1–3)

The Bible always turns us about-face. Hurts are tokens of God's love to God's people, says the Word. Struggle is the natural life of a believer. Uncompleted success is evidence of the Christians' stunning victory acoming!

It is this truth of Proverbs (3:11–12) and Hebrews that the orthodox humanist calls a lie, opium to rationalize failure. This whole business is a "comfort" that inactive, well-to-do believers in a church find farfetched. And for those who truly keep the faith, battling their own sin as well as the opposition of men not honoring Jesus Christ, for them too it often does not seem to be good news.

But the Holy Scriptures clearly say so: *suffering for Christ's sake defines believers; if you do not live in such New Testament turmoil, you are bastards and not sons of God.*

The early Christians written to here were in a fix. Years before things had been worse but clear-cut: believing Jews were imprisoned and their property was confiscated (Hebrews 10:32–34). Right now they were not yet afflicted by a bloody martyrdom. They were suffering a kind of twilight persecution—subtle threats, intimidations, legal harassment. Roman authorities were inhibiting free exercise of the Christian faith in society by restrictive sanctions and ominous pressures, all in the name of civil peace and economic welfare.

Such twilight persecution began to wear on those Christians of long ago. It is the hardest persecution to bear because it is indecisive, intangible, leaves you alive, intact but hurting, and lets the oppressive ruling forces think they are somewhat tolerant.

The early Christians were hurting to the quick. So some left the body of Christ and made their peace with the world. Others withdrew their faith into a church-tight compartment and let it go at that, confident that was enough to be approved of God; and they continued to make a living as best as they morally could in a semi-tolerant world. Some persevered at bringing Christ concretely into the marketplace, and were forced to keep on suffering for it. And these Christians were wondering whether the cost of discipleship (=Christ's discipline) was worth the trouble. Was Jesus Christ not supposed to be the answer to our problems? The end of our difficulties, harbinger of peace, good will, and security?

No, says Hebrews. Faith in Christ means fight in an evil world. And fight means you will be struck by the evil doers in the world. But remember (and Hebrews uses the Old Testament to back up its exhortation), remember that whoever is in trouble for the sake of Jesus Christ is a son of God. In fact, if you are not in trouble because of Jesus Christ's lordship you are a bastard. And the Bible knows better than any St. Lawrence Seaway dockworker what bastard means: you are illegitimately there on the face of God's earth; you are there but have no right to be there.

This is the choice and the comfort! of the Word of God.

One reproach that a reform movement receives in history from those already established in power, those determining the social order, or who mean to be disinterested critics, is this: you are fanatics looking for trouble, bigoted crusaders bucking (since "democracy" became the formula) the will of the majority; get wise and live with the existing set-up, or get out!

And often "reform movements" have simply been a new minority of revolutionaries willing to operate by hook and crook until they take control, when with the cynical piety of their erstwhile overlords they can institute a new brand of social activity as the genuine legal order. Groups of Christians too have sometimes been unholy troublemakers, seeking their own profit in God's name, inflated with a self-appointed Messianic calling or carping perversely with a martyr complex—as if trouble were evidence of sanctification just because the trouble met following Christ is a mark of God's care.

But this reproach of divisive intolerance aimed at squelching reformation is utterly mistaken when secular powers level it at God's people seeking Christ's rule in society, fighting against sin. It is sin that divides man against man; and Power devoid of biblical sensitivity is what cannot tolerate variety of opinion and different ways of life. Just because Christ-believers have to stand up to unjust coercion or perjure their religious conviction does not make them troublemakers in society. And just because Bible-believers know that the perspective of pagan Roman rule or of the increasingly secular, modern North American rule violates the peace and freedom Jesus Christ brings to earth: because Bible-believers have to say so in word and deed does not mean they are bigots. It means they are obeying God's Word rather than men. That such obedience entails hard knocks they know too.

What distinguishes God's people persisting in tears at the fight of faith for Christ's rule from bellwether sects and motley revolutionaries is the patience, prayer, and comforted *self*-denial that characterizes their doings.

This is what Hebrews has to say, the Word of God that organized Christian endeavors must hear: not the threat of secular power brokers or the counsel of churchmen fearful of "extremes."

Self-denial is built in to biblical practice of the Christian faith. By faith Abraham went to the extreme of sacrificing Isaac; by faith Moses extricated himself from Egyptian wisdom and culture (Hebrews 11:24–26). By faith Gideon saw that God did not need large numbers of men to win; by faith the sinful Samson learned all power comes from the Lord alone; by faith David gave up building a temple for Yahweh because God's timing ordained it for the next generation; by faith the original New Testament Christians, some of them, because they could not do otherwise, suffered twilight persecution, weakly struggling to articulate Christ's rule in a hostile world.

We too, in the presence of their historical witness and before many potential witnesses now living, must be prepared to deny ourselves and suffer failures in faith. It is so tempting to want more birds in the hand than in the bush. And it is so aggravating to have hurts—saints bleed too when cut, have nerves that give way, know the agony of frustration. But if every little completed coming of Christ's kingdom in our lives is the blessing of Almighty God upon our labors, so too every disappointment, obstruction, and evil encountered privately or as an association in pursuit of Christ's glory: such hurts are to be affirmed, by faith, as touches of God's love, training in God's holiness.

Training us in holiness comes by the Lord's teaching us not to covet success, not to suppose God's kingdom is dependent upon our efforts, by originating in us the sense of patient passionate dependence upon God's Word and Holy Power. This is what counts also for Christian school societies, Christian task forces in the market place, and organizations like Citizens for Public Justice: to be right before God and rightly (=legitimately) at work in educational, socioeconomic, and political affairs before it is altogether night.

So live the sons and daughters of God: meek before God, bold before men in the power of the Holy Spirit mocked, oppressed, patiently suffering for Christ's sake, in joy, comforted by the fact that we cannot lose! We who obey the Lord shall inherit the earth (Matthew 5:5, Hebrews 10:35–37)!

In the coming years, as the twilight persecution grows more grim, may the Christian organizations in Canada continue, nevertheless, fearlessly to pose the decision to the Canadian world: will you recognize Christ and God's freedom in areas of public concern and the realm of economic activity or not? The nation's response shall bring blessing to the land or foreshadow judgment. And let everyone banded together in committed Christian enterprises quietly yet determinedly in love shame the bastards comfortable in Zion to self-examination, repentance, and active prayer (comfortable believers are bastards)—if official, stereotyped believers could only be led to pray sincerely and openly for the work of the Institute for Christian Studies and Citizens for Public Justice, in time they will be won for active participation. Such an arousing ministry just might be used by our Father in Heaven to rejuvenate many church communions within hearing, or force them more consciously to the decision to pass by on the other side of the road.

Let us all too, everyone in his place, aware of the choice and the comfort! before us, be constant in pleading for the perseverance of those suffering so noiselessly under the violence of unseen hands. Trembling at the power of the Evil One who exploits our mistakes and pride to hurt us so grievously, let us implore the Lord to come quickly and establish our Savior's throne upon the earth so that all nations and peoples will be God's footstool.

If blood must be spilled—if the reformation and praise of God, which God's adopted sons and daughters gathered in the communal clusters of people dedicated to following Jesus Christ breathe into the cultural world of twentieth century Canada, eventually be snuffed out, violently or quite properly, by well-meaning or evil-meaning men, no matter: even then we will serve the Lord. For God's Word alone is our life.

OPERATION FISH AND BREAD FOR THE ONTARIO GOVERNMENT

Proverbs 25–29 is a short biblical treatise on leadership in God's world of history. I shall read at the beginning and at the end of my remarks the brief portions that give structure to those chapters in the biblical book of Proverbs.

This is the Word of God:

> **If hunger troubles the person hating you, give that one bread to eat, and if thirst gripes your enemy, give him or her water to drink: although you will be stoking coals of fire on your adversary's head, the LORD God will finish it off for you and make it whole.** (Proverbs 25:21–22)

This injunction is the key passage of chapters 25–29 of Proverbs. The imperative—do good to those trying to do evil to you!—sums up both the instruction of Moses (Leviticus 19:9–18) and the teaching of Christ (Matthew 5:38–48) on loving your neighbor. To do something concrete that serves a vital need of even those who are intent upon making your life miserable epitomizes the kind of mature obedience to the LORD most of us have difficulty with. We'd rather pay people back in kind, or avoid disagreeable confrontations. But this biblical injunction stands as our calling if we want to heed Proverbs 25–29 on becoming God-fearing leaders with the humbled self-control, expectant joy, and wisdom necessary for doing what is right on earth.

Paul quotes this same choice imperative from Proverbs just before he begins the famous chapter Romans 13 on Christians' respecting the government. Political rulers have the office to be servants of God for the good of the nation's citizens (Romans 13:3–4). And christian citizens

---

Meditation presented at the Institute for Christian Studies on 18 June 1982, two weeks after Bill 137 was introduced in the Ontario Legislature, which would have forced the ICS to close its doors and cease to exist. This piece was published in *Calvinist Contact*, 2 July 1982, p. 10.

ought to give the state authorities what is due them—taxes, deference, the honor they are worth (Romans 13:7). Do what is right by governing officials, says God's Word (1 Peter 2:13–17). Do what is good, not what is evil. Give your government what it needs, even if Caesar oppresses you.

Since more and more governments around the world seem to be betraying their office of serving God by not doing good for their citizens, we comfortable Christians need to re-examine what we owe such governments. As the spirit of secularism hardens people's hearts who set ruling policies to treat their subjects ever more ruthlessly, violating human lives by fear and torture, or simply constricting human life by legal force, we need to know more surely as a body of Christ what does Caesar deserve from us.

Those who conceived and gave birth to the Institute for Christian Studies did not believe Christ's enigmatic reply to the Pharisees meant you pay off Caesar with his tax monies and as little else as possible, and you partition the rest of your life in dedication to God (cf. Matthew 22:15–22). The legacy of the Reformation, in its genius that the whole life of society needs to be integrated and permeated by a people faithful to the Rule of Jesus Christ—even though reformers often disagreed and failed historically to practice in love what they believed: that Reformational legacy confesses that Caesar has coming to him not just money (begrudged money, because my conscience is continually violated), but Caesar has coming to him the Word of the LORD for governing society.

The fact that the Institute for Christian Studies is confronted by the Davis government of Ontario with Bill 137 (the old Bill 4) that threatens to exterminate us as a legal, degree-granting, graduate educational institution is a marvelous gift of God, an opportunity for us to make the Scriptural claims of a *just government* public in a poignant, concrete way.

It is unjust for the provincial government to deny us a charter because our biblical vision gives a focus to our graduate studies that is christian. We are more than willing to be tested by academic peers on the academic quality of our work. But we are not willing to call our christian philosophical endeavor a parochial theology or "biblical studies." And we are not willing to give up our faith-identity and be incorporated like stray atoms into existing, secular compounds. We want to serve the LORD with our own integrity, to serve our neighboring, secular professional colleagues and the many evangelical students who come to us for Reformed backbone in their studies of philosophy, history, political science, theology and aesthetics: we want to be a bona fide educational institution with bona fide degrees granted and recognized in freedom of religion, so we may provide sound christian schooling in Canada. To be denied that full, responsible right in name or fact by a political act is unjust, and injustice is not good for Canadian society.

Proverbs 25 says: give the unfriendly Davis government the biblical Word about justice in language they understand, because they need it. The Honorable Bette Stephenson acts like your enemy, but she's in a bad way, hungering and thirsting for genuine justice, it may be, but drinking what leaves her thirsty. Be adamant, only give her water that is unpolluted, clear as crystal on what the score is, that maybe will even quench her thirst! That is, witness to the truth of what you stand for educationally, single-mindedly live for, and, so help you God, would be willing to be padlocked for.

Why not? Such a joyful, rallying witness to the Spirit that drives us on to be good professional researchers, educators, and graduate students—an exuberant testimony that we are thankfully engaged together in quality education for the sake of Christ's Rule, loving our neighbor, supported by the world-wide body of Christ: this is what we should unswervingly do and pray for. Our concern is not first of all whether we can insure that we get what is just for our circumstances. God will take care of that, not the Davis government. We may persevere in faith asking for that justice as tenaciously as the widow in Christ's parable did before her unjust judge (cf. Luke 18:1–8). But we must seek first of all that *the Word for justice in education* be delivered to Queen's Park with the firm love, reckless wisdom, selfless dedication, and principled insight that will make God's ordinances for schooling known and legally protected for practice in Ontario as well as elsewhere in Canada. Such testimony, pressure, and existential fact will seem like burning coals on Davis and Stephenson heads, says Proverbs 25, but don't worry. The Lord will make it right, *shalom* it, bring it off, full-fill what good is done.

You could understand the crux of our mission this way: people using Christ's Name have dirtied it with "degree mills" in this province; the government of Ontario is now saying, such use of religion means fraudulent education, and we are called upon to stop it; here is Bill 137.

We reply: yes, but you are offering stones instead of bread, and have slipped in a scorpion for our bag-lunch instead of fish (cf. Luke 11:5–13). This is why we are mounting **Operation Fish and Bread for the Ontario Government** instead of its handout of scorpion and bag of stones. We don't want cake, Honorable Stephenson and Davis. We want to give you fresh fish and good bread to eat.

A person intent upon injustice is a stinking outrage to those

who live innocently doing what is just: whoever walks straight and has a habit of doing what is right is anathema to the godless one. To be awed by somebody (in power) sets you up for getting caught in a trap: but whoever holds on tight to the LORD God shall be kept protectively safe. May people are busy trying to get what they want from the strong-armed person who rules: but what a woman or man rightly has coming to them shall come indeed from the LORD.

(Proverbs 29:27, 25–26)

Father in heaven,
We pray that you will make us indeed as innocent as doves and as streetwise as snakes as we deal with the honorable Ontario government, for Jesus Christ's sake, Amen.

Babylon Streams Received Our Tears

1. Babylon streams received our tears: Zion, the holy city, gone. Exiles, we cried beneath the trees. Harps hung in silence many years.
2. Our captors laughed, "Perform your praise! Merrily dance, Jerusalem!" How could we chant the LORD God's songs while we were crushed by heathens' ways?
3. So help us, God, you may destroy our working hands if we deny— strike our mouths mute if we neglect to make your city our chief joy.
4. Remember, LORD, the awful day violent Edom cursed your folk: "Babylon, break Jerusalem! Raze to the ground, strip her away!"
5. God give you evil for reward. Blest be the one who brings your fall. Babylon great— your seed be smashed! Vengeance shall come from God our LORD.

Text: Psalm 137; vers. Calvin Seerveld, 1982, ©
Tune: Griffith Hugh Jones, 1890

LM
LLEF

THE TENDER, TOUGH MYSTERY OF (MARRIED) LOVE

It is integral to the faith tradition of the historical Reformation to realize you don't just worship God in a church service. A believer can praise God at the birth of a child, rejoicing with the mother, father, and midwife. A middle-aged child can receive strength when the faithful community surrounds you at the grave side of your parent and sing Psalm 23, 42, or 84.

When you fall in love, it is the time to sing a joyful song.

But what is a Christian supposed to do? To sing one of Schumann's *Liederkreis* like *Mondnacht* (May 1840) would be a bit much, you need to find a good pianist too, and it would not quite fit with our casual clothing. A Puccini or Mozart aria like Don Giovanni's serenade, "*Deh! Vieni alla fienstra o mio Tesoro*" (1787) sung under a balcony might be an unusual adventure, but most young women have other interests in a young man than whether he be a budding baritone or tenor, and they don't usually appear on balconies today.

[#62] Inès Cécile Naudin ten Cate, engaged to be married, 1956, The Hague

If a teenage girl is happy at a prospective beau, it would probably be a bit aggressive, even in our day, for her to sing him "*Let's give 'em something to talk about*" in a Bonnie Reitt voice (1990s). And so many "love songs" on the current pop charts, or like Leonard Cohen's old classic of "*Suzanne among the oranges*" (1966), are pregnant with hyped up

---

First published in the *Christian Courier* no.2826 (22 October 2007), 10.

sexual overtones. You really need a more circumspect approach, since courtship still best begins in friendship.

Of course, a fellow could always begin casually with Ina Lohr's simple melody in *The Greatest Song* (1963): Arise, beloved, by beautiful one, come wander away with me. . . .

The pickings for love songs celebrating married love are fairly slim, as if romance wears out quite soon after the knot is tied. Fixing daily meals, cleaning diapers, snoring in bed, and putting your kids through college if you are middle-class, are not so romantic. Sometimes it takes a birthday, or an anniversary, or the death of a spouse to help you remember the enrichment unspoken married love can provide a single person.

Years ago in the Vancouver Art Museum (1981), my wife and I toured an exhibit of Renaissance musical instruments with an audio pack that played appropriate music of that period before each exhibit case—recorder, viol, sackbut, cornett, crumhorn. We were enthralled.

I have gradually come to think such happy, dance-like tunes—you sometimes hear them in a good Shakespeare production—have a pristine spirit of Christian joy. Not church solemnity like a Palestrina motet, nor courtly frivolity like a troubadour lai; but simply jubilant artless melodic artistry that is gentle and exuberant.

So I have tried to capture the lilting, bell-like "Renaissance" quality of a counter-tenor or chaste soprano voice in this tune named INÈS. I hear the song accompanied by an angel playing a lute [#63]. Quiet guitar would do, I suppose, but a banjo twang is not appropriate. A sure a cappella voice or soft keyboard chords chiming in would do in a pinch. The text witnesses to the mystery of married love, which can weather ups and downs, misunderstandings, sins of neglect, and forgiveness, sadness, aging, and times of sweet nourishing peace.

[#63] Vittore Carpaccio, detail of *Presentation of Jesus in the temple*, c. 1505–1510

To know married love that lasts is a humbling experience, a very special gift of the LORD to some of us human creatures, and deserves a good song.

Written for my wife after 51 years of married love.
Thanks to James Leach and Emmy Honig for musical research help.

The Tender, Tough Mystery of (Married) Love

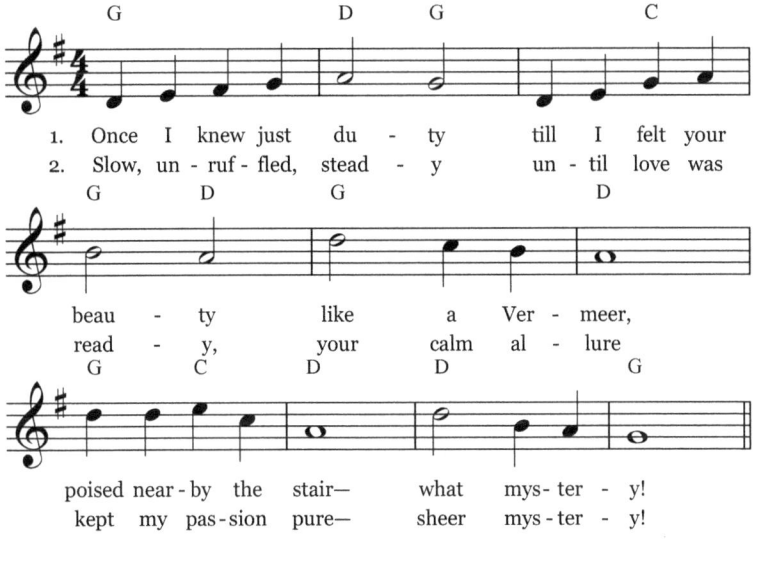

1. Once I knew just du-ty / till I felt your beau-ty / like a Vermeer, / poised near-by the stair— / what mys-ter-y!
2. Slow, un-ruf-fled, stead-y / un-til love was read-y, / your calm al-lure / kept my pas-sion pure— / sheer mys-ter-y!

Ending for final stanza

(6) ten-der, tough mys-ter-y!

3. Wedded love courts trouble:
   fear and faults are double.
   Yet simple grace
   touched our long embrace—
   strong mystery!

4. No caress can cover
   all two lives shall suffer.
   Shared joys and pains
   permutate the strains—
   fine mystery!

5. As our bodies altered,
   when love's patience faltered,
   your quiet peace
   let respect increase—
   strange mystery!

6. Married vows are brilliant
   cues to be resilient:
   helped us rehearse
   "better and the worse"—
   tender, tough mystery!

Aire for lute accompaniment or (unmiked) acappella voice

Text: Calvin Seerveld © 1998
Tune: Calvin Seerveld © 1998

66 454
INÉS

The Rare Gift of a Friend

Text and Tune and Harmonization: Calvin Seerveld, 1998 ©
Arrangement by Carson P. Cooman, 2002

13 13 6 5 13
PHYL

— The Tender, Tough Mystery of (Married) Love —

— Biblical Studies and Wisdom for Living —

Marriage photo of Inès Cécile Naudin ten Cate and
Calvin Seerveld, Den Haag, Netherlands, 1956

A Morning Weather Hymn

It is peculiarly human to sing, and to sing together. It is a heartening exercise when done communally on a theme you believe in, as the protest marchers for civil rights understood in the '60s with "We Shall Overcome." Such singing was not the same as Doo-wop entertainment or pop songs with the Supremes orchestrated by the Motown machine. Street singing had a different cachet too than Fanny Crosby's old-time revival hymns. If you yourself enter a non-professional group singing a song that is solid and well-known, it invigorates you.

But times have changed. Outside the church, people seldom sing together. The silent sing-along with MP3 players I see happening on the subway consists of bobbing heads and tensed facial muscles mimicking the jolting beat in their ears. And usually some soloist consummates the moment before the beginning of a big competitive sports event using the national anthem, with few in the stands joining in. "Happy Birthday" is about the most many of us ever voice with others.

It is probably too much to hope that families will ever sing together at home. But a few families still do. If you are a guest at such a family meal, you experience an unexpected blessing, as if angels are indeed mysteriously present. That's what our family experienced in 1980 visiting our Lutheran pastor friend, Gerhard Goebel, in Dresden while East Germany was still under communist control: the Goebels ended the simple meal by singing a German chorale in four-part harmony.

Saint Benedict's "Rule" (c. AD 528) had monks chanting psalms together at sunrise every morning (Lauds), beginning with Psalms 67 and 51. Less rigorous (Anglican) communions later on would have a "morning song" and an "evensong" to begin and end the day singing praise to God.

The Psalms also celebrate God's sunshine (Psalm 19:4b–6) and how the animals thrive in all kinds of God's weather (Psalm 104:7–10). The

---

First published in *Reformed Worship* 84 (2007): 33. Reprinted with permission © Faith Alive Christian Resources.

rhythm of seedtime and harvest and changing seasons, including snow and frost, is a covenantal promise by the Lord of the universe (Genesis 8:20–22; Psalm 148:7–10). So why not celebrate such a common gracious reality?

I wonder whether there might not be parachurch occasions—early morning Bible study groups, vacation Bible school, maybe a church school class, a prayer breakfast, or even a committee meeting—where a rousing song about the weather outside would be a unifying ice-breaker, bringing smiles to faces and relating sun and rain to God who graciously gives it.

God controls the weather. Even secular insurance companies recognize and bank on that fact. After a particularly disastrous storm, the insurance company will not pay damages. Small print in the policy exempts their liability from "acts of God."

Perhaps *Reformed Worship* readers might want to try out "A Morning Weather Hymn" for size. The weather God sends is always with us. The melody of this new song is upbeat. Its range is about an octave, very singable. It should be sung at a sprightly tempo. If you use the excellent harmony, there is the opening dissonance of a second (D against E), which tells you we are not living in the nineteenth century, but thanking God today, AD 2007, rain or shine. The musical accompaniment has a solid moving bass line against just enough syncopation in the melody to highlight a good regularity amid surprise in the developing tune—much like the weather. And the song ends with a full harmonic A major chord, snug, the way a good poem or hymn verse should conclude.

If your group tries "A Morning Weather Hymn" five times and is still not edified after you know it—a smile does a lot to a human face—drop me a line. I'll take you out for coffee at the nearest coffee shop and we'll sing together. After all, all of life is meant to be a song for God.

A Morning Weather Hymn

1. Come, greet the morning sunshine and laugh to see the rain.
   No matter what the weather, God's grace remains the same.
2. Wild beasts slink to the forest, the birds bestir the trees,
   while we awake like flowers to pray on bended knees.
3. The day is new with wonder despite how we may feel.
   The faithful Lord sent *winter to teach us what is real:
4. though times are fraught with troubles and ruled by hatefulness,
   providing us the seasons attests God's faithfulness.

5. So count your daily blessings,
   persist within the strife
   to benefit your neighbor,
   and praise the Lord of life!

6. Come, greet the morning sunshine,
   and laugh to see the rain. .
   No matter what the weather,
   God's grace remains the same.

*select springtime, summer, autumn, winter *as appropriate.*

Text: Calvin Seerveld. © 2004, Calvin Seerveld 7676
Music: Carson Cooman. © 2002, Carson Cooman RHINECLIFF

READING THE BIBLE LIKE A GROWN-UP CHILD

I was teaching philosophy at Trinity Christian College in Palos Heights, Illinois, back in the 1960s when one of my students came to me and said, "I'd like to learn how to read the Bible."

OK, I said. So Patsy Bylsma and I met every week for about an hour to read the Bible together. I think we started with Isaiah 40. We would read a chapter or so out loud to one another. Then we'd stop and comment on what was written:

"Why in the world would God say that?"

"'You little worm of Jacob'—is that a term of endearment?"

"How come God likes this Persian-army guy Cyrus so much?"

"That can't be in Chapter 54, can it? God offers you something for nothing? It's just like the come-on of hard-sell advertisers!"

We would let our imaginations follow the narrative. We'd ask questions and not worry too much about conclusions.

It started to be fun. We never knew what to expect next. And slowly we began to listen, intently, to reread earlier passages and to remember things. We'd hear this amazing covenant Lord with whom the poetic Isaiah was interacting speak things that were intriguing. We felt we could just take hold of God and pull for blessings.

Read it for what it is

It is not easy to read the Bible. It's easier to read it wrong or not to read it at all. To read the Bible the way it is written takes some coaching (Acts 8:26–31). But a lot of people don't want that. They want an easy fix, and after a while they give up on Bible reading.

That's because we often read the Bible for what it's not and seldom read it for what it is. Here's what it is not: It is not a book you use to prove a point. Neither is it a book written to solve your personal problems. Here's what it is: It is the true story of what God has really done in history. It is a true account of how God works and what God wants

---

First published in *The Banner* 130 (26 June 1995): 12–14.

done on earth.

To read the Bible the way it is written, you have to give up your own agenda. You have to dwell in the text and see the whole woven tapestry of the Bible from Genesis to Revelation. When you do, you will find that God speaks to you and with you.

Shaken by the Word
I learned that in a deeply experiential way as a graduate student in Basel, Switzerland in 1956. I was scheduled to take an exam the day after spring break. Oscar Cullmann was going to examine me on the book of Romans. That meant he would pick a passage and I would translate the Greek into German on the spot and exegete it out loud. So for ten days and nights, I literally closeted myself with food and drink, a cot and a toilet, and the book of Romans.

At about day eight, I had worked myself through the text up to the powerful conclusion in chapter 8. That's Paul's impassioned argument that we are saved from evil and sin only through faith in Jesus Christ. Paul says Christ's Spirit indwells in us, causing us to cry out "Daddy!" to the living God.

Suddenly I became afraid of the book in my hand as if it throbbed with the very presence of the holy Lord God Almighty. It was like a burning bush that had just spoken directly to me. So I put the Bible on a chair, got down on my knees and prayed, shaken and awed by the power of what was written there. That sense of the Bible has never left me.

A mistaken way of reading the Bible
Gaining that sense of the Bible takes giving up some mistaken ways of reading it. One mistake we make is to read the Bible to prove a point. It can be a point about doctrine (the millennium, for example) or liturgy (the form of baptism) or mores (whether to refer to God as "he"). It can be a point about your pet peeve (smarmy gospel-praise tunes), your pet project (a new church building), church policy (evangelistic priority over education), or church polity (synods have the last word). Whatever the point is, if you read Scripture in order to prove it to your neighbor or opponent, you are treating the Bible like a lawyer's codebook.

That's the way the scribes, the Pharisees and Sadducees, and the trained lawyers and leaders of God's people misread God's book in Jesus' day. They could twist texts to prove that dishonoring parents was obedience to the Lord (Matthew 15:1–9). They could argue immaturely about things like the laying on of hands while the church went apostate

(Hebrews 5:11–6:8). Jesus told them, in effect, "you search the Scriptures all right—to line up your insurance for eternal life. But you miss letting these booked writings convict you of my gracious, all-encompassing rule. If you did hear these words for what they are, they would instill selfless love of neighbor and exuberant praise of God in you as a body of saved sinners" (John 5:31–47).

Don't get me wrong. You can base doctrines and lifestyle on Bible study. But to read the Bible like a prosecuting attorney, marshaling evidence and scoring points, is to squeeze the juice of compelling mystery out of God's living Word. It is to leave it behind like a dried-out shell, as exhibit A or exhibit B. Whenever a do-it-yourself theology or even an official partisan theology calls on biblical texts as evidence to set somebody else straight, someone has lost the key to Bible reading. And that can lovelessly bind burdens on other people's backs (Luke 11:37–54).

What's crucial is not to treat the Bible like a block of wood that you cut and shape and customize for your own project. When you do that, you read the Bible with an obscuring veil over your eyes (2 Corinthians 3:12–18). Reading the Bible argumentatively also ruins the fun and scariness of hearing God's voice, which can caress your cheek lightly or suddenly hit you in the solar plexus.

The Bible is not for solving problems
It is also a mistake, I think, to read the Bible to solve your personal problems. We are all sometimes tempted to use the Bible like the yellow pages of a telephone book. We want it to list God's various numbers to call about troubles, accidents, joys, sorrow, perplexity, indecision. We want answers, so we put out the fleece, page through the Bible, and wait for a sign.

And God stoops to our weakness. Even if the Bible is not a collection of "Dear Abby" answers straight from God's mouth, the Scriptures do dispense specific comfort or wisdom.

It is also true that once a Scripture passage has seared your consciousness, you can recall its treasured message the way lovers remember special times of past embraces or track runners relive moments of memorable tension, success, or failure.

I'll never forget Psalm 146:3 because in 1939, after a week of poor swimming lessons, the instructor threw me off the end of the pier. Then, as I went under the water for the third time, he had to jump in and rescue me. I stumbled home, crying under my breath, "Put no confidence in princes, nor for help on man depend." So special portions of Scripture become dear to a person. This is the way Christ remembered Scripture, in contrast to the devil's prooftexting misuse of the Bible (Luke 4:1–13).

But it is an error to reduce the Bible to recipes for one's needs. The Gideon hotel Bible lists places where strangers can find one-sentence answers to pinpointed questions. Because we are often in a hurry, the *Family Altar* devotional booklet offers a brief homily on a couple of verses to focus our attention for a few minutes. But the Bible is not a fast read. The Bible is not a pacifier, and it is not an inspired almanac of God's solutions for what ails you. It is not the mother of all self-help books. And it was not written, I believe, to make us feel good.

The Bible is, instead, a true account of what God has done in history and the way the Lord does things and wants things done on earth. So to read the Bible aright, you have to set aside your own agenda and hurried pace. You must delve into the book, dwell in the text, become acquainted with the whole woven tapestry of the Bible from Genesis to Revelation. You can't just pull on a single thread and be fair to God's booked Word.

Reading the Bible rightly

It takes time, quality time, to read the Bible the way it is written. I'd wager that if you read a book of the Bible for ten days and nights straight, something extraordinary will happen to you, too. It would help if you took along certain good notes—Martin Luther on Galatians, John Calvin on the Psalms, Cornelis Van Gelderen on the Older Testament prophets, Herman Ridderbos on the Gospels, Klaas Schilder on Revelation. Once you catch the spoken-word character of the Bible, God's Word is a red-hot goad and a tender hug. The point is to actually hear God's voice—not just the scripted words—and meet the Lord's ongoing, connected, and promising deeds happening now.

If you don't have ten days to spare, then sit down regularly with somebody who knows better than you do how to read the Bible. Begin discovering with them what is written there. This is what preaching used to be about: understanding specific scriptural passages in their redemptive-historical context, focused in Jesus Christ. The Holy Spirit would then work out the Word flexibly in daily lives.

I assume your Bible-reading teacher would have earphones tuned by Augustinian monks, by Luther and Calvin, by Abraham Kuyper and Schilder. This Bible-reading tradition of the Reformation breathes the vision of Jesus Christ's rule over all of life. It knows in its bones the Melchizedekian calling of women, men, and children to be faithful, joyful stewards.

I also assume your teacher will follow the Spirit in hearing God's voice. That way, submissive to what is written (1 Corinthians 4:6), you will be gentle with others. After all, once you confess that you "believe without doubt all things contained in the Scriptures" (*Belgic Confession,* Article 5), you are free to relax in the communion of saints and let your imagination follow the text as a grown-up secure in someone's love. And so you become a wide-eyed child again, hanging on to God's words, so full of surprises for sinners.

Reading the Bible, like swimming, is not easy until you know how. And you cannot read the Bible rightly if you are in a hurry. But once you take the time to learn how, no matter how evil you have been and are, God will speak to you and with you. It is so exciting—and it can change your life—to hear God's voice intimately whispering through the tones of Moses, Job, Deborah, Hannah, David, Asaph, Isaiah, Mary, and the apostles Peter, Paul, and John. The Bible is an amazing book of life and forgiveness when you read it like a grown-up-turned-child, believing expectantly on your knees.

Epilogue: A personal testimony

It is not part of my tradition to be personal before 1,000 people. When I struggle with God alone, I'm jealous that it stay intimate, and not be hooked into a media event. Also, God often seems to strike down lately those who parade their faith in public. So I think this assignment is very dangerous, and makes me uncomfortable. If you are curious about me, it makes me feel like the scene of an accident.

However, because I love the people who lead the Coalition under the banner of JUBILEE, I agreed to tell you part of my ordinary story, which I have received as a gift from God.

My young life was unusual. I had good parents who were really christian and wise. Somehow they gave me biblical structure **and** room for myself to find the Way. Maybe it was how my Mother read us a Bible story and a fairy tale at night before bedtime. Maybe it was watching my Father cut up fish before the face of the LORD in the fish market all of us children came to work in: no tracts, just fresh fish, with a holy smell. Anyhow, I've never had to rebel against my parents, or the church into which I was born. That's unusual.

The Calvinist church communion we were part of on Long Island, New York, didn't dance, play cards, or go to the movies. But I never experienced it as prohibition, thanks to my parents, I believe. As country boys we played a lot of baseball among the cow flops in the pasture at the end of the street; you didn't seem to need manufactured entertainment. And at the secular high school, as long as you could play basketball and run distance track, such eccentricities were overlooked in those days. If you can imagine it, when I went away to Calvin College, it was still the

---

The Pittsburgh Coalition for Christian Outreach, every February since 1977, holds a three-day conference called "Jubilee," which many college students in that area and the Midwest USA attend. Seerveld was asked to address a plenary gathering in the ballroom of the Hilton, to give his personal testimony of faith in Jesus Christ. This is the text of what he said on 27 February 1988.

unwritten rule back then that students didn't go to movies. That was a time after the flood, but before you were born. The week after I graduated from Calvin, I went to see a movie. It didn't look so sinful, I recall, just superficial.

After a Master's degree in classics and English literature at the University of Michigan, I spent five faith-formative years as a footloose country boy studying christian philosophy, Old Testament theology, and art in Europe. One summer I hitch-hiked from Holland over the Alps to Italy to learn the language. I found out that hitch-hiking alone in a foreign country is not completely safe, but God's angels are on patrol. Left one night in a border village, I enquired for the local cemetery. I figured nobody would bother me sleeping there. Nobody did. I remember praying the childhood prayer,

> Now I lay me down to sleep;
> I pray Thee, Lord, my soul to keep.
> If I should die before I wake,
> I pray Thee, Lord, my soul to take.

I knew the prayer's theological-anthropological weaknesses as to its dichotomized view of soul and body, but it seemed very reassuring to me then in the dark, as I took a tombstone for my pillow and went to sleep, soundly, until waked at dawn by a church bell tolling for prayers.

These were the years when I met God in a special way that maybe I dare tell about. I was learning Hebrew in Basel, Switzerland, for fun, but also agreed to take an oral exam on *Romans* from Oscar Cullmann. That meant translating the Greek into German and interacting with his lecture notes from the past semester. I had a two-week vacation period of solitary confinement, with the sinecure of baby-sitting an empty house, to get ready for the exam.

It was wonderful—I was still behaviorally a Stoic in those days, before Inès and I married: I took in supplies of fresh bread, butter, jam, and milk, pulled down the shades so I wouldn't know or care whether it was day or night, and read *Romans*. Tired you slept, hungry you ate—the only rhythm—otherwise: *Romans*, Greek into German.

After ten days straight I got into chapter 8. Then it happened. Maybe it was the crazy intensity of the whole business, but suddenly I had a sense that the New Testament Greek text I was holding in my hand was veritably GOD before me. So I put it carefully on the stool, got down on my knees, and prayed. The sense that the Bible is my God talking to me live has never left me.

My professional calling from God has been to teach and to join with others in shaping small christian educational institutions to be a witness of jubilee in our world so like the days of Noah. I spent a year at Belhaven College in Mississippi, 13 years at Trinity Christian College near Chicago, and now 16 years at the graduate Institute for Christian Studies in Toronto, where I finally have been blessed with the time to work at a redemptive aesthetic theory of allusivity (=play, imaginativity, style, history of the arts).

"You spend too much time in your study," some people say. "What about life?"

That's one thing I have learned from the Lord: study is life too. Ideas can kill people, or make them alive. Simple words can be seductive, brutal, or give direction and bring healing. The whole world of cultured history with all its sin, vanity, lust, and waste pass before me in my study. I sometimes have felt like St. Anthony in those paintings, tempted all alone by incredible visions of grandeur that are threatening monsters, appearing like genii out of the rubbed bottles of my books. Does anyone these days pray for scholars living and dying in their studies?

My wife and I worked through Corinthians at the supper table the first year we were married, more than thirty years ago. Our image for the mutuality of head and body Paul recommends for a christian marriage is "the umbrella": the wife is the mainstay that holds up the ensemble; the husband is the fabric meant to be exposed first to the rain. Without the reassuring steadiness of my wife, I think I'd long be gone. That may not interest you, but it's a very personal reality brimful with God's love.

I mention one more thing. It's been a happy surprise for my wife and me to learn about the christian faith from our children. Walking to church one Sunday morning with our eldest daughter I wondered a bit about her clothes. It looked like a rainbow had shattered, and collected its fragments in her skirt. "You always taught us to dress for God, to make God happy," she said. "God likes colors." I walked down the church aisle that morning in my drab suit next to her very happy: rainbows for a fallen world!

As you can tell from my story I have been incredibly protected from evil—I've never had to learn to kill people with a gun, or lived under Nazi occupational rule as my Dutch wife did as a teenager. But time fails for me to tell, as Hebrews puts it: the vow I once made to God that changed my life, the day I met an angel, God's humor in making our second daughter a dance choreographer, and our son one who is learning to make documentary films. . . .

If you are a young Christian and want to mature, if you are an older uncertain believer, if you are an unbeliever looking for direction and the fullness of a meaningful life on earth, grab somebody by the collar who can read the Bible with you until you hear the living God revealed in Jesus Christ speak the truth to you of repentance and forgiveness and the Lord God's Rule over your daily life. Then the Jubilee begins.

List of illustrations•

© – copyright granted or purchased
AP – reproduced with the artist's permission
CS – photograph by Calvin Seerveld
CSU – © status unknown
PD – in the public domain

1 A Fireball of Energy (NASA). PD

2 Castle Geyser's Steam in Yellowstone National Park. Photo by Brocken Inaglory. CC

3 Wonderful icicles testifying of poor house insulation. CS

4 Oklahoma Tornado (NOAA). PD

5 Curious tree in Bath, England. CS

6 Fan-shaped fern, Indonesia. CS

7 Huge aloe plant in South African *veld*. CS

8 Glorious cover of dandelions, suburb of Toronto. CS

9 Peacock at close range, Australia. CS

10 Canadian walrus. Photo by Max Smith. PD

11 Praying mantis. Photo by Mark Williamson. CC

12 A larval Luna Moth. Photo by Benny Mazur Benimoto. CC

13 Luna Moth. Photo by Geoff Gallice. CC

14 Marble Canyon, Arizona. Photo by Realbrvvhrt at en.wikipedia. CC

15 Polar bear. Photo by Ansgar Walk. CC

16 Refugees in South Sudan. Photo by Robert Stansfield, Department of International Development. CC

17 Ernst Barlach, *Schwebender Gottvater* (1922), unglazed Böttger stonewear. PD

18 Susanna Oppliger, *Der Engel mit Elia* (1998), red and white clay. AP

19 Jacob Epstein, *Jacob wrestling with the Angel* (1940), alabaster, Tate Gallery, U.K. CS

20 *Christus Pantokrator*, apse of Monreale cathedral, Sicily (c.1180–1194), mosaic. Photo by Giuseppe. CC

• Links to many of these illustrations in full color can be easily accessed at www.dordt.edu/DCPimagesSeerveld

21 Masaccio, *Adam and Eve Expelled from Paradise* (1424–1425), fresco in Brancacci chapel, Chiesa Santa Maria del Carmine, Florence. PD

22 Matthias Grünewald, *The Small Crucifixion* (c.1505–1519), oil on panel, 2.41 x 1.81 in, National Gallery of Art, Washington, D.C. PD

23 Abraham Rattner, *There was a Darkness over All of the Land* (1942), oil on canvas, 32 x 39 in. CSU

24 Warren Breninger, example of *Gates of Prayer* (1993–2008). AP

25–27 Joan Cots, ceramic stele in his studio, Torrelles de Llobregat, Province of Barcelona. CS (1995)

28 Käthe Kollwitz, *Sleeping Child and Child's Head* (1903), charcoal, brush, and black ink, pastels, on brownish grey cardboard, 50.9-50 x 60.9-63.5 cm. © 2013 Artists Rights Society (ARS), New York / VG Bild-Kunst, Bonn

29 Henk (Senggih) Krijger, *"I will not let thee go except thou bless me"* (1972), three-color serigraph. AP

30 Egyptian Coptic Woman, c.1950, photographer unknown.

31 Jean Siméon Chardin, *La Pourvoyeuse* (1739), 47 x 38 cm, Musée du Louvre. PD

32 Johannes Vermeer, *The Lacemaker* (1669–70), oil on canvas, 24 x 21 cm, Louvre Museum, Paris. PD

33 Letitia Van Tielen (1955). CS

34 Ruth Huber (1988). CS

35 Inès Cécile Naudin ten Cate (1981). CS

36 Mature Malbec grapes on the vine. Photo by IanL. CC

37 Author undergoing massage from a Registered Massage Therapist. Photo by Inès

38 Victoria University administration building, University of Toronto, Canada (c.1835). CS

39 *Bocca della verità,* porch of Santa Maria in Cosmedin, Florence, Italy (300s BC). Photo by Manel Zaera. CC

40 Georges Rouault (1871–1958), *Il serait si doux d'aimer* [It would be so sweet to love] (1948), plate 13 of *Miserere et Guerre* series, aquatint, etching, and engraving, 21½ x 19 7/8 in. 58.1.13. Gift of Mr. Leonard J. Scheller. Collection of the Haggerty Museum of Art, Marquette University. © 2013 Artists Rights Society (ARS), New York / ADAGP, Paris

41 Thomas Cole, *Voyage of Life: Youth* (1842), 134.3 x 194.9 cm. PD

— List of Illustrations —

42 Rands Afrikaans Universiteit student mural [detail] (1992). CS
43 Dayton Castleman, *The End of the* Tunnel (2005). AP
44 Homeless shelter in Pilsen district, "HOPE Respect JOBS," Chicago. Photo by John Bakker
45 Britt Wikström, *Caritas* (2006). AP
46 Carlos Martinez, mime artist, based in Barcelona, Spain, 2009. AP
47 Thomas A. Dorsey, Gospel song-writer and performer. CSU
48 Mahalia Jackson practices with gospel legend Thomas A. Dorsey. CSU
49 The Barrett Sisters. CSU

Movie advertisement

50 Mahalia Jackson, Gospel singer (1962). Photo by Carl Van Vechten. PD
51 Mahalia Jackson and two deacons from Salem Baptist Church in Chicago meeting Hans Rookmaaker (1961). CS
52 First Church of the Deliverance on the Southside of Chicago. CS
53 A home in Alikalia, 200 km inland, Sierra Leone. CS
54 Roadway bridge of tree trunks over an inland stream, Sierra Leone. CS
55 A God-sent angel who saved Angie Hoolsema's life from the viper's lunging strike, Sierra Leone. CS
56 Native children gesticulating before a large mosque in Makeni, inland city of Sierra Leone. CS
57 Praise singer playing the *balangi* he makes, in Sumbana, Bendugu, Sierra Leone. CS
58 Tie-dying entrepreneur in Freetown, capital of Sierra Leone. CS
59 Kekura, enabled to walk by the love and skill of a christian community, Sierra Leone. CS
60 Agnes, agent of hope, delivering medicine for CES in Sierra Leone. CS
61 CRWRC Jan Disselkoen and Francis Saion Kamara before the CES literacy office in Alikalia, Sierra Leone. CS
62 Inès Cécile Naudin ten Cate, engaged to be married, 1956, Den Haag, Netherlands. CS
63 Vittore Carpaccio, detail of *Presentation of Jesus in the temple*, c.1505–1510. PD

Index

aging   204, 206, 210, 212-13
allusivity   121, 218-27, 411
  ambiguity   17, 267
  elliptical   17, 220, 252
  parabolic   17, 224
  suggestion-rich   220, 227. 295

Babylon   93-5, 127, 177, 330, 391
Bach, J.S.   91
balangi   355-6
Bartholomew, C.   291-3
bastards   381-3, 385
beauty   78, 128, 346, 363; (B)163, 226
body/soul   80, 82, 88, 158-64, 187, 252, 339, 360, 410
Buber, M.   15-16, 28, 33, 52, 76, 115, 215, 217-8, 222, 224-5, 228

Card, M.   319-24
the Cat   354-5, 362
Christ, body of   42, 119, 164, 169-72, 177, 179, 194, 244-6, 249-50, 252-6, 269, 286, 289, 342, 377, 388-9
christian life   245, 300, 323, 367; see way-of-life
Christian philosophy   175, 203, 215, 285, 377
CLAC – Christian Labour Association of Canada   52, 176, 279, 286
CRC – Christian Reformed (church)   233-4, 237, 240-4, 246, 248-50, 253-6, 258-61, 312, 314
  CRWRC – World Relief Committee   17, 343ff.
Christian(s)   38, 65, 172, 179, 207, 246, 351-2, 375
church   16, 79, 88, 95, 152, 164-5, 168, 171, 177, 199, 244, 303, 341, 370; see also CRC
  holy catholic   179, 245-6
  control   197-8
  hypocrisy   237-244, 250-1, 253
  musicians   78-80, 93, 313-4
  institutional   170, 172-3
college(s), christian   155-6, 180, 271
common sense   331-4
corporeality, our   158-64, 207, 376

Cots, J.   21-2
creation   78-9, 151-2, 154-8
creatures, non-human   2-5, 7-8, 18-9, 77-9, 151-7; see glossolalia

death   120-1, 206-9, 212-3
devil(s)   179, 187-8, 214, 336-8, 343, 348, 406
Disselkoen, J.   156, 177, 343, 347, 353-4, 362, 366, 372
Dorsey, T.A.   303-4, 307, 312

Empedocles   1-2, 7
enemies   41, 57, 265, 325, 335-7
Evangelicalism   149-50, 173-6
Evangelical(s)   65, 101, 151, 155-6, 158, 163-8, 178-9, 197, 237-8, 240, 288, 311, 377, 388
evangelism   16, 79, 171, 177, 247, 252, 297, 352, 356-7, 367
  Reformed   359-63, 366, 369, 371-2

faith   passim
  act of   244, 244, 249, 260-1
  christian   16, 151, 266, 300, 382, 384, 411
  Muslim   157, 349-50
fundamentalism(s)   65, 79, 150, 158, 167-8; 91, 173, 175

Genevan psalms   49, 64-7, 70, 72, 301, 310, 316
glocal   19, 272-3, 275-8
glossolalia   4, 7-8, 12, 18, 33, 76, 78-9, 88, 95, 142, 151, 154-7, 161, 176, 178, 244, 304
Gospel song   176, 303-7, 309, 311-2, 319
government   165, 173, 198-9, 388
Grenz, S.   150, 176
Griffioen, S.   150, 204, 214, 288
grit   40, 46, 66, 100, 128, 158, 200, 234, 256, 313, 319, 361

heart, human   121, 136, 161-2, 195
Heidelberg Catechism   37, 44, 172, 246, 252, 376

–417–

Herder, J.G. von 133-48
human nature 13, 145, 158-61, 163

ICS (Institute for Christian Studies)
  279-86, 288-9, 387-8, 411
integrity 118-20, 212, 226, 267
interpretation 104, 106, 141-4, 146-8,
  225, 292-3; see translation

Job's friends 111, 219, 329-31
justice 8, 13, 15-7, 21-3, 65, 118, 121,
  153-4, 169, 200, 211-2, 215-16,
  217, 352-3, 389
  restorative 122, 171-3

kill-joy spirit 188
kingdom of God 15-17, 22, 171, 173,
  177, 237, 241, 244-6, 339, 357, 384
Kuranko tribe 332, 343, 345, 347-9,
  351, 353-7, 362-3, 365, 367-8
Kuyper, A. 175, 261, 280, 288, 406

lament 13, 19, 21, 56, 94, 97-8, 100,
  114, 319-26, 334
  a congregational 57-9
leadership 106-8, 111, 127, 210, 242-3,
  254, 313, 387
  principles for sound 284-5

Martinez, C. 295-6
mission(arie)s, christian 156, 326, 342,
  357, 371
most important psalm 42-5, 65-7

neighbors 15-6, 21-2, 118, 159-60, 176-
  8, 284-5, 334-6, 360-1
Neo-Idealistic spirit 175-6

omnitemporal tense 9
ora et labora 91
ordinances, creational 5-6, 32, 49, 76-7,
  79, 112, 118, 122, 155-6, 216, 220-
  1, 225, 227, 250, 389
organizations, christian 252, 254, 279,
  283-4, 286-7, 384

pain 97, 159, 186, 194, 213, 323
Pharisees 188-9, 239-41, 331
philosophy, christian 156-8, 175, 377

pietism 150, 253, 300
pilgrim(s) 177, 373-5, 378
pleasure 185, 187-90, 337, 350, 375
poetry 10, 27, 44-7, 104-6, 112-23,
  134-44, 146-7, 218-20, 222
prayer 2-30, 46, 91, 98, 177, 260-1,
  298-300, 306, 323, 350, 410
preaching 249-52, 256, 261, 298, 313,
  315-6, 406
priorities, weighing 272, 289, 343, 361,
  365
the prodigal God 18, 68
proverbs 102-6, 111, 354-5
  as paragraphs 101, 104-6, 112-5, 117-
  20, 122-3, 220
Psalter 28, 30, 42, 46

reconciliation 18, 45, 68, 170, 252, 256
refuge, cities of 165, 376-9
Regime of God 245-7, 250-3, 255, 260-
  1; see kingdom of God
resourceful woman 125-32
revelation, creational 6, 154, 156-7
Rule of Christ 200, 244, 269, 284, 287-
  8, 359, 378, 383-4, 389, 406
Rule of God 6, 16, 19, 34, 37, 164, 171,
  212, 327-39

salvation 152, 156, 238, 252, 269, 333
Schilder, K. 239, 257, 406
school(s), christian 197-201, 250, 254
  teachers 199, 286-7
shalom 8, 19, 21, 76, 112, 120, 122,
  155, 171, 211, 213, 218, 226, 341,
  359, 377, 389
singing 51, 70, 136-7, 313, 321, 399
snake-mature childlike-doves 177, 220,
  264-9, 390
soul/body 159, 161-4, 177, 206-7, 252,
  360, 366, 410
Spirit of God 29-30, 45, 90-1, 108, 141,
  171-2, 195, 200, 256, 265, 313,
  333, 338-9
storytelling 310, 313, 354-5, 357, 370
Sunday worship 91, 251, 261, 311-13,
  315-16, 321

text, literary 146, 220, 222-3, 291
theologician(s) 18, 28, 45, 236, 241,

252
theology 102-3, 122, 144, 151, 157, 256-7, 291, 293, 341, 405
  systematic 45, 155, 357
thievery, christian response to 358-9
torah 15, 31-6, 47, 49, 76-7, 128, 245
translation 12, 115, 144-5, 147-8, 221-5, 295
truth 215-17, 225-6, 237, 267
  artistic 221-2, 226-8

Vandezande, G. 149, 156, 279-80, 285
voice of God 12, 19, 21, 27-8, 78, 405-7
Vollenhoven, D.H.T. 205, 207, 209, 279, 284

way-of-the-Lord 15-7, 22, 65, 211-2, 357
way-of-life 203-12, 214, 312, 360, 367, 371

Daoic 209-10
Muslim 349-50
North American 205-6, 376
Stoical 207
Webber, R. 150, 163, 176
winsome 35, 180, 196, 221. *285*, 287, 311, 339
wisdom 101-4, 110, 115, 120-1, 127-8, 154, 156, 205, 211, 219-20, 267, 284, 293
Wisdom woman 121
"the wise" 105-6, 109-12, 114-15, 122
wise women 108-9, 111, 126-7
wolves 265-7
world-and-life-view 203
world-and-life-vision 156, 190, 211, 370
worldview 28, 45, 106, 292, 376
worship 160, 163, 170, 172, 177, 298-300, 312-7, 326

"yes, but" pedagogy 111-4, 122, 219-20

Translated Bible passages printed in these books:

Genesis 2:23   *RA* 16
Genesis 11:1–9   *CE* 132–3
Deuteronomy 31:28–32:47 *CE* 81–6
1 Samuel 13:19–22   *RA* 83
Job 19:25–7   *BSt* 329
Psalm 1   *BSt* 31 & 49–50
Psalm 2   *BSt* 35–6
Psalm 8   *RA* 149
Psalm 19:1–4   *BSt* 3–4
Psalm 23   *BSt* 40
Psalm 30   *BSt* 81–2
Psalm 39   *CE* 150–1
Psalm 78:7–8   *CE* 41
Psalm 91   *NA* 262
Psalm 96   *BSt* 86–7
Psalm 110   *BSt* 43–4
Psalm 111   *RA* 145–6
Psalm 115   *CE* 76–7, *BSt* 25–6 & 52-4
Psalm 147   *NA* 233–4
Proverbs 8:22–36   *NA* 255–6
Proverbs 10:1–22   *BSt* 115–7
Proverbs 25:21–2   *BSt* 387
Proverbs 29:27, 25–6   *BSt* 389–90
Proverbs 31:10–31   *BSt* 125–6
Isaiah 28:23–9   *BSt* 331–2
Isaiah 54:1–3   *CP* 35–6
Isaiah 54:2–3   *BSt* 289

Isaiah 61:1–3   *CE* 61–2
Isaiah 61:1–4, 8–9, 11   *BSt* 89–90
Jeremiah 29:7   *RA* 107
Amos 8:11–2   *BSt* 234
Micah 6:8   *BSt* 15

Matthew 10:16   *BSt* 264
Matthew 23:23   *BSt* 239
Luke 10:25–37   *CP* 1–2
Luke 11:24–6   *BSt* 263
Luke 14:25–35   *CE* 105
Acts 2:1–13   *CE* 141
Acts 4:23   *BSt* 38–9
Romans 12:2, 6, 9, 14–5, 20–1   *BSt* 334
1 Corinthians 14:20   *BSt* 268
2 Corinthians 2:14–3:6   *BSt* 192
Galatians 6:2   *BSt* 15
Ephesians 3:8b–10   *BSt* 238
Philippians 2:12–6   *BSt* 269
Hebrews 5:11–6:3   *BSt* 149–50
Hebrews 6:4–12   *BSt* 180
Hebrews 12:4–11, 1–3   *BSt* 381–2
2 Peter 1:20–1   *BSt* 30
Revelation 18:21–4   *RA* 83 & 47–8
Revelation 18:21–19:8   *BSt* 92–3

Psalms, hymns, and spiritual songs printed in these books:

A Christian School Song for Parents and Teachers (PTA) *BSt* 201
A Congregational Lament *BSt* 58–9
A Congregational Paean *BSt* 72–3
A Morning Weather Hymn *BSt* 401
Babylon Streams Received Our Tears (Psalm 137) *BSt* 391
Blues 92 *CP* 32 and *BSt* 63
Did Love Hurt Heloise *CE* 72–3
Genevan Psalm 92 *BSt* 64
Genevan Psalm 141 *NA* 281
God Keeps My Tears in a Bottle (Psalm 56) *BSt* 61–2
I Worship You, O Lord (Psalm 30) *BSt* 85
Psalm 8 *BSt* 50
Psalm 110 *BSt* 67
The Rare Gift of a Friend *BSt* 396–7
The Resourceful Woman Song: Proverbs 31:10–31 *BSt* 131–2
The Shepherd Psalm Today (Psalm 23) *BSt* 55
The Tender, Tough Mystery of (Married) Love *BSt* 395
When God Brought Zion's Remnant Band (Psalm 126) *BSt* 69
When you Pass Through Rough Waters *CE* 76
Whoever Shelters with the Lord (Psalm 91) *NA* 271

NA *Normative Aesthetics*
RA *Redemptive Art in Society*
CP *Cultural Problems in Western Society*
AH *Art History Revisited*
CE *Cultural Education and History Writing*
BSt *Biblical Studies and Wisdom for Living*

Selected Bible translations by Calvin Seerveld published elsewhere:

BFOL   *Bearing Fresh Olive Leaves: Alternative steps in understanding art* (Carlisle & Toronto: Piquant & Tuppence Press, 2000).

CCAL   *A Christian Critique of Art and Literature* (Sioux Center & Toronto: Dordt College Press & Tuppence Press, rev. 3rd edition, 1995).

GSp   *How to Read the Bible to Hear God Speak* (Sioux Center & Toronto: Dordt College Press & Tuppence Press, 2003).

IFoL   *In the Fields of the Lord: A Calvin Seerveld reader.* ed. Craig Bartholomew (Carlisle & Toronto: Piquant Press & Tuppence Press, 2000).

OBH   *On Being Human: Imaging God in the modern world* (Burlington: Welch Publishing Company, 1988).

R   *Rainbows for the Fallen World: Aesthetic life and artistic task* (Toronto: Tuppence Press, 1980/2005).

RWJ   *For God's Sake Run with Joy* (Toronto & Chicago: Wedge Publishing Foundation & Trinity Pennyasheet Press, 1972). Out of print.

TGS   *The Greatest Song: In critique of Solomon* (Toronto: Tuppence Press, rev. ed., 1988).

THGP   *Take Hold of God and Pull* [new edition] (Carlisle: Pater Noster Press, 1999).

VGP   *Voicing God's Psalms* (Grand Rapids: Eerdmans, 2005).

[all publications except *RWJ* are available at www.seerveld.com/tuppence.html]

Older Testament

Genesis 32:22–31	*THGP* 11
Exodus 3:1–8, 10–15, 19–20 & 4:10–12	*IFoL* 260–1
Exodus 19:25–20:21	*RWJ* 11
Leviticus 19:1–4, 15–18	*OBH* 25
Leviticus 21:17–22:9, 17–25, 31–33	*RWJ* 14–15
Numbers 22–24	*GSp* 1–13
Judges 5	*VGP* 131–4
1 Samuel 2:1–10	*THGP* 232–3; *VGP* 121–2
2 Samuel 6:12–23	*RWJ* 174–5
1 Kings 3:3–14	*THGP* 3–4
2 Kings 22; 23:1–6	*RWJ* 202–4
2 Chronicles 34:29–33	*RWJ* 203–4
Job 1:6–21 & 27:1–12	*THGP* 25–7
Job 19	*VGP* 41–3; *RWJ* 47–8
Psalm 1	*THGP* 17; *VGP* 4
Psalm 2	*BFOL* 117–18; *VGP* 19–20
Psalm 3	*VGP* 33
Psalm 5	*VGP* 34–5; *RWJ* 57–8
Psalm 6	*VGP* 50
Psalm 8	*THGP* 43–4; *VGP* 5–6
Psalm 13	*VGP* 65
Psalm 19	*R* 10–11; *VGP* 8–9
Psalm 22	*THGP* 212–14; *VGP* 36–38
Psalm 23	*THGP* 198; *VGP* 87; *RWJ* 73

Psalm 25	*THGP* 155–7; *VGP* 67–8
Psalm 30	*IFoL* 49–50; *VGP* 97–8
Psalm 32	*VGP* 51–2
Psalm 34	*VGP* 124–5
Psalm 38	*VGP* 54–5
Psalm 39	*THGP* 47–8; *OBH* 35–6; *VGP* 69–70
Psalm 42–43	*VGP* 73–5; *RWJ* 61–2
Psalm 51	*THGP* 51–2; *VGP* 56–7
Psalm 56	*VGP* 99–100
Psalm 62	*VGP* 103–4
Psalm 78:1–8	*IFoL* 209–10
Psalm 81	*VGP* 126–7; *RWJ* 166–7
Psalm 86	*THGP* 56–7; *VGP* 78–9
Psalm 89:6–19, 47–53	*R* 73–5
Psalm 90	*VGP* 88–9; *RWJ* 66–7
Psalm 91	*THGP* 181–2; *VGP* 90–1
Psalm 92	*VGP* 106–7
Psalm 100	*VGP* 162
Psalm 103	*THGP* 61–2; *VGP* 142–3
Psalm 104:24–35	*R* 20–1
Psalm 110	*OBH* 75–6; *VGP* 22
Psalm 115	*IFoL* 71–2; *VGP* 24–5; *RWJ* 69–70
Psalm 116	*THGP* 68–9; *VGP* 110–11
Psalm 121:3–8	*GSp* 50
Psalm 126	*R* 58–9; *THGP* 228; *VGP* 144; *RWJ* 76
Psalm 130	*VGP* 58; *RWJ* 76
Psalm 137	*IFoL* 73
Psalm 139	*THGP* 75–7; *OBH* 15–16; *VGP* 80–1
Psalm 141	*VGP* 128–9
Psalm 146	*IFoL* 238
Psalm 147	*BFOL* 38–40
Psalm 148	*R* 40–1; *CCAL* 73–4; *IFoL* 146–7; *BFOL* 20–1; *VGP* 146–7
Psalm 149	*R* 201; *OBH* 50–1; *BFOL* 7–8; *IFoL* 315
Psalm 150	*IFoL* 315; *VGP* 148
Proverbs 1:7	*R* 96
Proverbs 1:20–33	*RWJ* 33–4
Proverbs 8:22–36	*R* 42–3
Proverbs 9	*THGP* 21–2
Proverbs 22:17–19, 22–29; 23:1–9, 12–18; 24:1–22	*RWJ* 37–40
Proverbs 30:15–23	*RWJ* 42–3
Ecclesiastes 2:18–19, 26	*IFoL* 283
Ecclesiastes 3:1–15	*THGP* 31–2; *VGP* 26–7

— BIBLICAL STUDIES AND WISDOM FOR LIVING —

Ecclesiastes 3:9–15, 7:13–14, 11:7–9	*OBH* 91–2
Ecclesiastes 11:1–7	*RWJ* 52
Ecclesiastes 11:9–12:8, 12–14	*THGP* 36–7
Song of Songs complete	*TGS* 23–65
Isaiah 1:10–20	*THGP* 100–1
Isaiah 5:1–2	*IFoL* 192
Isaiah 5:1–7; 2:6–3:5, 8–9.13–17, 25–26; 4:2–6	*RWJ* 110–14
Isaiah 6:1–9	*IFoL* 279
Isaiah 6:1–13	*THGP* 223–4
Isaiah 9:2–7	*THGP* 168–9
Isaiah 11:1–10	*VGP* 135–6; *RWJ* 150–1
Isaiah 29	*RWJ* 122–5
Isaiah 34:1–4, 16–17 & 35:1–10	*THGP* 147–9
Isaiah 38:1–6, 9–20	*THGP* 6–7
Isaiah 40	*RWJ* 81–3
Isaiah 52:13–53:12	*THGP* 117
Isaiah 53:2–5	*CCAL* 25; *BFOL* 1
Isaiah 54	*RWJ* 101–2
Isaiah 55	*THGP* 123–4
Isaiah 56:9–57:1	*THGP* 219
Isaiah 60:1–3, 19–62:5	*RWJ* 196–8
Isaiah 61:1–3	*OBH* 61–2
Isaiah 66:1–5, 10–14	*THGP* 202–3
Jeremiah 2:14–37	*THGP* 104–7
Jeremiah 13:1–17	*THGP* 88–9
Jeremiah 14:1–15:2	*RWJ* 133–6
Jeremiah 15:3–12, 15–21	*RWJ* 138–40
Jeremiah 18:1–17	*THGP* 91–2
Lamentations of Jeremiah 3:22–59	*THGP* 187–9
Ezekiel; 37:1–14	*THGP* 96–7
Ezekiel 19; 18:30–32	*RWJ* 105–6
Daniel 2:19–23, 26–28, 31–45	*RWJ* 155–6
Hosea 2:18–23	*THGP* 110–12
Joel 2:11b–32	*THGP* 207–9
Jonah 2	*VGP* 112–13; *RWJ* 170
Micah 4:6–5:4	*THGP* 173–4
Micah 6–7	*RWJ* 90–3
Habakkuk 1:2–4; 2:2–4; 3:2–19	*RWJ* 190–3
Zephaniah 3	*RWJ* 160–2
Zechariah 1:7–17	*THGP* 83–4
Zechariah 7:1–14	*THGP* 194–5
Zechariah 8:1–8	*IFoL* 68–70
Zechariah 9:9–17	*THGP* 162–3
Malachi 3:13–4:6	*IFoL* 211–12

Newer Testament

Matthew 3:1–12	*IFoL* 281
Matthew 5:1–16	*VGP* 10–11; *RWJ* 27

Matthew 6:33–34	*THGP* 141
Matthew 10:16–23, 26–39	*RWJ* 190–1
Matthew 11:16–19, 25–30	*RWJ* 145
Matthew 12:38–41	*RWJ* 171
Matthew 13:52	*TGS* 67
Matthew 21:28–32, 42–43	*OBH* 26–7
Matthew 22:15–21	*IFoL* 178
Mark 9:38–43	*CCAL* 113
Mark 10:28–32	*THGP* 134–5
Mark 14:1–11	*BFOL* 1–2
Luke 5:37–39	*CCAL* 1
Luke 10:25–42	*OBH* 59–61
Luke 12:22–30	*THGP* 140–1
Luke 12:1b, 8–9, 49, 51–59	*IFoL* 261–2
Luke 14:16–24	*THGP* 131
Luke 18:2–8	*RWJ* 50
Luke 19:1–10	*THGP* 134
John 3:12, 16	*R* 33
John 3:14–21	*VGP* 92
John 7:37–8	*THGP* 140
Acts 8:29–31	*TGS* 9
Romans 8:12–23	*OBH* 49–50
Romans 11:36–12:2	*IFoL* 244
Romans 15:4	*TGS* 67
1 Corinthians 12:1–10, 29–14:1, 20	*RWJ* 22–3
2 Corinthians 4:1–2	*TGS* 21
2 Corinthians 5:1–10	*OBH* 36–7
2 Corinthians 5:15, 17–19	*THGP* 141
2 Corinthians 5:17–19	*R* 32
2 Corinthians 5:17–21, 10:3–5	*OBH* 76–7
Galatians 5:16–6:2	*VGP* 12–13
Ephesians 2:8–10	*OBH* 49
Ephesians 4:7, 12–15	*R* 38
Ephesians 4:7, 12–16	*IFoL* 248–9
Ephesians 5:1–12, 15–20	*RWJ* 19
Ephesians 5:15–20	*IFoL* 51
Philippians 3:2–3	*THGP* 219
Philippians 4:2–7	*OBH* 17
1 Timothy 4:1–5	*R* 36–7
1 Timothy 4:1–8	*CCAL* 113–14
Hebrews 3:4–4:3a, 9–16	*RWJ* 181–2
Hebrews 5:11–6:12	*RWJ* 186
James 3:13–18	*VGP* 28; *RWJ* 43
1 Peter 2:9–10	*OBH* 76
1 Peter 4:10–11	*R* 38
1 John 4:1–6	*IFoL* 168–9
Revelation 18:21–24	*BFOL* 23; *IFoL* 316
Revelation 21:1–8	*OBH* 92–3

www.ingramcontent.com/pod-product-compliance
Lightning Source LLC
Chambersburg PA
CBHW050118170426
43197CB00011B/1631